PRAXIS®

2009 Edition

PRAXIS®

2009 Edition

KAPLAN

PUBLISHING

New York

This publication is designed to provide accurate and authoritative information in regard to the subject matter covered. It is sold with the understanding that the publisher is not engaged in rendering legal, accounting, or other professional service. If legal advice or other expert assistance is required, the services of a competent professional should be sought.

© 2009 by Kaplan, Inc.

Published by Kaplan Publishing, a division of Kaplan, Inc.
1 Liberty Plaza, 24th Floor
New York, NY 10006

Printed in the United States of America

2009
10 9 8 7 6 5 4 3 2 1

ISBN-13: 978-1-4195-5177-2

Kaplan Publishing books are available at special quantity discounts to use for sales promotions, employee premiums, or educational purposes. Please email our Special Sales Department to order or for more information at kaplanpublishing@kaplan.com, or write to Kaplan Publishing, 1 Liberty Plaza, 24th Floor, New York, NY 10006.

TABLE OF CONTENTS

SECTION TWO: PRAXIS I: PPST Practice Tests and Explanations

SECTION THREE: PRAXIS II: Principles of Learning and Teaching

Chapter Four: Review of the Principles of Learning and Teaching (PLT) 269

SECTION FOUR: Elementary Education Practice Tests and Explanations

Chapter Five: Review of the Content Area Exercises (0012) 327

SECTION FIVE: PRAXIS II: Subject Assessments

PRAXIS RESOURCES

Available Online

FOR ANY TEST CHANGES OR LATE-BREAKING DEVELOPMENTS

kaptest.com/publishing

The material in this book is up-to-date at the time of publication. However, the Educational Testing Service may have instituted changes in the test or test registration process after this book was published. Be sure to carefully read the materials you receive when you register for the test.

If there are any important late-breaking developments—or any changes or corrections to the Kaplan test preparation materials in this book—we will post that information online at **kaptest.com/publishing**. Check to see if there is any information posted there for readers of this book.

FEEDBACK AND COMMENTS

kaplansurveys.com/books

We'd love to hear your comments and suggestions about this book. We invite you to fill out our online survey form at **kaplansurveys.com/books**. Your feedback is extremely helpful as we continue to develop high-quality resources to meet your needs.

If you picked up this book, you're probably preparing to take a PRAXIS exam in the near future. Everything you need to get you over this minor hurdle in your life is right in your hands.

I know what you're thinking: PRAXIS doesn't seem like a minor hurdle, it seems like a huge barricade that might prevent you from getting or keeping the teaching job of your dreams. However, like so many things, the PRAXIS tests get less and less intimidating with familiarity. As the test prep adage goes, familiarity breeds success.

First things first, PRAXIS isn't a single exam; it's a series of exams. This book provides preparation for the PRAXIS I: PPST tests and for several key PRAXIS II exams. It is essential that you know which tests are required in the state(s) you plan on teaching in before registering and beginning your preparation for the tests. Understanding these requirements will guide your use of this book as a preparation tool. Check out the State Certification Information Table in the appendix.

PRAXIS I: PPST

This book is divided into five sections that refer to different areas in the PRAXIS Series of exams. The first two sections deal with the PRAXIS I: Pre-Professional Skills Test (PPST). These tests cover basic reading, mathematics, and writing skills and are normally taken by undergraduates in education programs or by noneducation majors seeking jobs in the classroom.

If you need to take tests from the PRAXIS I PPST Series, then the first section of this book will provide you with the content review you need. The second section contains two PPST practice tests that will help you get ready for the real thing.

PRAXIS II: PLT

The rest of this book is dedicated to several key tests that fall into the PRAXIS II category. Among these are the Principles of Learning and Teaching (PLT) and several elementary education tests. Once again, you should refer to the requirements for the state in which you plan on teaching to determine which of these tests you will need to take. You can find this information by looking at the table in the appendix.

In section three of this book, you'll find a PLT review section that applies both to the PLT tests and to the several elementary education tests included in the following section. In addition to the review, there is a full-length practice test for the PLT. This test applies to all four versions of the PLT: Early Education (0521); Grades K–6 (0522); Grades 5–9 (0523); and Grades 7–12 (0524).

PRAXIS II: ELEMENTARY EDUCATION TESTS

If you are required to take any of the tests listed below, then the fourth section of this book will provide valuable preparation for your exam(s).

- Elementary Education: Curriculum, Instruction, and Assessment (0011)
- Elementary Education: Curriculum, Instruction, and Assessment K-5 (0016)
- Elementary Education: Content Area Exercises (0012)
- Elementary Education: Content Knowledge (0014)

PRAXIS II: SUBJECT ASSESSMENTS

In addition to the reviews and full-length practice tests for the PLT and Elementary Education tests, this book provides you with additional preparation for certain PRAXIS II: Subject Assessments. This additional preparation comes in the form of brief overviews of key English, Science, Social Studies, and Mathematics tests followed by question banks testing content knowledge related to these fields.

If you are required to take any of the tests discussed in this section, these overviews and question banks provide helpful preparatory materials.

The PRAXIS tests can get confusing, and there's quite a bit of material contained in this book. It's up to you to determine which exams you need to take and which portions of the book will help you to make the most out of your preparation for the PRAXIS series exams. If you have any questions regarding which tests you will need to take to teach in a given state, be sure to refer to the State Certification Information Table, which appears at the back of this book.

Good luck in your preparation for the PRAXIS series of exams!

A NOTE ABOUT SCORING

At this time, ETS does not provide scoring information for PRAXIS. A passing score will vary depending on who is requiring you to take the test. Please contact the state licensing board, organization, institution, or teacher training program that will receive your scores for information about their score requirements.

REGISTERING FOR PRAXIS

To register for the PRAXIS tests, you will need to complete the registration form and send it to the Educational Testing Service to receive your test admission ticket. You will not be allowed to enter the testing site without this ticket. The registration form can be found in the PRAXIS Bulletin, which is usually available at the end of July. Most university departments of education will have copies of the bulletin, but you can also request one at **ets.org/praxis** or by writing to the address below. You could also register online at this same web address. If you register online, you will not be mailed an admission ticket. You must print out an e-ticket from the online registration site.

Whichever route you choose, be sure to check the test dates and locations and choose a location where you will feel the most comfortable. Also, look at up-to-date information about the state in which you plan to teach. A helpful list of relevant state addresses and websites appears in the Appendix at the back of this book.

Educational Testing Service
Praxis Series
Box 6051
Princeton, NJ 08541-6051
Telephone: 609-772-9476
Fax: 609-530-0581
Website: ets.org/teachingandlearning
Email: praxis@ets.org

Section One

PRAXIS I: PPST SUBJECT REVIEW

Introducing the PRAXIS I: Pre-Professional Skills Test (PPST)

The PRAXIS I: Pre-Professional Skills Test (PPST) consists of three exams: one in Reading, one in Mathematics, and one in Writing. These tests measure basic academic skills and are normally taken by undergraduates in education programs. Also, some noneducation majors are required to take these exams to be certified to teach in some states.

In a nutshell, the PPST is a test most teachers will have to pass to be certified to teach.

This section is devoted to preparing you for the PPST. The review sections and practice tests that follow provide comprehensive and thorough preparation for each of these tests. Be sure to understand your strengths and weaknesses as a test taker before working through these sections. You will need to pass all three tests to be certified to teach in many PRAXIS states. As a result, it's important to know where you need the most help so that you can focus most of your preparatory energies where they are most needed.

PRAXIS I: PPST PAPER AND PENCIL VERSUS CBT

Note that the PPST is offered in both paper and pencil and computer-based formats. This book focuses primarily on the paper and pencil version of these tests. If you are taking the Computer Based Test (CBT), the prep sections that follow are still applicable to your test.

Both the computer based and paper and pencil tests are scored the same way and test the same content. The primary differences between the two tests besides mode of delivery are the number of questions and timing for each section. The table below outlines these differences:

PPST Subject Test	Paper and Pencil	CBT
Reading	40 questions, 60 minutes	46 questions, 75 minutes
Mathematics	40 questions, 60 minutes	46 questions, 75 minutes
Writing	38 questions, 30 minutes 1 essay, 30 minutes	44 questions, 38 minutes 1 essay, 30 minutes

In all other respects, the same concepts and the same strategies apply to both tests. If you are taking a computer-based PPST, be aware that you will have several additional questions and some additional time to complete each test.

CHAPTER ONE

PRAXIS READING

INTRODUCING PRAXIS READING

Reading comprehension tests are the "bread and butter" of standardized tests, and the PRAXIS PPST is no exception. According to ETS, the PRAXIS Reading test measures "the ability to understand and to analyze and evaluate written messages." That sounds straightforward enough. In fact, if you're reading this book, you're demonstrating some reading comprehension. But it's more than just reading and comprehending. It's reading to answer multiple-choice questions.

There are three basic components to this reading test: the passages, the questions, and the answer choices. Each component can be handled strategically and can be squeezed for all it's worth for maximum point payoff.

KNOW WHAT TO EXPECT

The PRAXIS PPST in Reading contains several passages of varying lengths. The lengthier passages are approximately 200 words. Shorter passages of 100 words or less also appear on the test. You will be required to answer 40 multiple-choice questions in 60 minutes. As with all PRAXIS exams, there is no penalty for incorrect answers, so be sure to answer every question, even if you have to guess.

Regardless of the length of the passage, the multiple-choice questions will be based exclusively on its content. You will never be expected to bring any outside knowledge to bear on the questions. In fact, it can be dangerous to add more to the passage than what is given. Keep your focus exclusively on what is stated in the passage. You may be required to make inferences or identify assumptions on the test, but these should be based on what is written in the passage and not on any outside knowledge you might have on a given subject.

The questions on the PPST in Reading fall into one of two basic categories: literal comprehension and critical and inferential comprehension. According to ETS, roughly 55 percent of questions focus on literal comprehension, whereas 45 percent of questions involve critical and inferential comprehension.

Literal comprehension questions require you to do a literal read of the passage itself. This might mean that you have to identify the main idea or gist of the passage to locate a specific detail or to describe the organization of the passage as a whole. These questions tend to be straightforward; the challenge is to find the correct answer as quickly and efficiently as possible. At their toughest, literal comprehension questions can consume valuable time. Trick answers on these questions generally distort the literal meaning of the passage or focus on a scope that is broader or narrower than what appears in the passage.

Critical and inferential comprehension questions require you to read between the lines of the passage. These questions might ask you to make inferences, identify assumptions, or assess the strengths, weaknesses, or relevance of an argument made within a passage. Although these questions do not refer directly to the literal language of the passage, they are always consistent with the overall gist, organization, and tone.

Regardless of the nature of the passage or questions you will encounter on your test, a systematic approach to handling the passages, questions, and answer choices will help you move through the test with speed, confidence, and efficiency.

HOW TO APPROACH PRAXIS READING

As we already mentioned, you have one hour to complete 40 questions based on passages of varying lengths. That translates to a little more than a minute per question. When you consider the fact that while you are reading the passage you are not answering questions, you quickly realize that this test does not give you a lot of time to work on each passage and question.

The lack of time makes it essential to always move forward on this test. Spending more than two or three minutes on a single question will jeopardize your ability to get a good look at every question. If a question gives you trouble, take a quick guess and move on. Circle the question in your test booklet, and return to it if you have time, but learn to let go, especially if there are other questions and passages you haven't seen yet.

Because there is no penalty for wrong answers on this exam, you should never leave any questions unanswered, even if that means taking random guesses at the end of the exam. Ideally, you will manage your time such that you get a decent look at every question. However, if you are pressed for time, guessing is the best option.

Also, be aware that short passages are normally accompanied by a single question. Longer passages may have four or more questions associated with them. That means you should spend more time on the passages that translate to the most points. Short passages and passages with only one or two questions can be skimmed more quickly.

How to Read for Points:

The passages on the PRAXIS Reading exam are drawn from a wide variety of topics, including everything from art and science to business, politics, biography, and history. If you were reading them for your leisure or recreation, you might take your time and re-read confusing portions or jargon. But on this test, you're reading for points, which is an entirely different proposition.

Almost all reading passages on the PPST, no matter what the length or subject matter, tend to share one important characteristic. Compared with typical reading material, these passages are extremely dense with information. This is one reason why they can be so difficult to slog through when you apply your usual reading skills. Not only is it useless to try to absorb everything you read on a PRAXIS reading passage, but doing so is likely to slow you down and hurt your score.

How NOT to Read:

1. Don't try to understand the passage thoroughly. It's a waste of time.
2. Don't get caught up in the details.
3. Don't treat every part of the passage the same. Search for the answer you are looking for, find it, and move on.

Never forget that your goal in this section is to answer the questions correctly. You get absolutely no points for having an especially thorough understanding of the passage. To get the score you're aiming for, you need to develop a method for handling questions quickly without getting bogged down with your reading of the passages. In fact, you need to learn to spend less time reading the passages so that you can spend more time understanding the questions and finding the correct answers. Let's quickly take a look at the components of a typical Reading question.

> The Taj Mahal was built by the Mughal emperor
> Shah Jahan as a burial place for his favorite consort,
> Arjumand Banu Bagam. She was known as Mumtaz
> *Line* Mahal, "the Elect of the Palace." Construction began
> *(5)* soon after her death in 1631. The Taj Mahal and the
> surrounding complex of buildings and gardens were
> completed around 1653. However, the Taj Mahal is
> much more than an expression of love and loss. It's a
> breathtakingly symmetrical representation of heaven.

1. Which of the following best describes what the passage is about?

    (A) The Taj Mahal as an expression of love and loss
    (B) The history of the building of the Taj Mahal
    (C) The Taj Mahal as an architectural representation of heaven
    (D) The balance between the building and the gardens in the Taj Mahal complex
    (E) The importance of the Taj Mahal to the Mughal empire

This passage is full of dates, names, and all sorts of other useless information. All those details are not worth sweating over unless there is a question about them, in which case you'd zero in on the specific detail to answer the question. However, this question isn't focused on the details; this question asks about the passage as a whole.

Each of the wrong answer choices focuses too narrowly on a detail. Only choice (B) is broad enough to address the whole passage, which is about the history of the building of the Taj Mahal.

Now that we've covered the basics of how to read for points, it's time to look at the Kaplan Method for Reading Comprehension.

THE KAPLAN FOUR-STEP METHOD FOR PRAXIS READING

If you approach every passage the same way, you will work your way through the Reading Section efficiently.

Step 1. Read the passage

Step 2. Decode the question

Step 3. Research the detail

Step 4. Predict the answer, and check the answer choices

Like the methods for the other question types, the Kaplan Four-Step Method for Reading requires you to do most of your work before you actually get around to answering the questions. It's very tempting to read the questions and immediately jump to the answer choices. Don't do this. The work you do up front not only saves you time in the long run but increases your chances of avoiding the tempting wrong answers.

Step 1 Read the Passage

The first thing you're going to do is to read the passage. This should not come as a big surprise. It's important to realize that whereas you do not want to memorize or dissect the passage, you do need to read it. If you try to answer the questions without reading it, you're likely to waste time and make mistakes. Although you'll learn more about how to read the passages later, keep in mind that the main things you're looking for when you read the passage are the Big Idea and the Paragraph Topics. Additionally, you're going to note where the passage seems to be going.

For example, if you saw the following passage, these are some of the things you might want to note…

The first detective stories, written by Edgar Allan Poe and Arthur Conan Doyle, emerged in the mid-nineteenth century at a time when there was an *Line* enormous public interest in scientific progress. The (5) newspapers of the day continually publicized the latest scientific discoveries, and scientists were acclaimed as the heroes of the age. Poe and Conan Doyle shared this fascination with the step-by-step, logical approach used by scientists in their (10) experiments and instilled their detective heroes with outstanding powers of scientific reasoning.	**This passage is basically about detective stories and science.**
	Poe and Conan Doyle seem to be important.
The character of Sherlock Holmes, for example, illustrates Conan Doyle's admiration for the scientific mind. In each case that Holmes (15) investigates, he is able to use the most insubstantial evidence to track down his opponent. Using only his restless eye and ingenious reasoning powers, Holmes pieces together the identity of the villain from such unremarkable details as the type of cigar (20) ashes left at the crime scene or the kind of ink used in a hand-written letter. In fact, Holmes' painstaking attention to detail often reminds the reader of Charles Darwin's *On the Origin of the Species*, published some 20 years earlier.	**Holmes is an example of a detective hero with a brilliant scientific mind.**
	Ways that Holmes uses a scientific approach.
	Comparison between Holmes and Darwin ◄

Again, you'll spend more time a little later learning how to read the passage. The point here is that the first thing you'll do is read through the entire passage, noting the major themes and a few details.

Step 2 Decode the Question

The first thing you'll need to do with each question is to decode it. In other words, you need to figure out exactly what is being asked before you can answer the question. Basically, you need to make the question make sense to you.

1. Which of the following is implied by the statement that Holmes was able to identify the villain based on "unremarkable details"?

    (A) Holmes' enemies left no traces at the crime scene.
    (B) The character of Holmes was based on Charles Darwin.
    (C) Few real detectives would have been capable of solving Holmes' cases.
    (D) Holmes was particularly brilliant in powers of detection.
    (E) Criminal investigation often involves tedious, time-consuming tasks.

Essentially, this question is asking why the author mentions "unremarkable details." Looking at it in this way makes the answer more clear. Again, you'll spend more time a little later learning how to read the passage. The point here is that the first thing you'll do is read through the entire passage, noting the major themes and a few details.

Step 3 Research the Details

This does not mean that you should start re-reading the passage from the beginning to find the reference to "unremarkable details." Focus your research. Where does the author mention Holmes? You should have noted when you read the passage that the author discusses Holmes in the second paragraph. So scan the second paragraph for the reference to "unremarkable details." (Hint: you can find the reference in line 19.)

Another mistake to avoid is answering questions based on your memory. Go back and do the research. Generally, if you can answer questions based on your memory, you have spent too much time on the passage.

Step 4 Predict the Answer, and Check the Answer Choices

When you find the detail in the passage, think about the purpose that it serves. Why does the author mention the "unremarkable details"? If you read the lines surrounding the phrase, you should see that the author is talking about how amazing it is that Holmes can solve mysteries based on such little evidence. Therefore, the reason the author mentions "unremarkable details" is to show how impressive Holmes is. Now scan your answer choices.

    (A) Holmes' enemies left no traces at the crime scene.

    (B) The character of Holmes was based on Charles Darwin.

    (C) Few real detectives would have been capable of solving Holmes' cases.

    (D) Holmes was particularly brilliant in powers of detection.

    (E) Criminal investigation often involves tedious, time-consuming tasks.

Answer choice (D) should leap out at you. Now that you've seen how to apply the Kaplan method, it's time to back up a little and look more specifically at how to deal with the passages.

THE PASSAGE

As you learned earlier, reading for points is not exactly like the reading that you do in school or at home. As a general rule, you read to learn or you read for pleasure. It's a pretty safe bet that you're not reading PRAXIS Reading passages for the fun of it. If you happen to enjoy it, that's a fabulous perk, but most people find these passages pretty dry. You should also be clear about the fact that you are not reading these passages to learn anything. You are reading these passages so that you can answer questions. That's it. Reading to answer a few questions is not the same thing as reading to learn.

The main difference between reading to learn and reading to answer questions is that the former is about knowledge and the latter is only about points. Anything that doesn't get you points is a waste of time for the purposes of the test. The PRAXIS Reading test is not a place to learn anything new. Therefore, your goal is to read in such a way that you maximize your chances of getting points on the questions. The questions will ask you about the main idea, a few details, and a few inferences. You need to get enough out of the passage to deal with these questions.

SEVEN PRAXIS READING STRATEGIES

1. Mark it Up.

You can write in the test booklet, so use this to your advantage. Do not take a lot of notes, but do not leave the passage and surrounding space blank! If you do not jot down notes and circle and underline anything, you are putting yourself at a disadvantage. These passages are boring and difficult to remember. Make it easy to find the stuff you'll need to answer the questions.

2. Focus on the First Third of the Passage.

You may find the passages boring. That's just a fact of the test. However, whereas you cannot count on being entertained, you can count on being presented with a well-organized passage. This means that the author is overwhelmingly likely to spell out most the important stuff in the beginning of the passage. Odds are that you'll be able to answer the main idea question based on the first third of the passage.

3. Look for the Big Idea.

All you really need to pick up is the gist of the passage, i.e., the main idea and the paragraph topics. Remember that you can research the details as you need them as long as you have an idea of where to look.

4. Use the Paragraph Topics.

On longer passages, the first two sentences of each paragraph should tell you what it's about. The rest of the paragraph is likely to be more detail heavy. Just as you should pay more attention to the beginning of the passage, you should also pay more attention to the beginning of each paragraph.

5. Don't Sweat the Details.

Don't waste time reading and re-reading parts you don't understand. As long as you have a general idea of where the details are, you don't have to really know what the details are. Remember, if you don't get a question about a detail, you don't have to know it. This is another place where marking up the passage comes in handy. You can always circle or underline details that seem like they may be important. Furthermore, as long as you have made a note of the paragraph topic, you should be able to go back and find the details. Details will always be consistent with the paragraph topics.

6. Make it Simple.

Sometimes you'll come across difficult language and technical jargon in the passages. As much as possible, try not to get bogged down by language you find confusing. The underlying topics are generally pretty straightforward. It can be very helpful to put confusing-sounding language into your own words. You don't have to understand every word in order to summarize or paraphrase. All you need is a very general understanding.

7. Keep Moving.

Aim to move quickly through each passage. Remember, just reading the passage doesn't get you points.

CRITICAL READING SKILLS

So far, you've learned a method by which to approach all Reading passages and questions. Additionally, you've been introduced to seven strategies that should help you work through the passages efficiently. Now, it's time to look a little more closely at the skills you'll need to use in this section of the test—summarizing, researching, and inferencing. (OK, "inferencing" is not exactly a real word, but you get the gist.) Practicing these skills will make you a more effective PRAXIS test reader.

Summarizing

For the purposes of the PRAXIS Reading test, summarizing means capturing in a single phrase what the entire passage is about. You can expect to get a question following each passage that deals with only one paragraph or some other subset of the passage. You need to recognize the choice that deals with the passage as a whole. If you're looking for the Big Picture the entire time you're reading a passage, you will be more likely to zero in on the correct answer to these kinds of questions right away.

> Whether as a result of some mysterious tendency in the collective psyche or as a spontaneous reaction to their turbulent
> *Line* historical experience after the breakup of
> (5) the Mycenaean world, the Greeks felt that to live with changing, unmeasured, seemingly random impressions—to live, in short, with what was expressed by the Greek word *chaos*—was to live in a state of constant
> (10) anxiety.
>
> If the apparent mutability of the human condition was a source of pain and bewilderment to the Greeks, the discovery of a permanent pattern or an unchanging
> (15) substratum by which apparently chaotic experience could be measured and explained was a source of satisfaction, even joy, which had something of a religious nature.

2. The author's primary purpose is to

   (A) evaluate conflicting viewpoints
   (B) challenge an accepted opinion
   (C) question philosophical principles
   (D) enumerate historical facts
   (E) describe a cultural phenomenon

There is only one answer choice that captures the purpose of the two paragraphs above. This passage is simply a description of a cultural phenomenon—the desire to seek out order and avoid chaos—that was prevalent in ancient Greece. Choice (E) fits right in line with this Big Picture.

(A) misses the point of the passage because there are no conflicting viewpoints described in the passage. Instead, two aspects of a single cultural phenomenon are described. (B) and (C) are out because the passage is not challenging or questioning anything. It simply attempts to describe the prevailing perspective for the Greek culture. Finally, (D) is out because it misses the point. This passage is less concerned with delineating historical facts than with the overall zeitgeist or collective spirit of a society.

As you can see, reading for the overall gist and purpose of a passage will save you the trouble of returning to the passage on Big Picture questions like this one. Big Picture questions require a broad, overarching sense of the passage. Once you've gotten this sense, you're ready to handle most Big Picture questions.

Researching

Researching is the flip side of summarizing, and it is a skill that comes into play on Detail questions. Researching is essentially about knowing where to look for details you didn't "sweat" during your first pass through a passage. As we've already discussed, you should take note of paragraph topics when you first read through a passage. Then, when you're faced with a Detail question like the one that follows, you'll know which part of the passage has the key phrases needed.

Ever since the giant panda was discovered in the middle of the 19th century, a debate has raged over its relation to other species.
Line Whereas the general public tends to view
(5) the panda as a kind of living teddy bear, biologists have not been sure how to classify this enigmatic animal. At different times, the panda has been placed alternately with bears in the Ursidae family, with raccoons in
(10) the Procyonidae family, and in its own Ailuropodidae family.

Biologists who classify animal species have tried to categorize the panda according to whether its traits are homologous or
(15) merely analogous to similar traits in other species. Homologous traits are those that species have in common because they have descended from a common ancestor. For instance, every species of cat has the
(20) homologous trait of possessing only four toes on its hind foot because every member of the cat family descended from a common feline ancestor. The greater number of such traits that two species share, the more
(25) closely they are related. An analogous trait is a trait that two species have in common not because they are descended from a common ancestor but because they have different ancestors that developed in similar ways in
(30) response to similar environmental

pressures. A cat and a lion have more homologous traits between them than a cat and a human, for example. So cats and lions are more closely related than cats and
(35) humans. A whale and a fish have analogous tail fins because they both evolved in aquatic environments, not because they share a common ancestor. The questions surrounding the classification of the giant
(40) panda are linked to whether certain traits are homologous or simply analogous.

3. According to the passage, which of the following is true of the classification of the giant panda?

    (A) The correct classification of the giant panda is in the Ursidae family.

    (B) The classification of the giant panda is based on analagous traits.

    (C) The classification of the giant panda has changed because of the rapid evolution of the species.

    (D) The classification of the giant panda has proved difficult for biologists because of traits pandas share with several different types of animals.

    (E) It is best classified by biologists as a kind of giant teddy bear.

The classification of the giant panda is discussed in the first paragraph. The answer to this question can be found in the second sentence of the first paragraph. According to this sentence, "biologists have not been sure how to classify this enigmatic animal." This is right in line with (D).

(A) contradicts the passage because the author never states which classification is correct. (B) is also incorrect because classification should be based on homologous, not analogous traits. (C) is never discussed in the passage. (E) is a comical distortion of the passage. Although the passage does state that the general public may view the panda as a giant teddy bear, that does not correspond to the biological classification of the animal, which is the focus of this question.

4. Which of the following is NOT possible using the homologous/analogous classification scheme?

   (A) two species sharing more than one homologous trait
   (B) two species sharing more than one analogous trait
   (C) two species sharing an analogous trait but have no common ancestor
   (D) two species sharing a homologous trait but have no common ancestor
   (E) two species that share no analogous or homologous traits

Homologous and analogous traits are discussed in depth in the second paragraph. The second sentence of the second paragraph defines homologous traits as traits linked to a common ancestor. Consequently, (D) is the correct answer here because two species with a homologous trait by definition possess a common ancestor.

(A), (B), (C), and (E) are all possible based on the description given in the second paragraph. Two species can share numerous homologous traits, choice (A). That would simply mean that they shared a common ancestor. Similarly, two species can share numerous analogous traits, choice (B). This would simply mean that they did not share a common ancestor. Choice (C) is consistent with the definition of analogous traits, so it can be eliminated. Finally, (E) can be eliminated because nowhere in the passage is it stated that two species must have analogous or homologous traits. (E) is therefore possible and can be eliminated.

Inference

Inference means you're looking for something that is strongly implied but not stated explicitly. In other words, "inferencing" means "reading between the lines." What did the author almost say but not say exactly?

Inferences will not stray too far from the language of the text. Wrong answers on inference questions will often fall beyond the subject matter of the passage.

Children have an amazing talent for learning vocabulary. Between the ages of 1 and 17, the average person learns the
Line meaning of about 80,000 words—about 14
(5) per day. Dictionaries and traditional classroom vocabulary lessons only account for part of this spectacular knowledge growth. More influential are individuals' reading habits and their interaction with
(10) people whose vocabularies are larger than their own. Reading shows students how words are used in sentences. Conversation offers several extra benefits that make vocabulary learning engaging—it supplies
(15) visual information, offers frequent repetition of new words, and gives students the chance to ask questions.

5. When is a child most receptive to learning the meaning of new words?

   (A) when the child reaches high school age
   (B) when the child is talking to other students
   (C) when the child is assigned vocabulary exercises
   (D) when the child is regularly told that he or she needs to improve
   (E) when vocabulary learning is made interesting

This short passage discusses how children learn vocabulary. The question asks when children are most receptive to learning new words. There is no sentence in the passage that states "Children are most receptive to learning new words...." In lines 8–11, however, the author mentions that reading and conversation are particularly helpful. Lines 12–14 note how conversation is engaging. This is consistent with (E)—children learn when vocabulary learning is made interesting.

There is nothing in the passage to suggest that children learn more at high school age (A). (B) might have been tempting, but it is too specific. There's no reason to believe that talking to students is more helpful than talking to anyone else. (C) contradicts the passage, and (D) is never mentioned at all.

PRACTICE EXERCISE

Now it's time to put some of this together. Take about three minutes to read the following passage. Then take about four minutes to answer the questions that follow. Answers are at the end of the chapter.

The poems of the earliest Greeks, like those of other ancient societies, consisted of magical charms, mysterious predictions,
Line prayers, and traditional songs of work and
(5) war. These poems were intended to be sung or recited, not written down, because they were created before the Greeks began to use writing for literary purposes. All that remains of them are fragments mentioned
(10) by later Greek writers. Homer, for example, quoted an ancient work song for harvesters, and Simonides adapted the ancient poetry of ritual lamentation, songs of mourning for the dead, in his writing.

(15) The different forms of early Greek poetry all had something in common: They described the way of life of a whole people. Poetry expressed ideas and feelings that were shared by everyone in a community—
(20) their folktales, their memories of historical events, and their religious speculation. The poems were wholly impersonal, with little emphasis on individual achievement. It never occurred to the earliest Greek poets to
(25) tell us their names or to try to create anything completely new.

In the "age of heroes," however, the content and purpose of Greek poetry changed. By this later period, Greek communities had become
(30) separated into classes of rulers and ruled. People living in the same community, therefore, had different, even opposed, interests; they shared fewer ideas and emotions. The particular outlook of the
(35) warlike upper class gave poetry a new content, one that focused on the lives of individuals. Poets were assigned a new task: to celebrate the accomplishments of outstanding characters, whether they were real or
(40) imaginary, rather than the activity and history of the community.

In the heroic age, poets became singers of tales who performed long poems about the fates of warriors and kings. One need only
(45) study Homer's *Iliad* and *Odyssey*, which are recorded examples of the epic poetry that was sung in the heroic age, to understand the influence that the upper class had on the poet's performance. Thus, the poetry of the
(50) heroic age can no longer be called a folk poetry. Nor was the poetry of the heroic age nameless, and in this period it lost much of its religious character.

1. Which of the following best tells what this passage is about?

   (A) how the role of early Greek poetry changed
   (B) how Greek communities became separated into classes
   (C) the superiority of early Greek poetry
   (D) the origin of the *Iliad* and the *Odyssey*
   (E) why little is known about early Greek poets

2. The earliest Greek poems were probably written in order to

   (A) bring fame to kings
   (B) bring fame to poets
   (C) express commonly held beliefs
   (D) celebrate the lives of warriors
   (E) tell leaders how they should behave

3. The term "folk poetry" (lines 50–51) refers to poetry whose contents depict mainly

    (A) the adventures of warriors
    (B) the viewpoint of a ruling class
    (C) the problems of a new lower class
    (D) the concerns of a whole culture
    (E) the fates of heroes

4. Which of the following did poetry of the heroic age primarily celebrate?

    (A) community life
    (B) individuals
    (C) religious beliefs
    (D) the value of work
    (E) common people

5. The passage suggests that, compared to communities in an earlier period, Greek communities during the heroic period were probably

    (A) less prosperous
    (B) less unified
    (C) better organized
    (D) more peaceful
    (E) more artistic

6. Which of the following situations is most like the one involving poets in the heroic age as it is presented in the passage?

    (A) A school of artists abandons portrait painting in favor of abstract art.
    (B) A sports team begins to rely increasingly on the efforts of a star player.
    (C) A species of wolf is hunted to the verge of extinction.
    (D) A group of reporters publicizes the influence of celebrities on historical events.
    (E) A novelist captures the daily lives of a rural community.

THE QUESTIONS

As you already know, Reading points come from answering the questions, not from the passages. This doesn't mean that it is not important to approach the passage strategically—it is. However, if you do not answer the questions correctly, the passage hasn't done you much good.

There are three basic question types in the Reading Section: Main Idea, Detail, and Inference questions.

Main Idea Questions

A Main Idea question asks you to summarize the topic of the passage. A key strategy for Main Idea questions is to look for a choice that summarizes the entire passage—not just a detail that's mentioned once or just a single paragraph.

    1. Which of the following best tells what this passage is about?

        (A) The history of American landscape painting

        (B) Why an art movement caught the public imagination

        (C) How European painters influenced the Hudson River School

        (D) Why writers began to romanticize the American wilderness

        (E) The origins of nationalism in the United States

Detail Questions

Detail questions are straightforward—all you have to do is locate the relevant information in the passage. The key strategy is to research the details by relating facts, figures, and names in the question to a specific paragraph.

    2. Which of the following is not mentioned as one of the reasons for the success of the Hudson River School?

        (A) American nationalism increased after the War of 1812.

        (B) Americans were nostalgic about the frontier.

        (C) Writers began to focus on the wilderness.

        (D) The United States wanted to compete with Europe.

        (E) City dwellers became concerned about environmental pollution.

Inference Questions

An Inference question, like a Detail question, asks you to find relevant information in the passage. However, once you've located the details, you've got to go one step further to figure out the underlying point of a particular phrase or example. The answer will not be stated, but it will be strongly implied.

3. Which of the following best describes what is suggested by the statement that the Hudson River School paintings "fitted the bill perfectly" (lines 32–33)?

(A) The paintings depicted famous battle scenes.

(B) The paintings were very successful commercially.

(C) The paintings reflected a new pride in the United States.

(D) The paintings were favorably received in Europe.

(E) The paintings were accurate in their portrayal of nature.

Now that you've been introduced to the question types, it's a good idea to take a closer look at them. Because you cannot really deal with questions unless you have an accompanying passage, take three to four minutes to read the passage on the next page. As usual, mark it up. Read it with the goal of answering questions afterward.

The first truly American art movement was formed by a group of landscape painters that emerged in the early nineteenth
Line century called the Hudson River School.
(5) The first works in this style were created by Thomas Cole, Thomas Doughty, and Asher Durand, a trio of painters who worked during the 1820s in the Hudson River Valley and surrounding locations. Heavily
(10) influenced by European Romanticism, these painters set out to convey the remoteness and splendor of the American wilderness. The strongly nationalistic tone of their paintings caught the spirit of the times, and
(15) within a generation the movement had mushroomed to include landscape painters from all over the United States. Canvases celebrating such typically American scenes as Niagara Falls, Boston Harbor, and the
(20) expansion of the railroad into rural Pennsylvania were greeted with enormous popular acclaim.

One factor contributing to the success of the Hudson River School was the rapid
(25) growth of American nationalism in the early nineteenth century. The War of 1812 had given the United States a new sense of pride in its identity, and as the nation continued to grow, there was a desire to
(30) compete with Europe on both economic and cultural grounds. The vast panoramas of the Hudson River School fitted the bill

perfectly by providing a new movement in art that was unmistakably American in
(35) origin. The Hudson River School also arrived at a time when writers in the United States were turning their attention to the wilderness as a unique aspect of their nationality. The Hudson River School
(40) profited from this nostalgia because they effectively represented the continent the way it used to be. The view that the American character was formed by the frontier experience was widely held, and
(45) many writers were concerned about the future of a country that was becoming increasingly urbanized.

In keeping with this nationalistic spirit, even the painting style of the Hudson River
(50) School exhibited a strong sense of American identity. Although many of the artists studied in Europe, their paintings show a desire to be free of European artistic rules. Regarding the natural landscape as a direct
(55) manifestation of God, the Hudson River School painters attempted to record what they saw as accurately as possible. Unlike European painters who brought to their canvases the styles and techniques of
(60) centuries, they sought neither to embellish nor to idealize their scenes, portraying nature with the care and attention to detail of naturalists.

Hopefully, you caught that this passage was about why the Hudson River School became so successful. You should have also noted that the second paragraph addresses how American nationalism contributed to the success of the Hudson River School, and the third paragraph discusses how nationalist sentiment was evident in the Hudson River School painting style.

Main Idea Questions

1. Which of the following best tells what this passage is about?

   (A) the history of American landscape painting
   (B) why an art movement caught the public imagination
   (C) how European painters influenced the Hudson River School
   (D) why writers began to romanticize the American wilderness
   (E) the origins of nationalism in the United States

Do you see which one of these answers describes the entire passage without being too broad or too narrow?

(A) is too broad, as is (E). The passage is not about all American landscape painting, it's about the Hudson River School. Nationalism in the United States is much larger than the role of nationalism in a particular art movement. (C) and (D) are too narrow. European painters did influence the Hudson River School painters, but that wasn't the point of the whole passage. Similarly, writers are mentioned in paragraph 2, but the passage is about an art movement. Only (B) captures the the essence of the passage—it's about an art movement that caught the public imagination.

Detail Questions

2. Which of the following is not mentioned as one of the reasons for the success of the Hudson River School?

   (A) American nationalism increased after the War of 1812
   (B) Americans were nostalgic about the frontier.
   (C) Writers began to focus on the wilderness.
   (D) The United States wanted to compete with Europe.
   (E) City dwellers became concerned about environmental pollution.

Four of the five answer choices are mentioned explicitly in the passage. (A) is mentioned in lines 23–25. (B) appears in line 40. (C) shows up in lines 35–38. (D) is mentioned in lines 26–30. Only (E) does not appear in the passage.

Inference Questions

3. Which of the following best describes what is suggested by the statement that the Hudson River School paintings "fitted the bill perfectly" (lines 32–33)?

   (A) The paintings depicted famous battle scenes.
   (B) The paintings were very successful commercially.
   (C) The paintings reflected a new pride in the United States.
   (D) The paintings were favorably received in Europe.
   (E) The paintings were accurate in their portrayal of nature.

First, read the lines surrounding the quote to put the quote in context. Paragraph 2 is talking about American pride—that's why Hudson River School paintings "fitted the bill." Hudson River School paintings were about America. (C) summarizes the point nicely. Note how this question revolves around the interplay between main idea and details. This detail strengthens the topic of the paragraph—the growing sense of nationalism in America. (A) superficially relates to the War of 1812, but does not answer the question. (B), (D), and (E) are way off base.

PRACTICE

Now it's time to practice some Reading passages and questions. Make sure you mark up the passage and note the Big Idea and the Paragraph topics. Research the details and predict your answers. Most importantly, remember that it's about the questions.

The painter Georgia O'Keeffe was born in Wisconsin in 1887 and grew up on her family's farm. At seventeen she decided she
Line wanted to be an artist and left the farm for
(5) schools in Chicago and New York, but she never lost her bond with the land. Like most painters, O'Keeffe painted the things that were most important to her, and nearly all her works are simplified portrayals of
(10) nature.

O'Keeffe became famous when her paintings were discovered and exhibited in New York by the photographer Alfred Stieglitz, whom she married in 1924. During
(15) a visit to New Mexico in 1929, O'Keeffe was so moved by the bleak landscape and broad skies of the Western desert that she began to paint its images. Cows' skulls and other bleached bones found in the desert figured
(20) prominently in her paintings. When her husband died in 1946, she moved to New Mexico permanently and used the horizon lines of the desert, colorful flowers, rocks, barren hills, and the sky as subjects for her
(25) paintings. Although O'Keeffe painted her best-known works in the 1920s, '30s, and '40s, she continued to produce tributes to the western desert until her death in 1986.

O'Keeffe is widely considered to have
(30) been a pioneering American modernist painter. Whereas most early modern American artists were strongly influenced by European art, O'Keeffe's position was more independent. She established her own
(35) vision and preferred to view her painting as a private endeavor. Almost from the beginning, her work was more identifiably American than that of her contemporaries

in its simplified and idealized treatment of
(40) color, light, space, and natural forms. Her paintings are generally considered "semi-abstract" because even though they depict recognizable images and objects, the paintings don't present those images in a
(45) very detailed or realistic way.

Rather, the colors and shapes in her paintings are often so reduced and simplified that they begin to take on a life of their own, independent of the real-life
(50) objects from which they are taken.

1. Which of the following best tells what this passage is about?

   (A) O'Keeffe was the best painter of her generation.
   (B) O'Keeffe was a distinctive modern American painter.
   (C) O'Keeffe liked to paint only what was familiar to her.
   (D) O'Keeffe never developed fully as an abstract artist.
   (E) O'Keeffe used colors and shapes that are too reduced and simple.

2. Which of the following is not mentioned as an influence on O'Keeffe's paintings?

   (A) her rural upbringing
   (B) her life in the west
   (C) the work of Mexican artists
   (D) the appearance of the natural landscape
   (E) animal and plant forms

3. The passage suggests that Stieglitz contributed to O'Keeffe's career by

   (A) bringing her work to a wider audience
   (B) supporting her financially for many years
   (C) inspiring her to paint natural forms
   (D) suggesting that she study the work of European artists
   (E) requesting that she accompany him to New Mexico

4. Which of the following is most similar to O'Keeffe's relationship with nature?

   (A) a photographer's relationship with a model
   (B) a writer's relationship with a publisher
   (C) a student's relationship with a part-time job
   (D) a sculptor's relationship with an art dealer
   (E) a carpenter's relationship with a hammer

5. Why have O'Keeffe's paintings been described as "semi-abstract" (lines 41–42)?

   (A) They involve a carefully realistic use of color and light.
   (B) They depict common, everyday things.
   (C) They show familiar scenes from nature.
   (D) They depict recognizable things in an unfamiliar manner.
   (E) They refer directly to real-life activities.

6. Why was O'Keeffe considered an artistic pioneer?

   (A) Her work became influential in Europe.
   (B) She painted the American Southwest.
   (C) Her paintings had a definite American style.
   (D) She painted things that were familiar to her.
   (E) Her work was very abstract.

ANSWERS AND EXPLANATIONS

Greek Poetry Passage

Main Idea: What the poems of the ancient Greeks were like.

Paragraph 2:   Ancient Greek poetry was an expression of the community, not individuals.

Paragraph 3:   How later ancient Greek poetry (in the "age of heroes") became more individualistic. (Note contrast keyword "however" signaling this change in line 27.)

Paragraph 4:   More changes in later Greek poetry.

1. A

Main idea. Only (A) captures paragraphs 1–4. (B) is beyond the scope of this passage. (C) expresses an extreme view that the author never takes. (D) mentions the *Iliad* and the *Odyssey*, which are discussed only in paragraph 4. (E) again does not address the purpose of the entire passage.

2. C

Paragraph topic. Refer to the topic of paragraph 2. (A), (B), (D), and (E) are never mentioned in this paragraph.

3. D

Inference. You need to use your inference skills to answer this question. The reference to lines 50–51 leads you to the fourth paragraph. Here "folk poetry" refers to the age before the "heroic age" when poetry was about the entire community and not just the warriors and kings. (A), (B), and (E) do not refer to the "folk" at all and are therefore incorrect. (C) mentions class conflict—something not discussed in this paragraph.

4. B

Paragraph topic. The answer is clearly stated in paragraph 3. "In the heroic age, poets became singers of tales who performed long poems about the fates of warriors and kings" (i.e., individuals).

5. B

Paragraph topic. Refer to the topic of paragraph 3, which focuses on the diversification (or "less unified") of the Greeks during the heroic period.

6. D

Inference. Here you are asked to apply the ideas of the passage to a hypothetical situation. Paragraphs 3 and 4 discuss the portrayal of individual heroes in later Greek poetry such as Homer's *Iliad*. Journalism focusing on celebrities is analogous.

O'Keeffe Passage

1. B

A Main Idea question. Looking at these choices in order, (A) is wrong because it's simply never stated that O'Keeffe was the best painter of her generation. (B) is accurate and may be the best choice, so keep it in mind. (C) is a bit tricky. It's true that O'Keeffe liked to paint things that were familiar to her—primarily certain nature images— but this is just one point about O'Keeffe covered in the passage. The broader, more important idea— the reason the passage was written—is that O'Keeffe was an important modern American painter. (D) is simply never suggested by the passage. (E) focuses too much on a detail and also distorts the "message" of the passage. The author never says that O'Keeffe's colors and shapes are "too" reduced and simple. O'Keeffe is never criticized. That leaves (B), which is both accurate and general enough without being so general that the meaning of the passage is lost. That's the kind of answer you always want to look for in main idea questions.

2. C

A detail question. You're looking for the factor that did not influence O'Keeffe. The third paragraph describes O'Keeffe's work as distinctly American in style, independent of European influences. Mexican influences are never even mentioned, so (C) is correct here. The four wrong choices are all true. As for (A), the passage's first few sentences make clear that her rural childhood had a lasting influence. (B), (D), and (E) are supported in the second half of the second paragraph: her work was greatly affected by her life in the West, particularly by its natural landscape with bleached animal bones, hills, and colorful flowers.

3. A

The first sentence of paragraph 2 states that O'Keeffe "became famous" when Stieglitz "discovered and exhibited" her work in New York City. You can infer, then, that Stieglitz helped O'Keeffe by bringing her work to a wider audience, choice (A). Whatever financial arrangement, if any, existed between Stieglitz and O'Keeffe, (B) is not mentioned in the passage. Paragraph 1 strongly implies that O'Keeffe was inspired to paint natural forms (C) long before she met Stieglitz. (D) contradicts paragraph 3, which states that O'Keeffe was not strongly influenced by European artists. As for (E), the circumstances leading to O'Keeffe's visit to New Mexico are not described.

4. A

First, ask yourself what O'Keeffe's relationship to nature was. O'Keeffe painted from nature—it was the subject of her work. Of the choices offered, which is most similar to the relationship between a painter and her subject? Choice (A) is best because a model is the subject of a photographer's work. (B) is wrong because a publisher is not the subject of a writer's work; a publisher simply prints and distributes a writer's work. Similarly, (C) is out because a part-time job is not a student's subject. It is not what a student bases her work on. Same with (D). An art dealer buys and sells a sculptor's work, but the art dealer is not the subject of the sculptor's work. Finally, a hammer is simply a carpenter's tool; it doesn't provide a carpenter with a subject or model, so (E) is out.

5. D

O'Keeffe's "semi-abstract" style is discussed in the passage's last two sentences. Was "semi-abstract" confusing to you? Hopefully not, because, as always, everything you need to know will be stated or clearly suggested. The next-to-last sentence states that O'Keeffe's paintings are thought of as semi-abstract because they depict recognizable images in a way that is not very detailed or realistic. (D) simply restates this. (A) and (E) are wrong because they refer to "realistic" or "real-life" qualities, which contradict the passage's explanation of "semi-abstract." Whereas (B) and (C) both describe O'Keeffe's work accurately, they are not reasons for her work being called "semi-abstract." They describe subjects of her paintings but not the semi-abstract style in which they were painted.

6. C

The first sentence of the third paragraph states that O'Keeffe is considered a pioneering modern American painter. The following two sentences say why—because her style was independent and identifiably American and not strongly influenced by European art. (C) restates the idea. (A) is never suggested. (B) and (D) are true of O'Keeffe's work but are not the reasons she was considered an artistic pioneer. (E) is not true of O'Keeffe's work, which is considered semi-abstract, not very abstract. Furthermore, (E) does not address the question of why O'Keeffe is considered an artistic pioneer.

CHAPTER TWO

PRAXIS MATHEMATICS

INTRODUCING PRAXIS MATHEMATICS

For some reason, not many people are neutral on the subject of mathematics. As a general rule, either you love or hate it. Either you derive a secret thrill out of doing a good math problem, or your third grade math teacher traumatized you to the point where the very sight of numbers and math symbols induces nausea and blurred vision. On whichever side of the great math divide you reside, we have some important news for you regarding math on the PRAXIS PPST.

First, a word to the math crackerjacks out there. You probably don't need us, but be careful. You should ace the PRAXIS Mathematics test, and yet somehow a lot of good math students don't. Why not? Perhaps it's because they think that the same skills that lead to success on other math tests necessarily translate to success on the PRAXIS. They're wrong.

On other math tests, solving a problem the way you've to been taught to in class is rewarded. On the PRAXIS Mathematics test, solving problems the correct way can slow you down or get you into trouble. On other math tests, if you do the work but accidentally miss a step, you'll still get partial credit. On the PRAXIS Mathematics test, you will not.

PRAXIS Mathematics is not very tough, but it can be tricky. Success on PRAXIS Mathematics requires learning to avoid careless errors and realizing that these errors are often the result of traps built into the questions. What we want to show you is a different approach to test taking, one that takes advantage of, instead of falling prey to, the nature of the PRAXIS.

Now a word to the math haters out there. You should view the PRAXIS Mathematics test as an opportunity. Here's where you can have your revenge on that math teacher who made your life miserable. After all, success is the best revenge. We'll show you how to avoid doing more math than is necessary on the PRAXIS. By taking advantage of the standardized test format of the PRAXIS, you too can get a very good PRAXIS math score. However, to do that, first you need to understand the nature of the test.

KNOW WHAT TO EXPECT

The PRAXIS PPST Mathematics test consists of 40 multiple-choice questions covering a wide range of math topics. You have one hour to complete this section, and there is no penalty for incorrect answers. Once again, it's essential that you manage your time so that you get a look at every question within the section and that you leave no question unanswered.

Whereas the Mathematics section of the PPST covers a wide range of topics, it does not delve too deeply into these subject areas. According to ETS, the test "measures those mathematical concepts that an educated adult might need." In fact, much of the Mathematics content that appears on the PRAXIS exam corresponds to math you'd see in eighth or ninth grade math classes. For some of you, that's great news. For those of you who haven't looked at the concepts covered in middle school math class since middle school, it's important that we take some time to review the basics and how they are tested on the PRAXIS exam.

As we already mentioned, PRAXIS Mathematics is most likely quite different from math you studied in school. Rather than asking you to show your work and demonstrate mastery of concepts, PRAXIS Mathematics is all about results. It doesn't matter how you get to the correct answer—all that matters is that you get to the correct answer, and get there quickly.

In short, PRAXIS Mathematics is multiple-choice math, so you have opportunities to use answer choices when you're in a pinch. In addition, there is no penalty for incorrect answers, so be sure to answer every question on the test. Even without reading a question, you've got a one-in-five chance of selecting the correct answer. After reading the question and plugging in an answer or two, you're well on your way to finding the correct answer, even on questions that cause trouble for you. We'll discuss how to make the most of these "backdoor" strategies later.

The following table provides a quick breakdown of the math content categories that appear on the PPST Mathematics test, with approximate number of questions per content area:

PRAXIS Mathematics Test	
Conceptual Knowledge and Procedural Knowledge	18 questions: 45%
Representations of Quantitative Information	12 questions: 30%
Measurement and Informal Geometry; Formal Mathematical Reasoning	10 questions: 25%

The terms used to describe the content areas on the PPST Mathematics test are somewhat vague. We'll touch on each of these areas and attempt to explain in concrete terms the kind of questions we're talking about.

Conceptual knowledge refers to a basic sense of how whole numbers, fractions, and decimals work. This includes comparing values of different numbers and understanding that the same number can be represented in several ways (e.g., as a fraction, a decimal, and a whole number). A rudimentary understanding of the order of operations, place value, and number properties fall under this category as well.

Procedural knowledge refers to knowledge of the basic procedures required to establish quantitative relationships and solve problems. This includes basic computations, estimation, ratios, proportions, percents, probability, equations, and algorithmic thinking.

Representations of quantitative information refers to the ability to interpret visual displays of quantitative information. This involves interpreting graphs and tables and making simple inferences and conclusions based on given graphs or sets of data.

Measurement and informal geometry refers to the knowledge of the basic units of measure used in the United States and comfort converting from one unit to another (e.g., feet to inches or hours to minutes). Simple geometric concepts like the Pythagorean theorem, perimeter, and area fall into this category as well.

Formal mathematical reasoning refers to the use of logical reasoning and language (if-then, some-all, etc.). These questions may also test your ability to identify assumptions and make simple inferences and deductions.

Whereas this may seem like a great deal of information to assimilate, you're probably comfortable with many of the concepts discussed above. We'll refresh your knowledge of key concepts on the test and attempt to keep things as concrete and question-based as possible as we go. Remember, you simply need to locate the correct answer from the choices given. You don't need to identify the concept or terminology in question.

As you work through this chapter, pay attention to which types of questions you are most comfortable with and which questions give you the greatest difficulty. For questions you have a natural knack for, it makes sense for you to work out your answers in a more straightforward fashion. For questions in areas that give you trouble, think about using the answer choices and working backwards. PRAXIS Mathematics is all about results, and the only results that matter are correct answer choices.

HOW TO APPROACH PRAXIS MATHEMATICS

The two most important things to remember when it comes to PRAXIS Mathematics are that PRAXIS Mathematics is not high school Mathematics and that you should never leave a question unanswered.

If you have not taken a practice Mathematics test, do so now. You can use the reviews in this chapter or one of the Practice Tests in this book. After completing the test, you should have a good sense of which areas you are most comfortable with and which areas cause you the most trouble.

Managing Your Time

Once you know your strengths and weaknesses, you can make more strategic use of your time on the test. If a question looks like one you can readily handle using a straightforward "textbook approach," work through it immediately and in a straightforward manner. If a question looks tough, don't waste time on it early on.

Plan on making one quick initial pass through the entire Mathematics test looking for questions you know you can handle. If a question looks like it will cause you trouble, use the answer choices to work backwards or take a quick guess and return to it later. Never leave a question unanswered, but always be moving forward through the test. After you've answered (or guessed on) every question, feel free to invest additional time on the questions that gave you trouble at first. Spending too much time on tough questions early can prevent you from taking a good crack at questions you can handle later on in the test.

THE KAPLAN THREE STEP-METHOD FOR PRAXIS MATHEMATICS

Step 1. Read through the question.

Step 2. Do it now or guess.

Step 3. Look for the fastest approach.

Step 1 Read Through the Question

Okay, this may seem a little too obvious. Of course, you're going to read through the question. How else can you solve the problem? In reality, this is not quite as obvious as it seems. The point here is that you need to read the entire question carefully before you start solving the problem. If you don't read the question carefully, it's incredibly easy to make careless mistakes. Consider the following problem:

1. At Blinky Burgers restaurant, two hamburgers and five orders of french fries cost the same as four hamburgers and two orders of french fries. If the restaurant charges $1.50 for a single order of french fries, how much does it charge for two hamburgers?

    (A) $2.25
    (B) $3.00
    (C) $4.50
    (D) $5.00
    (E) $6.00

It's crucial that you pay close attention to precisely what the question is asking. This question contains a classic trap that's very easy to fall into if you don't read the question carefully. Can you spot the trap?

Notice that you're being asked to find the cost of two hamburgers, not one. Many students will get this question wrong by finding the price for one hamburger and then forgetting to double it. It's a careless mistake to make, but it's easy to be careless when you're working quickly. That's why you always have to make sure you know what's being asked.

Step 2. Do It Now or Guess

Another reason to read carefully before answering is that you probably shouldn't solve every problem on your first pass. A big part of taking control of your PRAXIS test experience is deciding which problems to answer and which ones to guess on and come back to later (if you have time).

Before you try to solve the problem, decide whether you want to do it now. If you have no idea how to solve the problem, or if you think the problem will take a long time to solve, you should take your best guess and circle the question in your test booklet. After you've taken a look at every question on the exam (and answered the questions that are easiest for you), you can return to the questions you circled and spend more time on them.

Don't worry about ones that got away. Sure it feels good to try to answer every question on a given math test, but if you end up not getting back to a question or two, don't feel bad. Take quick guesses, bank your time, and let go. By spending more time on the questions you can answer, you're more likely to get a great score, even if you have to guess blindly at a few questions.

Step 3. Look For the Fastest Approach

Once you've understood what the question asks and have decided to tackle it now, it's time to look for shortcuts. Sometimes the "obvious" way to solve the problem is the long way. For instance, let's return to the Blinky Burger problem.

1. At Blinky Burgers restaurant, two hamburgers and five orders of
   french fries cost the same as four hamburgers and two orders of
   french fries. If the restaurant charges $1.50 for a single order of french
   fries, how much does it charge for two hamburgers?

   (A) $2.25
   (B) $3.00
   (C) $4.50
   (D) $5.00
   (E) $6.00

Here many students would turn this word problem into two algebraic equations: $2H + 5F = 4H + 2F$ and $F = 1.50$. From there you could substitute 1.50 for F in the first equation, solve for H, and then multiply your answer by 2.

However, if you think carefully, there's often an easier approach. Here, for instance, if two hamburgers and five orders of fries cost the same as four hamburgers and two orders of fries, take away all the items that are the same in the two orders and you're left with three orders of fries costing the same as two hamburgers. Because one order of fries costs $1.50, three orders cost $4.50, so $4.50 must also be the cost of two hamburgers. The correct answer is (C), and you didn't even have to set up any algebraic equations.

Textbook Approaches Versus Backdoor Strategies

We've mentioned a few times that the PRAXIS Mathematics Test is not like the math tests you took in high school. That's because on most high school tests, you are expected to show your work and demonstrate your ability to work step by step from the information given to the correct answer.

PRAXIS Mathematics doesn't work like that. Whereas you're welcome to work through a problem in a straightforward way, you are by no means required to do so. In fact, frequently it pays to use an alternative approach. Let's apply the Kaplan Method for PRAXIS Mathematics to a few practice problems to see what we mean.

The 40 questions that make up the PRAXIS Mathematics test contain many word problems with five answer choices containing numbers, percents, or fractions. PRAXIS Mathematics also tests basic algebra, and occasionally the answer choices will contain variables. In either case, it's important to note that the answer is right in front of you—you just have to find it.

Two methods in particular are extremely useful when you don't see—or would rather not use—the textbook approach to solving the question. We call these strategies backsolving and picking numbers. These strategies aren't always quicker than more traditional methods, but they're a great way to make confusing problems more concrete. If you know how to apply these strategies, you're guaranteed to nail the correct answer every time you use them. Let's examine these strategies now.

Backsolving

Because many questions contain only numbers in the answer choices, often you can use this to your advantage by "backsolving." This just means that sometimes it's easiest to work backwards from the answer choices than straight ahead from the question.

Here's how it works. When the answer choices are numbers, you can expect them to be arranged from small to large (or occasionally from large to small). What you want to do is start with choice (C). If that number works when you plug it into the problem, then that's the answer, and you're done. If it doesn't work, you can usually figure out whether to try a larger or smaller answer choice next. By backsolving strategically this way, you usually don't have to try out more than two answer choices before you zero in on the correct answer. If this seems confusing, check out the following problem and explanation.

2. In a certain school, the ratio of boys to girls is 3:7. If there are 84 more girls than boys, how many boys are there?

   (A) 48
   (B) 54
   (C) 63
   (D) 84
   (E) 147

The correct answer should yield a ratio of boys to girls of 3:7, so let's try out choice (C).

If there are 63 boys, there are $63 + 84 = 147$ girls, so the ratio of boys to girls is $\dfrac{63}{147} = \dfrac{9}{21} = \dfrac{3}{7}$, which is just what we want. That means we're done.

Okay, so that was a bit easy. The answer isn't always the first choice you pick. But usually, when you start with (C) and that answer doesn't work, you'll know which direction to go. Choice (C) will be too big or too small, leaving you with only two answers that could possibly be correct.

Let's try another one.

3. A tailor has 20 yards of shirt fabric. How many shirts can she complete if each shirt requires $2\dfrac{3}{4}$ yards of fabric?

   (A) 6
   (B) 7
   (C) 8
   (D) 10
   (E) 14

You could, of course, divide 20 by $2\frac{3}{4}$ to solve this question, but backsolving might be less painful. Start with choice (C). If the tailor could complete 8 shirts, that would require at least $2\frac{3}{4} \times \frac{11}{4} \times 8 = 22$ yards of fabric. That's too much fabric, so the correct answer must be less than 8. Eliminate (C), (D), and (E). You could multiply $2\frac{3}{4}$ by 7 at this point, or you could reason the problem out. If 8 shirts require 22 yards of fabric, and each shirt takes $2\frac{3}{4}$ yards, you know that 7 shirts would take less than 20 yards of fabric because $22 - 2\frac{3}{4}$ would be less than 20. (B) is correct.

Let's quickly recap the steps involved in backsolving:

Step 1: Start with choice (C), and plug it in. If the numbers work out, choose (C) and move on.

Step 2: If (C) doesn't work, eliminate it along with other choices you know are too big or too small.

Step 3: Keep going until you find the choice that works.

Picking Numbers

Sometimes a math problem can seem more difficult than it actually is because it's general or abstract, particularly on the Mathematical Knowledge section. You can make a question like this more concrete—and easier—by substituting numbers for the variables. Here's what we mean by picking numbers to make an abstract problem concrete.

4. When n is divided by 14, the remainder is 10. What is the remainder when n is divided by 7?

    (A) 1
    (B) 2
    (C) 3
    (D) 4
    (E) 5

Speed Tip

When picking a number on a remainder problem, add the remainder to the number you're dividing by and pick that number.

For starters, you might note that just because the question contains numbers in the answer choices, that doesn't mean that you can always backsolve. Here, backsolving doesn't make any sense. The problem is confusing because the question contains an annoying unknown value, n, rather than an actual number. So, to make this abstract question concrete, you should pick a number for n that leaves a remainder of 10 when divided by 14. The easiest strategy is to pick $n = 24$ (because $14 + 10 = 24$). Now try your number out: $24 \div 7 = 3r3$ (the "r" means remainder). Thus, the answer is (C).

Picking numbers works great on word problems that contain variables. This is great news because these problems can be especially confusing on the PRAXIS Mathematics test. Give the following example a try:

5. Four years from now, Ron will be twice as old as his sister will be then. If Ron is now R years old, how many years old is his sister?

   (A) $\dfrac{R-4}{2}$

   (B) $R-4$

   (C) $\dfrac{R+4}{2}$

   (D) $R-2$

   (E) $R+2$

Now, maybe you just love to translate word problems into algebra equations. Fine then, do it your way. But keep in mind, picking numbers can be much, much easier and quicker on questions like this one. Here's how you do it. Begin by picking a number for R, Ron's age now. Make it a nice and simple round number such as $R = 10$. Now substitute 10 for R in the question and the answer choices, and you're left with the following, much simpler problem:

Four years from now, Ron will be twice as old as his sister will be then. If Ron is now 10 years old, how many years old is his sister?

   (A) $\dfrac{10-4}{2}$, or 3

   (B) $10-4$, or 6

   (C) $\dfrac{10+4}{2}$ or 7

   (D) $10-2$, or 8

   (E) $10+2$, or 12

Now let's see. Ron is now 10 years old, so in four years he'll be 14, which means his sister will be seven years old then. Because she'll be seven in four years, that means she must be three years old now. The correct answer must be (A).

Percent questions that do not specify a value are another instance where picking numbers is an effective strategy. In cases like these, pick 100 as your value because it is easy to calculate percents of 100.

Give the following example a try.

6. The value of a certain stock rose by 30 percent from March to April
    and then decreased by 20 percent from April to May. The stock's value
    in May was what percentage of its value in March?

    (A) 90%
    (B) 100%
    (C) 104%
    (D) 110%
    (E) 124%

Notice that although the question involves the value of a certain stock, that value is never given. As a result, the question is pretty abstract. To make it more concrete and manageable, we can pick a number for the initial value of the stock. As we already mentioned, 100 is a great number to pick on percent questions. Let's say the stock originally cost $100. If it rose by 30 percent from March to April, its value in April would have been $130. If the value decreased by 20 percent in May, that decrease would be $0.20 \times \$130 = \$26$. Subtract $26 from $130 to find the answer: $130 − $26 = $104, choice (C).

You can see that working backwards can come in handy on PRAXIS Mathematics questions. Get comfortable with these strategies and be flexible in your approach to new problems. It's essential that you figure out which techniques work best for you for the wide range of problems you'll see on the test.

The remainder of this chapter will provide a quick review of the basic mathematical concepts that are tested on the PRAXIS Mathematics test.

INTRODUCING THE MATHEMATICS CONTENT REVIEW

All right. Now that we've laid out the basic math strategies, it's time to provide you with a review of the concepts that you are expected to know for the PRAXIS Mathematics exam. It's important that you keep a few things in mind as you work through this chapter.

First off, quite a bit of content is covered in this chapter. Depending on your mathematical strengths and weaknesses, you may be able to move quickly through some areas and focus on others that tend to give you trouble.

Before working through this chapter, be sure that you have taken a practice Mathematics test and noted those areas that you have the greatest difficulty with. Based on those problem areas, you can develop a plan of attack for this chapter and the wide range of content contained herein.

One last point before we begin the review—although this chapter is a content review, there will be many times when the strategies we covered in the previous chapter will come into play. Get comfortable using the answer choices or picking numbers to get to the correct answer as quickly as possible. You may find with time that you are more comfortable using textbook strategies for certain types of questions and backdoor strategies for other types. That's fine. Remember, the only rule that applies is that you need to find as many correct answers as you can in a short period of time. Shore up your weaknesses in this chapter now, and be ready to play to your strengths when test day rolls around.

Review One

THE DECIMAL SYSTEM

Decimals are numbers that use place value to show amounts less than one. You already use decimals when working with money. For example, in the amount $10.25, you know that the digits to the right of the **decimal point** represent cents, or hundredths of a dollar.

The first four decimal place values are labeled on the chart below.

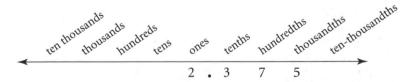

The number 2.375 is shown on the chart. Read *and* in the place of the decimal point. After reading the decimal part, say the place value of the last decimal digit. This number would be read, "two *and* three hundred seventy-five *thousandths*."

Comparing and Ordering

Comparing decimals is similar to comparing whole numbers.

1. Matt ran the 400-meter race in 45.8 seconds. Alonzo ran the same race in 45.66 seconds. Which runner had the faster time?

   | 45.80 |
   | 45.66 |

   - Line up the decimal points. Add a zero at the end of 45.8 so that both times have the same number of digits after the decimal.

   - Compare the decimal parts of the numbers as though they were whole numbers. **Alonzo's time was faster**.

   > 80 is greater than 66, so
   > 45.8 is greater than 45.66

When you compare more than two numbers, it is helpful to compare one place-value column at a time, working left to right.

2. Arrange the numbers 0.85, 1.8, 0.8, and 0.819 in order from greatest to least.

   | 0.850 |
   | 1.800 |
   | 0.800 |
   | 0.819 |

   - Write the numbers in a column, lining up the decimal points. Add zeros so that the numbers have the same number of decimal places.

   - Compare the digits, working from left to right. Only 1.8 has a whole number part—a number greater than zero to the left of the decimal point—so it is the greatest. The remaining numbers each have 8 in the tenths column. Looking at the hundredths column, 0.85 is next, followed by 0.819. The least number is 0.8.

   > In order:
   > 1.8
   > 0.85
   > 0.819
   > 0.8

DECIMAL OPERATIONS

Addition and Subtraction

Adding decimals is much like adding whole numbers. The trick is to make sure you have lined up the place-value columns correctly. You can do this by writing the numbers in a column and carefully lining up the decimal points.

1. Add 0.37 + 13.5 + 2.638

   - Write the numbers in a column, lining up the decimal points.
   - You may add placeholder zeros so that the decimals have the same number of decimal places.

   | 0.370 |
   | 13.500 |
   | + 2.638 |

   - Add. Start on the right, and add each column. Regroup, or carry, as you would with whole numbers.

   - Place the decimal point in the answer directly below the decimal points in the problem.

   | 1 1 |
   | 0.370 |
   | 13.500 |
   | + 2.638 |
   | 16.508 |

To subtract decimals, write the numbers in a column with the greater number on top. Make sure the decimal points are in a line.

2. Find the difference between 14.512 and 8.7

    $$\begin{array}{r} 14.512 \\ -8.700 \\ \hline \end{array}$$

    - Write the numbers in a column, lining up the decimal points. Add placeholder zeros so that the numbers have the same numbers of decimal places.
    - Subtract. Regroup, or borrow, as needed. Place the decimal point in the answer directly in line with the decimal points in the problem.

    $$\begin{array}{r} {}^{13\ 15} \\ \cancel{14.5}12 \\ -8.700 \\ \hline 5.812 \end{array}$$

The greater number may have fewer or no decimal places. In the next example, a decimal is subtracted from a whole number.

3. What does 9 minus 3.604 equal?

    $$\begin{array}{r} 9.000 \\ -3.604 \\ \hline \end{array}$$

    - Line up the place-value columns. Put a decimal point after the whole number 9 and add placeholder zeros.
    - Subtract, regrouping as needed. Place the decimal point in the answer directly below the decimal points in the problem.

    $$\begin{array}{r} {}^{8\ \ 9\,9\,10} \\ \cancel{9.000} \\ -3.604 \\ \hline 5.396 \end{array}$$

Multiplication and Division

The rules you use to multiply whole numbers can be used to multiply decimals. You don't have to line up the decimal points. You will wait until you are finished multiplying before you place the decimal point in the answer. The number of decimal places in the answer equals the total number of decimal places in the numbers you are multiplying.

1. Find the product of 2.6 and 0.45

    $$\begin{array}{r} 2.6 \\ \times 0.45 \\ \hline \end{array}$$

    - Set up the problem as though you were multiplying the whole numbers 26 and 45.
    - Ignore the decimal points while you multiply.
    - Now count the decimal places in the numbers you multiplied. The number 2.6 has one decimal place, and 0.45 has two decimal places, for a total of three.
    - Starting from the right, count three decimal places to the left and insert the decimal point.

    $$\begin{array}{r} 2.6 \\ \times 0.45 \\ \hline 130 \\ 1040 \\ \hline 1.170 \end{array}$$

When you divide decimals, you must figure out where the decimal point will go in the answer before you divide.

2. Divide 14.4 by 6

    - Set up the problem. Because the divisor (the number you are dividing by) is a whole number, place the decimal point in the answer directly above the decimal point in the dividend (the number you are dividing).
    - Divide. Use the rules you learned for dividing whole numbers.

$$
\begin{array}{r}
2.4 \\
6\overline{)14.4} \\
-12 \\
\hline
2\ 4 \\
-2\ 4 \\
\hline
0
\end{array}
$$

If the divisor is also a decimal, you must move the decimal points in both the divisor and the dividend before you divide.

3. Divide 4.9 by 0.35

    - Set up the problem. There are two decimal places in the divisor, which is 0.35. Move the decimal point in both the divisor and the dividend, 4.9, two places to the right. Note that you need to add a zero in the dividend to move the decimal two places.
    - Place the decimal point in the quotient directly above the decimal point in the dividend.
    - Divide.

$$
0.35\overline{)4.90}
$$

$$
\begin{array}{r}
14. \\
35\overline{)490.} \\
-35 \\
\hline
140 \\
-140 \\
\hline
0
\end{array}
$$

FRACTIONS

A fraction uses two numbers to represent part of a whole. The bottom number, called the **denominator**, indicates how many equal parts are in the whole group or how many parts into which one item is divided. The top number, called the **numerator**, indicates how many parts you are working with.

- There are 4 equal parts in this rectangle. Because 3 are shaded, we say that $\frac{3}{4}$ of the rectangle is shaded.

In a proper fraction, the numerator is less than the denominator. A **proper fraction** represents a quantity less than 1. An **improper fraction** is equal to or greater than 1.

- There are 6 equal parts in the figure below, and 6 are shaded; therefore, $\frac{6}{6}$ of the figure are shaded: $\frac{6}{6} = 1$

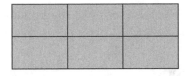

- In this grouping, each figure is divided into 2 equal parts. A total of 3 parts are shaded, so the fraction of the shaded area of the figures is $\frac{3}{2}$.

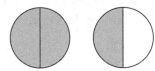

A **mixed number** is another way to show an amount greater than 1. It consists of a whole number and a proper fraction. Another name for the shaded portion in the last figure is $1\frac{1}{2}$. The improper fraction $\frac{3}{2}$ equals the mixed number $1\frac{1}{2}$.

You can also change an improper fraction to a whole number or mixed number.

1. Change $\frac{16}{5}$ to a mixed number.
   - Divide the numerator (16) by the denominator (5). Because 16 is not evenly divisible by 5, there is a remainder. In this case, the remainder is 1.

     $$16 \div 5 = 3r1$$

   - The answer becomes the whole number, and the remainder becomes the numerator of the proper fraction. The denominator is the same as the original fraction.

     $$\frac{16}{5} = 3\frac{1}{5}$$

You can also change a mixed number to an improper fraction.

2. Change $7\frac{2}{3}$ to an improper fraction.
   - Multiply the whole number (7) by the denominator of the fraction (3), and add the numerator (2).

     $$7 \times 3 = 21$$
     $$21 + 2 = 23$$

   - Write the sum over the denominator of the original fraction.

     $$7\frac{2}{3} = \frac{23}{3}$$

To perform operations with fractions, you need to be able to write equal fractions in higher or lower terms. The terms are the numerator and the denominator. A fraction is **reduced to lowest terms** when the two terms do not have any common factor except 1.

- To **raise** a fraction, multiply both terms by the same number: $\frac{3}{4} = \frac{3 \times 3}{4 \times 3} = \frac{9}{12}$

- To **reduce** a fraction, divide both terms by the same number: $\frac{10}{15} = \frac{10 \div 5}{15 \div 5} = \frac{2}{3}$

FRACTION OPERATIONS

Additions and Subtraction

You can add or subtract like **fractions**. Like fractions have a **common denominator**. In other words, the numbers below the fraction bar are the same.

1. Add $\frac{3}{10} + \frac{5}{10}$
   - Because the denominators are the same, add the numerators.

     $\frac{3}{10} + \frac{5}{10} = \frac{8}{10}$

   - Reduce the answer to lowest terms.

     $\frac{8}{10} = \frac{8 \div 2}{10 \div 2} = \frac{4}{5}$

2. Subtract $\frac{2}{9}$ from $\frac{7}{9}$

   - Subtract the numerators. The answer is already in lowest terms.

     $\frac{7}{9} - \frac{2}{9} = \frac{5}{9}$

If the denominators are not the same, convert one or both fractions to equivalent fractions so that they become like fractions.

3. Add $\frac{5}{6} + \frac{1}{4}$

   - One way to find a common denominator is to list the multiples of both denominators.

     Multiples of 6: 6, $\boxed{12}$, 18

     Multiples of 4: 4, 8, $\boxed{12}$, 16

     The lowest common multiple of the denominators is 12.

   - Convert each fraction to an equivalent fraction with a denominator of 12.

     $\frac{5 \times 2}{6 \times 2} = \frac{10}{12}, \frac{1 \times 3}{4 \times 3} = \frac{3}{12}$

   - Add the like fractions.

     $\frac{10}{12} + \frac{3}{12} = \frac{13}{12}$

Multiplication and Division

It is not necessary to find a common denominator to multiply and divide fractions. To multiply fractions, simply multiply the numerators and then the denominators. Reduce the answer to lowest terms, if necessary.

1. What is the product of $\frac{7}{8}$ and $\frac{1}{2}$?
   - Multiply the numerators together, and then multiply the denominators.

$$\frac{7}{8} \times \frac{1}{2} = \frac{7 \times 1}{8 \times 2} = \frac{7}{16}$$

Before multiplying a mixed number, change it to an improper fraction.

2. What is $\frac{1}{3}$ of $3\frac{3}{4}$?

$$3\frac{3}{4} = \frac{15}{4}$$

   - Change $3\frac{3}{4}$ to an improper fraction.
   - Multiply the numerators and the denominators.

$$\frac{1}{3} \times \frac{15}{4} = \frac{1 \times 15}{3 \times 4} = \frac{15}{12}$$

   - Change to a mixed number and reduce to lowest terms.

$$\frac{15}{12} = 1\frac{3}{12} = 1\frac{1}{4}$$

You will need one additional step to divide fractions. Before dividing, **invert** the divisor (the fraction you are dividing by). To invert a fraction, switch the numerator and the denominator. Finally, change the division symbol to a multiplication symbol and multiply.

3. Jim has an 8-pound bag of nuts. He wants to fill smaller, $\frac{1}{2}$ pound bags using the nuts. How many $\frac{1}{2}$ pound bags can he fill?
   - Divide 8 by $\frac{1}{2}$. Set up the division problem. Always write the whole or mixed numbers as improper fractions.

$$8 \div \frac{1}{2} = \frac{8}{1} \div \frac{1}{2} =$$

   - Invert the fraction you are dividing by, and change the operation sign to multiplication. Multiply, following the rules for multiplying fractions. **Jim can fill 16 small bags**.

$$\frac{8}{1} \times \frac{2}{1} = \frac{16}{1} = 16$$

RATIOS

Ratios represent the proportion of one quantity to another.

Ratios are usually written in the form *c:d*. A ratio does not, by itself, tell you the number of each item present.

1. The ratio of blue marbles to green marbles in a bag is 5:3.

This does *not* necessarily mean that there are 5 blue marbles and 3 green marbles in the bag. All it means is that for every 5 blue marbles, there are 3 green marbles. It is possible that there are 10 blue marbles and 6 green marbles, 50 blue marbles and 30 green marbles, or any other combination in which the proportion of blue marbles to green marbles is 5:3.

Ratios can also be written as fractions. To write a ratio as a fraction, put the number associated with the *of* in the numerator (on top) and put the number associated with the word *to* in the denominator (on the bottom) and reduce.

2. The ratio of 20 apples to 12 oranges is $\frac{20}{12}$, which reduces to $\frac{5}{3}$.

Part-to-Part Ratios versus Part-to-Whole Ratios

A ratio can either express the relationship of a part to whole of which it is a part, or it can express the relationship of a part to another part of the same whole.

The examples above both express part-to-part ratios. In the case of the marbles, there are two parts: blue marbles and green marbles. If all marbles in the bag are either blue or green, they make up the whole, that is, all of the marbles in the bag. If we wanted to express the ratio of blue marbles to all the marbles in the bag, we would have to add the blue and green marbles together.

1. If the ratio of blue marbles to green marbles in a bag is $\frac{5}{3}$, then the ratio of blue marbles to all marbles is $\frac{5}{3+5} = \frac{5}{8}$.

PROPORTIONS

A **proportion** is an equation that shows that two ratios are equal. The cross products in a true proportion are equal. In other words, when you multiply diagonally across the equal sign, the products are equal.

1. The directions on a can of powdered drink mix say to add 3 cups of water to every 2 scoops of drink mix. Mike adds 12 cups of water to 8 scoops of drink mix. Did he make the drink correctly?

    *   Write the proportion, making sure the terms of the ratios are in the same order.

        $$\frac{\text{cups}}{\text{scoops}} \quad \frac{3}{2} = \frac{12}{8}$$

    *   Cross multiply and compare the products. Because the products are the same, the ratios are equal. **Mike made the drink correctly**.

        $$3 \times 8 = 24$$
        $$2 \times 12 = 24$$

In most proportion problems, you are asked to solve for a missing term.

2. A map scale says that 2 inches = 150 miles. What actual distance would a map distance of 5 inches represent?

    *   Write a proportion with both ratios in the same form: inches to miles. The variable x represents the unknown distance in miles.

        $$\frac{\text{inches}}{\text{miles}} \quad \frac{2}{150} = \frac{5}{x}$$

    *   Locate the term in the first ratio that is diagonal from the known term in the second ratio. Cross multiply.

        $$\frac{2}{150} = \frac{5}{x}$$
        $$150 \times 5 = 750$$

    *   Divide the result by the remaining known term to find the value of x.

        $$x = 750 \div 2 = 375$$

RATES

Some proportion problems ask you to find a **rate**. A rate compares the number of units of one item to one unit of another item. When a rate is written in fraction form, its denominator is always one unit. In word form, rates are often expressed using the word *per*.

1. Connie drove 276 miles on 12 gallons of gasoline. How many miles per gallon did she get on the trip?

    $$\frac{\text{miles}}{\text{gallons}} \quad \frac{276}{12} = \frac{x}{1}$$

    *   Gas mileage is one kind of rate. You need to find how many miles Connie drove on 1 gallon of gasoline.

        $$(276)(1) = 12x$$
        $$x = 276 \div 12 = 23$$

    *   Solve. **Connie got 23 miles per gallon on the trip.**

PERCENTS

Percent means "per hundred" or "out of one hundred." For example, if you have $100 and you spend $25, you spent $25 of $100 or 25% of your money.

Because a percentage is a way of showing part of a whole, it has much in common with fractions, decimals, and ratios. In fact, percentages are just a specific type of fraction, one in which the denominator is 100.

- To convert a percent to a fraction, write the percent over 100 and reduce. To convert percents to decimals, drop the percent symbol and move the decimal point two places to the left.

<table>
<tr><td align="center">**Percent to Fraction**</td><td align="center">**Percent to Decimal**</td></tr>
<tr><td align="center">$25\% = \dfrac{25\%}{100\%} = \dfrac{25}{100} = \dfrac{1}{4}$</td><td align="center">$25\% = .25 = 0.25$</td></tr>
</table>

In any percent problem, there are three elements: the whole, the part, and the percent. The whole is the amount that the problem is about. The **part** is a portion of the whole. The **percent** is a number followed by the percent symbol (%).

1. At a restaurant, Janice's bill is $20. She gives the waiter a tip of $3, which is 15% of her bill. Identify the whole, part, and percent in this situation.

   - The entire bill of $20 is the whole. The $3 tip is the part, and the percent is 15%.

   - One way to think of a percent problem is as a proportion. In this example, there are two ratios. The $3 tip is figured as a part of the $20, and 15% is the same as $\dfrac{15}{100}$. Because the two ratios are equal, they can be written as a proportion.

     $$\dfrac{part}{whole}\ \dfrac{3}{20} = \dfrac{15}{100}$$

   - Cross multiply to prove that the ratios are equal.

     $$20 \times 15 = 300$$
     $$3 \times 100 = 300$$

You can solve percent problems by using the equation Percent $= \dfrac{part}{whole}$ and solving for the missing element. Sometimes you will want to use the equation in the form Part = percent × whole. Just remember to express the percent as a number over 100.

2. At a plant that manufactures lighting fixtures, it is expected that approximately 2% of the fixtures assembled each day will have some type of defect. If 900 fixtures are completed in one day, how many are expected to be defective?

   - We are given the percent and the whole, and we want to find the part. So we will use the equation Part = percent × whole.
     Here, 2% = 0.02

   - Find the part. 2% of 900 = 0.02 × 900 = 18. **The company can expect about 18 defective fixtures.**

PROBABILITY

The numerical representation of the likelihood of an event or events occurring is termed **probability**.

Probability is the ratio of the number of favorable outcomes possible to the total number of outcomes possible, or, in fractional form,

$$\text{Probability (Event)} = \frac{\text{\# of favorable outcomes possible}}{\text{total \# of possible outcomes}}$$

1. If you flip a coin, what are the odds that it will fall with the heads side up?

   • The probability that the coin will land heads up is $\frac{1}{2}$ because there is one outcome favorable to your result (heads up), and there are two possible outcomes (heads or tails).

FACTORS, PRIMES, AND DIVISIBILITY

Multiples

An integer that is divisible by another integer is a **multiple** of that integer.

   • 12 is a multiple of 3 because 12 is divisible by 3; $12 = 3 \times 4$

The multiples of a number can be thought of as those numbers that you would get if you "counted" by that number. For example, if you counted by 6, you would get: 6, 12, 18, 24, 36, 42, 48, and so on. All of these numbers are multiples of 6.

Remainders

The **remainder** is what is left over in a division problem. A remainder is always smaller than the number you are dividing by.

   • 17 divided by 3 is 5 with a remainder of 2

This means that you can divide 17 into 5 equal parts, all of which have 3 units, plus 2 leftover units.

Factors

The **factors** of a number are the positive integers that evenly divide into that number.

- 36 has nine factors: 1, 2, 3, 4, 6, 9, 12, 18, and 36.

These factors can be grouped into pairs:

$$1 \times 36 = 2 \times 18 = 3 \times 12 = 4 \times 9 = 6 \times 6$$

Divisibility Tests

There are several tests to determine whether a number is divisible by 2, 3, 4, 5, 6, or 9.

A number is divisible by 2 if its last digit is divisible by 2.

- 138 is divisible by 2 because 8 is divisible by 2

A number is divisible by 3 if the sum of its digits is divisible by 3.

- 4,317 is divisible by 3 because $4 + 3 + 1 + 7 = 15$, and 15 is divisible by 3
- 239 is **not** divisible by 3 because $2 + 3 + 9 = 14$, and 14 is not divisible by 3

A number is divisible by 4 if its last two digits are divisible by 4.

- 1,748 is divisible by 4 because 48 is divisible by 4

A number is divisible by 5 if its last digit is 0 or 5.

- 2,635 is divisible by 5, but 5,052 is **not** divisible by 5

A number is divisible by 6 if it is divisible by both 2 and 3.

- 4,326 is divisible by 6 because it is divisible by 2 (last digit is 6) and by 3 $(4 + 3 + 2 + 6 = 15)$

A number is divisible by 9 if the sum of its digits is divisible by 9.

- 22,428 is divisible by 9 because $2 + 2 + 4 + 2 + 8 = 18$, and 18 is divisible by 9

Prime Number

A prime number is an integer greater than 1 that has no factors other than 1 and itself. The number 1 is not considered a prime. The number 2 is the first prime number and the only even prime. (This is fairly evident. Every other even number is divisible by two and therefore is not prime.) The first ten prime numbers are 2, 3, 5, 7, 11, 13, 17, 19, 23, and 29.

THE COORDINATE PLANE

A coordinate grid is a way of locating points that lie in a **plane** or flat surface. The grid is formed by two intersecting lines, an *x*-axis, and a *y*-axis. The *x*-axis is actually a horizontal number line. The point at which the two axes intersect is called the **origin**.

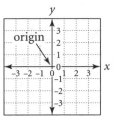

Each point on the grid can be named using a set of two numbers called an **ordered pair**. The first number is the distance from the origin along the *x*-axis. The second number is the distance from the origin along the *y*-axis. The numbers are written in parentheses and are separated by a comma: (x, y).

1. Write the ordered pairs for points *M* and *P*.

    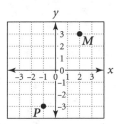

    • Point *M* lies 2 spaces to the right of the origin along the *x*-axis and 3 spaces above the origin along the *y*-axis. The coordinates are $(2, 3)$.

    • Point *P* lies 1 space to the left along the *x*-axis and 3 spaces down along the *y*-axis. The coordinates are $(-1, -3)$.

To plot points on the grid, use the number lines located at the axes. Remember that right and up are the directions for positive numbers, and left and down are the directions for negative numbers.

2. Point *A* is located at $(-2, 1)$, and point *B* is located at $(3, -2)$. Plot these points on a coordinate grid.

    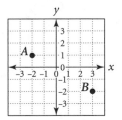

    • To plot *A*, start at the origin. Count 2 spaces left along the *x*-axis. Count 1 space up along the *y*-axis.

    • To plot point *B*, start at the origin. Count 3 spaces right along the *x*-axis. Count 2 spaces down along the *y*-axis.

Review One Practice

Round these numbers as directed.

1. Round 3.75 to the tenths place.

2. Round 5.908 to the ones place.

Which number is greater?

3. 0.45 or 0.449

4. 0.008 or 0.08

Write these numbers from least to greatest.

5. 5.6   5.08   5.8   5.802

6. 0.1136   0.12   0.2   0.115

Solve.

7. $\begin{array}{r} 4.025 \\ +3.971 \\ \hline \end{array}$

8. $\begin{array}{r} 8.5 \\ -1.074 \\ \hline \end{array}$

9. $\begin{array}{r} 17.52 \\ + 3.8 \\ \hline \end{array}$

10. James ran three miles. His times for the individual miles were 7.2 minutes, 6.8 minutes, and 8.25 minutes. How long did it take him, in minutes, to run the three-mile distance?

    (A)   9.65
    (B)   22.25
    (C)   22.7
    (D)   23.35
    (E)   96.5

11. $\begin{array}{r} 5.3 \\ \times\, 0.5 \\ \hline \end{array}$

12. $8\overline{)28.8}$

13. $\begin{array}{r} 9.62 \\ \times\, 1.005 \\ \hline \end{array}$

14. One container of floor cleaner holds 3.79 liters. If Zachary bought 4 containers, how many liters of cleaner did he buy?

    (A) 0.9475
    (B)   7.79
    (C)   9.48
    (D) 12.83
    (E) 15.16

Write the proper fraction for the shaded portion of each figure.

15.    16.

Write an improper fraction and a mixed number for the shaded portion of each group of figures.

17. 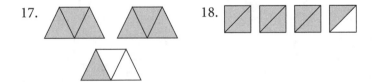   18.

Write improper fractions as mixed numbers and mixed numbers as improper fractions.

19. $\dfrac{17}{3} =$

20. $2\dfrac{5}{12} =$

Write an equal fraction with the given denominator.

21. $\dfrac{3}{4} = \dfrac{}{16}$

22. $\dfrac{3}{8} = \dfrac{}{40}$

Reduce each fraction to lowest terms.

23. $\dfrac{21}{28} =$

24. $\dfrac{4}{24} =$

25. Eighteen of every 24 people surveyed say they went to at least one movie in December. What fraction of the people surveyed went to a movie in December?

   (A) $\dfrac{3}{4}$

   (B) $\dfrac{2}{3}$

   (C) $\dfrac{1}{2}$

   (D) $\dfrac{1}{3}$

   (E) $\dfrac{1}{4}$

26. $5\dfrac{5}{6} + 2\dfrac{2}{3} =$

27. $\dfrac{3}{8} + \dfrac{7}{12} + 1\dfrac{2}{3} =$

28. To make the top of a dining room table, Craig glued a piece of oak that is $\frac{5}{16}$ inch thick to a piece of pine that is $\frac{7}{8}$ inch thick. What is the total thickness, in inches, of the tabletop?

    (A) $\frac{1}{2}$

    (B) $\frac{9}{16}$

    (C) $1\frac{3}{16}$

    (D) $1\frac{1}{4}$

    (E) $1\frac{9}{16}$

29. $\frac{2}{3} \times \frac{1}{4} =$

30. $2\frac{1}{3} \times 3\frac{2}{5} =$

31. A pygmy kangaroo needs to cross a highway that is 10 meters across. If the kangaroo covers exactly $1\frac{1}{4}$ meters each time it hops, how many hops would it take for the kangaroo to cross the highway?

    (A) 5
    (B) 6
    (C) 7
    (D) 8
    (E) 9

Write each ratio as a fraction in lowest terms.

32. Stan made 24 sales in 6 hours. What is the ratio of sales to hours?

33. Carol's monthly take-home pay is $1,500. She spends $250 a month on food. What is the ratio of food costs to take-home pay?

34. A toy rocket travels 180 feet in 15 seconds. What is the ratio of feet to seconds?

35. Soan made a $400 down payment on a washer and dryer that cost a total of $1,200. What is the ratio of the amount paid to the amount owed after making the down payment?

    (A) 1 to 4
    (B) 1 to 3
    (C) 1 to 2
    (D) 2 to 3
    (E) 3 to 4

36. $\dfrac{2}{3} = \dfrac{x}{18}$

37. $\dfrac{4}{\$2.12} = \dfrac{7}{x}$

38. The Bay City Cardinals have won 5 of 8 games. At the same rate, how many games will they have to play to win 60 games?

    (A) 190
    (B) 180
    (C) 120
    (D) 96
    (E) 12

39. What is 20% of $25?

40. Find 90% of 200.

41. Pat called 120 customers to offer a software upgrade. Of those he called, 72 purchased the upgrade. What percent agreed to the purchase?

    (A) 6%
    (B) 40%
    (C) 48%
    (D) 60%
    (E) 66%

For each situation, identify and label the whole, part, and percent.

42. Victor owes his uncle $1,000. Recently, he gave his uncle $200. The payment was 20% of the money he owes.

43. On a test with 80 problems, Sophie got 72 problems correct. In other words, she answered 90% of the problems correctly.

Express probability as a fraction, decimal, and percent.

44. A game has 50 wooden tiles. Players draw tiles to spell words. If 20 of the tiles are marked with vowels, what is the probability of drawing a vowel from the tiles?

45. There are four red, four blue, and two green marbles in a bag. If one marble is chosen from the bag, what is the probability that the marble will be green?

46. What is the greatest integer that will divide evenly into both 36 and 54?

    (A) 6
    (B) 9
    (C) 12
    (D) 18
    (E) 27

47. Which of the following is not a factor of 168?

    (A) 21
    (B) 24
    (C) 28
    (D) 32
    (E) 42

Write the ordered pair for each point.

48. Point A

49. Point B

50. Point C

51. Point D

52. Point E

53. Point F

54. Point G

55. Point H

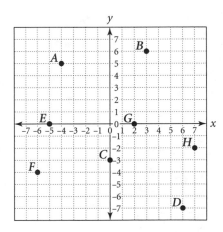

Plot the points on the coordinate grid.

56. Plot the following points:

> *J* at $(-3, -2)$
> *K* at $(4, 0)$
> *L* at $(1, -3)$
> *M* at $(-4, 2)$

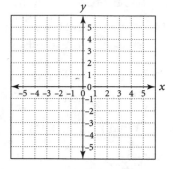

Review One Answer Key

1. 3.8

2. 6

3. 0.45

4. 0.08

5. 5.08, 5.6, 5.8, 5.802

6. 0.1136, 0.115, 0.12, 0.2

7. 7.996

8. 7.426

9. 21.32

10. (B) 22.25

Add the times: $7.2 + 6.8 + 8.25 = 22.25$ minutes. You do not need to use the three-mile distance to solve the problem.

11. 2.65

12. 3.6

13. 9.6681

14. (E) 15.16

Multiply 3.79 liters by 4. Then $3.79 \times 4 = 15.16$ liters.

15. $\frac{3}{5}$

16. $\frac{2}{4}$, or $\frac{1}{2}$

17. $\frac{7}{3}$, or $2\frac{1}{3}$

18. $\frac{7}{2}$, or $3\frac{1}{2}$

19. $5\frac{2}{3}$

20. $\frac{29}{12}$

21. $\frac{12}{16}$

22. $\frac{15}{40}$

23. $\frac{3}{4}$

24. $\frac{1}{6}$

25. (A) $\frac{3}{4}$

Of those surveyed, $\frac{18}{24}$ went to at least one movie. Reduce the fraction to lowest terms.

$\frac{18 \div 6}{24 \div 6} = \frac{3}{4}$

26. $8\frac{1}{2}$

27. $2\frac{5}{8}$

28. (C) $1\frac{3}{16}$

Add to find the total.

$\frac{5}{16} + \frac{7}{8} = \frac{5}{16} + \frac{14}{16} = \frac{19}{16} = 1\frac{3}{16}$ inches

29. $\frac{1}{6}$

30. $7\frac{14}{15}$

31. (D) 8

Divide 10 by $1\frac{1}{4}$ because the kangaroo needs to cover 10 meters with a series of jumps each $1\frac{1}{4}$ meters in length. When dividing by a mixed number like $1\frac{1}{4}$, it's easier to work with an improper fraction. $1\frac{1}{4} = \frac{5}{4}$, so you need to divide 10 by $\frac{5}{4}$. Remember, when dividing by a fraction, you flip the divisor and then multiply. So, $10 \div \frac{5}{4} = 10 \times \frac{4}{5} = \frac{40}{5} = 8$. It would take the kangaroo exactly 8 hops to cross the highway, so choice (D) is correct.

32. $\dfrac{24}{6} = \dfrac{4}{1}$

33. $\dfrac{\$250}{\$1,500} = \dfrac{1}{6}$

34. $\dfrac{180}{15} = \dfrac{12}{1}$

35. (C) 1 to 2

Subtract to find the amount owed.
    $1,200 − $400 = $800.
Write the ratio and reduce.
    400 to 800 = 1 to 2

36. 12

37. $3.71

38. (D) 96

$\dfrac{5}{8} = \dfrac{60}{x}$

$8 \times 60 \div 5 = 96$

39. $5

40. 180

41. (D) 60%

$72 \div 120 = 0.6 = 60\%$

42. whole = $1,000
    part = $200
    percent = 20%

43. whole = 80
    part = 72
    percent = 90%

44. $\dfrac{2}{5}$, 0.4, 40%

45. $\dfrac{1}{5}$, 0.2, 20%

46. (D) 18

47. (D) 32

48. (−4, 5)

49. (3, 6)

50. (0, −3)

51. (6, −7)

52. (−5, 0)

53. (−6, −4)

54. (2, 0)

55. (7, −2)

56.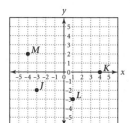

Review Two

THE ORDER OF OPERATIONS

When a mathematical expression contains more than one operation, its value may depend on the order in which the operations are performed. To avoid confusion, mathematicians have agreed to perform operations in a certain order.

The Order of Operations

1. Parentheses or any other grouping symbols that enclose operations

2. Exponents and roots

3. Multiplication and division, working from left to right

4. Addition and subtraction, working from left to right

Study the following example to see how to apply the order of operations. Notice that the parentheses are used in two places in the expression; however, only the first set of parentheses encloses an operation.

1. Evaluate the expression $\dfrac{(5+3)^2}{4} + 3(-1)$

   - Perform the addition in parentheses.

     $$\dfrac{(8)^2}{4} + 3(-1)$$

   - Raise 8 to exponent 2.

     $$\dfrac{64}{4} + 3(-1)$$

   - Divide, then multiply.

     $$16 + (-3)$$

   - Add.

     $$13$$

The value of the expression $\dfrac{(5+3)^2}{4} + 3(-1)$ is 13.

The division bar is also a grouping symbol. Before you divide, perform any operations shown above and below the bar.

2. Evaluate the expression $\dfrac{15+25}{2(5)} + 6$

   - Perform the operations above and below the fraction bar.
   - Divide, then add.

     $$\dfrac{15+25}{2(5)} + 6$$

     $$\dfrac{40}{10} + 6$$

     $$4 + 6 = 10$$

ALGEBRAIC EXPRESSIONS

An **algebraic expression** uses numbers, operations, and variables to show number relationships. **Variables** are letters (such as x and y) that represent unknown numbers. Each time the same letter is used within the same expression, it represents the same number.

Here are some examples of algebraic expressions in both words and symbols:

Algebraic expressions in words	In symbols
the product of 5 and a number	$5x$
a number decreased by 12	$x - 12$
the sum of 3 and the square of a number	$3 + x^2$
6 less than the quotient of a number and 2	$\frac{x}{2} - 6$
one-half a number increased by 15	$\frac{1}{2}x + 15$
4 times the difference of -3 and a number	$4(-3 - x)$
a number less another number	$x - y$
10 less the square root of a number plus 3	$10 - \sqrt{x} + 3$

SIMPLIFYING AND EVALUATING EXPRESSIONS

Simplifying an expression means performing all the operations you can within an expression. When working with variables, you must remember an important rule: You can add or subtract like terms only.

A **term** is a number, a variable, or the product or quotient of numbers and variables. A term cannot include a sum or a difference.

$$5x \quad 3y^2 \quad 13 \quad x^3 \quad \frac{x}{2}$$

Like terms have the same variable raised to the same power. For example, $3x^2$ and $5x^2$ are like terms; $8y$ and $4y$ are also like terms. However, $6x$ and $2x^2$ are *not* like terms because the variables are not raised to the same exponent.

To simplify an expression, combine like terms.

- Simplify $2x - 5 + 4x^2 - 8 + 6x$

$$2x - 5 + 4x^2 - 8 + 6x$$
$$= (2x + 6x) + (-5 + (-8)) + 4x^2$$
$$= 8x + (-13) + 4x^2$$
$$= 4x^2 + 8x - 13$$

It is customary to write the term with the greatest exponent first and to continue in descending order.

The **distributive property** allows you to remove grouping symbols to simplify expressions. We can state the distributive property using symbols.

$$a(b + c) = ab + ac \text{ and } a(b - c) = ab - ac$$

In other words, each term inside the parentheses is multiplied by the term outside the parentheses, and the results are added or subtracted depending on the operation inside the parentheses. The next example applies the distributive property.

1. Simplify $4x - 3(x + 9) + 15$.

   • Change the subtraction of $3(x + 9)$ to the addition of a negative number.

   • Use the distributive property. Multiply -3 by each term in the parentheses.

   • Combine like terms. (*Note:* $1x$ means x.)

$$\begin{aligned} &4x - 3(x + 9) + 15 \\ &= 4x + -3(x + 9) + 15 \\ &= 4x + (-3x) + (-3)(9) + 15 \\ &= 4x + -3x + -27 + 15 \\ &= (4x + -3x) + (-27 + 15) \\ &= 1x - 12 \\ &= x - 12 \end{aligned}$$

Evaluating an expression means finding its value. To evaluate an expression, substitute a given number for each variable.

2. Find the value of the expression $\dfrac{3x + 2y}{4}$ when $x = 6$ and $y = 5$.

   • Replace the variables with the corresponding values given in the problem.

$$\frac{3x + 2y}{4} = \frac{3(6) + 2(5)}{4}$$

   • Perform the operations above the fraction bar.

$$\frac{3(6) + 2(5)}{4} = \frac{18 + 10}{4} = \frac{28}{4} = 7$$

Note: To remove parentheses from an operation that follows a minus sign, imagine that the parentheses are preceded by 1. Then use the distributive property.

$$\begin{aligned} &-(2x + 3) \\ &= -1(2x + 3) \\ &= -1(2x) + (-1)(3) \\ &= -2x + (-3) \text{ or } -2x - 3 \end{aligned}$$

EQUATIONS

An **equation** is a mathematical statement that two expressions are equal.

$$3 + 5 = 4 \cdot 2 \qquad 10 - 1 = 3^2 \qquad 5(3 + 5) = 40$$

An equation can contain one or more variables. Solving an equation means finding a value for each variable that will make the equation true.

$$\begin{array}{ccc} 4 + x = 11 & 3x = 24 & x - 5 = -2 \\ x = 7 & x = 8 & x = 3 \end{array}$$

The basic strategy in solving an equation is to isolate the variable on one side of the equation. You can do this by performing **inverse**, or opposite, operations. However, you must always follow one basic rule: Whatever you do to one side of the equation, you must also do to the other side.

Solve $x - 23 = 45$

On the left side of the equation, the number 23 is subtracted from x. The inverse of subtraction is addition. Add 23 to both sides of the equation.

$$x - 23 = 45$$
$$x - 23 + 23 = 45 + 23$$
$$x = 68$$

To check your work, replace the variable with your solution and simplify. When $x = 68$, the equation is true.

Check:
$$x - 23 = 45$$
$$68 - 23 = 45$$
$$45 = 45$$

The following examples use the inverse operations of multiplication and division.

Solve $\frac{x}{2} = 17$

The variable x is divided by 2. Because multiplication is the inverse of division, you must multiply each side of the equation by 2.

$$\frac{x}{2} = 17$$
$$2\left(\frac{x}{2}\right) = 2(17)$$
$$x = 34$$

To check your work, replace the variable with your solution and simplify.

When $x = 34$, the equation is true.

Check:
$$\frac{34}{2} = 17$$
$$17 = 17$$

Solve $5x = 75$

Because the variable x is multiplied by 5, divide both sides of the equation by 5.

$$5x = 75$$
$$\frac{5x}{5} = \frac{75}{5}$$
$$x = 15$$

ALGEBRA WORD PROBLEMS

Algebra problems describe how several numbers are related. One number is the unknown, which you will represent with a variable. Using the relationships described in the problem, you can write an equation and solve for the variable.

1. There are twice as many women as men in a class on auto repair. If there are 24 students in the class, how many are women?

    *   Express the numbers in the problem in terms of the *same* variable. Let x represent the number of men. Because there are twice as many women, let $2x$ represent the number of women.

    *   Write and then solve an equation. The total number of men and women is 24, so $x + 2x = 24$. Solve:

        $$x + 2x = 24$$
        $$3x = 24$$
        $$x = 8$$

Because $x = 8$, $2x = 2(8) = 16$. There are 8 men and 16 women in the class.

Consecutive numbers are numbers that follow in the counting order. For example, 1, 2, and 3 are consecutive numbers. The numbers 2, 4, and 6 are consecutive even numbers, and 1, 3, and 5 are consecutive odd numbers.

2. The sum of three consecutive numbers is 105. What is the greatest of the three numbers?

   - Let x represent the first number, and $x + 1$ and $x + 2$ represent the other numbers.

   - Write an equation and solve:

   - Find the answer. The variable x represents the first number in the sequence, so the three numbers are 34, 35, and 36. The problem asks for the greatest number, which is 36.

$$x + (x + 1) + (x + 2) = 105$$
$$3x + 3 = 105$$
$$3x = 102$$
$$x = 34$$

PATTERNS AND FUNCTIONS

A **pattern** is a series of numbers or objects whose sequence is determined by a particular rule. You can figure out what rule has been used by studying the terms you are given. Think: What operation or sequence of operations will always result in the next term in the series? Once you know the rule, you can continue the pattern.

1. Find the seventh term in the sequence: 1, 2, 4, 8, 16,…

   - Determine the rule. Each number in the sequence is two times the number before it.

   - Apply the rule. You have been given five terms and must find the seventh. Continue the pattern. The sixth term will be $16 \times 2 = 32$, and the seventh term will be $32 \times 2 = 64$.

A **function** is an algebraic rule that shows how the terms in one sequence of numbers are related to the terms in another sequence. For example, a sidewalk vendor charges $1.50 for a slice of pizza. The chart below shows how much it would cost to buy one to six slices.

Number of Pizza Slices	1	2	3	4	5	6
Cost	$1.50	$3.00	$4.50	$6.00	$7.50	$9.00

Each number in the first row corresponds to a price in the second row. We could say that the amount a customer will pay is a function of (or depends on) the number of slices the customer orders. This function could be written:

Cost = number of slices × $1.50, or C = n($1.50).

If you know the function and a number in the first set of numbers, you can solve for its corresponding number in the second set.

2. Using the function $y = 3x + 5$, what is the value of y when $x = -3$?

   - Substitute the given value of x.
   - Solve for y.

$$y = 3(-3) + 5$$
$$y = -9 + 5$$
$$y = -4$$

3. Using the function $n = 100 - 4(3 + m)$, what is the value of n when $m = 6$?

   - Substitute the given value of m.

$$n = 100 - 4(3 + 6)$$

   - Solve for n.

$$n = 100 - 4(9)$$
$$n = 100 - 36$$
$$n = 64$$

Solving Function Word Problems

Functions are used in many business applications. For instance, they can be used to calculate profit, cost, employee wages, and taxes.

Anderson Advertising is finishing a series of print ads for a client. Finishing the project will cost $2,000 per day for the first seven days and $3,500 per day after seven days. When finishing the project takes seven days or longer, the finishing costs can be found using the function $C = \$2,000d + \$1,500(d - 7)$, where C = the cost of finishing the project and d = the number of days. If the project takes 12 days to complete, what will the project cost?

Use the function to solve the problem.

$$C = \$2,000d + \$1,500(d - 7)$$
$$= \$2,000(12) + \$1,500(12 - 7)$$
$$= \$24,000 + \$1,500(5)$$
$$= \$24,000 + \$7,500$$
$$= \$31,500$$

Nita decides to join a health club. She gets brochures from two health clubs and compares the plans. Anytime Fitness charges a one-time membership fee of $250 and $8 per month. Freedom Health Center charges $25 per month. At both health clubs, the price (P) Nita will pay is a function of the number of months (m) she attends the club. The functions are:

| Anytime Fitness | $P = \$250 + \$8m$ |
| Freedom Health Center | $P = \$25m$ |

1. Nita plans to move in 18 months. If she attends a health club until she moves, which one offers the better price?

   - Find the price at Anytime Fitness:

$$P = \$250 + \$8m$$
$$= \$250 + \$8(18)$$
$$= \$250 + \$144$$
$$= \$394$$

   - Find the price at the Freedom Health Center:

   - Compare the results. Even though Nita will have to pay a large amount up front, **Anytime Fitness** offers the better price for 18 months of membership.

$$P = \$25m$$
$$= \$25(18)$$
$$= \$450$$

MEAN, MEDIAN, AND MODE

Suppose you were asked how much money you usually spend on groceries in a week. Some weeks you may spend a great deal; other weeks, much less. You would probably choose an amount in the middle to represent what you typically spend. This middle value is called a **measure of central tendency.**

The most common type is the **mean**, or the arithmetic average.

1. In five football games, a team scored 14, 21, 3, 20, and 10 points. What is the mean, or average, score per game?

   - Add the values.

     $14 + 21 + 3 + 20 + 10 = 68$

   - Divide by the number of items in the data set.

     $68 \div 5 = 13.6$ points per game.

Although it is impossible for a football team to score 13.6 points in one game, the number represents the average of the scores from the five games.

Another measure of central tendency is the median. The **median** is the middle number in a list of data when the number of items in the list is odd.

2. During a seven-hour period, a bookstore recorded the following numbers of sales. Find the median number of sales.

Hour 1	Hour 2	Hour 3	Hour 4	Hour 5	Hour 6	Hour 7
43	28	24	36	32	37	48

   - Arrange the values in ascending (or descending) order.

     24, 28, 32, 36, 37, 43, 48

   - Find the middle number.

     24, 28, 32, 36, 37, 43, 48

If there is an even number of values, the median is the mean of the two middle values.

3. Robert has the following test scores in his math class: 90, 72, 88, 94, 91, and 80.

   - Arrange the values in ascending order and find the middle.

     72, 80, 88, 90, 91, 94

   - Find the mean of the two middle values. The median score is 89.

     Add: $88 + 90 = 178$
     Divide by 2: $178 \div 2 = 89$

The **mode** is the value that occurs most often in a set of data. A set of data could have more than one mode if several items occur the same number of times and these items occur more often than any other items. If each item of data occurs only once, there is no mode.

Six weather stations recorded the following temperatures at 3 P.M.: 45°, 44°, 45°, 47°, 46°, and 45°. What is the mode of the data?

The temperature 45° occurs the most often (three times). The mode is 45°.

TABLES AND PICTOGRAPHS

Data are facts and information. By analyzing data, we can make predictions, draw conclusions, and solve problems. To be useful, data must be organized in some way. A **table** organizes data in columns and rows. The labels on the table help you understand what the data means.

1. The table below shows population figures for selected counties in 1990 and 2000 and the land area in square miles for each county.

County	Adams	Bell	Cook	Davis	Evans
1990 Pop.	11,128	25,199	6,532	82,204	139,519
2000 Pop.	15,295	22,707	6,518	90.834	130,748
Land Area in Sq. Miles	4,255	2,532	2,398	1,139	321

Which county showed the greatest percentage of increase in population from 1990 to 2000?

- **Read the labels.** The first row shows the county names. The second and third rows show population figures. The fourth row shows land area data. You do not need the land area data to answer this question.
- **Analyze the data.** Only Adams and Davis counties show increases from 1990 to 2000.
- Use the data. Find the percent of increase for Adams and Davis counties.

Adams: $\dfrac{15,295 - 11,128}{11,128} \approx 0.374 \approx 37\%$ Davis: $\dfrac{90,834 - 82,204}{82,204} \approx 0.105 \approx 10\%$

Adams County shows the greatest percent increase in population from 1990 to 2000.

A **pictograph** is another way to display data. Pictographs use symbols to compare data. A key shows what value each symbol represents.

2. A city has three public library branches. A librarian kept track of the numbers of books checked out from each branch in a week. He used the data to create the pictograph below.

Branches	Books checked out from 3/4 to 3/10
North	📖 📖 📖 📖 📖 📖 📖
South	📖 📖 📖 📖 📖
West	📖 📖 📖 📖 📖 📖 📖 📖 📖

Key: 📖 = 150 books

From March 4 to March 10, how many books were checked out from the South and West branches combined?

- There are $4\frac{1}{2}$ symbols for the South Branch and 9 symbols for the West Branch. Add.

$$4\frac{1}{2} + 9 = 13\frac{1}{2} \text{ symbols}$$

- Find the value of the symbols. The key states that each symbol equals 150 books. Multiply $13\frac{1}{2}$ by 150.

$$13\frac{1}{2} \times 150 = 2{,}025 \text{ books}$$

Review Two Practice

1. $4(3) - 2 + (6 + 4 \cdot 2)$

2. $5^2 - (5 - 7)(2)$

3. In the expression $5 + 2\left[7\left(\frac{10^2}{10}\right) + (6 - 2)(3)\right]$, what is the last operation you should perform to find the value of the expression?

   (A) Multiply by 3.
   (B) Subtract 2 from 6.
   (C) Add 5.
   (D) Multiply by 2.
   (E) Find the square of 10.

Write an algebraic expression for each description. Use the variables x and y.

4. a number decreased by seven   _____

5. the product of 3 and the square of a number increased by that number

6. the amount that -3 multiplied by a number is greater than the product of 2 and another number

7. A minor-league baseball team is giving a local charity the sum of $1,500 and $0.50 for each ticket over 2,000 sold for one game. Let x represent the number of tickets sold, where $x > 2,000$. Which of the following expressions could be used to find the amount of the donation?

   (A) $\$1,500 + \$0.50x$
   (B) $\$1,500 + \$0.50(2,000)$
   (C) $\$1,500 + \$0.50(2,000 - x)$
   (D) $\$1,500 + \$0.50(x - 2000)$
   (E) $\$1500(2,000 - x)(\$0.50)$

8. $5 + x^2 - 3 + 3x$

9. $2y + 5 + 17y + 8$

Evaluate each expression as directed.

10. Find the value of $6(x + 2) + 7$ when $x = 2$.

11. Find the value of $3x^2 + 3(x + 4)$ when $x = 3$.

12. Which of the following expressions is equal to $3x^2 + 3(x - 3) + x + 10$?

    (A) $x^2 + 9x + 1$
    (B) $3x^2 + 4x + 19$
    (C) $3x^2 + 2x - 19$
    (D) $3x^2 - 2x + 19$
    (E) $3x^2 + 4x + 1$

Solve for the variable in each equation.

13. $7x = 63$ 14. $23 + m = 51$

15. $-13 = y - 12$ 16. $\frac{x}{4} = -16$

17. When a number is divided by 4, the result is 32. What is the number?

    (A) 8
    (B) 28
    (C) 36
    (D) 128
    (E) 512

18. Two houses are for sale on the same street. The second house has 1,000 square feet less than twice the square feet of the first house. Together the houses have 4,400 square feet. What is the square footage of the first house?

19. The Bulldogs won twice as many games as they lost. If they played a total of 36 games, how many did they win?

20. Sylvia scored 10 points better than Wiley on their science exam. Greg scored 6 points less than Wiley. Altogether the students earned 226 points. How many points did Sylvia earn?

    (A) 68
    (B) 74
    (C) 78
    (D) 84
    (E) 94

21. Which number should come next in the following pattern?

    $-12, -9, -6, -3,$ _____

22. Each term in the second row is determined by the function $y = 2x - 1$.

x	1	2	3	4	5	...	12
y	1	3	5	7	9	...	

    What number belongs in the shaded box?

23. The price per scarf is a function of the number of scarves purchased. The original price per scarf, $5.00, is reduced by 25 cents starting with the second scarf. The table shows the price per scarf for purchases of up to four scarves.

Number (n) of scarves	1	2	3	4
Cost (c) per scarf	$5.00	$4.75	$4.50	$4.25

    Which of the following was used to determine the prices shown in the table?

    (A) $c = n(\$5.00 - \$0.25)$
    (B) $c = \$5.00 - \$0.25(n - 1)$
    (C) $c = \$5.00 - \$0.25n$
    (D) $c = \$5.00n - \$0.25$
    (E) $c = \$5.00n - \$0.25n$

24. The Chimney Sweep charges $25 for a chimney inspection. If the customer purchases additional services, $15 of the inspection fee is deducted. Let $s =$ the cost of any additional services. The total cost (C) of an inspection and services can be determined by the function $C = \$25 + (s - \$15)$.

    a. Jan has her chimney inspected and purchases a smoke guard for $89. How much will she be charged?

    b. After an inspection, Ahmed decides to have a new damper installed for $255. How much will he pay?

25. Alicia is considering three job opportunities. At all three jobs, weekly pay (P) is a function of the number of hours (h) worked during the week. The functions are shown below:

    Job 1 $P = \$9.75h$

    Job 2 $P = \$70 + \$8.40h$

    Job 3 $P = \$380 \times \dfrac{h}{38}$

If Alicia works 30 hours in a week, how much more will she earn at Job 2 than at Job 1?

(A) $5.33
(B) $29.50
(C) $40.50
(D) $59.00
(E) Not enough information is given.

For each data set, find the mean, median, and mode. Round calculations to the nearest hundredth or cent.

26. Golf score for 18 holes: 76, 82, 75, 87, 80, 82, and 79

27. Sales totals for 6 weeks: $5,624; $10,380; $8,102; $6,494; $12,008; and $8,315

28. What is the median value of $268, $1,258, $654, $1,258, $900, $1,588, and $852?

    (A) $1,258
    (B) $960
    (C) $900
    (D) $913
    (E) $852

Use the table on page 68 to answer questions 29 and 30.

29. On average, how many people were there per square mile in Bell County in 2000?

30. To the nearest percent, what was the percent decrease in Evans County's population from 1990 to 2000?

Question 31 refers to the following table.

Percentage of three-year-old children with school-readiness skills for the years 1994 and 2000		
	1994	2000
Recognizes all letters	13%	15%
Counts to 20 or higher	37%	41%
Writes own name	22%	24%
Reads or pretends to read	68%	70%

31. A community had 350 three-year-old children in 2000. Based on the table, how many were able to write their own names?

(A) 22
(B) 77
(C) 84
(D) 140
(E) 273

Review Two Answer Key

1. 24

2. 29

3. (C) Add 5

The operations in the brackets must be performed first. Once these are completed, you would multiply by 2 and then add 5. Notice that it is not necessary to find the value of the expression to answer the question.

4. $x - 7$

5. $3x^2 + x$

6. $-3x \quad 2y$

7. (D) $\$1,500 + \$0.50(x - 2,000)$

Here, x represents the number of tickets sold. The expression $x - 2,000$ is the number of tickets over 2,000 sold. Multiply this expression by $0.50 to find the amount donated based on ticket sales, and add $1,500. Only option (D) performs these operations.

8. $x^2 + 3x + 2$

9. $19y + 13$

10. 31

11. 48

12. (E) $3x^2 + 4x + 1$

Simplify the expression.

$$3x^2 + 3(x - 3) + x + 10$$
$$= 3x^2 + 3x - 9 + x + 10$$
$$= 3x^2 + 4x + 1$$

13. $x = 9$

14. $m = 28$

15. $y = -1$

16. $x = -64$

17. (D) 128

When x is divided by 4, the result is 32. Solve for x.

$$\frac{x}{4} = 32$$
$$4 \cdot \frac{x}{4} = 4 \cdot 32$$
$$x = 128$$

18. 1,800 sq ft

19. 24 games

20. (D) 84

Let x = Wiley's points, $x + 10$ = Sylvia's points, and $x - 6$ = Greg's points. Write and solve an equation:

$$x + x + 10 + x - 6 = 226$$
$$3x + 4 = 226$$
$$3x = 222$$
$$x = 74$$

The question asks for Sylvia's points, so: $x + 10 = 74 + 10 = 84$

21. 0

22. 23

23. (B) $c = \$5.00 - \$0.25(n - 1)$

24. a. $99
   b. $265

25. **(B)** $29.50

Use the functions for the two jobs, substituting 30 hours for h.

Job 1: $P = \$9.75h$

$\qquad = \$9.75(30)$

$\qquad = \$292.50$

Job 2: $P = \$70 + \$8.40h$

$\qquad = \$70 + \$8.40(30)$

$\qquad = \$70 + \$252$

$\qquad = \$322$

Subtract. $322 − $292.50 = $29.50

26. mean: 80.14
    median: 80
    mode: 82

27. mean: $8,487.17
    median: $8,208.50
    mode: none

28. **(C)** $900

The median is the middle number. Arrange the amounts in order and find the middle value.

29. 9

30. 6%

31. **(C)** 84

In 2000, 24% of three-year-old children could write their own name. Find 24% of 350. $0.24 \times 350 = 84$

Review Three

INTERPRETATION OF GRAPHS

Bar and Line Graphs

A **bar graph** uses bars to represent values. Bar graphs have two axis lines. One line shows a number scale, and the other shows labels for the bars. By comparing the length of a bar to the scale, you can estimate what value the bar represents.

1. A national corporation made a bar graph (shown below) to show the number of discrimination complaints made by employees during a six-year period. About how many more complaints were made in 1999 than in 1998?

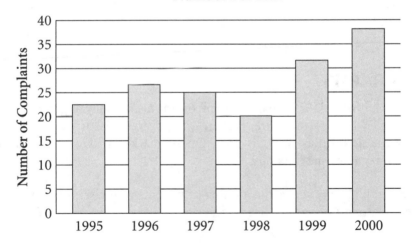

Employee Discrimination Complaints
Number Per Year

- **Read the labels.** Each bar represents the number of complaints made within a year. The years are shown beneath the bars.
- **Analyze the data.** Compare the bars for 1998 and 1999 to the scale. There were 20 complaints in 1998 and about 32 complaints in 1999.
- **Use the data.** Subtract: $32 - 20 = 12$. There were about 12 more complaints in 1999 than in 1998.

A **double-bar graph** compares more than one type of data.

2. A studio released four films in one year. The graph below compares the cost of making each movie to its box-office receipts, or ticket sales. Film B's cost is approximately what percent of its box-office receipts?

Profit Analysis for Four Films

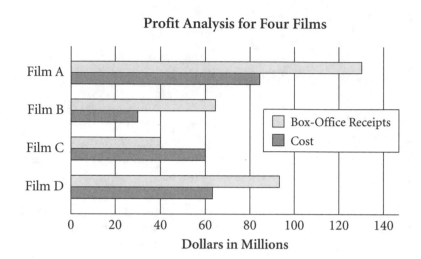

- **Read the labels.** Read the key to find the meaning of the bars. Notice that the scale represents millions of dollars.
- **Analyze the data.** Film B's cost is about $30 million. It brought in about $65 million in receipts.
- **Use the data.** Find what percent $30 is of $65.

> The percent that $30 is of $65 is
> $$\frac{\$30}{\$65} \approx 0.462 \approx 46\%$$

LINE GRAPHS

A **line graph** is useful for showing changes over time. By analyzing the rise and fall of the line, you can tell whether something is increasing, decreasing, or staying the same. Like a bar graph, a line graph has two axis lines. One is marked with a scale; the other is (usually) marked in regular time intervals.

The graph below shows the number of patients who visited an emergency room for the treatment of scooter-related injuries.

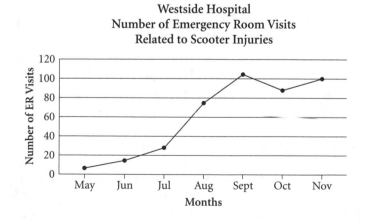

During what month was there a decrease in the number of emergency room visits for scooter-related injuries from the previous month?

The points on the graph are positioned above the months, which are arranged in calendar order. By examining the line that connects the points, you can tell whether there was an increase or decrease from one month to the next.

You can tell a lot about the information in a line graph even if you don't look at the exact values. Because the scale on the vertical axis increases from bottom to top, a line that slopes up from left to right shows an increase over time. Likewise, a line that slopes down from left to right shows a decrease during that period of time.

In this graph, there is only one segment that does not slope up from left to right—the segment from September to October. This means that there was a decrease in scooter-related injuries in October from September.

The steepness of a line can also be informative. A steeper line indicates a faster rate of change than a flatter line. In this graph, the line from July to August is the steepest, indicating that the largest one-month increase occurred during that period. (This can be confirmed by actually reading off the values and comparing them.)

If a line graph has more than one line, a key will tell you what each line represents.

1. The graph below shows the changes in ticket prices for two amusement parks.

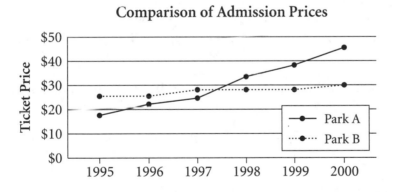

Comparison of Admission Prices

What was the last year in which the admission price to Park B was greater than the admission price to Park A?

*   The admission prices for Park A are represented by a solid line. Park B's prices are shown with a dotted line. The graph begins in 1995. In 1995, Park B's ticket price is greater than Park A's. Follow the two lines to the right. Between 1997 and 1998, the lines cross, and Park A's prices climb higher than Park B's. **The year 1997 was the** last time that Park B charged more than Park A for a ticket.

CIRCLE GRAPHS

A **circle graph**, or **pie chart**, is used to show how a whole amount is broken into parts. The sections of a circle graph are often labeled with percents. The size of each section corresponds to the fraction it represents. For example, a section labeled 25% will be $\frac{1}{4}$ of the circle.

1. A graph below shows how a children's sports camp spends its weekly budget.

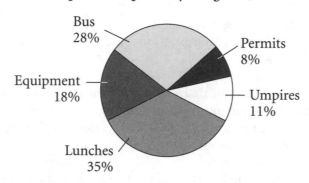

Sports Camp Weekly Budget $2,250

How much does the sports camp spend on lunches each week?

- **Analyze the graph.** According to the heading, the entire circle represents the camp's weekly budget of $2,250. Find the section labeled "lunches." According to the section label, lunches make up 35% of the weekly budget.

- **Use the data.** To find the amount spent on lunches, find 35% of $2,250.
  $2,250 \times 0.35 = \$787.50$

A circle graph may also be labeled using fractions or decimals. One common kind of circle graph labels each section in cents to show how a dollar is used.

2. According to the graph, what percentage of the average energy bill is spent on drying clothes, lighting, and heating water?

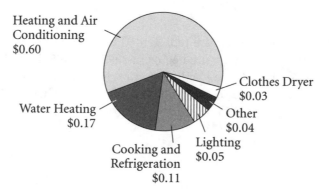

Where Do Your Energy Dollars Go?

- **Analyze the graph.** The entire circle represents $1. The amounts in the sections mentioned in the problem are $0.03, $0.05, and $0.17.
- **Use the data.** Add the amounts: $0.03 + $0.05 + $0.17 = $0.25. Because $0.25 is 25% of a dollar, **25% of an average bill is spent on these items.**

THE NUMBER LINE AND SIGNED NUMBERS

Signed numbers include zero, all positive numbers, and all negative numbers. Zero is neither positive nor negative. On a number line, the positive numbers are shown to the right of zero, and the negative numbers are shown to the left.

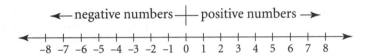

A positive number may be written with a plus (+) sign. If a number has no symbol, it is assumed to be positive. A negative number *must* be preceded by a minus (–) sign.

A signed number provides two important facts. The sign indicates the direction from zero on a number line, and the number indicates the distance from zero. For example, –5 lies five spaces to the left of zero, and +4 lies four spaces to the right of zero.

ADDING AND SUBTRACTING SIGNED NUMBERS

You can use a number line to model the addition of signed numbers.

$1 + (-4) = -3$

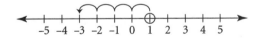

Begin at +1; move 4 units in a negative direction (left).

$-5 + 4 = -1$

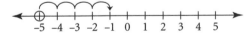

Begin at –5; move 4 units in a positive direction (right).

$-2 + (-3) = -5$

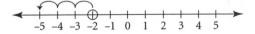

Begin at –2; move 3 units in a negative direction (left).

To add without a number line, follow these steps:

- If numbers have like signs, add the numbers, and keep the same sign.
- If the numbers have unlike signs, find the difference between the two numbers, and use the sign of the larger number.

1. Add $15 + (-25)$

   - Because the numbers have unlike signs, subtract. $25 - 15 = 10$
   - Use the sign from the larger number. $15 + (-25) = -10$

Subtraction is the opposite of addition. To rewrite a subtraction problem as an addition problem, change the operation symbol to addition and change the sign on the number you are subtracting. Then apply the rules for adding signed numbers.

2. Subtract $3 - 8$

   - Change the operation and the sign of the number you are subtracting.
     $3 - 8$ becomes $3 + (-8)$
   - Add. $3 + (-8) = -5$

POWERS AND ROOTS

Powers are a special way to show repeated multiplication. For example, suppose you need to multiply $5 \times 5 \times 5 \times 5$. This series of operations can be expressed as "five raised to the exponent 4." In other words, the number 5 appears in the expression 4 times.

We can write the operations using **exponents.** In the expression $5 \times 5 \times 5 \times 5$, the number 5 is the base. The exponent, a number written slightly above and to the right of the base, indicates how many times the base is repeated: $5 \times 5 \times 5 \times 5 = 5^4$.

To evaluate an expression, perform the multiplication indicated by the exponent.

Find the value of 2^5

Write the base out the number of times indicated by the exponent and multiply.

$2^5 = 2 \times 2 \times 2 \times 2 \times 2 = 32$

There are certain instances of exponents to make note of:

1. A number raised to the exponent 1 equals itself. $8^1 = 8$

2. A number other than zero raised to the exponent zero equals 1. $6^0 = 1$

3. A number raised to a negative exponent is equal to a fraction with a numerator of 1.

$$4^{-2} = \frac{1}{4^2} = \frac{1}{4 \times 4} = \frac{1}{16}$$

A square root of a number n is a number that when squared equals the number n. Every positive number has two square roots. One square root of a positive number is positive, and one square root of a positive number is negative. For example, the square roots of 25 are 5 and –5. This is because $5^2 = 25$ and $(-5)^2 = 25$. The number 0 has only one square root, 0,

By convention, if x is positive, $\sqrt{x}$ means the positive square root of x. Whenever there is a $\sqrt{}$ symbol, this means the positive square root. We have mentioned that 25 has two square roots, which are 5 and –5. However, $\sqrt{25}$ is unambiguous; it means the positive square root of 25. We write $\sqrt{25} = 5$.

4. Find the value of $\sqrt{144}$.

- We know that $12 \times 12 = 144$.
- So $\sqrt{144} = 12$.
- Note that $\sqrt{144}$ is unambiguous. It means 12.

INEQUALITIES

An **inequality** is a mathematical statement that connects two unequal expressions. The inequality symbols and their meanings are:number is pos

> greater than $\geq$ greater than or equal to

< less than $\leq$ less than or equal to

An inequality is solved much like an equation. Use inverse operations to isolate the variable.

1. Solve for x in the inequality $3x + 2 < 8$.

- Subtract 2 from both sides.
- Divide both sides by 3.

$$3x + 2 < 8$$
$$3x < 6$$
$$x < 2$$

The solution $x < 2$ states that any number less than 2 makes the inequality true. Check by substituting 1 (a number less than 2) for x: $3(1) + 2 < 8$, which simplifies to $5 < 8$, a true statement.

PERIMETER, AREA, AND VOLUME

Perimeter is the distance around a figure. To find the perimeter, simply add the lengths of the sides. For common figures, you can apply a formula to find the perimeter.

square	Perimeter = 4 × side	$P = 4s$
rectangle	Perimeter = 2 × length + 2 × width	$P = 2l + 2w$
triangle	Perimeter = side$_1$ + side$_2$ + side$_3$	$P = a + b + c$

A rectangle is 16 inches long and 9 inches wide. What is the perimeter of the rectangle?

Use the formula:

$$
\begin{aligned}
\text{Perimeter} &= 2 \times \text{length} + 2 \times \text{width} \\
&= 2 \times 16 + 2 \times 9 \\
&= 32 + 18 \\
&= 50 \text{ inches}
\end{aligned}
$$

Area is the measure of the space inside a flat figure. Area is measured in square units. For example, if the sides of a figure are measured in inches, its area will be measured in square inches. The formulas for finding area are shown below.

square	Area = side^2	$A = s^2$
rectangle	Area = length × width	$A = lw$
parallelogram	Area = base × height	$A = bh$
triangle	Area = $\frac{1}{2}$ × base × height	$A = \frac{1}{2}bh$
trapezoid	Area = $\frac{1}{2}$(base$_1$ + base$_2$) × height	$A = \frac{1}{2}(b_1 + b_2)h$

Three of the formulas mention two new measures: base and height. The **base** is one side of the figure. The **height** is the length from a vertex to the base, forming a right angle to the base.

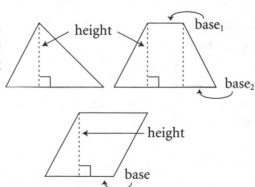

1. Find the area of polygon *ABCD*

    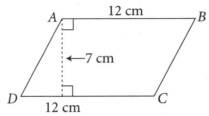

    - Identify the figure. *ABCD* is a parallelogram.
    - Find the data that you need. To use the formula for finding the area of a parallelogram, you need to know the height and the length of the base. You do not need to know the length of sides *BC* or *AD*.
    - Use the formula: Area = base × height.

    > Area = 12 × 7
    > = 84 sq cm or 84 cm^2

CIRCLES: CIRCUMFERENCE AND AREA

A **circle** is a closed, linear figure all of whose points are the same distance from a single point, the center of the circle. The **circumference** of a circle is its perimeter, or the distance around the circle. The area of a circle is the space inside the circle.

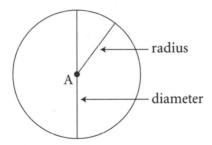

To find the circumference and area of a circle, you need to know certain measurements of the circle. The **diameter** is a line segment with endpoints on the circle that passes through the center of the circle. The **radius** is a line segment that connects the center of the circle to a point on the circle. The radius is one-half the diameter.

The formulas for the circumference and area of a circle use a special quantity called **pi** (π). Pi is the ratio of the circumference to the diameter. Pi is approximately 3.14. The formula for the circumference of a circle is: Circumference = π × diameter, or $C = \pi d$. The circumference C of a circle is related to the radius r of the circle by $C = 2\pi r$. The formula for the area of a circle is: Area = π × radius^2, or $A = \pi r^2$.

1. A china plate has a gold rim. If the plate's diameter is 10.5 inches, what is the distance around the rim to the nearest tenth of an inch?

    - Use the formula:

    > $C = \pi d$
    > $\approx 3.14(10.5)$
    > $= 32.97$, or about 33 inches

2. The circular surface of a satellite component must be covered with heat-resistant tiles. If the radius of the circular surface is 4 meters, what is the area of the circular surface in square meters?

  • Use the formula:

$$A = \pi r^2$$
$$= 3.14(4^2)$$
$$= 3.14(16)$$
$$= 50.24 \text{ square meters}$$

3. What is the circumference of circle *B* to the nearest tenth of a centimeter?

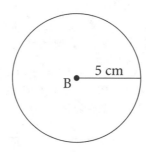

  • The radius of the circle is 5 cm. Therefore, the diameter is 2 × 5, or 10 cm.
  • Use the formula $C = 2\pi r$

$$C = 2\pi r$$
$$\approx 2(3.14)(5)$$
$$= 3.14(10)$$
$$= 31.4 \text{ cm}$$

VOLUME

Volume is the measure of space inside a three-dimensional object. Volume is measured in cubic units. For example, if the sides of an object are measured in inches, the volume is the number of cubes with an edge of one inch that would be needed to fill the object.

Many common three-dimensional objects have at least two identical and parallel faces. Think of a cereal box or soup can. Both objects have identical faces at the top and bottom. Either of these faces can be called the base of the object. To find the volume of any container with identical bases, multiply the area of one base by the height of the object: Volume = area of base × height.

Another way to find the volume of an object is to use the formula that applies specifically to that object. Three common regular solids are rectangular solids, cubes, and cylinders.

rectangular solid	Volume = length × width × height	$V = lwh$
cube	Volume = edge^3	$V = e^3$
cylinder	Volume = pi × radius^2 × height	$V = \pi r^2 h$

A **rectangular solid** has two identical rectangular bases. The remaining sides of the solid are also rectangles.

1. A cardboard box has the dimensions shown in the diagram. What is the volume of the box in cubic feet?

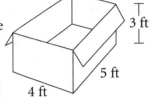

3 ft

5 ft

4 ft

   • Use the formula:
   $$V = lwh$$
   $$= 5(4)(3) = 60 \text{ cubic feet}$$

A **cube** is a rectangular solid with six identical faces. In a cube, each edge is the same length.

2. A wood block measures 2 inches on each edge. What is the volume of the block?

   • Use the formula:
   $$V = e^3$$
   $$= 2^3 = 2 \times 2 \times 2 = 8 \text{ cubic inches}$$

A **cylinder** has two circular bases. The bases are connected by a curved surface. Cans, barrels, and tanks are often in the shape of cylinders.

3. A storage tank has a radius of 1.5 meters. What is the volume of the tank to the nearest cubic meter?

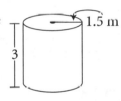

1.5 m

3

   • Use the formula:
   $$V = \pi r^2 h$$
   $$\approx 3.14(1.5^2)(3) = 21.195 \text{ m}^3,$$
   which rounds to 21 cubic meters

WORKING WITH IRREGULAR FIGURES

An irregular figure combines geometric figures to form a new shape. To find the perimeter of an irregular figure, simply add the lengths of all the sides. You may need to deduce the lengths of some of the sides using the measures given for the other sides.

1. A family room has the dimensions shown in the diagram. All measurements are in feet. What is the perimeter of the room?

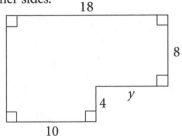

18

8

y

4

10

   • Find the missing measurements. Measurement x equals the combined lengths of the two opposite walls: $x = 8 + 4 = 12$ ft. You also know that $18 - 10 = y$, so $y = 8$ ft.

- Add all of the distances to find the perimeter. $12 + 18 + 8 + 8 + 4 + 10 = 60$ ft

To find the area of an irregular figure, break the figure into parts. Then apply the correct formula to each part.

2. What is the area of this figure in square centimeters?

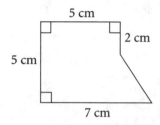 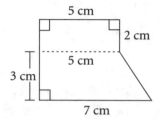

- Divide the figure into two shapes, and find any missing measurements. Here, the figure is divided into a trapezoid and a rectangle.
- Calculate the area of each shape.

Rectangle: $A = lw$
$$= 2(5) = 10 \text{ sq cm}$$

Trapezoid: $A = \frac{1}{2}(b_1 + b_2)h$
$$= \frac{1}{2}(5 + 7)(3) = \frac{1}{2}(12)(3)$$
$$= 6 \times 3 = 18 \text{ sq cm}$$

- Combine. $10 + 18 = 28$ sq cm

Review Three Practice

For questions 1 and 2, use the bar graph entitled, "Employee Discrimination Complaints" on page 77.

1. To the nearest ten, how many employee discrimination complaints were there in 1995 and 1996 combined?

2. About how many more complaints were there in 2000 than in 1995?

Questions 3 and 4 refer to the following graph.

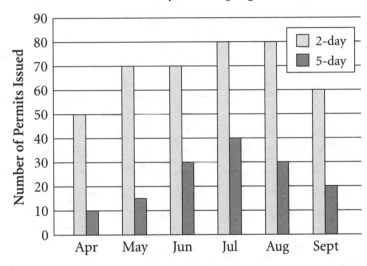

Echo Canyon Camping Permits

3. In May, what was the ratio of the number of 2-day permits to the number of 5-day permits?

   (A) 2:5
   (B) 3:14
   (C) 3:17
   (D) 14:3
   (E) 14:17

4. In which month was there a total of 80 permits issued?

   (A) May
   (B) June
   (C) July
   (D) August
   (E) September

For questions 5 and 6, use the graph from Westside Hospital on page 78.

5. In which month did the number of scooter-related injuries increase by the greatest amount over the previous month?

6. To the nearest ten, how many emergency room visits were caused by scooter injuries in August, September, and October?

Questions 7 and 8 refer to the graph below.

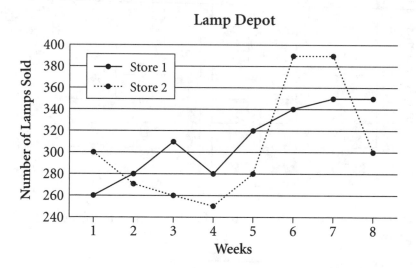

7. About how many more lamps were sold at Store 2 than at Store 1 in Week 6?

   (A) 110
   (B) 50
   (C) 40
   (D) 25
   (E) 20

8. During which week did Store 1 experience the greatest increase in sales over the week immediately before?

   (A) Week 2
   (B) Week 3
   (C) Week 4
   (D) Week 5
   (E) Week 6

For question 9, use the sports camp budget graph on page 80. For question 10, use the circle graph on energy on page 80.

9. What percentage of the total sports camp budget is spent on equipment and umpires?

10. Which section is greater than 50% of an energy dollar?

Question 11 refers to the following graph.

   The employees of National Bank are given the following graph to explain how their retirement fund is invested.

How Your Retirement Dollar Is Invested

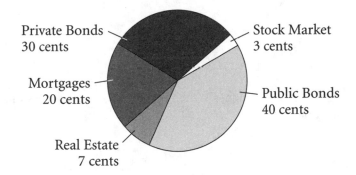

11. What percentage of each retirement dollar is invested in real estate and the stock market?

   (A) 4%
   (B) 10%
   (C) 40%
   (D) 90%
   (E) 100%

12. $8 + (-3)$

13. $-1 + 2$

14. $6 - (-3) + (-5) + 8$

15. At noon, the temperature in the high desert was 92°F. A scientist observed the following temperature changes over the course of the next two hours: $+12°, -5°, +6°, -3°$, and $+13°$. What was the temperature at the end of the two-hour period?

    (A) 53°
    (B) 95°
    (C) 103°
    (D) 115°
    (E) 131°

Find each expression.

16. 3^2

17. 4^1

18. $\sqrt{49}$

19. A cube has an edge length of 6 inches Which of the following expressions represents the volume of the cube?

    (A) 6^2
    (B) $6(12)$
    (C) $6(4^2)$
    (D) 6^3
    (E) $3(6^3)$

20. $3x - 7 > 5$

21. $\dfrac{4 + x}{5} \leq 8$

22. $-4(x + 2) < 24$

Choose the one best answer to each question.

23. Three added to the product of −4 and a number *x* is less than 5 added to the product of −3 and the number. Which of the following is a graph of the solution set of *x*?

(A)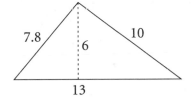

(B)

(C)

(D)

(E)

Find the area and perimeter of each figure.

24.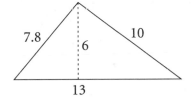

25.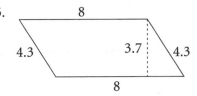

26. The four sides of a parallelogram measure 9 feet, 6 feet, 9 feet, and 6 feet. What is the area of the parallelogram in square feet?

(A) 30

(B) 36

(C) 54

(D) 81

(E) Not enough information is given.

Find the approximate circumference and area of each circle. Round answers to the nearest tenth.

27.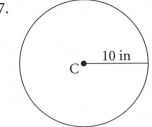

Question 28 refers to the following drawing.

 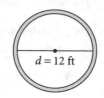

28. If workers lay a tile border around the edge of the fountain shown in the diagram, how many feet long will the border be to the nearest foot?

(A)   19
(B)   36
(C)   38
(D)   57
(E) 113

29. On the target below, the 5- and 10-point bands are each 2 inches wide, and the inner circle has a diameter of 2 inches.

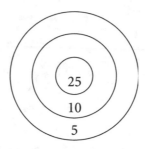

To the nearest inch, what is the outer circumference of the 10-point band?

(A)   6
(B)   13
(C)   19
(D) 113
(E) Not enough information is given.

Find the volume of each object to the nearest whole unit.

30.

31.

32. A wooden crate measures 5 feet along each edge. What is the crate's volume in cubic feet?

   (A)   15
   (B)   25
   (C) 125
   (D) 150
   (E) Not enough information is given.

33. Find the perimeter and area of the figure.

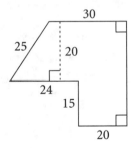

34. Find the volume of the figure to the nearest cubic unit.

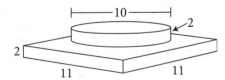

Review Three Answer Key

1. 50

2. about 15

3. (D)　14:3

Write a ratio and simplify. $\frac{70}{15} = \frac{14}{3}$

4. (E) September

Add the 2-day and 5-day permits for each month. Only September's permits equal 80. In September, there were 60 + 20 = 80 permits

5. August

6. 270

7. (B) 50

There were 390 sales in Store 2 and 340 sales in Store 1 in the sixth week. 390 − 340 = 50

8. (D) Week 5

The steepest line segment is for the time period for Week 4 (between Week 4 and Week 5), an increase of 40 sales.

9. 29%

10. heating and air conditioning

11. (B) 10%

Add. 3 cents + 7 cents = 10 cents, and 10 cents out of 100 cents is $\frac{10}{100}$, or 10%.

12. 5

13. 1

14. 12

15. (D) 115°

Begin with 92°. Then perform the following operations: 92° + 12° − 5° + 6° − 3° + 13° = 115°

16. 9

17. 4

18. 7

19. (D) 6^3

The volume of a cube is the length of an edge cubed. The volume of this cube is 6^3.

20. $x > 4$

21. $x \le 36$

22. $x > -8$

23. (D)

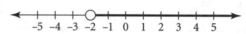

Solve the inequality:

$$-4x + 3 < -3x + 5$$
$$-x < 2$$
$$x > -2$$

To graph the solution $x > -2$, place an open circle at −2 because −2 is not included in the solution. Then extend the line to the right to include all values greater than −2.

24. area: 39 sq units
　　perimeter: 30.8 units

25. area: 29.6 sq units
　　perimeter: 24.6 units

26. (E) Not enough information is given.

From the measures of the sides, you cannot determine the height of the parallelogram.

27. $C = 62.8$ in., $A = 314$ in.^{2}

28. (C) 38

Use the formula $C = \pi d$, where $d = 12$.
$12(3.14) \approx 37.7 \approx 38$

29. (C) 19

You need to find the circumference of the 10-point band. First, find the diameter that passes through the inner circle. Add the width of the 10-point band twice and the diameter of the inner circle: $2 + 2 + 2 = 6$ inches. Now you can use the formula for circumference to get $6(3.14) = 18.84$, which rounds to 19 inches.

30. 160 cubic units

31. 236 cubic units

32. (C) 125

If each edge measures 5 feet, then the figure is a cube: $5^3 = 125$

33. $P = 149$ units

$A = 1,040$ sq units

34. $V \approx 399$ cubic units

Review Four

POINTS, LINES, AND ANGLES

A **point** is a single location in space. We assign a name to a point by writing a letter next to it. A **plane** is a two-dimensional flat surface. In the drawing, point *A* lies in plane *P*.

A **line** is a one-dimensional straight path that extends indefinitely in two directions. A line may be named by a single letter or by two points on the line.

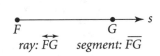
line s or $\overleftrightarrow{CD}$

A **ray** is part of a line that begins at the endpoint and extends indefinitely in one direction. A portion of a line with two endpoints is called a **line segment**. Both rays and line segments are named using two points.

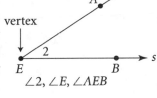
ray: $\overrightarrow{FG}$ *segment:* $\overline{FG}$

When two rays share an endpoint, they form an **angle**. The shared endpoint is the vertex of the angle. An angle can be named in different ways: by a number or letter written inside the angle, by the name of the vertex, or by the vertex and a point on each ray. The symbol ∠ means angle.

∠2, ∠E, ∠AEB

Angles are measured in degrees, indicated by a number and the degree symbol (°).

A **right angle** forms a square corner and measures 90°. A right angle is often identified by a small square drawn inside it.

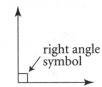
right angle symbol

An **obtuse angle** is greater than 90° but less than 180°.

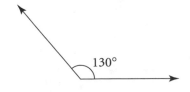
130°

An **acute angle** is less than 90°.

30°

A **straight angle** measures 180°.
180°

A **reflex angle** has a measure greater than 180° but less than 360°.

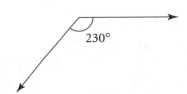
230°

When the sum of two angles is 90°, the angles are **complementary**. When the sum of two angles is 180°, the angles are **supplementary**. You can use this information to solve for a missing angle measure.

1. In the drawing, $\angle AOB$ and $\angle BOC$ are complementary. What is the measure of $\angle AOB$?

   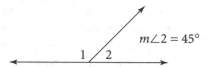

   - The measure of angle BOC is given as 23°, or $m\angle BOC = 23°$. The sum of the angles is 90°. Therefore, $\angle AOB$ measures 67°.

   $$m\angle AOB + 23° = 90°$$
   $$m\angle AOB = 90° - 23°$$
   $$m\angle AOB = 67°$$

2. In the drawing, $\angle 1$ and $\angle 2$ are supplementary. What is the measure of $\angle 1$

   - $\angle 2$ measures 45°. The sum of the angles is 180°. $\angle 1$ measures 135°.

   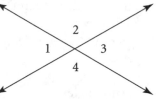

PARALLEL LINES AND TRANSVERSALS

When two lines intersect, they form two pairs of vertical angles. **Vertical angles** have the same angle measure. In the drawing, $\angle 1$ and $\angle 3$ are vertical angles, as are $\angle 2$ and $\angle 4$.

Intersecting lines also form adjacent angles. **Adjacent angles** share a common ray. For example, $\angle 1$ and $\angle 2$ are adjacent angles. The adjacent angles in this figure are supplementary angles because their sum is the measure of a straight angle. If you know the measure of one angle, you can find the measure of the other three angles.

1. In the figure above, $m\angle 1 = 35°$. What are the measures of $\angle 2$, $\angle 3$, and $\angle 4$?

   - $\angle 1$ and $\angle 2$ are supplementary, so their sum equals 180°. Solve for $\angle 2$.

   $$m\angle 2 + 35° = 180°$$
   $$m\angle 2 = 145°$$

   - Angles 1 and 3 are vertical, so both measure 35°. Angles 2 and 4 are vertical, so both measure 145°.

Parallel lines are lines that never intersect. This means that their distance from each other remains constant. The symbol for parallel is ‖. A **transversal** is a line that intersects two or more other lines. When a transversal intersects two parallel lines, special angle relationships are formed.

In the drawing, $M \| N$. The transversal, line P, forms eight angles.

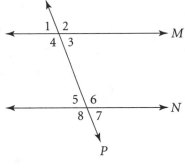

Each angle matches another angle in the same position on the transversal. These angles, called **corresponding angles,** always have the same measure. The corresponding angles are $\angle 1$ and $\angle 5$, $\angle 2$ and $\angle 6$, $\angle 3$ and $\angle 7$, and $\angle 4$ and $\angle 8$.

Alternate exterior angles, which are also equal in measure, are on opposite sides of the transversal and are on the outside of the parallel lines. One pair of alternate exterior angles is $\angle 1$ and $\angle 7$, and the other is $\angle 2$ and $\angle 8$.

Alternate interior angles are on opposite sides of the transversal and are inside the parallel lines. One pair of alternate interior angles is $\angle 3$ and $\angle 5$, the other is $\angle 4$ and $\angle 6$. Alternate interior angles are always equal in measure.

2. In the figure, $C \| D$. If $m\angle 4 = 48°$, what is the measure of $\angle 5$?

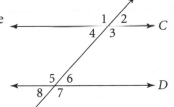

- There are many ways to solve the problem. Here is one way: $\angle 4$ and $\angle 8$ are corresponding angles, so $m\angle 8 = 48°$.

- $\angle 8$ and $\angle 5$ are supplementary angles, so $m\angle 5 + 48° = 180°$, and $m\angle 5 = 132°$.

TRIANGLES

A **triangle** is a closed three-sided figure. From the definition, we can infer other properties. Because a triangle has three sides, it must also have three interior angles and three vertices.

A triangle is named by writing its vertices in any order. The triangle shown at the right could be named $\triangle DEF$. Its sides are DE, EF, and DF.

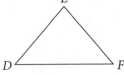

Triangles can be classified by the lengths of their sides and by the measures of their angles. In the figures on the next page, sides with the same number of marks are equal.

Triangles Classified by Side Lengths

equilateral triangle

All sides are equal in length. Note that the angles are equal as well.

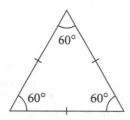

isosceles triangle

Exactly two sides are equal in length. Note that the two angles opposite these sides are equal.

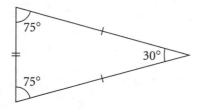

scalene triangle

No sides are equal in length, and no angles are equal.

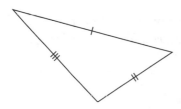

Triangles Classified by Angle Measures

right triangle

One angle measures 90°.

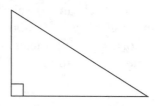

acute triangle

All angles measure less than 90°.

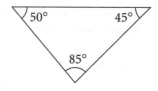

obtuse triangle

One angle is greater than 90°.

Each triangle can be classified in two ways.

1. What kind of triangle is $\triangle PQR$?

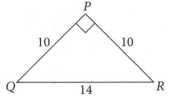

- Classify by its sides: Two sides have the same length, so $\triangle PQR$ is an isosceles triangle.

- Classify by its angles: $\angle P$ is a right angle, so $\triangle PQR$ is a right triangle.

$\triangle PQR$ is a **right isosceles triangle.**

The sum of the measures of the interior angles for any triangle is 180°. We can use this fact to solve for a missing angle.

2. In $\triangle ABC$, $\angle A$ measures 55° and $\angle B$ measures 100°. What is the measure of $\angle C$?

- Write an equation and solve.

$$55° + 100° + \angle C = 180°$$
$$155° + \angle C = 180°$$
$$\angle C = 25°$$

The measure of $\angle C$ is 25°.

COMPARING TRIANGLES

Figures are **congruent** (indicated by the symbol ≅) when they have exactly the same size and shape. In other words, two figures are congruent if their corresponding parts (the angles and sides) are congruent. You can often tell that two geometric shapes are congruent by sight. However, in geometry, you must be able to prove that figures are congruent.

Two triangles are congruent if the following corresponding parts are congruent:

Side-Side-Side (SSS)   The side measures for both triangles are the same.

Side-Angle-Side (SAS)   Two sides and the angle between them are the same.

Angle-Side-Angle (ASA)   Two angles and the side between them are the same.

1. Are triangles ABD and BCD congruent?

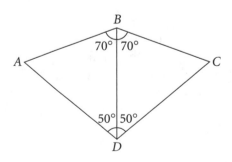

- Find the known corresponding parts: $\angle ABD \cong \angle CBD$ and $\angle ADB \cong \angle CDB$. Both triangles share side BD.

- Is this enough information to prove that the triangles are congruent? Yes, two angles and the side between them are equal. Using the ASA rule, $\triangle ABD \cong \triangle BCD$.

UNDERSTANDING SIMILARITY

Figures are **similar** (shown by the symbol ~) when the corresponding angles are congruent and the corresponding sides are in proportion. In other words, similar figures always have the same shape, but they do not have to be the same size.

There are two rules that you can use to prove that two triangles are similar:

Rule 1: If two angle measures in the first triangle are equal to two angle measures in the second triangle, the triangles are similar.

Rule 2: If all corresponding sides have the same ratio, the triangles are similar.

1. Are triangles *JKL* and *MNO* similar?

    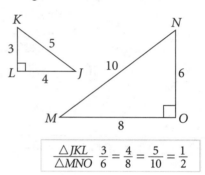

    -   Compare corresponding angles. Because only one angle measure is given, you cannot use Rule 1 to prove that the triangles are similar.

    -   Write ratios comparing the sides in the first triangle to the corresponding sides in the second triangle. Each ratio is equal to $\frac{1}{2}$.

    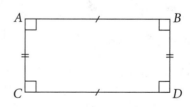

    $$\frac{\triangle JKL}{\triangle MNO} \quad \frac{3}{6} = \frac{4}{8} = \frac{5}{10} = \frac{1}{2}$$

Because the ratios are equal, the triangles are similar: $\triangle JKL \sim \triangle MNO$.

QUADRILATERALS

A **quadrilateral** is a closed shape with four sides.

A **rectangle** is a four-sided figure with four right angles. The opposite sides (sides across from each other) are the same length, and they are parallel.

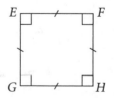

A **square** is actually a kind of rectangle. It, too, has four right angles with parallel opposite sides. However, a square has one additional property: its four sides are all the same length.

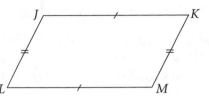

A **parallelogram** is a four-sided figure whose opposite sides are parallel and the same length. In addition, its opposite angles (the angles diagonally across from each other) are also equal in measure. A special parallelogram, called a **rhombus** (not shown), has four sides of equal length.

All quadrilaterals have one important property in common. The sum of the measures of the interior angles is 360°. You can use this fact to find a missing angle measure.

1. In figure *ABCD,* the opposite sides are parallel. What is the measure of ∠*A?*

   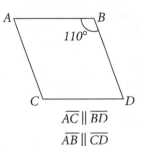

   $AC \parallel BD$

   $AB \parallel CD$

   • Identify the figure. The notation on the drawing tells you that the opposite sides are equal in measure. Because the opposite sides are parallel, the figure is a parallelogram.

   • Find the measure of ∠*C.* The opposite angles of a parallelogram are equal in measure; therefore, $m\angle C = m\angle B$. Both ∠*B* and ∠*C* measure 110°.

   • Because all of the angles in the figure will total 360° and ∠*A* and ∠*D* are equal, you can solve for ∠*A.*

$$2 \times m\angle A + 110° + 110° = 360°$$
$$2 \times m\angle A = 140°$$
$$m\angle A = 70°$$

THE ENGLISH SYSTEM OF MEASUREMENT

Measurements are used to describe an object's length, weight, or volume. We also use measurement to describe a quantity of time. The United States uses the English, or standard, system of measurement. Study the table below to learn the common standard units and their abbreviations.

Measurement Equivalencies

Length
1 foot (ft) = 12 inches (in.)
1 yard (yd) = 3 ft

Weight
1 pound (lb) = 16 ounces (oz)
1 ton (t) = 2,000 lb

Volume
1 cup (c) = 8 fluid ounces (fl oz)
1 pint (pt) = 2 c
1 quart (qt) = 2 pt
1 gallon (gal) = 4 qt

Time
1 minute (min) = 60 seconds (sec)
1 hour (hr) = 60 min
1 day = 24 hr
1 week = 7 days
1 year (yr) = 12 months (mo) = 365 days
(leap year = 366 days)

To change a larger unit of measurement to a smaller one, you need to multiply.

1. A picture frame is 3 feet 8 inches long. What is the length of the frame in inches?

   • Change 3 feet to inches using the fact that 1 foot = 12 inches. | 3 ft × 12 = 36 in. |

   • Add the remaining 8 inches. | 36 + 8 = 44 in. |

The picture frame is 44 inches in length.

To change a smaller unit of measure to a larger one, divide using the appropriate measurement equivalency.

2. A package weighs 84 ounces. What is the weight of the package in pounds?

   • Change 84 ounces to pounds. Because 1 pound = 16 ounces, divide by 16.

$$\begin{array}{r} 5 \\ 16\overline{)84} \\ -80 \\ \hline 4 \end{array}$$

   • The remainder is in ounces, the same unit you started with. Therefore, the package weighs 5 lb 4 oz. You can also express the remainder as a fraction:

$$5\frac{4\text{ oz}}{16\text{ oz}} = 5\frac{1}{4}\text{ lb}$$

In a measurement problem, you may need to add, subtract, multiply, or divide measurements. When finding a sum or a difference, remember that you can only add or subtract like measurement units.

3. A deck requires pieces of railing that are 5 feet 9 inches, 15 feet 4 inches, and 8 feet 6 inches. What is the total length of railing needed?

   - Write the measurements in a column, aligning like units of measure.

   - Add like units.

5 ft 9 in.
15 ft 4 in.
+ 8 ft 6 in.
28 ft 19 in.

   - Simplify the answer. (Change 19 inches to 1 feet 7 inches, and add to 28 feet.)

The deck requires 29 feet 7 inches of railing.

When you subtract, you may need to regroup, or borrow.

4. How much more is 4 pounds 3 ounces than 2 pounds 8 ounces?

   - Align the values in the problem. Because you cannot subtract 8 ounces from 3 ounces, regroup 1 pound from the pounds column, and add it to the ounces column as 16 ounces.

   $$\begin{array}{r} \overset{3}{\cancel{4}} \text{ lb } \overset{19}{\cancel{3}} \text{ oz} \\ - 2 \text{ lb } 8 \text{ oz} \\ \hline 1 \text{ lb } 11 \text{ oz} \end{array}$$

   - Subtract. The difference is 1 pound 11 ounces.

To multiply a measurement by a whole number, multiply the units of measure separately. Then simplify the result.

5. Tony has five lengths of plastic pipe, each measuring 6 feet 10 inches. What is the combined length of the five pieces of pipe?

   - Multiply each part of the measurement by 5.

   - Simplify using the fact 1 feet = 12 inches.

6 ft 10 in.
×   5
30 ft 50 in. =
30 ft + 4 ft 2 in. =
34 ft 2 in.

The combined length is 34 feet 2 inches.

To divide a measurement, you can divide each part of the measurement and then add the results. However, it will usually be faster to rewrite the measurement in terms of the smallest unit of measure. Then divide and simplify.

6. John has 1 pint 8 fluid ounces of liquid lawn fertilizer. He has plans to mix one-third of the liquid with two gallons of water and apply it to his lawn. How many fluid ounces of fertilizer will he use?

   - Change the amount to ounces.

1 pt = 2 c = 16 fl oz
1 pt + 8 fl oz = (16 + 8) fl oz = 24 fl oz

   - To find one-third, divide by 3.

24 fl oz ÷ 3 = 8 fl oz

   - John will use 8 fluid ounces of lawn fertilizer.

THE METRIC SYSTEM

The **metric system** is the measurement system used in most of the countries of the world. The main unit of length in the metric system is the **meter** (m). The **gram** (g) is the basic metric measure of mass (or weight). The basic unit of volume is called the **liter** (*l*).

The units of measurement in the metric system are named by combing prefixes to the basic units. The prefixes have specific meanings:

milli- means one-thousandth
centi- means one-hundredth
deci- means one-tenth

deka or *deca-* means ten
hecto- means hundred
kilo- means one thousand

Therefore, a kilometer (km) equals 1,000 meters, a milligram (mg) equals one one-thousandth gram, and a centiliter (cl) equals one one-hundredth liter.

As in the decimal place-value system, each column on the chart below is 10 times the column to its right. To convert between metric units, count the number of times that you must move to the right or left from the unit you are converting from to the unit you are converting to. Then move the decimal point that number of place values in the same direction.

kilo- (km) 1,000 m	hecto- (hm) 100 m	deka- (dam) 10 m	meter (m) 1 m	deci- (dm) 0.1 m	centi- (cm) 0.01 m	milli- (mm) 0.001 m

Note: Although the chart uses the meter as the basic unit, the chart can also be used with liters and grams.

1. How many millimeters (mm) are equal to 3 centimeters (cm)?

   - Find *milli-* and *centi-* on the chart. The prefix *milli-* is one place to the right of the prefix *centi-*; therefore, you need to move the decimal point one place to the right to convert from centimeters to millimeters.

   - For example, 3 cm = 3.0 cm = 30 mm.

2. How many grams (g) are equal to 6,400 (mg)?

   - Start in the *milli-* column. The basic unit is three columns to the left. Move the decimal point three place-value columns to the left.

   - For example, 6,400 mg = 6,400. mg = 6.4 g.

Metric measurements are written as decimal numbers. Therefore, you can perform operations with metric measurements using the rules for adding, subtracting, multiplying, and dividing decimals.

3. Three metal rods measure 1.5 meters, 1.85 meters, and 450 centimeters. What is the total length of the rods in meters?

    - The first two measures are in meters. Convert the third measure to meters. 450 cm = 4.5 m

    - Add using the rules for adding decimals. The total is 7.85 meters.

$$
\begin{array}{r}
1\\
1.5\\
1.85\\
+\,4.5\\
\hline
7.85
\end{array}
$$

Follow the same steps to subtract.

4. Tanya is jogging in a city park. The park has a path for joggers that is 2 kilometers in length. When she reaches the 750-meter checkpoint, how many kilometers does she have left to run?

    - You need to find the distance she has left in kilometers.

    - Change 750 meters to kilometers. 750 m = 0.75 km

    - Subtract using the rules for subtracting decimals.

$$
\begin{array}{r}
1\ 9\ 10\\
2.\cancel{0}\cancel{0}\\
-0.75\\
\hline
1.25
\end{array}
$$

Tanya has 1.25 kilometers left to run.

Multiplying and dividing is easy in the metric system. Follow the rules for multiplying and dividing decimals.

5. Alex is a buyer at Rugs Plus. He plans to order 25 acrylic rugs to sell in the store. The shipping weight for each rug is 7.8 kilograms. What is the shipping weight in kilograms of the entire order?

    - Multiply the weight of one rug (7.8 kilograms) by 25.

    - The weight of 25 rugs is 195 kilograms. Notice that the answer has the same unit of measure as the number you multiplied.

$$
\begin{array}{r}
7.8\\
\times\ 25\\
\hline
390\\
1560\\
\hline
195.0
\end{array}
$$

6. At a food-processing plant, a tank holds 92.4 liters of a fruit drink. It takes three hours for a machine to empty the tank into small containers. How many liters of fruit drink are processed per hour?

    - To find the number per hour, divide 92.4 liters by 3.

    - The machine can process 30.8 liters per hour.

$$
\begin{array}{r}
30.8\\
3\overline{)92.4}\\
9\\
\hline
2\ 4\\
2\ 4\\
\hline
\end{array}
$$

ESTIMATION

Some questions ask for an **estimate** rather than an exact value. Here are some estimation techniques to practice.

1. Approximately how many people attended the 3-game series if attendance was 33,541, 35,045, and 34,092?

   - The problem asks *approximately* how many people; therefore, you can estimate. Notice that all three amounts are close to 35,000.

     $$33,541 \approx 35,000$$
     $$35,045 \approx 35,000$$
     $$34,095 \approx 35,000$$

   - Multiply 35,000 by 3 to find the approximate attendance for the 3-game series.

     $$35,000 \times 3 = 105,000$$

2. If Ambrose wanted to save enough money to make a $1,159 purchase in a year's time, approximately how much should he save per month?

   - The problem asks *approximately* how much; therefore, you can estimate. Divide to find how many equal parts are in the total money to be saved. Because 1 year = 12 months, the numbers you need to solve the problem are 12 and $1,159.

   - Round one or both of the numbers so that they are easy to divide. Round $1,159 to $1,200, then divide.

     $$\$1,200 \div 12 = \$100 \text{ per month}$$

Estimation can also be used to help you narrow down answer choices in multiple-choice problems or to check your calculations.

3. Souvenir sales are $389, $205, and $276 at each of three booths. What is the total amount in sales?

   (A) $92
   (B) $615
   (C) $828
   (D) $870
   (E) $2,621

Strategy 1:

You can estimate an answer by rounding values to the nearest hundred. That eliminates options (A), (B), and (E); 900 is closest to option (D) $870.

$$\$400 + \$200 + \$300 = \$900$$

Strategy 2:

You can calculate an answer and then check it against an estimate to see if your answer makes sense. The solution (D) $870 is close to an estimate of $900.

$$\$389 + \$205 + \$276 = \$870$$

Review Four Practice

Classify each angle based on its angle measure.

1. 55°

2. 270°

Questions 3 and 4 refer to the drawing at the right.

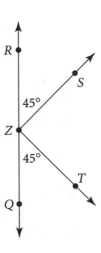

3. ∠*QZR* is a straight angle. What is the measure of ∠*QZS*?

(A) 135°
(B) 125°
(C) 90°
(D) 60°
(E) 45°

4. What kind of angle is ∠*SZT*?

(A) acute
(B) obtuse
(C) right
(D) straight
(E) reflex

Using the figure shown at the right, solve as directed.

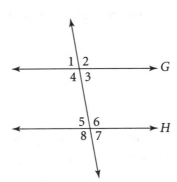

5. List one pair of alternate interior angles.

6. Which angle corresponds to ∠7?

7. Which of the following is a true statement about corresponding angles?

(A) They are also vertical angles.
(B) They are also supplementary angles.
(C) They are in the same position from one parallel line to the other.
(D) They are also alternate interior angles.
(E) They are also alternate exterior angles.

Question 8 refers to the following figure.

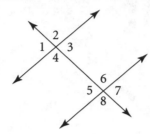

8. The measure of ∠7 is 115°. What is the measure of ∠4?

   (A) 25°
   (B) 65°
   (C) 115°
   (D) 245°
   (E) Not enough information is given.

Classify the triangle in two ways.

9.

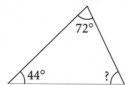

Find the measure of the unknown angle in the triangle.

10.

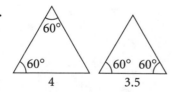

Decide whether the pairs of triangles are congruent. Write *Yes*, *No*, or *Not Enough Information*.

11.

12.

<u>Question 13</u> refers to the figure at the right.

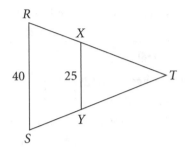

13. If $XY \parallel RS$, $m\angle S = 68°$, and $m\angle T = 48°$, then what is the measure of $m\angle TXY$?

    (A) 48°

    (B) 64°

    (C) 68°

    (D) 116°

    (E) 135°

List the names of quadrilaterals with the following properties. Write *None* if no quadrilateral has the given property.

14. four right angles

15. opposite sides are equal in length

16. exactly one pair of parallel sides

<u>Question 17</u> refers to the figure at the right.

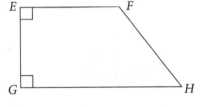

17. $\angle F$ is 20° more than three times the measure of $\angle H$. What is the measure of $\angle F$?

    (A) 40°

    (B) 60°

    (C) 120°

    (D) 140°

    (E) 180°

18. How many inches are equal to 4 feet?

19. How many minutes are equal to 420 seconds?

Question 20 refers to the following information.

> **Portable Air Cooler**
> Duracool R612
> 3.75 gallon capacity
> Runs 6 hours without refilling
> width: 27 in.; depth: 16 in.
> height: $13\frac{3}{4}$ in.
> shipping weight: 26 lb

20. Bob wants to buy an air cooler. He knows the capacity of several other models in quarts. Which of the following expressions could he use to find the capacity for this model in quarts?

    (A) 3.75×2
    (B) $3.75 \div 2$
    (C) 3.75×4
    (D) $3.75 \div 4$
    (E) 3.75×8

21.　　3 hr 30 min
　　　　4 hr 20 min
　　　+ 2 hr 45 min
　　　───────────

22.　　3 gal 1 qt
　　　− 1 gal 3 qt
　　　──────────

23. Nydia works in a photo lab. She uses 1 pint 6 fluid ounces of film developer from a full container. If the capacity of the container is 3 quarts, how much developer is left in the container?

    (A) 2 qt 10 fl oz
    (B) 2 qt 6 fl oz
    (C) 2 qt 2 fl oz
    (D) 2 qt
    (E) 1 qt 10 fl oz

24. How many meters equal 5 kilometers?

25. Six hundred centimeters equal how many meters?

26. How many milligrams equal 4 grams?

27. In a vitamin supplement, each capsule contains 500 milligrams of vitamins. How many grams of vitamins are found in each capsule?

    (A) 5,000
    (B) 500
    (C)   50
    (D)   5
    (E) 0.5

Solve as directed. Pay special attention to the label given for each answer.

28. 5.4 cm + 19 cm + 2.85 cm = _____ cm

29. 12 kg + 10.5 kg + 120 g = _____ g

30. To make a carbonated punch, Kay Lynn adds six cans of club soda to 2 liters of cranberry juice. If each can holds 355 milliliters, how many liters of punch has Kay Lynn made?

    (A) 4.13
    (B) 4.26
    (C) 5.55
    (D) 23.3
    (E) 37.5

Review Four Answer Key

1. acute

2. reflex

3. (A) 135°

$m\angle RZS + m\angle QZS = 180°$. Because $\angle RZS$ measures 45°, $\angle QZS$ must measure 135°.

4. (C) right

Because $m\angle RZQ = 180°$, subtract the two known angles to find the measure of $\angle SZT$: $180° - 45° - 45° = 90°$. Because $\angle SZT$ measures 90°, it is a right angle.

5. $\angle 4$ and $\angle 6$, $\angle 3$ and $\angle 5$

6. $\angle 3$

7. (C)

They are in the same position from one parallel line to the other.

8. (B) 65°

$\angle 7$ and $\angle 3$ are corresponding angles, so $m\angle 7 = m\angle 3$; therefore, $m\angle 3 = 115°$. $\angle 3$ and $\angle 4$ are adjacent angles, which means that $115° + m\angle 4 = 180°$. $m\angle 4 = 65°$

9. equilateral, acute

10. 64°

11. No

12. Not enough information

13. (B) 64°

Because XY is parallel to RS and $m\angle S = 68°$, then $m\angle TYX = 68°$. $m\angle TYX + m\angle T + m\angle TXY = 180°$. Substitute and solve. $68° + 48° + m\angle TXY = 180°$ and $m\angle TXY = 64°$.

14. rectangle, square

15. parallelogram, rectangle, square, rhombus

16. trapezoid

17. (D) 140°

Let x = the measure of $\angle H$. $3x + 20° = m\angle F$. The sum of the angles of a quadrilateral is 360°, so $3x + 20° + x + 90° + 90° = 360°$. Solve the equation.

$$4x + 200° = 360°$$
$$4x = 160°$$
$$x = 40°$$

so $3x + 20° = 140°$

18. 48 in.

19. 7 min

20. (C) 3.75×4

4 qt = 1 gal, so multiply the number of gallons by 4 to find the number of quarts.

21. 10 hr 35 min

22. 1 gal 2 qt

23. (A) 2 qt 10 fl oz

3 qt = 2 qt 2 pt = 2 qt 1 pt 16 fl oz

Subtract.

$$\begin{array}{r} 2 \text{ qt 1 pt 16 fl oz} \\ - \quad \text{1 pt 6 fl oz} \\ \hline 2 \text{ qt 10 fl oz} \end{array}$$

24. 5,000 m

25. 6 m

26. 4,000 mg

27. (E) 0.5

There are 1,000 milligrams in 1 gram.

$500 \div 1,000 = 0.5$ g

28. 27.25 cm

29. 22,620 g

30. (A) 4.13

Multiply the number of milliliters of soda in a can by the number of cans. 355 ml × 6 = 2,130 ml Convert to liters. 2,130 ml ÷ 1,000 = 2.13 *l*. Add the liters of soda and juice. 2.13 *l* + 2*l* = 4.13 *l*.

CHAPTER THREE

PRAXIS WRITING

INTRODUCING PRAXIS WRITING

The PRAXIS Writing test consists of two sections that test two very different kinds of writing skills. The first section tests your ability to read sentences and locate and correct grammatical errors. The second section tests your ability to write a clear, coherent essay in a certain amount of time.

Keep in mind this test is not designed to discover the next Ernest Hemingway or Maya Angelou. Instead, this test assesses your ability to adhere to the basic rules of written English and to avoid common grammatical errors and traps.

Your approach to the Writing test should vary depending on the section. Like all other sections on the PRAXIS PPST, strategic time management and understanding what the test maker is looking for are the keys to success.

KNOW WHAT TO EXPECT

The key to success on any test is knowing what you can expect. The PRAXIS Writing test is no exception. Here's what you'll be up against:

PRAXIS Writing Test	
Section 1: 30 Minutes Usage and Sentence Correction	38 Multiple-Choice Questions • Grammatical Relationships • Structural Relationships • Idiom/Word Choice, Mechanics, No Error
Section 2: 30 Minutes	1 Essay Question Write a coherent, well-structured essay responding to the essay prompt

As you can see, there are two different sections to the PRAXIS Writing test, and they require different approaches. However, keep in mind that the same rules of standard written English are applicable to both the short answer questions and the essay component of the Writing test. We'll cover the grammar rules that are tested most frequently and give you the proven Kaplan strategies for each question type you'll see on your test.

PPST WRITING: MULTIPLE-CHOICE QUESTIONS

Ironically, the multiple-choice section of the PRAXIS Writing test does not require you to do any writing at all. You won't be tested on the names of grammatical terms. You won't need to identify nouns, pronouns, verbs, participles, or gerunds. Whereas a vague sense of how you diagrammed sentences back in the day may help a bit, it's not an essential skill on these questions.

What the multiple-choice Writing questions do test is your ability to recognize the elements of good writing, including basic grammar, sentence structure, agreement, and word choice.

As you prepare for the test, read everything—and we mean everything—with an eye toward sentence structure. Look for fragments in advertisements. Find run-on sentences in emails from your friends. Ferret out misplaced modifiers in your school newspaper. Develop "proofreader's eyes" as you read, read, read your way to success.

As you hone your eyes and get ready to spot errors on the PRAXIS exam, be sure to fine-tune your ears as well. Develop a more critical ear that notes errors and awkward constructions when you hear them. Frequently, you will have to trust your ear to identify errors and avoid trap answers on test day.

Introducing the Question Types

Because these question types may be new to you, you should begin by becoming familiar with the structure of the questions and the direction for each question type you will see on your test. Remember, you only have 30 minutes to answer 38 questions on the multiple-choice section of the PRAXIS Writing test. Getting familiar with the directions and the basics of each question type ahead of time will give you an edge when test day rolls around.

Usage Questions

There are approximately 19 Usage questions on the Writing test. The directions for Usage questions look like this:

> <u>Directions:</u> For each of the following questions, choose the best answer from the given choices and darken the corresponding oval.
>
> The following sentences contain problems in grammar, usage, diction (choice of words), and idiom. Some sentences are correct. None of the sentences contains more than one error. The error, if there is one in the sentence, is underlined and lettered. Parts of the sentence that are not underlined are correct and cannot be changed. In selecting answers, follow the requirements of standard written English. If there is an error, choose the <u>one underlined part</u> that must be changed to make the sentence correct and fill in the corresponding oval on your answer grid.
>
> If there is no error, fill in oval E.

Here's what a sample question might look like:

> 1. <u>Even though</u> he <u>had to</u> supervise a large staff, his salary <u>was no greater</u>
>   A   B   C
>   than <u>a clerk</u>. <u>No error</u>
>   D   E

The game you're playing with Usage questions is "Spot the Mistake!" You'll see a sentence like this one with words and phrases underlined. Look at each underlined part and decide which part is incorrect. Some sentences are correct as written. On average, approximately 5 of the 19 Usage questions contain no error. For those questions, you should choose choice (E), "No error."

The test makers put Usage questions in the Writing Skills section to test your ability to catch words or phrases that are frequently used incorrectly in student essays. If you can spot these types of errors, the test makers assume that you can use appropriate words and phrases in your own writing.

In the example above, the correct answer is (D). The current wording makes it sound as though the size of the subject's salary is being compared to the size of a clerk; in fact, the subject's salary should be compared to the size of a clerk's *salary*.

Keep in mind that you only have 30 minutes to answer 38 questions and that there is no penalty for incorrect answers. That means you need to move quickly through the 19 Usage questions to allow for the more time-consuming questions. Aim to spend roughly 10 minutes on the Usage questions. That means you need to answer between two and three questions per minute.

Speed is of the essence in this section, and wrong answers have no impact on your score. Practice moving quickly through the practice sets we've provided, and learn to trust your ear on your first read of a question. Always choose an answer on your first read through. If nothing sounds wrong, choose (E) and move on. Make a note in your test booklet next to the questions you are unsure of, and return to them if you have time. Never leave a question unanswered on the PPST.

Sentence Correction Questions

There are approximately 19 Sentence Correction questions on the PPST Writing test. The directions for Sentence Correction questions look like this:

> <u>Directions:</u> The following sentences test accuracy and effectiveness of expression. In selecting answers, follow the rules of standard written English; in other words, consider grammar, choice of words, sentence construction, and punctuation.
>
> In each of the following sentences, a portion or all of the sentence is underlined. Under each sentence you will find five ways of phrasing the underlined portion. Choice A repeats the original underlined portion; the other four choices provide alternative phrasings.
>
> Select the choice that best expresses the meaning of the original sentence. If the original sentence is better than any of the alternative phrasings, choose A; otherwise, select one of the alternatives. Your selection should construct the most effective sentence—clear and precise with no awkwardness or ambiguity.

Here's what a sample question might look like.

2. The experts from the Fish and Wildlife Department could not decide which one of eight possible nesting sites along the Platte River <u>will provide the best habitat into which to release the cranes</u>.

   (A) will provide the best habitat
   (B) would be providing the better habitat
   (C) would provide the better habitat
   (D) would provide the best habitat
   (E) is providing the best habitat

In the question above, (D) is correct. A quick scan of the answer choices reveals that this question tests verb tense. The nonunderlined portion of the sentence is in the past tense, so you need to use the past form of *will*, which is *would*. Thus, choices (A) and (E) are out. More scanning reveals another split between *best* and *better*. Better/best is a frequently tested idiom: you use *better* to compare two things, *best* to compare more than two. There are eight possible nesting sites, so the experts need to find the best one. Eliminate (B) and (C). (D) is correct because it is the only answer choice that uses *would* and *best*. Quickly scanning your answer choices for differences like these will help you identify what the question is testing and allow you to locate the correct answer quickly and efficiently.

Sentence Correction questions tend to take more time than Usage questions, and you should budget your time accordingly. Nonetheless, to perform well on the Writing section, you need to continue to move quickly and avoid getting stuck on any single question. Again, trust your ear and your instincts, and continue to move forward throughout the test. Getting one question wrong is not nearly as harmful as agonizing for five or six minutes on a question, regardless of whether you get it right. Always choose an answer on your first read through. If the sentence sounds good to begin with, choose (A) and move on. Don't waste time re-reading choice (A)—you already know what it says. As you move through the test, make a note in your test booklet next to the questions you are unsure of, and return to them if you have time.

You should spend no more than a minute to a minute and a half on Sentence Correction questions.

HOW TO APPROACH PRAXIS WRITING

Earlier in this chapter, you learned about the importance of developing an eye for mistakes and trusting your ear to help you locate and fix potential errors. You then read about the various question types you'll encounter on your test. Now we're going to show you how to put your search-and-repair tactics to work on real PPST Writing Skills questions. Start with these three simple steps.

THE KAPLAN THREE-STEP METHOD FOR PRAXIS WRITING

Step 1. Read the sentence *listening* for a mistake.

Step 2. Identify the error.

Step 3. Check the answer choices.

This method will serve you well for all types of Writing Skills questions, although we'll show you how to refine it slightly to suit each question type.

THE USAGE SECTION

Usage is a great place for the Writing Skills test to begin because you don't have to fix anything. You just have to point out what's wrong. Pretend you're a teacher with a big red pencil and get to it!

Try using the Three-Step Method on this question. First, read the sentence *listening* for a mistake. Note: In preparation for test day, you should get used to reading silently and listening to the voice in your head. No, don't listen to the bad voices. Just listen to the one that's reading the sentence.

3. The <u>club members</u> are so busy <u>studying</u> for exams that attendance is
     A   B

<u>rare</u> more <u>than 50 percent</u>. <u>No error</u>
 C   D   E

When you read the sentence, did you hear an error? If so, you're all set. You don't need to figure out how you would fix the error. You just need to fill in the right bubble and move on. If you didn't hear the mistake, read the sentence again. There's no problem with the phrase *club members. Studying* is OK here. How about *rare*? There's the clunker. The correct construction here would be "rarely more than 50 percent." Choice (C) is correct.

This question is a classic example of an adjective/adverb error. Let's look at some other classic errors that appear in the Usage section.

Verb Tense Errors

As you know, the verb is the action part of the sentence. The verb's tense tells you when the action is taking place. You won't need to identify verb tenses by name on the test, but you will need to recognize the difference between correct and incorrect verb tenses.

  When David was in Holland, he was seeing many windmills.

You don't need to know the rules about proper use of the past tense to know that something's wrong here. Your ear should have told you that the verbs don't sound right. Try this instead:

  When David was in Holland, he saw many windmills.

That sounds better, and it's correct. Now let's look at a testlike question that has a verb tense error.

4. <u>Unsatisfied</u> with the ending, the director <u>considering</u> <u>reshooting</u>
  A   B   C

<u>the entire</u> film. <u>No error</u>
  D   E

Did this sentence make sense to you? If not, where did the confusion come in? We don't know when the director's action took place because *considering* isn't a complete verb. You could substitute *is considering* or *was considering* or even *considered*. Because choice (B) contains the error in this sentence, it's the answer.

Subject-Verb Agreement Errors

Your grammar book tells you that the subject and the verb of a sentence must agree in number. Put simply, this means that a singular subject takes a singular verb, and a plural subject takes a plural verb. Subject and verb also have to agree in person. This simply means that you need to use the right form of the verb depending on whether the subject is first person, second person, or third person.

You do this correctly a million times a day, and it's not as tricky as it sounds. Take a look at these sentences:

> The 4:05 train to Boston leave from the north platform.
>
> Henry's dog are brown with a white tail.
>
> The ballerinas practices for eight hours a day.
>
> You spends too much time thinking about subject-verb agreement.

Did you find the agreement errors? The sentences on the PPST won't be quite this easy, but with a little practice, you'll be able to spot agreement errors in any sentence. You may have to learn to be on the lookout for the three classic subject-verb agreement traps. Let's take a look.

Trap 1: Collective Nouns

A very common trap that appears on the PPST Writing Skills section uses collective nouns to try to trick you.

Words such as *group*, *audience*, or *committee* require a singular verb.

> The group has decided to plan a trip to a chocolate factory.
>
> The audience was moved to throw rotten vegetables at the mime.
>
> The committee votes to clean up the waterfront every year.

All of these sentences are correct. Now try the following out for size.

5. That <u>particular</u> gang of pirates <u>were</u> often <u>referred to</u> as the <u>scourge of</u>
          A   B   C   D
      the seven seas. <u>No error</u>
                       E

Even with advance warning, this one was kind of tricky. The correct answer here is (B) because the subject was the collective singular noun *gang*. Making the error harder to spot in this case was the prepositional phrase *of pirates*, which was thrown in to the sentence just to confuse you. This brings us to Trap 2.

Trap 2: Intervening Phrases

The test makers will often try to confuse the issue of subject-verb agreement by inserting an intervening phrase between the subject and verb. Try this one.

6. Tax evasion, <u>a crime</u> that <u>has been documented</u> in many modern
           A   B

   novels and films, <u>remain</u> a relatively <u>uncommon offense</u>. <u>No error</u>
                C   D   E

Did you pick choice (C)? You're right. The verb *remain* goes with *evasion*, a singular word, which requires the verb form *remains*. Don't be fooled by the plural nouns *novels* and *films*, which are part of the intervening phrase. Also, if you have trouble identifying the subject and verb, try ignoring all the extra adjectives, prepositional phrases, and subordinate clauses.

Trap 3: Subject After Verb

Another way that the test makers try to confuse you is by placing the subject after the verb. Take a look at this example.

7. <u>Although</u> nutritionists have <u>criticized pizza</u> for being too high in fat,
       A   B

   there <u>is</u> many people <u>who</u> continue to enjoy it. <u>No error</u>
        C   D   E

People is the subject of the verb *to be*, and it requires a plural subject:...*There are many people*...Choice (C) is correct.

Pronoun Errors: Case and Number

You're sure to see at least a few questions on your PPST that test the use of pronouns. The key thing to remember about pronouns is that they must agree with their antecedents in case and number.

Who is *He*? What is *It*?

Every pronoun must have an antecedent. The *antecedent* is the noun that corresponds to the pronoun in the sentence. Look at this sentence: Beck is a great singer, and he is also a fine songwriter. "Beck" is the antecedent and "he" is the pronoun.

Case refers to the form in which the word appears in the sentence. If the pronoun refers to the subject, it has a different case than if it refers to an object.

Sally dances, and *she* also sings.

Bob praised Sally, and he also applauded *her*.

These sentences are correct.

The **number** of a pronoun is just what it sounds like: singular or plural.

Give this question a try:

8. A student <u>who</u> applies for a part-time job assisting Dr. Frankenstein
        A

<u>may get</u> more than <u>they</u> asked <u>for</u> in the bargain. <u>No error</u>
  B   C   D   E

Did you see the error here? The antecedent here is *a student* and the pronoun is *they*. To make the plural pronoun agree with its singular antecedent, you would have to use *he* or *she*, or even possibly *he or she*. Jeez, no wonder the author used *they*.

This example demonstrates a common grammatical mistake. Many people use "they" in spoken English to refer to a single person of unknown gender. However, this is not grammatically correct in standard written English because "they" is plural. Watch out for "they" and "them" on test day!

Pronoun Errors: Ambiguous Reference

Another common pronoun problem you'll find on the PPST Writing Skills section is ambiguous reference. As you just read, every pronoun must have a clear antecedent.

Give this question a try:

9. To expand the newspaper's <u>coverage</u> of local politics, <u>they</u> transferred
                          A   B

a <u>popular</u> columnist <u>to</u> the City desk. <u>No error</u>
   C   D   E

This one may have been easy because you knew what you were looking for. Choice (B), *they*, is a pronoun without a clear antecedent. Who transferred the columnist? The sentence doesn't tell us. Choice (B) is correct.

Questions like this one can be tricky because they read smoothly, with no bumpy parts to jar your ear. Keep an eye out for ambiguous references in sentences that seem too good to be true.

Idioms

The test makers also occasionally like to test whether students can recognize the proper use of idioms. This can be especially bad news for non-native speakers of English because idioms are the hardest thing to learn in any foreign language. This is because idioms are simply word combinations that have become part of the language. They're correct, but there's no particular rhyme or reason why they're correct. Most— although certainly not all—native speakers will know the proper idiom to use simply because their ear tells them what combination sounds correct.

Prepositions are the typically short words—such as *by, at, among,* and *before*—that link prepositional phrases to the rest of the sentence. Most preposition issues tested on the PPST are idiomatic. This means that you'll be listening for word combinations that frequently go together. Use your ear to catch prepositions that just don't sound right.

Give the following question a try. Be sure to use the Kaplan Three-Step Method.

> 10. Many people are <u>desensitized to</u> violence on TV shows, <u>but</u> this does
>   A   B
>
> not mean that they are not sensitive <u>of</u> the real-life violence around
>   C
>
> <u>them</u>. <u>No error</u>
> D   E

There are two idiomatic uses of prepositions in this sentence. Did you spot them? *Desensitized to* and *sensitive of* are choices (A) and (C). *Sensitive of* simply isn't idiomatic, and choice (C) is correct. If you're not a native speaker of English or you don't have a good ear for idioms, you'll need to immerse yourself in idioms as you study for the test.

Comparison Errors

Another error that frequently shows up on the PPST Writing Skills section involves comparisons. This one can be a little sneaky because some of these sentences may sound OK to your ear. It's time to bring your brain into the picture!

When you compare two or more parts of speech, like nouns or verb phrases, the parts of speech must be in the same form.

Take a look at this example:

> The producer agreed that casting a drama series is harder than comedy.

If you heard this sentence, you'd probably understand what it means, although it's not crystal-clear. *Casting a drama series* is harder than . . . what exactly? The sentence would be clearer if it were written as follows:

> The producer agreed that casting a drama series is harder than casting a comedy series.

Both parts of the comparison are in the same form, making the sentence easier to understand and grammatically correct.

See if you can spot the mistake in the next question.

11. Even though <u>he</u> is a Nobel Laureate, <u>Elie Wiesel's name</u> is still
         A   B

     <u>less well known</u> than <u>last year's</u> Heisman Trophy winner. <u>No error</u>
           C   D   E

This is a bit subtle. Did you spot the faulty comparison? The sentence compares *Elie Wiesel's name* with the *Heisman Trophy winner*. If we change choice (B) to read simply *Elie Wiesel*, the comparison is parallel and easier to understand.

Adjective and Adverb Errors

You probably haven't thought about adjectives and adverbs since those junior high sentence diagrams. The good news is that you probably use adjectives and adverbs correctly all the time.

> That painting is beautiful.
> The artist painted it skillfully.

In the first sentence, *beautiful* is an adjective modifying *painting*, a noun. In the second sentence, *skillfully* is an adverb modifying *painted*, a verb form.

Know Your Modifiers

An adjective modifies a noun or pronoun. An adverb modifies a verb, an adjective, or another adverb. Most but not all adverbs end in –ly.

Now take a look at how adjectives and adverbs might be tested in the Usage section.

12. <u>Since the onset</u> of <u>his</u> blindness, the artist <u>has sculpted</u> more <u>slow</u> than
             A   B   C   D

     before. <u>No error</u>
                  E

Choice (D) is correct. The adverb *slowly* is required to modify the verb form *has sculpted*.

Double Negatives

In standard written English, it's incorrect to use two negatives in a row. Just as in math, two negatives added together create a positive.

> I won't have none of that backtalk, young lady!

This sentence, if you cancel the negatives, translates to:

> I'll have that backtalk, young lady!

You'll find an occasional double negative question in the Usage section, although the sentences are a bit tougher than the one above. Give this one a try:

13. The town hasn't <u>hardly any</u> money left in <u>its</u> budget <u>because of</u> the
               A   B   C
    unexpected snowplow <u>costs</u>. <u>No error</u>
                          D   E

The words *hasn't* and *hardly any* cancel each other out, making it sound as if the town doesn't have money problems. We can figure out from the rest of the sentence that the author's trying to tell us that the town does have money problems because of the unexpected costs. Changing choice (A), *hardly any*, to *much* would help to eliminate one of the negatives, clearing up the meaning of the sentence.

> The town hasn't much money left in its budget because of the unexpected snowplow costs.

THE SENTENCE CORRECTION SECTION

Sentence Correction questions test the same skills as Usage questions. You'll still be using your eyes and ears to spot errors and oddities in sentences. Here's the difference: now you have to fix the mistakes you find. As you probably remember from earlier in this chapter, each Sentence Correction question has an underlined phrase. You need to decide whether the sentence is OK as is, in which case you should pick choice (A), or whether the underlined portion should be replaced by one of the answer choices.

Take a look at the Kaplan Three-Step Method for Sentence Corrections. It'll help you keep your focus as you tackle the Sentence Corrections in this section.

Step 1. Read the sentence listening for a mistake.

Step 2. Predict a correction.

Step 3. Select the answer choice that matches your prediction, and eliminate clearly wrong answer choices.

Now apply the Three-Step Method to this Sentence Correction.

14. Hoping to receive a promotion, <u>the letter he received instead informed Burt</u> that he had been fired.

    (A) the letter he received instead informed Burt

    (B) the letter having been received, instead informed Burt

    (C) Burt instead received a letter informing him

    (D) information from the received letter instead told Burt

    (E) Burt, instead informed by the letter he received

First, read the sentence, listening for a mistake. Something sounds wrong. Burt hoped to receive the promotion, but this makes it sound as if the letter hoped to receive the promotion. Next, predict a correction. You should put Burt at the beginning of the second phrase. Now, select the choice that fits your prediction, eliminating wrong choices. Choices (C) and (E) both put Burt at the beginning of the phrase, but choice (C) is the clearest and most succinct choice, so it's correct.

Whereas any of the errors discussed previously could also appear in the Sentence Correction question set, there are some errors that are much more likely to appear in this section. Let's review them.

Sentence Fragments

Sentence fragments are incomplete sentences. To be complete, a sentence requires a main subject and a main verb. Some sentences are fragments because they lack the necessary elements to make logical sense or have an unnecessary connector like *that* or *because*.

Here are some fragments. How would you repair them?

    Stereo equipment on sale at the mall today!

    The busload of tourists that wandered curiously around the ancient ruins.

    Because Myrna likes the Adirondacks, frequently taking photos of them.

Did you get an empty feeling when you read these fragments? Watch for that feeling on test day, and you'll be able to spot the fragments.

Give this example a try, using the Kaplan Three-Step Method:

> 15. Last of the world's leaders to do so, the prime minister admits that terrorist threats <u>credible enough to warrant</u> the imposition of stringent security measures.
>
> (A) credible enough to warrant
> (B) credible enough warrant
> (C) are credible enough to warrant
> (D) credible enough, warranting
> (E) are credible enough to be warranted

That empty feeling sets in right in the middle of the sentence. The subject is *terrorist threats*, but where's the verb? *Credible* is the adjective modifying *terrorist threats*, so adding *are*, as choices (C) and (E) do, repairs the fragment. Choice (E), however, introduces a new problem with the phrase *to be warranted*, which is confusing. Choice (C) clearly fixes the fragment and is correct.

Run-On Sentences

A run-on sentence occurs when two complete sentences that should be separate are joined together.

Here are some examples:

> Jane was the preeminent scientist in her class her experiments were discussed across campus.
>
> Jane was the preeminent scientist in her class, her experiments were discussed across campus.

You can tell that this is a run-on sentence because it sounds like it should be two separate sentences. There are three ways to fix a run-on sentence.

1. Use a period.
Jane was the preeminent scientist in her class. Her experiments were discussed across campus.

2. Use a conjunction, making one sentence dependent.
Because Jane was the preeminent scientist in her class, her experiments were discussed across campus.

3. Use a semicolon.
Jane was the preeminent scientist in her class; her experiments were discussed across campus.

Use the Kaplan Three-Step Method and the information you just learned to solve this question:

16. <u>Jonas Salk was born in East Harlem, New York, the developer of the polio vaccine.</u>

    (A) Jonas Salk was born in East Harlem, New York, the developer of the polio vaccine.
    (B) Jonas Salk being the developer of the polio vaccine and was born in East Harlem, New York.
    (C) Being the developer of the polio vaccine, Jonas Salk was born in East Harlem, New York.
    (D) Jonas Salk was the developer of the polio vaccine, having been born in East Harlem, New York.
    (E) Jonas Salk, who was born in East Harlem, New York, was the developer of the polio vaccine.

Because the entire sentence is underlined, you know that either it's correct or there's a better rewrite among the choices. What's wrong with the sentence? Well, it's clearly a run-on because there are two independent thoughts that aren't joined in any way. It's also a bit confusing because it sounds as if Salk was born the developer of the vaccine. (He probably had to grow up a bit and go to school for a while before he developed the vaccine.) Choice (E) fixes the problem by making the facts about Salk's birthplace dependent thus clearing up the meaning and fixing the run-on problem.

Coordination and Subordination Errors

Sometimes a sentence won't make sense because it contains clauses that aren't logically joined. There are two types of errors involving the improper joining of clauses in a sentence: coordination and subordination errors.

Definition Alert

Clauses are groups of words that contain a subject and a verb. Dependent, or *subordinate*, clauses need to be linked to an independent clause by a conjunction, such as *because*, *although*, or *since*, in order for the sentence to express a complete thought.

Proper **coordination** expresses the logical relationship between two clauses. Misused conjunctions can bring about faulty coordination and make a sentence confusing or nonsensical.

Because he was very thirsty, he refused to drink the water.

This sentence doesn't make much sense (unless we're dealing with a very stubborn or confused person, but let's not over-rationalize things too much). What would be a better conjunction?

> Although he was very thirsty, he refused to drink the water.

This is better. We still don't know why he won't drink the water, but the conjunction *although* sets up the contrast between the two clauses that makes the sentence make sense.

Problems with **subordination** occur when a group of words contains two or more subordinate clauses (also known as dependent clauses) but no independent clause.

> Since the advent of inexpensive portable stereos, because of a boom in the manufacture of light, powerful headphones has resulted.

Connective words like *since, because, so that, if,* and *although* introduce subordinate clauses. As it stands, this sentence consists of two dependent clauses, with no independent clause. We can eliminate *because of* in order to make this a grammatically correct sentence.

> Since the advent of inexpensive portable stereos, a boom in the manufacture of light, powerful headphones has resulted.

Try the following two questions, using the Kaplan Three-Step Method.

17. New restaurants appeared on the <u>waterfront, however merchants</u> were finally able to convince diners of the area's safety.

    (A) waterfront, however merchants
    (B) waterfront; merchants
    (C) waterfront, yet merchants
    (D) waterfront, because merchants
    (E) waterfront, although merchants

However is a conjunction that indicates contrast. This sentence is about cause-and-effect. Choice (D) is correct because the use of the conjunction because shows the relationship between the appearance of the new restaurants and the merchants' ability to convince diners that the area was safe.

18. Because Megan was unable to finish her tax forms before April 15, <u>so she filed</u> for an extension.

    (A) so she filed
    (B) but she was filing
    (C) she filed
    (D) and this led to her filing
    (E) and she filed

This question tests subordination. The sentence contains two dependent clauses, each beginning with a linking word. Choice (C) eliminates the linking word and fixes the problem by creating an independent clause.

Misplaced Modifier Errors

Modifiers are phrases that provide information about nouns and verbs in a sentence. A modifier must appear next to the word or words that it's modifying. Otherwise, things can get a bit confusing (not to mention ungrammatical).

Spot the Trouble Early On!

Most misplaced modifier errors on the PPST occur in sentences that begin with a modifying phrase. When a short phrase followed by a comma begins a sentence, make sure that what follows the comma is who or what the phrase is supposed to modify.

Take a look at this example.

> Dripping on his shirt, Harvey was so eager to eat his hamburger that he didn't notice the ketchup.

As it's written, it sounds as if Harvey was dripping on his shirt, which isn't a very pleasant image. In fact, it's the ketchup that's dripping on his shirt.

Misplaced modifiers are easy to fix. As long as you can spot them, these questions are usually quite easy to answer.

> Harvey was so eager to eat his hamburger that he didn't notice the ketchup dripping on his shirt.

This clears up the confusion and is a logical sentence.

Now let's look at a testlike question that tests misplaced modifiers.

19. <u>Flying for the first time, the roar of the jet engines intimidated the elderly man as the plane sped down the runway.</u>

    (A) Flying for the first time, the roar of the jet engines intimidated the elderly man as the plane sped down the runway.

    (B) The roar of the jet engines intimidated the elderly man as the plane, flying for the first time, sped down the runway.

    (C) Flying for the first time, the elderly man was intimidated by the roar of the jet engines as the plane sped down the runway.

    (D) The plane sped down the runway as, flying for the first time, the roar of the jet engines intimidated the elderly man.

    (E) As the plane sped down the runway, flying for the first time, the elderly man was intimidated by the roar of the jet engines.

We need a choice that makes it clear that the elderly man is the one who is flying for the first time. Choice (C) accomplishes this by placing the modifier *flying for the first time* next to *the elderly man*. Note that choice (E) also places the two phrases next to each other, but the modifier is sandwiched between two phrases, making it unclear which phrase it is meant to modify. Choice (C) is correct.

Parallelism Errors

Parallelism is very much like comparison, which we covered earlier. Essentially, whenever you list items, they must be in the same form.

Take a look at this sentence:

> On Saturday, Ingrid cleaned her apartment, bought her plane tickets for France, and was deciding to go out to dinner.

The first two verbs set us up to expect a parallel verb, but we get blindsided at the end with a nonparallel construction.

> On Saturday, Ingrid cleaned her apartment, bought her plane tickets for France, and decided to go out to dinner.

In this corrected sentence, *cleaned*, *bought*, and *decided* are all in the same form, so the parallel structure is correct.

Try the following question and see how you do:

20. Changing over from a military to a peacetime economy means producing tractors rather than tanks, radios rather than rifles, and producing running shoes rather than combat boots.

   (A) producing running shoes rather than combat boots
   (B) the production of running shoes rather than combat boots
   (C) running shoes rather than combat boots
   (D) replacing combat boots with running shoes
   (E) running shoes instead of combat boots

Choice (C) does the trick by maintaining the parallel structure of the sentence: *tractors rather than tanks, radios rather than rifles, running shoes rather than combat boots.*

Practice Questions

Now it's time to practice some writing questions. Make sure to use the Three-Step Method when working through this quiz.

1. The first woman aviator <u>to cross</u> the English Channel, Harriet Quimby, <u>flown</u>
                   A   B
   <u>by monoplane</u> from Dover, England, to Hardelot, France, <u>in</u> 1912. <u>No error</u>
       C   D   E

2. The reproductive behavior of sea horses <u>is notable</u> <u>in respect of</u> the male, <u>who,</u>
                                       A   B   C
   <u>instead of</u> the female, carries the fertilized eggs. <u>No error</u>
      D   E

3. Early <u>experience</u> of racial discrimination <u>made</u> an <u>indelible</u> <u>impression for</u> the late
        A   B   C   D
   Supreme Court Justice Thurgood Marshall. <u>No error</u>
                                  E

4. More journalists <u>as</u> you would suspect are <u>secretly</u> writing plays or novels, <u>which</u> they
                 A   B   C
   hope someday <u>to have published</u>. <u>No error</u>
               D   E

5. <u>As long ago as</u> the twelfth century, French alchemists <u>have</u> perfected techniques
      A   B
   <u>for refining</u> precious metals <u>from</u> other ores. <u>No error</u>
      C   D   E

6. Galileo begged Rome's indulgence for his <u>support of</u> a Copernican system <u>in which</u> the
                                          A   B
   Earth circled the sun <u>instead of</u> <u>occupied</u> a central position in the universe. <u>No error</u>
                         C   D   E

7. Arthur Rubinstein was long ranked <u>among</u> the world's finest pianists, <u>although</u> he was
                                  A   B
    sometimes known <u>as playing</u> several wrong notes <u>in a single</u> performance. <u>No error</u>
                       C   D   E

8. The new office complex is beautiful, but <u>nearly</u> two hundred longtime residents
                                               A
    <u>were forced</u> to move when <u>they</u> <u>tore down</u> the old apartment buildings. <u>No error</u>
      B   C   D   E

9. Neither the singers <u>on stage</u> <u>or</u> the announcer in the wings <u>could be heard</u> <u>over</u> the
                          A   B   C   D
    noise of the crowd. <u>No error</u>
                           E

10. <u>Many of</u> the organic farms in the country <u>are</u> based on rotating crops <u>so that</u> there is
      A   B   C
    <u>hardly</u> no soil erosion. <u>No error</u>
      D   E

11. None of this injury <u>to life</u> and damage to property <u>wouldn't have</u> happened if the
                          A   B
    amateur pilot <u>had only</u> heeded the weather forecasts and <u>stayed</u> on the ground.
                       C   D
    <u>No error</u>
      E

12. The doctor recommended that young athletes <u>with a history</u> of severe asthma <u>take</u>
                                           A   B
    <u>particular</u> care <u>not to exercise</u> alone. <u>No error</u>
      C   D   E

13. <u>Amelia Earhart was born in Kansas the first person to fly from Hawaii to California.</u>

    (A) Amelia Earhart was born in Kansas the first person to fly from Hawaii to California.
    (B) Amelia Earhart being the first person to fly from Hawaii to California and was born in Kansas.
    (C) Being the first person to fly from Hawaii to California, Amelia Earhart was born in Kansas.
    (D) Amelia Earhart was the first person to fly from Hawaii to California and was born in Kansas.
    (E) Amelia Earhart, who was born in Kansas, was the first person to fly from Hawaii to California.

14. Beethoven bridged two musical eras, in that <u>his earlier works are essentially Classical; his later ones, Romantic.</u>

    (A) his earlier works are essentially Classical; his later ones, Romantic
    (B) his earlier works are essentially Classical, nevertheless, his later ones are Romantic
    (C) his earlier works being essentially Classical; his later are Romantic
    (D) whereas essentially, his earlier works are Classical, his later ones would be Romantic
    (E) despite his earlier works' being essentially Classical; his later are more Romantic

Practice Questions Answers and Explanations

1. B

The use of the word *flown* isn't right. *Flown,* the past participle form of *fly,* can't be used as a main verb without a form of the verb *have.* What's needed here is the simple past form of *fly,* which is *flew.*

2. B

In respect of doesn't sound quite right. Something like *with respect to* would be better.

3. D

Does something make an *impression for* someone? No, it makes an *impression on* someone.

4. A

The correct comparative form is *more...than,* not *more...as.*

5. B

This sentence describes events prior to a time in the past, so instead of the present perfect *have perfected,* it should use the past perfect *had perfected.*

6. D

Instead of takes a participle: *occupied* should be corrected to *occupying.*

7. C

The correct answer is *to play.*

8. C

Who tore down the old buildings? Surely not the *longtime residents.* The antecedent—some group such as "landlords" or "developers"—is missing.

9. B

Neither calls for *nor.*

10. D

The phrase *hardly no* creates a double negative. If *hardly* is removed, the sentence will be correct.

11. B

To see the double negative more easily, remove the intervening words: *None of this … wouldn't have happened.* The correct phrase should say *would have.*

12. A

In this sentence, the plural noun *athletes* is modified by the prepositional phrase *with a history of severe asthma.* But the athletes don't have a collective medical history; each athlete has his or her own. The sentence should read either *young athletes with histories of severe asthma* or *a young athlete with a history of severe asthma.* Because the prepositional phrase is underlined, it must be changed.

13. E

The original sentence is a run-on. Choice (E) provides the best fix by introducing a subordinate clause.

14. A

The original sentence is best. (B) is a comma splice. (C) removes the parallelism and the verb of the *that* clause. (D) is wordy and misuses the conditional. (E) turns *works* into a possessive adjective modifying the gerund *being,* so it can't serve as an antecedent for *later.* (E) is also punctuated incorrectly.

PRAXIS ESSAY

Introducing the PRAXIS Essay

Essay writing evokes an immediate reaction from nearly everyone, and prospective teachers are no exception. Generally speaking, you either love to write or you see it as a chore. Either way, the PRAXIS PPST will require you to do a bit of it.

Also, keep in mind, even the best writers can have problems with the unique nature of the PRAXIS exam. You must respond directly to the topic, and you have to generate your essay in a short period of time. Overly ambitious or flamboyant essayists can run short on time or run too far afield from the topic at hand.

Rather than indulging in unnecessarily creative writing, the kind of writing you're required to do is a highly specialized type of writing known as essay writing. Creativity and improvisation are not the goals of an essay. Instead, an essay is defined as a short literary composition on a single subject, usually presenting the personal view of the author. That definition can take you a long way towards effective essay writing on the PRAXIS exam.

First, the PRAXIS essay is meant to be short. You only have 30 minutes to read and digest the essay prompt, put together the essay, and proof it for errors and clarity. That's not a lot of time. A brief, clear essay is what the test maker is looking for.

Second, the PRAXIS essay is meant to be on a *single subject.* Although tangents, allusions, and digressions make for good fiction, they'll send you into dangerous territory on the PRAXIS exam. Be sure whatever you include on your essay pertains to the subject at hand. Keep your essay on point. If a sentence or idea does not relate directly to the topic of the essay, it should be omitted.

Finally, the PRAXIS essay is an opportunity for you *to express your views on a topic*. What this means is that you will need to express and support an opinion or argument. Remember, you will have to do more than simply express your views on this exam; you will be expected to provide illustrations, examples, and generalizations that support your view.

Keeping all three of the points above in mind as you put your essay together will put you well on your way to success on the PRAXIS PPST. Of course, the key to effective preparation is knowing what you're up against.

Know What to Expect

As we already mentioned, the essay section of the PPST in Writing tests your ability to put together a clear, coherent essay in a limited period of time. The essay topic will require you to draw from personal experiences and observations to support a stance on a given issue. The topics are selected such that any educated person should be able to draw from their experience to answer the question, and no specialized knowledge is required.

The essay section makes up one-half of the Writing test. You have only 30 minutes to write your essay, so effective time management is key. Be sure to complete your essay in the time allotted. Even a well-crafted essay that abruptly ends without a conclusion will lose valuable points.

Speaking of points, the essay section is scored differently from the other sections of the PRAXIS exam. Instead of receiving a score based on the number of questions you answered correctly, your essay is scored "holistically" on a scale of 0 to 6. A score of 6 indicates "a high degree of competence in response to the assignment." A score of 4 or 5 also demonstrates competence, but to a lesser degree. A score of 3 or lower may show some competence but also demonstrates organizational flaws, poor mechanics, or other significant errors.

HOW TO APPROACH THE PRAXIS ESSAY

As we already mentioned, you're working against the clock as you write your essay. Even though you have only 30 minutes to complete your essay, you should take time to organize your thoughts before writing about a topic, and take time to proof your essay after writing it.

Writing for the PRAXIS exam is a two-stage process. First, you decide what you want to say about a topic. Second, you figure out how to say it. If your writing style isn't clear, your ideas won't come across no matter how brilliant they are. Good PRAXIS English is not only grammatical, but also clear and concise. By using some basic principles, you'll be able to express your ideas clearly and effectively on your essay.

Four Principles of Good Essay Writing

1. Your Control of Language Is Important

Writing that is grammatical, concise, direct, and persuasive displays the "superior control of language" that earns top scores. This involves using the same good grammar that is tested in the multiple-choice questions. It also involves good word choice or diction and sentence structure.

2. It's Better to Keep Things Simple

Perhaps the single most important thing to bear in mind when writing a PRAXIS essay is to keep everything simple. Because you are aiming to pass this test and get it out of your life, there is no reason to be overly wordy or complex as you write your essay. Simplicity is essential whether you are talking about word choice, sentence structure, or organization. Complicated sentences are more likely to contain errors. Complicated organization is more likely to wander off topic. Keep in mind that simple doesn't mean simplistic. A clear, straightforward approach can convey perceptive insights on a topic.

3. Minor Grammatical Flaws Won't Kill You

Small mistakes are bound to happen when working under the kind of pressures you face on this exam. So don't panic. Essay readers expect minor errors, even in the best essays. That doesn't mean you should include an error or two to keep them happy. It means you should be aware of the kinds of errors you tend to make. If you have trouble with parallelism, double-check how you listed groups of things. Knowing your strengths and weaknesses should help you proof your essay before completion.

4. Keep Sight of Your Goal

Remember, your goal isn't to become a prize-winning stylist. Write a solid essay and move on. Write well enough to address the topic and demonstrate that you can write. Remember, essay graders aren't looking for rhetorical flourishes, they're looking for effective expression. Express your ideas clearly and simply, and you'll be well on your way to success.

THE KAPLAN FIVE-STEP METHOD FOR THE PRAXIS ESSAY

Step 1. Digest the Issue

Step 2. Select the points you will make

Step 3. Organize

Step 4. Write type

Step 5. Proofread

By now you should know what you're up against on the essay portion of the PRAXIS PPST in Writing. You need to demonstrate that you can think quickly and organize an essay under time pressure. The essay you write is supposed to be logical in organization and clear and concise in its use of written English. To toss in a couple cliches (something you should avoid doing on the PRAXIS exam), PRAXIS essay writing is not about bells and whistles; it's about bread and butter. Nothing fancy—just answer the question in clear language.

The real challenge is to write an effective essay in a short period of time. With that goal in mind, we've developed a proven five-step method that will help you make the most of your time.

Step 1 Digest the Issue

- Read the prompt and get a sense of the scope of the issue
- Note any ambiguous terms that need defining
- Crystallize the issue

Step 2 Select the Points You Will Make

- Think of arguments for both sides of the issue, and make a decision as to which side you will support

Step 3 Organize

- Outline your essay
- Lead with your best arguments
- Think about how the essay will flow as a whole

Step 4 Write/Type

- Be direct
- Use paragraph breaks to make your essay easy to read
- Make transitions, and link related ideas
- Finish strongly

Step 5 Proofread

- Save enough time to allow for one final read through of the entire essay
- Have a sense of the errors you are likely to make, and seek to find and correct them

Now that we've quickly outlined the five steps to effective PRAXIS essay writing, it's time to see how these steps work in action.

Applying the Kaplan Five-Step Method to the Issue Essay

Let's use the Kaplan Five-Step method on one of the sample issue topics we saw before:

The drawbacks to the use of nuclear power mean that it is not a long-term solution to the problem of meeting ever-increasing energy needs.

Step 1 Digest the Issue

It's simple enough. The person who wrote this believes that nuclear power is not a suitable replacement for other forms of energy.

Step 2 Select the Points You Will Make

Your job, as stated in the directions, is to decide whether or not you agree and to explain your decision. Some would argue that the use of nuclear power is too dangerous, whereas others would say that we can't afford not to use it. So, which side do you take? Remember, this isn't about showing the admissions people what your deep-seated beliefs about the environment are—it's about showing that you can formulate an argument and write it down. Quickly think through the pros and cons of each side, and choose the side for which you have the most relevant things to say. For this topic, that process might go something like this:

Arguments for the use of nuclear power:

- Inexpensive compared to other forms of energy
- Fossil fuels will eventually be depleted
- Solar power still too problematic and expensive

Arguments against the use of nuclear power:

- Radioactive hyperproducts are deadly
- Safer alternatives like nuclear fusion may be viable in the future
- Solar power already in use

Again, it doesn't matter which side you take. Let's say that in this case you decide to argue against nuclear power. Remember, the question is asking you to argue *why* the cons of nuclear power outweigh the pros—the inadequacy of this power source is the end you're arguing toward, so don't list it as a supporting argument.

Step 3 Organize

You've already begun to think out your arguments—that's why you picked the side you did in the first place. Now is the time to write them all out, including ones that weaken the opposing side.

Nuclear power is not a viable alternative to other sources of energy because:

- Radioactive, spent fuel has leaked from storage sites (too dangerous)
- Reactor accidents can be catastrophic—Three Mile Island, Chernobyl (too dangerous)
- More research into solar power will bring down its cost (weakens opposing argument)
- Solar-powered homes and cars already exist (alternatives proven viable)
- No serious effort to research other alternatives like nuclear fusion (better alternatives lie undiscovered)
- Energy companies don't spend money on alternatives; no vested interest (better alternatives lie undiscovered)

Step 4 Write/Type

Remember, open up with a general statement and then assert your position. From there, get down your main points. Your essay for this assignment might look like the following:

Sample Essay 1

At first glance, nuclear energy may seem to be the power source for the future. It's relatively inexpensive, it doesn't produce smoke, and its fuel supply is virtually inexhaustible. However, a close examination of the issue reveals that nuclear energy is more problematic and dangerous than other forms of energy production.

A main reason that nuclear energy is undesirable is the problem of radioactive waste storage. Highly toxic fuel left over from nuclear fission remains toxic for thousands of years, and the spills and leaks from existing storage sites are hazardous and costly to clean up. Even more appalling is the prospect of accidents at the reactor itself: Incidents at the Three Mile Island and Chernobyl power plants have proven that the consequences of a nuclear meltdown can be catastrophic and have consequences that are felt worldwide.

Environmental and health problems aside, the bottom line for the production of energy is profit. Nuclear power is a business just like any other, and the large companies that produce this country's electricity and gas claim they can't make alternatives like solar power affordable. Yet—largely because of incentives from the federal government—there exist today homes that are heated by solar power, and cars that are fueled by the sun have already hit the streets. If the limited resources that have been devoted to energy alternatives have already produced working models, a more intensive effort is likely to make those alternatives less expensive and problematic.

Options like solar power, hydroelectric power, and nuclear fusion are far better in the long run in terms of cost and safety. The only money required for these alternatives is for the materials required to harvest them: Sunlight, water, and the power of the atom are free. They also don't produce any toxic byproducts for which long-term storage—a hidden cost of nuclear power—must be found. Also, with the temporary exception of nuclear fusion, these sources of energy are already being harnessed today.

Whereas there are arguments to be made for both sides, it is clear that the drawbacks to the use of nuclear power are too great. If other alternatives are explored more seriously than they have been in the past, safer and less expensive sources of power will undoubtedly prove to be better alternatives.

Step 5 Proofread

Take that last couple of minutes to catch any glaring errors.

HOLISTIC SCORING

The PPST writing tests are scored by hand, not by computer. Holistic scoring uses a single letter or a number—on the PPST it's a number from zero to six—to provide an overall evaluation of an essay as a whole. A holistic score emphasizes the interrelation of different thinking and writing qualities in an essay (such as content, organization, or syntax) and tries to denote the unified effect that all of these elements combine to produce.

6: "Outstanding" Essay

- Insightfully presents and convincingly supports an opinion on the issue or a critique of the argument
- Ideas are very clear, well organized, and logically connected
- Shows superior control of language: grammar, stylistic variety, and accepted conventions of writing; minor flaws may occur

5: "Strong" Essay

- Presents well-chosen examples, and strongly supports an opinion on the issue or a critique of the argument
- Ideas are generally clear and well organized; connections are logical
- Shows solid control of language: grammar, stylistic variety, and accepted conventions of writing; minor flaws may occur

4: "Adequate" Essay

- Presents and adequately supports an opinion on the issue or a critique of the argument
- Ideas are fairly clear and adequately organized, logical connections are satisfactory
- Shows satisfactory control of language: grammar, stylistic variety, and accepted conventions of writing; some flaws may occur

3: "Limited" Essay

- Succeeds only partially in presenting and supporting an opinion on the issue or a critique of the argument
- Ideas may be unclear and poorly organized
- Shows less than satisfactory control of language: contains significant mistakes in grammar, usage, and sentence structure

2: "Weak" Essay

- Shows little success in presenting and supporting an opinion on the issue or a critique of the argument
- Ideas lack clarity and organization
- Meaning is impeded by many serious mistakes in grammar, usage, and sentence structure

1: "Fundamentally Deficient" Essay

- Fails to present a coherent opinion and/or evidence on the issue or a critique of the argument
- Ideas are seriously unclear and disorganized
- Lacks meaning because of widespread severe mistakes in grammar, usage, and sentence structure

0: "Unscorable" Essay

- Completely ignores topic

You Be the Evaluator

You've now seen what the essay looks like, and you know more about the criteria used to evaluate essays. With this information in mind, review your own practice essays, and see how you think they measure up.

For this exercise, it's not critical that you assign the "right" grade. It's more important that you understand whether the essay is well written and how well it fulfills the required tasks.

Section Two

PRAXIS I: PPST PRACTICE TESTS AND EXPLANATIONS

Practice Test One
Answer Sheet

Remove (or photocopy) this answer sheet and use it to complete the practice test. (See answer key following the test when finished.)

If a section has fewer questions than answer spaces, leave the extra spaces blank.

Reading—60 minutes

1 Ⓐ Ⓑ Ⓒ Ⓓ Ⓔ	11 Ⓐ Ⓑ Ⓒ Ⓓ Ⓔ	21 Ⓐ Ⓑ Ⓒ Ⓓ Ⓔ	31 Ⓐ Ⓑ Ⓒ Ⓓ Ⓔ
2 Ⓐ Ⓑ Ⓒ Ⓓ Ⓔ	12 Ⓐ Ⓑ Ⓒ Ⓓ Ⓔ	22 Ⓐ Ⓑ Ⓒ Ⓓ Ⓔ	32 Ⓐ Ⓑ Ⓒ Ⓓ Ⓔ
3 Ⓐ Ⓑ Ⓒ Ⓓ Ⓔ	13 Ⓐ Ⓑ Ⓒ Ⓓ Ⓔ	23 Ⓐ Ⓑ Ⓒ Ⓓ Ⓔ	33 Ⓐ Ⓑ Ⓒ Ⓓ Ⓔ
4 Ⓐ Ⓑ Ⓒ Ⓓ Ⓔ	14 Ⓐ Ⓑ Ⓒ Ⓓ Ⓔ	24 Ⓐ Ⓑ Ⓒ Ⓓ Ⓔ	34 Ⓐ Ⓑ Ⓒ Ⓓ Ⓔ
5 Ⓐ Ⓑ Ⓒ Ⓓ Ⓔ	15 Ⓐ Ⓑ Ⓒ Ⓓ Ⓔ	25 Ⓐ Ⓑ Ⓒ Ⓓ Ⓔ	35 Ⓐ Ⓑ Ⓒ Ⓓ Ⓔ
6 Ⓐ Ⓑ Ⓒ Ⓓ Ⓔ	16 Ⓐ Ⓑ Ⓒ Ⓓ Ⓔ	26 Ⓐ Ⓑ Ⓒ Ⓓ Ⓔ	36 Ⓐ Ⓑ Ⓒ Ⓓ Ⓔ
7 Ⓐ Ⓑ Ⓒ Ⓓ Ⓔ	17 Ⓐ Ⓑ Ⓒ Ⓓ Ⓔ	27 Ⓐ Ⓑ Ⓒ Ⓓ Ⓔ	37 Ⓐ Ⓑ Ⓒ Ⓓ Ⓔ
8 Ⓐ Ⓑ Ⓒ Ⓓ Ⓔ	18 Ⓐ Ⓑ Ⓒ Ⓓ Ⓔ	28 Ⓐ Ⓑ Ⓒ Ⓓ Ⓔ	38 Ⓐ Ⓑ Ⓒ Ⓓ Ⓔ
9 Ⓐ Ⓑ Ⓒ Ⓓ Ⓔ	19 Ⓐ Ⓑ Ⓒ Ⓓ Ⓔ	29 Ⓐ Ⓑ Ⓒ Ⓓ Ⓔ	39 Ⓐ Ⓑ Ⓒ Ⓓ Ⓔ
10 Ⓐ Ⓑ Ⓒ Ⓓ Ⓔ	20 Ⓐ Ⓑ Ⓒ Ⓓ Ⓔ	30 Ⓐ Ⓑ Ⓒ Ⓓ Ⓔ	40 Ⓐ Ⓑ Ⓒ Ⓓ Ⓔ

Math—60 minutes

1 Ⓐ Ⓑ Ⓒ Ⓓ Ⓔ	11 Ⓐ Ⓑ Ⓒ Ⓓ Ⓔ	21 Ⓐ Ⓑ Ⓒ Ⓓ Ⓔ	31 Ⓐ Ⓑ Ⓒ Ⓓ Ⓔ
2 Ⓐ Ⓑ Ⓒ Ⓓ Ⓔ	12 Ⓐ Ⓑ Ⓒ Ⓓ Ⓔ	22 Ⓐ Ⓑ Ⓒ Ⓓ Ⓔ	32 Ⓐ Ⓑ Ⓒ Ⓓ Ⓔ
3 Ⓐ Ⓑ Ⓒ Ⓓ Ⓔ	13 Ⓐ Ⓑ Ⓒ Ⓓ Ⓔ	23 Ⓐ Ⓑ Ⓒ Ⓓ Ⓔ	33 Ⓐ Ⓑ Ⓒ Ⓓ Ⓔ
4 Ⓐ Ⓑ Ⓒ Ⓓ Ⓔ	14 Ⓐ Ⓑ Ⓒ Ⓓ Ⓔ	24 Ⓐ Ⓑ Ⓒ Ⓓ Ⓔ	34 Ⓐ Ⓑ Ⓒ Ⓓ Ⓔ
5 Ⓐ Ⓑ Ⓒ Ⓓ Ⓔ	15 Ⓐ Ⓑ Ⓒ Ⓓ Ⓔ	25 Ⓐ Ⓑ Ⓒ Ⓓ Ⓔ	35 Ⓐ Ⓑ Ⓒ Ⓓ Ⓔ
6 Ⓐ Ⓑ Ⓒ Ⓓ Ⓔ	16 Ⓐ Ⓑ Ⓒ Ⓓ Ⓔ	26 Ⓐ Ⓑ Ⓒ Ⓓ Ⓔ	36 Ⓐ Ⓑ Ⓒ Ⓓ Ⓔ
7 Ⓐ Ⓑ Ⓒ Ⓓ Ⓔ	17 Ⓐ Ⓑ Ⓒ Ⓓ Ⓔ	27 Ⓐ Ⓑ Ⓒ Ⓓ Ⓔ	37 Ⓐ Ⓑ Ⓒ Ⓓ Ⓔ
8 Ⓐ Ⓑ Ⓒ Ⓓ Ⓔ	18 Ⓐ Ⓑ Ⓒ Ⓓ Ⓔ	28 Ⓐ Ⓑ Ⓒ Ⓓ Ⓔ	38 Ⓐ Ⓑ Ⓒ Ⓓ Ⓔ
9 Ⓐ Ⓑ Ⓒ Ⓓ Ⓔ	19 Ⓐ Ⓑ Ⓒ Ⓓ Ⓔ	29 Ⓐ Ⓑ Ⓒ Ⓓ Ⓔ	39 Ⓐ Ⓑ Ⓒ Ⓓ Ⓔ
10 Ⓐ Ⓑ Ⓒ Ⓓ Ⓔ	20 Ⓐ Ⓑ Ⓒ Ⓓ Ⓔ	30 Ⓐ Ⓑ Ⓒ Ⓓ Ⓔ	40 Ⓐ Ⓑ Ⓒ Ⓓ Ⓔ

Writing—60 minutes

1 Ⓐ Ⓑ Ⓒ Ⓓ Ⓔ	11 Ⓐ Ⓑ Ⓒ Ⓓ Ⓔ	21 Ⓐ Ⓑ Ⓒ Ⓓ Ⓔ	31 Ⓐ Ⓑ Ⓒ Ⓓ Ⓔ
2 Ⓐ Ⓑ Ⓒ Ⓓ Ⓔ	12 Ⓐ Ⓑ Ⓒ Ⓓ Ⓔ	22 Ⓐ Ⓑ Ⓒ Ⓓ Ⓔ	32 Ⓐ Ⓑ Ⓒ Ⓓ Ⓔ
3 Ⓐ Ⓑ Ⓒ Ⓓ Ⓔ	13 Ⓐ Ⓑ Ⓒ Ⓓ Ⓔ	23 Ⓐ Ⓑ Ⓒ Ⓓ Ⓔ	33 Ⓐ Ⓑ Ⓒ Ⓓ Ⓔ
4 Ⓐ Ⓑ Ⓒ Ⓓ Ⓔ	14 Ⓐ Ⓑ Ⓒ Ⓓ Ⓔ	24 Ⓐ Ⓑ Ⓒ Ⓓ Ⓔ	34 Ⓐ Ⓑ Ⓒ Ⓓ Ⓔ
5 Ⓐ Ⓑ Ⓒ Ⓓ Ⓔ	15 Ⓐ Ⓑ Ⓒ Ⓓ Ⓔ	25 Ⓐ Ⓑ Ⓒ Ⓓ Ⓔ	35 Ⓐ Ⓑ Ⓒ Ⓓ Ⓔ
6 Ⓐ Ⓑ Ⓒ Ⓓ Ⓔ	16 Ⓐ Ⓑ Ⓒ Ⓓ Ⓔ	26 Ⓐ Ⓑ Ⓒ Ⓓ Ⓔ	36 Ⓐ Ⓑ Ⓒ Ⓓ Ⓔ
7 Ⓐ Ⓑ Ⓒ Ⓓ Ⓔ	17 Ⓐ Ⓑ Ⓒ Ⓓ Ⓔ	27 Ⓐ Ⓑ Ⓒ Ⓓ Ⓔ	37 Ⓐ Ⓑ Ⓒ Ⓓ Ⓔ
8 Ⓐ Ⓑ Ⓒ Ⓓ Ⓔ	18 Ⓐ Ⓑ Ⓒ Ⓓ Ⓔ	28 Ⓐ Ⓑ Ⓒ Ⓓ Ⓔ	38 Ⓐ Ⓑ Ⓒ Ⓓ Ⓔ
9 Ⓐ Ⓑ Ⓒ Ⓓ Ⓔ	19 Ⓐ Ⓑ Ⓒ Ⓓ Ⓔ	29 Ⓐ Ⓑ Ⓒ Ⓓ Ⓔ	
10 Ⓐ Ⓑ Ⓒ Ⓓ Ⓔ	20 Ⓐ Ⓑ Ⓒ Ⓓ Ⓔ	30 Ⓐ Ⓑ Ⓒ Ⓓ Ⓔ	

Practice Test One
Pre-Professional Skills Test (PPST)

This timed practice serves as a diagnostic tool. It provides an opportunity for you to apply, in a test-like setting, what you already know, and identify areas of weakness.

Reading

Time—60 Minutes
40 Questions

Directions: Each statement or passage in this test is followed by a question or questions based on its content. After reading a statement or passage, choose the best answer to each question from among the five choices given. Answer all questions following a statement or passage on the basis of what is stated or implied in that statement or passage; you are not expected to have any previous knowledge of the topics treated in the statements and passages.

Be sure to mark all your answers on your answer sheet, and fill in completely the lettered space with a heavy, dark mark so that you cannot see the letter.

Remember, try to answer every question.

Questions 1–2

In modern society, a new form of folk tale has emerged: the urban legend. These stories persist both for their entertainment value and for the transmission of popular values and beliefs. Urban legends are stories we all have heard; they are supposed to have happened but cannot be verified. The people involved can never be found. Researchers of urban legends call the elusive participant in these supposedly "real-life" events a FOAF (friend of a friend).

One classic urban legend involves alligators in the sewer systems of major metropolitan areas. According to the story, before alligators were a protected species, people vacationing in Florida purchased baby alligators to take home as souvenirs. After the novelty of having a pet alligator wore off, people would flush their souvenirs down the toilet. The baby alligators found a perfect growing environment in city sewer systems, where to this day they thrive on an ample supply of rats.

1. The passage suggests that real-life participants of urban legends

   (A) can be difficult to track down
   (B) are usually barely known by the teller
   (C) seem believable but, in fact, do not exist
   (D) are the original tellers of the stories
   (E) would often travel to Florida

2. According to the passage, the successful urban legend contains all of the following characteristics EXCEPT

   (A) the capacity to entertain
   (B) messages that conform to popular values
   (C) a degree of plausibility
   (D) a basis in reality
   (E) qualities of a folk tale

3. Halley's Comet has been around since at least 240 B.C. and possibly since 1059 B.C. Its most famous appearance was in A.D. 1066 when it appeared right before the Battle of Hastings. It was named after the astronomer Edmund Halley, who calculated its orbit. He determined that the comets seen in 1530 and 1606 were the same object following a 76-year orbit. Unfortunately, Halley died in 1742, never living to see his prediction come true when the comet returned on Christmas Eve 1758.

   It can be inferred from the passage that the last sighting of the Halley's Comet recorded before the death of Edmund Halley took place in

   (A) 1066
   (B) 1530
   (C) 1606
   (D) 1682
   (E) 1758

4. Both alligators and crocodiles can be found in southern Florida, particularly in the Everglades National Park. Alligators and crocodiles do look similar, but there are several physical characteristics that differentiate the two giant reptiles. The most easily observed difference between alligators and crocodiles is the shape of the head. The crocodile's skull and jaws are longer and narrower than the alligator's. When an alligator closes its mouth, those long teeth slip into sockets in the upper jaw and disappear. When a crocodile closes its mouth, the long teeth remain visible, protruding outside the upper jaw. In general, if you can still see a lot of teeth when the animal's mouth is closed, you are looking at a crocodile.

   One can distinguish a crocodile from an alligator

   (A) only when the animal's mouth is closed
   (B) by the location in Florida where the animal is found
   (C) by its thick, heavily armored skin
   (D) by its size when full grown
   (E) by the narrower snout found on a crocodile

GO ON TO THE NEXT PAGE

Questions 5–7

The following passage is excerpted from a historian's account of the development of European classical music.

During the first half of the 19th century, the political and social currents in Europe in the aftermath of the French Revolution
Line brought with them significant developments
(5) in the world of music. The elevated status of the middle-class increased the participation of women in the musical field, which had traditionally been associated with men. Bourgeois families encouraged their
(10) daughters to take advantage of the new-found leisure time by studying voice or piano because this would improve their marriage possibilities and thus be an asset in the family's climb to social acceptance.

(15) Society was only beginning to enlarge its concept of appropriate musical education and activities for women, however. Female musical professionals were still very uncommon. The advice and support of a
(20) man was still a necessity in the musical career of a woman no matter how talented she was.

Many prominent 18th century writers believed that women did not possess the
(25) intellectual and emotional capacity to learn or to create as artists. Furthermore, it was held to be unnecessary and even dangerous for women to acquire extensive musical knowledge, because such knowledge could
(30) only detract from the business of being a wife and mother.

Even the great Clara Schumann, who was exceptional in that she was encouraged both by her husband and by the musical public to
(35) compose, entertained doubts about her creative ability. In 1839 she wrote, "I once believed that I possessed creative talent, but I have given up this idea; a woman must not desire to compose." Schumann was, in fact, a
(40) trailblazer—one of the very first female composers to construct a large-scale orchestral work.

5. The first paragraph of the passage suggests that for the majority of bourgeois women, their increased participation in music in the 19th century was

(A) consistent with their traditional roles in the family

(B) burdensome because they were now obliged to become involved

(C) groundbreaking in that women had never become professional musicians before

(D) discouraged by men because playing as an amateur was socially inappropriate

(E) justified, considering that women had shown talent equal to men in music

6. The statement that the "advice and support of a man was still a necessity" (lines 19–20) for a woman musician no matter how talented she was suggests primarily that women musicians

(A) were more emotionally fragile than their male counterparts

(B) accepted the fact that they had little experience in making decisions

(C) were as critical of themselves as the men in the family were of them

(D) generally conformed to accepted norms of behavior

(E) did not need ability so long as they were well connected

7. If Schumann was a trailblazing composer, why, according to the author, did she write in 1839 that she no longer thought she had creative talent?

   (A) She was compelled by her husband to do so in order to preserve the family's social status.

   (B) She was not receiving the praise that she once had.

   (C) She had not produced anything of significance by that time.

   (D) She had been influenced by society's view of women.

   (E) She felt she had exhausted her talent in the creation of *Piano Concerto in A Minor*.

8. When Joe attends orchestra rehearsal, he plays the first violin part. When Joe is not at rehearsal, Carl and Sonya compete for the first violin part.

   Based only on the information above, which of the following is a valid conclusion?

   (A) Joe is considered the best violinist in the orchestra.

   (B) Carl and Sonya are equally talented as musicians.

   (C) Joe is frequently unable to attend orchestra rehearsal.

   (D) If Carl misses a rehearsal, Sonya plays the first violin part.

   (E) If Joe and Carl both attend rehearsal, Joe plays the first violin part.

9. A talent agent analyzed her company's records in an attempt to determine why it was placing so few actors in roles. She attributed the company's poor performance to the fact that often the actors sent to an audition were completely inappropriate for the role.

   It can be inferred from the passage that the agent believes that

   (A) certain actors are inappropriate for certain roles

   (B) the actors her company represents are not very good

   (C) it is difficult to predict how appropriate an actor will be for a role

   (D) her company does not send enough actors to audition for major roles

   (E) directors often cast actors who are inappropriate for the role

GO ON TO THE NEXT PAGE

Questions 10–12

At the end of the 19th century, a new wave of immigration caused a massive population explosion in the United States.
Line Few immigrants of this period found life in
(5) America easy, however. Many of those who lacked professional skills and did not speak English found themselves living in slum conditions in the sprawling cities of the northeast, exploited by their employers, and
(10) trapped at the poverty level.

Two groups had ideas about how to go about assimilating these immigrants. A conservative group called the Daughters of the American Revolution approached
(15) immigrants with the expectation that newcomers should completely adopt American customs and culture. Consequently, they supported laws that required immigrants to take oaths of loyalty
(20) and to pass English language tests.

Another conception of assimilation came from the experience of reformers such as Jane Addams. In 1889, Addams founded a volunteer organization in Chicago called
(25) Hull House that attempted to improve conditions in the city's poor immigrant neighborhoods and provided local government services, including medical care, legal assistance, and adult education.
(30) Fundamental to the "settlement house" philosophy was a respect for the cultural heritage of the new arrivals.

10. Which of the following best tells what this passage is about?

(A) the story of immigration to the United States
(B) the cultural contributions offered by immigrants
(C) how to assimilate immigrants into American life
(D) how immigrants changed life in U.S. cities
(E) two different concepts of assimilating immigrants

11. The conservatives' methods of assimilation are most similar to those of someone who renovates a house

(A) to look more expensive than it really is
(B) to reveal the structural elements of the house
(C) to look like all of the other houses on the block
(D) to make it stand out from the rest of the houses on the block
(E) to preserve the original style of design

12. The services provided by the settlement houses were intended to

(A) supplement the services provided by local government
(B) discourage the use of foreign languages in schools
(C) enable immigrants to open similar settlement houses elsewhere
(D) instruct immigrants in the beliefs of the reformers
(E) teach immigrants to conform to rigid standards

13. The youngest employee of the financial consulting firm makes $25,000 per year. Matthew only makes $9,000 per year.

    Based only on the information above, which of the following must be true?

    (A) Matthew does not work for the financial consulting firm.
    (B) Matthew is not the youngest employee of the financial consulting firm.
    (C) The size of an employee's income is related to the employee's age.
    (D) Other employees in the financial consulting firm make more than $25,000 per year.
    (E) The youngest employee of the financial consulting firm makes less money per year than any other employee.

14. European nations are starting to decrease the percentage of their foreign aid that is "tied"—that is, given only on the condition that it be spent to obtain goods and materials produced by the country from which the aid originates. By doing so, European nations hope to avoid the ethical criticism that has been recently leveled at some foreign aid donors, notably Japan.

    Which of the following can most reasonably be inferred from the passage?

    (A) Many non-European nations give foreign aid solely for the purpose of benefiting their domestic economies.
    (B) Only ethical considerations, and not those of self-interest, should be considered when foreign aid decisions are made.
    (C) Many of the problems faced by underdeveloped countries could be eliminated if a smaller percentage of the foreign aid they obtained was "tied" to specific purchases and uses.
    (D) Much of Japan's foreign aid returns to Japan in the form of purchase orders for Japanese products and equipment.
    (E) Non-European nations are unwilling to offer foreign aid that is not "tied" to the purchase of their own manufactures.

GO ON TO THE NEXT PAGE

15. When a movie panned by most film critics is a popular success, this is often seen as a sign of poor taste of the part of general audiences. But film critics belong to a fairly homogeneous class, and their preferences are often rooted in the prejudices of that class. Their opinions are no more likely to be an unerring guide to quality than those of the average moviegoer.

The passage above best supports which of the following conclusions?

(A) Judgments of film quality by professional film critics are usually wrong.
(B) Judgments of quality applied to movies are meaningless.
(C) Film critics usually consider popular movies to be of poor quality.
(D) Professional critics generally agree on the quality of any given movie.
(E) When critics and general audiences disagree about a movie's quality, the critics' opinion is not necessarily more accurate.

Questions 16–17

The four brightest moons of Jupiter were the first objects in the solar system discovered through the use of the telescope.
Line Their proven existence played a central role
(5) in Galileo's famous argument in support of the Copernican model of the solar system, in which the planets are described as revolving around the Sun. For several hundred years after their discovery by
(10) Galileo in 1610, scientific understanding of these moons increased fairly slowly. It was the spectacular series of photographs sent back by the 1979 Voyager missions that forever changed our impressions of these
(15) bodies.

16. Which of the following best tells what this passage is about?

(A) Galileo's invention of the telescope
(B) the discovery of the Galilean moons
(C) scientific knowledge about the solar system
(D) the damage caused by asteroid bombardment
(E) Jupiter's four brightest moons

17. This passage suggests that Galileo was one of the first scientists to

(A) attack the Copernican theory of the solar system
(B) make accurate measurements of the diameters of Jupiter's moons
(C) engage in studies of stars
(D) compare the various densities of the four Galilean moons
(E) make important use of the telescope

GO ON TO THE NEXT PAGE

18. The tomato originated in the new world. It was first domesticated around A.D. 700 by the Aztec and Incan civilizations. In the 16th century, European explorers were so appreciative of the tomato that they introduced it to the rest of Europe. Although the French, Spanish, and Italians quickly began to adapt their recipes to the tomato, the English considered it poisonous. This myth continued into the American colonial period, and it wasn't until the mid-1800s that the tomato began to gain acceptance in the United States.

According to the passage, Americans did not start using the tomato until the mid-19th century because

(A) it was unavailable in the new world
(B) they lacked recipes for using it
(C) they believed it to be poisonous
(D) it was viewed as a Mediterranean food
(E) it tasted bitter, unlike the modern tomato

19. The presidential election in November 2000 showed once again how important it is for all Americans to take advantage of their right to vote. The election was so close that it took weeks to finalize the tally, and the controversy surrounding chads, voting machines, and the court system only served to reinforce the sentiment that each vote counts.

The main idea of the passage is that

(A) voting machines are not adequate
(B) the Supreme Court should decide the president
(C) voting is a right that can be taken away
(D) every voter should exercise his right and vote
(E) if fewer Americans had voted, there would have been less controversy

20. Four years ago, the governor came into office seeking to change the way politics were run in this state. Now, it seems he has been the victim of his own ambitious political philosophy. Trying to do too much has given him a reputation as being pushy, and the backlash in the state has let him accomplish little. He may very well lose in his reelection bid.

The governor's approach to politics was

(A) business as usual
(B) overly idealistic
(C) careless and sloppy
(D) undeterred by critics
(E) unduly cautious

GO ON TO THE NEXT PAGE

Questions 21–24

For thousands of years, smallpox was one of the world's most dreaded diseases. Ancient Chinese medical texts show that the
Line disease was known as long ago as 1122 B.C.
(5) Yet, as recently as 1967, more than 2 million people died of smallpox in one year.

The first method developed to combat smallpox was an attempt to immunize healthy patients. In a procedure called
(10) variolation, a healthy patient's skin was deliberately scratched with infectious material from a person with a mild case of smallpox. If the treatment was successful, the patient suffered a mild smallpox
(15) infection and then became immune to the disease. Unfortunately, the patient could still spread smallpox to others.

A safer method of conferring immunity was discovered in 1796 by an English doctor
(20) named Edward Jenner. Jenner was fascinated by the fact that people who caught cowpox, a harmless disease spread by cattle, became immune to smallpox. He tested this seeming connection on a young
(25) boy, and it was successful. Jenner wrote a paper describing his results, but the Royal Society of Physicians rejected it. Jenner published his findings independently, and his paper became a bestseller. Within a
(30) matter of years, the new procedure known as vaccination was in general use throughout Europe and the United States, and the fight against smallpox was underway. However, it was not until 1966
(35) that the World Health Organization was able to find the resources to launch a worldwide campaign to wipe out the disease altogether.

21. Which of the following best tells what this passage is about?

(A) how to treat viral diseases
(B) the dangers of variolation
(C) how Edward Jenner discovered vaccination
(D) the history of the fight against smallpox
(E) early efforts at controlling infectious diseases

22. As discussed in this passage, one disadvantage of variolation was that

(A) the inoculated patient could still spread smallpox
(B) variolation did not give immunity to cowpox
(C) immunity wore off after a time
(D) variolation was hard to perform
(E) many doctors refused to use the procedure

23. The passage implies that Jenner began to experiment with vaccination because he

(A) was suffering from a mild case of smallpox himself
(B) had noticed a relationship between two diseases
(C) wanted to be accepted into the Royal Society of Physicians
(D) had attempted variolation without success
(E) preferred unconventional approaches to scientific problems

GO ON TO THE NEXT PAGE

24. When did vaccination against smallpox become widespread?

    (A) as soon as Jenner wrote a report of his findings

    (B) several years after Jenner's discovery

    (C) only in countries where variolation was not practiced

    (D) early in the 20th century

    (E) when adopted by the World Health Organization in 1966

25. The question of whether a child's personality is the result of genetic material inherited from the parents or the nurturing and environment provided by the parents is a perennial subject of debate. Whereas no one would deny that environment and upbringing play a limited role, the genetic traits that a child inherits provide some sort of basic blueprint for who and what that child becomes. After all, if one plants tomatoes, _____ .

    Which of the following best completes this passage?

    (A) one must tend them carefully in order to gather good vegetables

    (B) one had better choose the variety and location with equal care

    (C) one will eventually get tomatoes but not necessarily good tomatoes

    (D) one must expect tomatoes to grow, not cucumbers or daffodils

    (E) one must be sure to tend them well, regardless of the quality of the seeds used

GO ON TO THE NEXT PAGE

Questions 26–27

The diamond is the hardest known material and has long been used in various industrial-shaping processes, such as cutting, grinding, and polishing. The diamond, sapphire, ruby (sapphire with chromium "impurities"), and garnet are increasingly important in various applications. For example, diamonds are used in sensors, diaphragms for audio speakers, and coatings for optical materials. The sapphire is used in gallium nitride-based LEDs, the ruby is used as wear parts in check valves, and synthetic garnet is used in lasers intended for applications in medical products.

26. An appropriate title for this passage would be

    (A) The Timeless Allure of Precious Stones
    (B) Nontraditional Uses of Diamonds
    (C) Industrial Uses for Precious Stones
    (D) Gem Hardness and Utility
    (E) The Use of Precious Gems in Cutting, Grinding, and Polishing Applications

27. It can be inferred from this passage that

    (A) diamonds are more precious than sapphires
    (B) rubies come from the same type of stone as sapphires
    (C) garnets are used in various industrial shaping processes
    (D) precious stones are more costly than ever
    (E) garnets and rubies are interchangeable in industrial applications

28. Our environment can stand only so much more "progress." We must take a few steps backward and accept some inconvenience if we want to secure the health and well-being of our planet. This is not merely a matter of using manual mowers instead of power mowers or foregoing a few outdoor barbecues. Something must be done about the 51.1 percent of total ozone that is contributed by vehicles and fuel. The percentage must be cut regardless of the cost or inconvenience. Such concerns are irrelevant here; what needs to be done must be done.

The author of the passage above makes which of the following arguments?

    (A) People will have to go back to living as they did a century ago if they want to save the environment.
    (B) If people would be willing to drive their cars less, pollution would be drastically reduced.
    (C) People can continue to use power lawn mowers and have barbecues as long as industry cuts down on its use of fuel.
    (D) People must accept drastic and costly measures because they are necessary to save the environment.
    (E) Lack of concern for the environment leads people to continue their overuse of the automobile.

GO ON TO THE NEXT PAGE

29. Although it is less well known than chess, "go" is an extremely popular game among mathematicians and game theorists. Unlike chess, go has only one type of playing piece. These pieces, or stones, are placed on a 19 by 19 grid. Each piece must be placed on one of the unoccupied vertices on the grid. The object of the game is to occupy space and surround your opponent's pieces according to prescribed rules. Despite the somewhat straightforward nature of the game, it has proven to be extremely difficult to map out or model with artificial intelligence or computers. It turns out to be a surprisingly tricky game to understand.

The author would be most likely to agree with which of the following?

(A) Chess is more complex than go.

(B) Game theorists prefer go to any other game.

(C) Computers will soon learn to play go better than the greatest go masters.

(D) In order to play go, each player must have 19 stones.

(E) Despite its simple appearance, go is surprisingly complex.

Questions 30–34

Many people dream about living on a coral island, but probably few of us would be able to describe one with any accuracy.
Line Popular books and films create a romantic
(5) image of these islands, and it is not always entirely justified if seen from sea level. However, beneath the waves, the coral island is a fantastic and very beautiful world, depending entirely on a complex web
(10) of interrelationships between plants and animals.

The main architect of the reef is the stony coral, a relative of the sea anemone that lives in tropical climates and secretes a skeleton of
(15) almost pure calcium carbonate. Its partner is the green alga, a tiny unicellular plant, which lives within the tissues of the coral. The two organisms coexist in a mutually beneficial relationship, with the algae consuming
(20) carbon dioxide given off by the corals, and the corals thriving in the abundant oxygen produced photosynthetically by the algae.

Many aspects of coral reefs still puzzle scientists, however. One mystery concerns
(25) the transformation of coral reefs into islands. It's suggested that many of today's reef islands resulted from a rise in sea level at the end of the last Ice Age. Scientists also believe that certain reef islands resulted
(30) from volcanic activity. Reefs that originally surrounded volcanic islands were transformed into atolls, or ring-shaped reef islands, as the volcanoes within gradually eroded and disappeared.

GO ON TO THE NEXT PAGE

30. The skeleton of the stony coral is mostly made up of what?

    (A) cartilage
    (B) stone
    (C) calcium carbonate
    (D) carbon dioxide
    (E) sediment

31. The relationship between the coral and the algae is best described as

    (A) unfriendly
    (B) competitive
    (C) predatory
    (D) cooperative
    (E) mysterious

32. What is the "puzzling" feature of coral reefs discussed in this passage?

    (A) their evolution into islands
    (B) their ability to support diverse communities of life
    (C) the ease with which they withstood the destructive effects of the last Ice Age
    (D) their evolution from isolated reefs into great land masses
    (E) the frequent appearance of new volcanoes in their vicinity

33. Which of the following is mentioned as resulting from volcanic activity?

    (A) barrier reefs
    (B) fringing reefs
    (C) land masses such as Australia
    (D) ring-shaped reef islands
    (E) barrier islands

34. What does the passage suggest about the image of coral islands in popular culture?

    (A) It is widely held but totally inaccurate.
    (B) It is justified except in the case of fringing reefs.
    (C) It is the product of divers with rich imaginations.
    (D) It is a perception most scientists would like to correct.
    (E) It is more accurate from an underwater perspective.

35. Proxemics is defined as the study of spatial distances between individuals in different cultures and situations. Edward Hall, founder of this field of study, coined the term. Hall studied how different cultures use space and spatial boundaries. His findings have influenced how diplomats are trained to engage members of different cultures.

Which of the following can be inferred from the passage?

(A) Edward Hall was an important diplomat

(B) Most cultures have the same norms for space and spatial boundaries

(C) The use of space and spatial boundaries is important to diplomats

(D) Proxemics is a field of study with few practical applications

(E) Diplomats are trained to engage all members of different cultures in the same way

36. Although some researchers have linked the modern game of basketball to Meso-American games that date back thousands of years, the current version of the game is generally credited to Dr. James Naismith who "invented" the game in Springfield, Massachusetts in 1891. In his initial version of the game, players would attempt to throw soccer balls into peach baskets perched at a standard height, hence the name "basketball."

The main idea of the passage is that

(A) Basketball was first played in Springfield, Massachusetts

(B) Naismith invented the current version of basketball in 1891

(C) Basketball is most popular in Meso-America

(D) Basketball got its name from peach baskets

(E) Basketball is a combination of soccer and other Meso-American games

GO ON TO THE NEXT PAGE

37. The earliest references to playing cards in Europe date back to the late 14th century, but cards must have originated elsewhere. Because paper was invented in China, it is likely that playing cards originated there as well. Playing cards then made their way west through the Islamic Empire en route to Europe. Consequently, the modern fifty-two card English deck is but one of many variants. The modern Italian deck, for instance, has no queens.

An appropriate title for this passage would be

(A) Chinese Playing Cards: Where It All Started
(B) The History of Playing Cards
(C) The Islamic Influence on Playing Cards
(D) Strange Decks of the World
(E) Paper and Playing Cards: Two Chinese Innovations

Questions 38–39

Animals that use coloring to safeguard themselves from predators are said to have "protective coloration." Many animals
Line change their protective pigmentation with
(5) the seasons. The caribou sheds its brown coat in winter, replacing it with white fur. The stoat, a member of the weasel family, is known as the ermine in winter, when its brown fur changes to the white fur prized by
(10) royalty. The chameleon, even more versatile than these, changes color in just a few minutes to match whatever surface it happens to be lying on or clinging to.

38. The author uses the caribou and the stoat as examples of animals that

(A) change their color according to the time of year
(B) are protected by disruptive coloring
(C) possess valuable white fur
(D) have prominent markings to warn predators
(E) protect themselves by constantly changing their coloring

39. The feature of the chameleon discussed in this passage is its ability to

(A) camouflage itself despite frequent changes in location
(B) cling to surfaces that are hidden from attackers
(C) adapt easily to seasonal changes
(D) use disruptive coloring to confuse predators
(E) change the colors of surfaces it is resting on

40. Tungsten is a metal with numerous industrial uses. One of its main uses is as filament in electric lights. It was discovered in 1783 in Spain by Fausto and Juan José de Elhuyar. Its name comes from the Swedish *tung sten* or heavy stone. Surprisingly, tungsten's symbol on the periodic table is W. This symbol comes from the German word for tungsten, *wolfram*.

    According to the passage, tungsten's name comes from

    (A) the names of its discoverers
    (B) the German language
    (C) its industrial uses
    (D) the Swedish language
    (E) its symbol on the periodic table

STOP!

If you finish before time is up, you may go back and check your work.

Mathematics

Time—60 Minutes
40 Questions

<u>Directions:</u> Each of the questions below is followed by five answer choices. Select the choice that best answers the question and fill the corresponding oval on your answer sheet. Remember, try to answer every question. Note: Figures are drawn to scale unless otherwise indicated. All figures can be assumed to lie in a plane, and all lines can be assumed to be straight unless otherwise indicated.

1. Nine paper slips are placed in a bag to be drawn as a science assignment. Each slip is labeled with the name of a planet: Mercury, Venus, Earth, Mars, Jupiter, Saturn, Uranus, Neptune, and Pluto. What is the probability of drawing at random a slip labeled with the name of a planet that does NOT start with the letter 'M'?

   (A) $\frac{2}{9}$

   (B) $\frac{2}{3}$

   (C) $\frac{4}{9}$

   (D) $\frac{6}{7}$

   (E) $\frac{7}{9}$

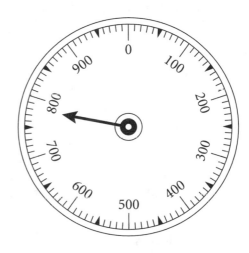

2. A picture of a scale is shown above. What is the current reading on the scale in pounds?

   (A) 820 pounds
   (B) 800 pounds
   (C) 780 pounds
   (D) 760 pounds
   (E) 740 pounds

3. Which of the following numbers is greatest?

   (A) 72.563
   (B) 73.526
   (C) 73.652
   (D) 72.536
   (E) 73.625

4. A measuring cup contains $1\frac{2}{3}$ cups of water. It needs to be filled to the $3\frac{3}{4}$ cup mark. How much water must be added?

   (A) A little less than 1 cup
   (B) A little more than 1 cup
   (C) A little less than 2 cups
   (D) A little more than 2 cups
   (E) A little less than 3 cups

5. The user's manual for a stereo set includes a scale diagram in which 2 scaled inches represent 8 actual inches. If the speakers of the stereo set measure 6 inches tall in the diagram, how tall are they in reality?

   (A) 1 foot 6 inches
   (B) 1 foot 8 inches
   (C) 1 foot 10 inches
   (D) 2 feet
   (E) 2 feet 2 inches

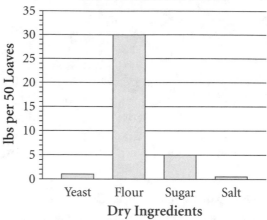

lbs of Dry Ingredients
Per 50 Loaves of Bread

6. In the bar graph above, the amounts of dry ingredients required by a bakery to produce 50 loaves of bread are shown. If 50 loaves contain 30 pounds of flour, how many pounds of sugar will the bakery need to produce 100 loaves of bread?

   (A) 30
   (B) 20
   (C) 15
   (D) 12
   (E) 10

7. One-fourth of the 1,600 sales representatives employed by a company work in its corporate headquarters. Of these, 62.5 percent met or exceeded their sales goals last year. Which computation shows the number of sales representatives working at the corporate office who failed to meet their sales goals last year?

   (A) 375 × 400
   (B) 37.5 × 400
   (C) 3.75 × 400
   (D) 0.375 × 400
   (E) 0.0375 × 400

GO ON TO THE NEXT PAGE

Average Monthly Temperature	
May 1996	65°F
Jun 1996	61°F
Jul 1996	57°F
Aug 1996	52°F
Sep 1996	54°F
Oct 1996	58°F
Nov 1996	65°F
Dec 1996	71°F
Jan 1997	73°F
Feb 1997	70°F
Mar 1997	68°F
Apr 1997	64°F

8. The chart above shows changes in temperature in a city between May 1996 and April 1997. Which of the following is true of the average temperature in this city between May 1996 and December 1996?

(A) The temperature increased continually.
(B) The temperature increased and then decreased.
(C) The temperature remained constant.
(D) The temperature decreased and then increased.
(E) The temperature decreased continually.

Peterson Family
Estimated Expenditures 2000

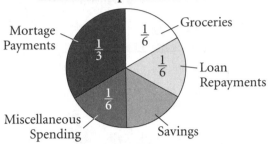

Annual Income = $42,000

9. The pie chart shown above represents the estimated expenditures of the Peterson family in 2000. If the Petersons' annual income in 2000 was $42,000, how much did they manage to save that year?

(A) $5,000
(B) $6,000
(C) $7,000
(D) $8,000
(E) $9,000

10. If the area of the rectangle above is 15, what is its perimeter?

(A)   5
(B)   8
(C) 15
(D) 16
(E) 21

11. If $26 - y = 2x + 14 + y$, what is the value of $x + y$?

(A) 1
(B) 2
(C) 3
(D) 6
(E) 8

GO ON TO THE NEXT PAGE

Questions 12–14 refer to the following graph.

Shampoo Sales in Blind Survey

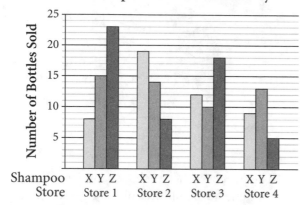

12. In how many of the stores surveyed were there at least twice as many bottles of Shampoo X sold as there were of Shampoo Z?

    (A) None
    (B) One
    (C) Two
    (D) Three
    (E) Four

13. What fraction of the total number of shampoo bottles sold at Store 3 were bottles of Shampoo Y?

    (A) $\frac{1}{4}$ (B) $\frac{1}{5}$ (C) $\frac{1}{6}$

    (D) $\frac{1}{8}$ (E) $\frac{1}{10}$

14. How many more bottles of Shampoo Z were sold at Store 2 than at Store 4?

    (A) 1
    (B) 2
    (C) 3
    (D) 4
    (E) 5

15. 525 is how many times 0.15?

    (A) 3.5
    (B) 35
    (C) 350
    (D) 3,500
    (E) 35,000

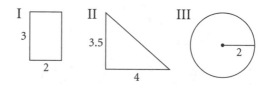

16. Which of the figures above has an area of 6?

    (A) I only
    (B) I and II
    (C) II and III
    (D) I and III
    (E) I, II, and III

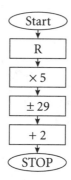

17. What is the result of the computation outlined in the chart above if $R = 5$?

    (A) −4
    (B) −2
    (C) 0
    (D) 2
    (E) 4

GO ON TO THE NEXT PAGE

18. Which of the following numbers, if any, are the same?

    I. 0.76×10^5
    II. $7,600 \times 10^{-4}$
    III. $\quad 7.6 \times 10^2$

    (A) None of them
    (B) I and II only
    (C) II and III only
    (D) I and III only
    (E) I, II, and III

19. Which of the following, when divided into 137, leaves a remainder of 5?

    (A) 12
    (B) 10
    (C) 9
    (D) 8
    (E) 4

20. Which of the following is greater than 1.25?

    (A) 125%
    (B) $\dfrac{3}{2}$
    (C) 0.125
    (D) 12.5%
    (E) $\dfrac{2}{3}$

21. A bus carries 15 sixth graders, 18 seventh graders, and 12 eighth graders. What fraction of the total number of students on the bus is seventh graders?

    (A) $\dfrac{1}{5}$
    (B) $\dfrac{2}{7}$
    (C) $\dfrac{2}{5}$
    (D) $\dfrac{3}{7}$
    (E) $\dfrac{3}{5}$

22. To find 36 times 4, you could multiply what number by 12?

    (A) 8
    (B) 10
    (C) 12
    (D) 14
    (E) 16

23. If T is 40% of 900, then $T =$

    (A) 300
    (B) 320
    (C) 360
    (D) 380
    (E) 400

24. What is the maximum number of points of intersection between a rectangle and a circle if both lie on a plane?

    (A) 1
    (B) 2
    (C) 4
    (D) 6
    (E) 8

GO ON TO THE NEXT PAGE

{15, 13, 6, 15, 8, 3, 24, 12, 5}

25. The median is the number that falls in the middle of an odd list of values arranged in increasing order or the average of the two middle numbers of an even list of values. What is the median of the above set?

(A)   6
(B)   8
(C) 12
(D) 13
(E) 15

Questions 26–27 refer to the following graph.

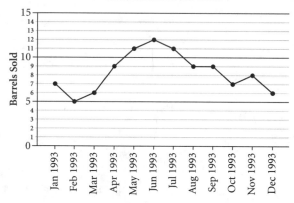

26. How many barrels of industrial solvent were sold in January 1993?

(A) 4
(B) 5
(C) 6
(D) 7
(E) 8

27. What number of barrels of industrial solvent was sold in June and July of 1993 combined?

(A) 16
(B) 19
(C) 23
(D) 25
(E) 28

28. What is the area of the isosceles right triangle shown above?

(A) 3
(B) 3.5
(C) 4
(D) 4.5
(E) 6

29. If $J + 2 = \dfrac{K}{4}$, then $J =$

(A) $K - 2$

(B) $2K - 2$

(C) $\dfrac{K}{2} - 4$

(D) $\dfrac{K}{4} - 2$

(E) $4K - 4$

30. Of the following expressions, which is NOT equivalent to the others?

(A) $4 \times 48 \times 8$
(B) $4 \times 8 \times 48$
(C) $4^2 \times 12 \times 8$
(D) $4^3 \times 12 \times 2$
(E) $4^3 \times 3 \times 2$

GO ON TO THE NEXT PAGE

31. Each of seven runners on a relay team must run a distance of 1.27 kilometers. What, most nearly, is the total combined number of kilometers run by the team in the race?

    (A) 10
    (B) 9
    (C) 8
    (D) 7
    (E) 6

32. A Ferris wheel has 12 cars that can seat up to 3 people each. If every car on the Ferris wheel is full except for 2 that contain 2 people and 1 that is empty, how many people are currently riding on the Ferris wheel?

    (A) 30
    (B) 31
    (C) 32
    (D) 36
    (E) 40

33. If $= J - (K \times H)$,

    then =

    (A) −12
    (B) −6
    (C) 0
    (D) 6
    (E) 12

34. The four shapes below are made up of identical equilateral triangles. Which of the five shapes, if any, has the *least* perimeter?

    (A) (B)

    (C) (D)

    (E) All have the same perimeter

35. Nine temperature readings are taken, one reading every four hours, with the first reading taken at 12:00 P.M. What will be the time at which the final reading is taken?

    (A) 12:00 A.M.
    (B) 8:00 A.M.
    (C) 12:00 P.M.
    (D) 4:00 P.M.
    (E) 8:00 P.M.

36. Which of the figures below, if any, has a perimeter value equal that is the same as the value of its area?

    (A) (B)

    (C) (D)

    (E) None has a perimeter equal to its area.

GO ON TO THE NEXT PAGE

37. If the length, *x*, of a rectangle is doubled and its width, *y*, is divided by 3, then the area of the new rectangle is given by the formula:

    (A) *xy*

    (B) 2*xy*

    (C) $\frac{2xy}{3}$

    (D) 3*xy*

    (E) 6*xy*

Apple pie is served only on every even-numbered day in February.

Ice cream is served only on every day in February that is numbered with a multiple of three.

---

38. If both statements above are true, then it is valid to conclude that both apple pie and ice cream are served on how many days in February?

    (A) 2

    (B) 3

    (C) 4

    (D) 5

    (E) 6

39. What is the average (arithmetic mean) of $\frac{3}{5}$ and $\frac{9}{2}$?

    (A) $\frac{45}{10}$

    (B) $\frac{51}{10}$

    (C) $\frac{45}{20}$

    (D) $\frac{51}{20}$

    (E) $\frac{45}{40}$

40. Which of the following represents 89,213 written in scientific notation?

    (A) 8921.3×10

    (B) 892.13×10^2

    (C) 89.213×10^3

    (D) 8.9213×10^4

    (E) 0.89213×10^5

STOP!

If you finish before time is up, you may go back and check your work.

Writing

Time—60 Minutes
38 Questions and Essay

<u>Directions:</u> For each of the following questions, choose the best answer from the given choices and darken the corresponding oval.

The following sentences contain problems in grammar, usage, diction (choice of words), and idiom. Some sentences are correct. None of the sentences contains more than one error. The error, if there is one in the sentence, is underlined and lettered. Parts of the sentence that are not underlined are correct and cannot be changed. In selecting answers, follow the requirements of standard written English. If there is an error, choose the <u>one underlined part</u> that must be changed to make the sentence correct and fill in the corresponding oval on your answer grid.

If there is no error, fill in oval E.

1. Before <u>the advent of</u> modern surgical techniques,
          A
   <u>bleeding patients</u> with leeches <u>were considered</u>
      B   C
   therapeutically <u>effective</u>. <u>No error</u>
              D   E

2. The <u>recent</u> establishment of "Crime Busters,"
       A
   officially sanctioned neighborhood block

   watching groups, <u>has</u> <u>dramatic</u> improved
              B   C
   relations <u>between</u> citizens and police. <u>No error</u>
         D   E

3. The masterpiece auctioned so <u>successfully</u> today
                     A
   depicts a Biblical scene in <u>which</u> the king is on
                     B
   his throne <u>with</u> his counselors <u>respectively</u>
          C   D
   standing below. <u>No error</u>
           E

4. <u>During</u> the election campaign, the major
     A
   political parties <u>have agreement</u> that minorities
                B
   must <u>be given</u> the opportunity <u>to advance</u> in
        C   D
   society. <u>No error</u>
          E

5. Most of the delegates <u>which</u> attended the
                 A
   convention <u>felt</u> the resolution was <u>too strongly</u>
           B   C
   worded, and the majority voted <u>against</u> it.
                        D
   <u>No error</u>
   E

6. <u>Lost in the forest</u> on a cold night,
      A

   <u>the hunters built</u> a fire <u>to keep themselves</u>
        B   C

   warm and <u>to frighten away</u> the wolves.
                D

   <u>No error</u>
     E

7. The effort to <u>create appropriate</u> theatrical
              A

   effects <u>often result</u> in settings that cannot be
          B

   <u>effective</u> without an imaginative <u>lighting</u> crew.
     C   D

   <u>No error</u>
     E

8. Every one of the shops in the town <u>were closed</u>
                         A

   on Thursday <u>because</u> of the <u>ten-inch</u> rainfall
            B   C

   that <u>had fallen</u> during the day. <u>No error</u>
       D   E

9. <u>According to</u> the directions on the package,
     A

   the contents <u>are</u> intended for external use
           B

   <u>only</u> and <u>should not hardly</u> be swallowed,
    C   D

   even in small quantities. <u>No error</u>
                   E

10. Mr. Webster's paper is <u>highly imaginary</u> and
                   A

    <u>very creative</u> <u>but</u> seems to be <u>lacking in</u>
       B   C   D

    cogency. <u>No error</u>
           E

11. The late president's <u>numerous</u> memoirs now
               A

    <u>about to be</u> published <u>promises</u> to be of
       B   C

    special <u>historical</u> interest. <u>No error</u>
          D   E

12. The point <u>on issue</u> was whether the dock
            A

    workers, <u>who</u> were <u>an extremely</u> vocal group,
         B   C

    <u>would decide to</u> return to work. <u>No error</u>
       D   E

13. <u>Raising</u> living costs, <u>together</u> with escalating
     A   B

    taxes, <u>have</u> proved to be a burden for
         C

    <u>everyone</u>. <u>No error</u>
      D   E

14. A number of <u>harried</u> department store
            A

    employees <u>were congregating</u> <u>around</u> the
           B   C

    water cooler <u>to compare and discuss</u> their
               D

    grievances. <u>No error</u>
           E

GO ON TO THE NEXT PAGE

15. The deep-sea diver <u>considered himself</u> not
    A
    only a <u>competent</u> barnacle scraper, but also
    B
    <u>capable for</u> collecting <u>interesting</u> specimens of
    C   D
    seashells. <u>No error</u>
                E

16. A round robin is a competition <u>in which</u> each
    A
    team <u>will have to</u> compete <u>against</u> every <u>other</u>
    B   C   D
    team. <u>No error</u>
            E

17. The voters were <u>dismayed</u> at <u>him retiring</u> from
    A   B
    <u>elected</u> office at such an early age, seemingly
    C
    <u>at the outset of</u> a brilliant career. <u>No error</u>
    D   E

18. <u>Having</u> a reasonable amount of intelligence and
    A
    steady persistence <u>assure</u> <u>one</u> of acquitting
    B   C
    oneself <u>creditably</u> in any undertaking. <u>No error</u>
    D   E

19. "Elementary, my dear Watson," <u>was</u> <u>frequent</u>
    A   B
    an observation <u>of</u> the <u>eminent</u> Sherlock
    C   D
    Holmes. <u>No error</u>
                E

GO ON TO THE NEXT PAGE

Directions: The following sentences test accuracy and effectiveness of expression. In selecting answers, follow the rules of standard written English; in other words, consider grammar, choice of words, sentence construction, and punctuation.

In each of the following sentences, a portion or all of the sentence is underlined. Under each sentence you will find five ways of phrasing the underlined portion. Choice A repeats the original underlined portion; the other four choices provide alternative phrasings.

Select the choice that best expresses the meaning of the original sentence. If the original sentence is better than any of the alternative phrasings, choose A; otherwise, select one of the alternatives. Your selection should construct the most effective sentence—clear and precise with no awkwardness or ambiguity.

20. In *War and Peace*, Tolstoy presented his theories on history and <u>illustrated them</u> with a slanted account of actual historical events.

    (A) illustrated them
    (B) also illustrating them
    (C) he also was illustrating these ideas
    (D) then illustrated the theories also
    (E) then he went about illustrating them

21. In the United States, an increasing number of commuters <u>that believe their families to be</u> immune from the perils of city life.

    (A) that believe their families to be
    (B) that believe their families are
    (C) believes their families are
    (D) who believe their families to be
    (E) believe their families to be

22. <u>Developed by a scientific team at his university</u>, the president informed the reporters that the new process would facilitate the diagnosis of certain congenital diseases.

    (A) Developed by a scientific team at his university
    (B) Having been developed by a scientific team at his university
    (C) Speaking of the discovery made by a scientific team at his university
    (D) Describing the development of a scientific team at his university
    (E) As it had been developed by a scientific team at his university

23. One ecological rule of thumb states that there is opportunity for the accumulation of underground water reservoirs <u>but in regions where vegetation remains undisturbed</u>.

    (A) but in regions where vegetation remains undisturbed
    (B) unless vegetation being left undisturbed in some regions
    (C) only where undisturbed vegetation is in regions
    (D) only in regions where vegetation remains undisturbed
    (E) except for vegetation remaining undisturbed in some regions

24. The Equal Rights Amendment to Islandia's constitution is dying a lingering political death, <u>many dedicated groups and individuals have attempted</u> to prevent its demise.

    (A) many dedicated groups and individuals have attempted
    (B) although many dedicated groups and individuals have attempted
    (C) many dedicated groups and persons has attempted
    (D) despite many dedications of groups and individuals to attempt
    (E) also, many dedicated groups and individuals have attempted

GO ON TO THE NEXT PAGE

25. The ancient Chinese were convinced that air was composed of two kinds of particles, <u>one inactive and one active, the latter of which they called yin and we today call oxygen</u>.

    (A) one inactive and one active, the latter of which they called yin and we today call oxygen
    (B) an inactive and an active one called yin, now known as oxygen
    (C) an inactive type and the active type they called yin we now know to be oxygen
    (D) inactive and active; while they called the active type yin, today we call it oxygen
    (E) contrasting the inactive type with the active ones they named yin and we call oxygen

26. Developing a suitable environment for house plants <u>is in many ways like when you are managing</u> soil fertilization for city parks.

    (A) is in many ways like when you are managing
    (B) is in many ways similar to when you are managing
    (C) in many ways is on a par with managing your
    (D) is in many ways similar to the managing of
    (E) is in many ways like managing

27. Most students would get better grades if <u>writing were to be studied by them</u>.

    (A) writing were to be studied by them
    (B) they studied writing
    (C) writing was studied by them
    (D) they would have studied writing
    (E) they were to have studied writing

28. <u>If they do not go into bankruptcy</u>, the company will probably survive its recent setbacks.

    (A) If they do not go into bankruptcy
    (B) Unless bankruptcy cannot be avoided
    (C) If they can avoid bankruptcy
    (D) If bankruptcy will be avoided
    (E) Unless it goes bankrupt

29. Now that I have read the works of both Henry and William James, I am convinced that Henry is <u>the best psychologist and William the best writer</u>.

    (A) the best psychologist and William the best writer
    (B) a better psychologist, William is the best writer
    (C) the best as a psychologist, William the best as a writer
    (D) the best psychologist, William the better writer
    (E) the better psychologist and William the better writer

30. When he arrived at the hospital, the doctor found that <u>several emergency cases had been admitted before</u> he went on duty.

    (A) several emergency cases had been admitted before
    (B) there were several emergency cases admitted prior to
    (C) two emergency cases were being admitted before
    (D) a couple of emergency cases were admitted before
    (E) several emergency cases was admitted before

GO ON TO THE NEXT PAGE

31. The variety of Scandinavian health care services offered to residents at reduced cost <u>far exceeds low-cost health programs</u> available in the United States.

    (A) far exceeds low-cost health programs
    (B) far exceeds the number of low-cost health programs
    (C) tends to be greater than low-cost programs
    (D) far exceed the number of low-cost health programs
    (E) are greater than comparable low-cost health programs

32. The politician is benefiting from behavioral <u>research, there are new techniques for them</u> to utilize and new broadcasting methods to experiment with.

    (A) research, there are new techniques for them
    (B) research; there are new techniques for them
    (C) research; he has new techniques
    (D) research, there are new techniques for him
    (E) research; they have new techniques

33. Laval, the first bishop of Quebec, exemplified aristocratic vigor and concern <u>on account of his giving up his substantial inheritance to become an ecclesiastic</u> and to help shape Canadian politics and education.

    (A) on account of his giving up his substantial inheritance to become an ecclesiastic
    (B) since he gave up his substantial inheritance to become an ecclesiastic
    (C) since giving up his substantial inheritance to become an ecclesiastic
    (D) because of his having given up his substantial inheritance for the purpose of becoming an ecclesiastic
    (E) as a result of becoming an ecclesiastic through giving up his substantial inheritance

34. James's ambition was <u>not only to study but also mastering</u> the craft of journalism.

    (A) not only to study but also mastering
    (B) not only studying but to try and master
    (C) not studying only, but also mastering
    (D) not only to study but also to master
    (E) to study and as well to master

35. The Islandian government, under pressure to satisfy the needs of consumers, <u>and loosening its</u> control of the economy.

    (A) and loosening its
    (B) by loosening its
    (C) is loosening their
    (D) but loosening their
    (E) is loosening its

GO ON TO THE NEXT PAGE

36. To the surprise of the school's staff, the new freshman class at Ridgewood High <u>being larger than last year's</u>.

    (A) being larger than last year's
    (B) is large, more so than last year
    (C) which is larger than the one last year
    (D) is larger than last year's
    (E) by far larger than the last

37. Night shift workers lead a strange life, working while the rest of us are sleeping, <u>then sleeping</u> while the rest of us are working.

    (A) then sleeping
    (B) after which they sleep
    (C) then they sleep
    (D) until they go to sleep
    (E) but soon they are sleeping

38. <u>The young couple eventually returned to the grassy spot where they had left their sandwiches, strolling hand in hand.</u>

    (A) The young couple eventually returned to the grassy spot where they had left their sandwiches, strolling hand in hand.
    (B) Eventually, the young couple returned to the grassy spot where they had left their sandwiches, strolling hand in hand.
    (C) Strolling hand in hand, the grassy spot where they had left their sandwiches was returned to by the young couple.
    (D) The young couple, returning to the grassy spot where they had left their sandwiches, while strolling hand in hand.
    (E) Strolling hand in hand, the young couple eventually returned to the grassy spot where they had left their sandwiches.

GO ON TO THE NEXT PAGE

SAMPLE DIRECTIONS FOR THE WRITTEN ASSIGNMENT

This section of the test consists of a written assignment. You are asked to prepare a written response of about 300–600 words on the assigned topic. *The assignment can be found on the next page.* You should use your time to plan, write, review, and edit what you have written for the assignment.

Read the assignment carefully before you begin to write. Think about how you will organize what you plan to write. You may use any blank space provided on the following pages to make notes, write an outline, or otherwise prepare your response. *However, your score will be based solely on the response you write in the space provided on pages 3, 4, 5, and 6 in the answer document.*

Your response to the written assignment will be evaluated based on your demonstrated ability to:

- Comprehend and focus on a unified, controlling topic
- Select and use a strategy of expression that is appropriate for the intended audience and purpose
- Present a reasoned, organized argument or exposition
- Use support and evidence to develop and bolster your ideas and account for the views of others
- Express yourself clearly and without distractions caused by inattention to sentence and paragraph structure, choice and use of words, and mechanics (i.e., spelling, punctuation, and capitalization)

Your response will be evaluated based on your demonstrated ability to express and support opinions, not on the nature or content of the opinions expressed. The final version of the response should conform to the conventions of edited American English. This should be your original work, written in your own words, and not copied or paraphrased from some other work.

Be sure to write about the assigned topic and use multiple paragraphs. Please write legibly. You may not use any reference materials during the test. Remember to review what you have written and make any changes you think will improve your response.

GO ON TO THE NEXT PAGE

Written Assignment

With more violent acts occurring in our schools, there is a call for more obvious security measures, such as metal detectors, security guards in the hallway, banning backpacks, and requiring students to wear uniforms.

Do you believe these or other security measures are a good idea or bad idea?

Write an essay to support your position.

STOP!

If you finish before time is up, you may go back and check your work.

Practice Test One (PPST) Answers and Explanations

READING

1. C	21. D
2. D	22. A
3. D	23. B
4. E	24. B
5. A	25. D
6. D	26. C
7. D	27. B
8. E	28. D
9. A	29. E
10. E	30. C
11. C	31. D
12. A	32. A
13. B	33. D
14. D	34. E
15. E	35. C
16. E	36. B
17. E	37. B
18. C	38. A
19. D	39. A
20. B	40. D

MATHEMATICS

1. E	21. C
2. C	22. C
3. C	23. C
4. D	24. E
5. D	25. C
6. E	26. D
7. D	27. C
8. D	28. D
9. C	29. D
10. D	30. E
11. D	31. B
12. B	32. B
13. A	33. E
14. C	34. B
15. D	35. E
16. A	36. C
17. B	37. C
18. A	38. C
19. A	39. D
20. B	40. D

WRITING

1. C	14. E	27. B
2. C	15. C	28. E
3. D	16. B	29. E
4. B	17. B	30. A
5. A	18. B	31. B
6. E	19. B	32. C
7. B	20. A	33. B
8. A	21. E	34. D
9. D	22. C	35. E
10. A	23. D	36. D
11. C	24. B	37. A
12. A	25. A	38. E
13. A	26. E	

READING EXPLANATIONS

Urban Legend Passage: Questions 1–2

1. C

This is an inference question, so the correct answer may be implied but not spelled out directly. The first paragraph talks about the sources of urban legends. It turns out that they can never be found. In other words, "the elusive participant in these supposedly 'real-life' events" does not actually exist, choice (C). Once you realize that urban legends are fictional, choices (A), (B), (D), and (E) cannot be correct.

2. D

This is an EXCEPT question, so you are looking for the one answer choice that does not characterize successful urban legends. Here again, if you were able to glean that urban legends are fictional, the correct answer choice (D) is clearly the correct answer. Otherwise, you could use the process of elimination on the wrong answer choices. The passage states that urban legends "persist both for their entertainment value and for the transmission of popular values and beliefs," so choices (A) and (B), which paraphrase this, are wrong. Urban legends must also, by inference, contain a degree of plausibility (C) because so many people believe them. Finally, the very first sentence describes urban legends as a new form of folk tale, so (E) is out.

3. D

This is a slightly tricky inference question because a lot of dates are mentioned in the passage. Nonetheless, the passage states that Halley determined that the comet followed a 76-year orbit. He never lived to see the comet that appeared in 1758, so it follows that the last time the comet appeared before his death took place 76 years earlier, or $1758 - 76 = 1682$, choice (D).

4. E

The passage discusses a few ways to distinguish a crocodile from an alligator. The first and most easily observed of these is the fact that the crocodile's head and jaws, and therefore snout, are longer and narrower, choice (E). Moreover, (A) is out because the animal's mouth does not necessarily have to be closed to distinguish one from the other. Choice (B) is out because both animals can be found in the Everglades National Park, and (C) and (D) are never discussed as ways to distinguish one giant reptile from the other.

Music History Passage: Questions 5–7

This passage focuses on the effect of societal currents on women's participation in music. It is not too dense, so you should read through it fairly quickly to get the gist, noting important themes in each paragraph as you go.

Paragraph 1 gives an overview of the social and political climate of the first half of the 19th century and the effect of this climate on the middle class, particularly with regard to music. In paragraph 2, the author explains that, despite the increased access to music that the middle class enjoyed at this time, it was still uncommon for women to participate in many musical activities. Paragraph 3 explains that negative opinions about women and music can be traced to 18th-century notions. Paragraph 4 discusses Clara Schumann and the part she played in creating ideological and professional roles for women in music.

5. A

In the first paragraph, we learn that women's involvement with music was thought to enhance their marriageability and their families' social status. This is best characterized by choice (A) because all of these forms of participation are consistent with women's traditional family roles.

6. D

Reread the second paragraph, including the cited lines. If you have trouble prephrasing an answer, test each of the choices. It's most reasonable to infer that because women at this time needed men's support and advice, they must have conformed to society's expectations. None of the other choices is supported by the passage.

7. D

The third paragraph focuses on society's negative view of women who performed music publicly or composed music. The topic of Clara Schumann, raised in this context, leads us to believe that her lack of confidence was a product of society's views. This idea is paraphrased in choice (D).

8. E

Let's go through the answer choices. (A) is tempting but wrong. You cannot be absolutely sure that the person playing the first violin part is considered the best violinist in the orchestra; maybe someone even better on the violin always plays another instrument when playing with the orchestra. There's no reason to think that Carl and Sonya are "equally talented," although they're probably pretty close, so (B) is incorrect. (C) is out because you don't know how often Joe misses rehearsal. (D) doesn't make sense because Joe may be there to play the first part when Carl misses the rehearsal. (E) is the correct choice: Joe always plays the first part when he attends rehearsal, regardless of who else is there.

9. A

On this question you are asked to infer what the agent believes. Clearly she must assume that certain actors are inappropriate for certain parts because if she didn't believe this, her conclusion would make no sense, and it would not be possible for an actor to audition for an inappropriate part. The actors'

talent (B) isn't questioned by the agent; she focuses on the types of roles. The agent never assumes the possibility that an actor's appropriateness for the part may be difficult to predict (C); in fact, if anything, such a belief would weaken her conclusion. Major roles (D) are never discussed in the passage, and if it were true that directors often cast the wrong actors (E), then the idea that the agency isn't doing well because it is sending out the wrong actors just doesn't wash.

Immigration Passage: Questions 10–12

This is a social sciences passage about immigration into the United States. Paragraph 1 introduces the topic, focusing on a period of massive immigration. Paragraph 2 tells us that there were two main aid organizations helping these immigrants assimilate to the United States and describes the approach of the Daughters of the American Revolution— encouraging immigrants to adapt to mainstream U.S. culture. Paragraph 3 portrays the contrasting approach of "settlement houses"—providing vital services and promoting a respect for the immigrants' original culture.

10. E

The passage starts off talking about immigration around the turn of the century. In paragraphs 2 and 3, the author gets even more specific, highlighting the contrasting efforts of two immigrant aid organizations. Choice (E) fits the focus best. Choices (A) and (D) are too broad—the passage isn't just about immigration in general, it's about a specific period and two specific ideas about assimilating immigrants. (B) only relates to paragraph 3. (C) is wrong because the passage doesn't recommend one way of assimilating immigrants—it just describes two concepts that occurred in the past.

11. C

This is an Application question about the conservatives' approach, described in paragraph 2. Basically, the conservative philosophy was that all immigrants should adopt American customs and culture (lines 15–17). Choice (C)—making a house look like all the other ones on the block—is the best analogy here. Choices (D) and (E) are wrong because they suggest preserving the nationality of immigrants.

12. A

Paragraph 3 describes the services offered by settlement houses. We're told in lines 27–29 that settlement houses aimed to offer whatever social services were not provided by local governments.

13. B

The assumption to avoid is that the younger an employee is, the less money she is going to make. There could be older employees of the firm making less money than the youngest employee, and Matthew could be one of them. It could even be the case that the youngest employee makes the most money, as far as you know. This eliminates every choice but (B). Because Matthew and the youngest employee of the firm don't make the same salary, they can't be the same person.

14. D

According to the passage, when foreign aid money is tied, nation A gives money to nation B with the understanding that B will use the money only to buy A's products. That way, nation A makes most of its money back. The author says that European nations are phasing out this practice in order to avoid criticism leveled at other donors, "notably Japan." The inference to be drawn here is that Japan has been criticized for tying its foreign aid, so (D) is the inference we're looking for. (A) isn't inferable because the passage discusses only *one* non-European nation, Japan, and its foreign aid policy. (E) says the same thing, that non-European nations are out for their own profit—one comment about

Japan doesn't let you make sweeping inferences about non-European nations. Choices (B) and (C) make statements of opinion—(B) about the role of ethical considerations and (C) about how to help underdeveloped countries—the author doesn't make any policy recommendations, so (B) and (C) are wrong.

15. E

In this inference question, you are asked to supply a conclusion that is best supported by the passage. The author seems to believe that critics' opinions aren't necessarily more significant than those of the average Joe, so (E), which restates this main idea, is easy to conclude.

Though the author says the critics' opinions aren't more correct than those of average moviegoers, he doesn't imply that they are usually incorrect, or choice (A). (B) is out because it's not that judgments are meaningless but that critics don't always make the right judgments. We don't know how frequently critics dislike popular movies (C), only that when they do, they may not be right. (D), which states that critics generally agree about any given movie, is too strong because the author only states that their opinions tend to reflect certain class prejudices.

Galilean Moons Passage: Questions 16–17

This is a science passage about four of Jupiter's moons, discovered by Galileo. The paragraph relates their discovery and role in debates about the solar system. It also introduces the main idea—scientists didn't know much about these moons until the 1979 Voyager missions "changed our impressions of these bodies."

16. E

Remember that the main idea of the passage is the choice that covers the whole passage. Here, it's the simplest choice that describes the passage best: Because the passage covers how Jupiter's moons were discovered when information became available about them from the Voyager mission, it is basically about Jupiter's four brightest moons (E). Choices (A) and (B) are wrong because they're not discussed in detail. Choice (C) is too broad; this passage isn't about the whole solar system. (D) is not mentioned at all.

17. E

Lines 1–3 tell us that the Galilean moons were the "first objects in the solar system discovered through the use of the telescope." Lines 3–6 go on to say that Galileo's discovery played a central role in a famous debate about the solar system. You can infer from this that Galileo was one of the first to "make important use of the telescope"—choice (E). (A) is wrong because Galileo supported Copernicus. (B) and (D) are wrong because accurate measurements of the moons didn't come until centuries later. (C) is out because there's no evidence that Galileo was one of the first astronomers ever.

18. C

This detail question asks why Americans did not start using the tomato until the mid-19th century. So what does the passage say? According to the passage, the English considered the tomato poisonous, and this myth continued to hold sway in America until the mid-19th century; in other words, they too believed it to be poisonous, choice (C). None of the other answer choices are supported by their statements in the passage.

19. D

The main idea of this brief passage is conveyed in its first sentence. The presidential election of 2000 is used as an example of how important it is for Americans to exercise their right to vote. This is consistent with (D). (A) and (E) are somewhat consistent with the passage, but they distort the point being conveyed. The author is not focused on the problems or controversy associated with the election but rather on the importance of each vote. (B) and (C) focus on issues that are outside the scope or focus of the passage.

20. B

The answer in this case is (B). From the information given, you should have seen that the governor was very determined to get things done his way. Specifics on how he pursued his policies are not discussed in the passage, and thus, (C) and (D) are not adequate as answers. (E) contradicts the passage. Only (B) is addressed in the paragraph.

Smallpox Passage: Questions 21–24

This is a social studies passage about smallpox, "one of the world's most dreaded diseases." Paragraph 1 gives us some historical background on the disease. Paragraph 2 describes one of the first attempts to protect people against the disease, a process called variolation that was painful and often unsuccessful. Paragraph 3 details Edward Jenner's discovery of a superior method—the process of vaccination.

21. D

Skimming paragraphs 2 and 3 should indicate that the focus of the passage is on the fight against smallpox, from the ninth century until the 1970s (D). Choices (A) and (E) are too broad—the passage isn't about all infectious or viral diseases. Choices (B) and (C) only relate to paragraphs 2 and 3, respectively.

22. A

What were the problems associated with variolation? According to the passage, variolation patients were sometimes fatally infected and could spread the disease to others even in successful inoculations. Choice (A) summarizes this second disadvantage. Cowpox (B) was an aspect of Jenner's treatment (paragraph 3). No description of variolation wearing off (C), being difficult to perform (D), or controversial among doctors (E) is given.

23. B

Lines 20–23 indicate that Jenner became "fascinated" by the fact that having had cowpox somehow immunized people to smallpox. Thus, he had noticed a relationship between cowpox and smallpox, and (B) is correct. (A) is never stated. Though we can infer that Jenner wanted his vaccination work to be recognized by the Royal Society of Physicians, there's no evidence that he did so in order to be accepted into the society (C). Jenner underwent variolation as a boy, but it's never implied that he worked with variolation himself (D). (E) goes too far: Jenner tried vaccination not because he preferred unconventional approaches in general, but because variolation was unsafe and only partially successful.

24. B

When did Jenner's vaccination process become widespread? It wasn't immediately (A) because Jenner's findings were initially rejected. (B) is the answer—Jenner's process became widespread "within a matter of years" after he published them (lines 29–30).

25. D

On this inference question, you are asked for the answer choice that best completes the author's line of thought. Because the author believes in the primacy of genetics, we need a completion involving tomatoes that illustrates this. If one plants tomatoes, then one will get tomatoes (that's genetics), not some other plant.

26. C

The passage here discusses industrial uses for precious stones, so the correct answer (C) should pretty much jump out at you. This passage is not about the "timeless allure" of these stones (A), and gem "hardness" is only mentioned in reference to diamonds, so (D) is out. (B) is wrong because the passage is not just about diamonds, not to mention that the industrial uses for diamonds that are mentioned are fairly traditional. Finally, (E) is wrong because the applications for precious stones that are mentioned go well beyond merely cutting, grinding, and polishing.

27. B

The passage notes parenthetically that a ruby is a sapphire with chromium "impurities," so one can logically infer that both gems come from the same kind of stone, choice (B). All the other answer choices are either never mentioned in the passage or directly contradict the passage, as choice (E) does: different applications for garnets and rubies are clearly mentioned in the passage.

28. D

The author argues that we must accept inconvenience if we want to secure the well-being of our world. Most pollution is caused by vehicle fuel, and according to the author, it "must be cut regardless of the costs." That's best summarized by (D). We must do what's necessary, no matter how drastic and costly, to save the environment. The closest choice is probably (B), but the if/then statement in (B) argues that a lower rate of car use would be sufficient to drastically reduce pollution. The author doesn't say that driving less is *sufficient* to cut pollution but rather that it is *necessary* to cut pollution. (C) brings in the use of fuel by industry, which is outside the scope here. Saying that we've got to go back to the 19th century (A) is too extreme to describe this argument. Finally, (E) states a causal relationship not implied in the stimulus—that people overuse their cars because they don't care about the environment. Again, (D) is correct.

29. E

You are asked to determine which statement the author would be most likely to agree with. This is another way of asking you to make an inference based on the passage. The passage is about the game go. The author compares go with chess but does not discuss the relative complexity of the games, so (A) is out. Although the passage states that go is extremely popular among game theorists, nowhere does it imply that game theorists prefer it to any other game;

that is an extreme statement, and (B) can be excluded. According to the passage, computers have a difficult time modeling the game, so (C) is off target. (D) is a distortion. The game is played with stones on a 19 by 19 grid, but the number of stones required to play is never discussed in the passage. Choice (E) is consistent with the tone and gist of the passage. Go is more complex than it seems.

Coral Reef Passage: Questions 30–34

This passage is a science passage about coral reefs. Paragraph 1 introduces the main idea, which is a focus on "the complex web of interrelationships between plants and animals." Paragraph 2 describes how reefs are formed out of the skeletons of the reefs' two main inhabitants, the stony coral and the green alga. Paragraph 3 describes several theories about how coral reefs are transformed into islands.

30. C

Paragraph 2 is the only place where the stony coral is discussed. Lines 14–15 indicate that the stony coral's skeleton is composed of "almost pure calcium carbonate."

31. D

Paragraph 2 outlines the relationship between the coral and the algae. The animals are described as "partners" that "coexist in a mutually beneficial relationship" (lines 17–18). Cooperative (D) is the choice that best summarizes this subsea partnership.

32. A

Paragraph 3 discusses the issue that scientists find "puzzling." Lines 24–26 indicate that scientists find the "transformation of reefs into islands" a mystery. Choice (A) summarizes the issue. Wrong choice (D) is a distortion—the passage talks about islands, not "great land masses."

33. D

Where is volcanic activity mentioned? The last few lines of the passage discuss volcanic activity as one possible way in which reefs are transformed into islands. Specifically, we're told that reefs are transformed into "atolls, or ring-shaped reef islands," (line 32–33), making (D) the correct answer.

34. E

The passage states that the popular perception of coral islands "is not always entirely justified. . .from sea level"—that is, on the surface. "Beneath the waves," however, coral islands are "fantastic and very beautiful". (A)'s "totally inaccurate" is too sweeping. (B) is not mentioned in the text. The author never suggests (C) that divers are waging a disinformation campaign about coral islands. As for (D), nothing here suggests that scientists are trying to dispel the romantic image of coral islands.

35. C

This passage describes the field of proxemics and concludes by linking studies of proxemics with how diplomats are trained to engage members of different cultures. This implies that the use of space and spatial boundaries is important to diplomats, so (C) is correct. (A) is a distortion. (B) is contradicted by the passage. If most cultures had the same spatial norms, Hall's studies would not have found anything of note or use. (D) is directly contradicted by the fact that diplomats have used Hall's findings to train diplomats—that is a practical application of proxemics. It seems likely that there would be others. (E) is an unlikely statement that receives no support within the passage.

36. B

This passage is about the origins of the current version of the game of basketball. Naismith began the current version of the game in 1891. (B) is correct. (A) and (D) are both mentioned in the passage, but each is too narrow in scope to address the passage as a whole. (C) is a distortion. Basketball's popularity in Meso-America is never discussed within the passage. (E) is also a distortion that fails to address Naismith's role in the creation of the current version of the game

37. B

This passage is about the history of playing cards. Consequently, (B) is the correct answer. (A) and (E) focus on one part of that history—the origin of playing cards in China. Similarly, (C) focuses too narrowly on one detail in the passage. (D) fails to address the historical focus of the passage.

Camouflage Passage: Questions 38–39

This is a science passage about the camouflage animals use to protect themselves from predators called "protective coloration."

38. A

The caribou and the stoat crop up in lines 5–9, where it is indicated that they are animals that "change their protective pigmentation with the seasons"—choice (A). Constant changes of color (E) are discussed later as a safeguard of the chameleon—but this isn't a seasonal change.

39. A

The chameleon's special talent is described in lines 11–12—it changes color to match the surface it rests on. Choice (A) summarizes this idea. Just clinging to surfaces (B) wouldn't make the chameleon noteworthy or protect it from attackers. (E) distorts the passage—the chameleon doesn't change the color of the surfaces it comes into contact with.

40. D

According to the passage, the word "tungsten" comes from the Swedish language. *Tung sten* means heavy stone in Swedish.

MATHEMATICS EXPLANATIONS

1. E

The probability of an event is equal to the number of favorable outcomes divided by the number of possible outcomes. In this case, the number of slips labeled with a planet name that does not start with the letter *M* will be the number of favorable outcomes. As two of the nine planets have names starting with *M*, seven do not. The number of favorable outcomes divided by the number of possible outcomes will be $\frac{7}{9}$, choice (E).

2. C

Referring to the image, it can be seen that the needle of the meter is pointing to a value between 750 and 800 pounds. Because the needle is pointing closer to 800 than to 750, answer (C) is correct.

3. C

Compare the values in each answer choice moving from left to right. In the tens place, all choices have sevens. In the ones place, (A) and (D) have twos, whereas the rest have threes, so (A) and (D) can be eliminated. In the tenths place, (B) has a value of five, whereas (C) and (E) have sixes, so (B) can be eliminated. Finally, the hundredths place value of (C) is five, whereas that of (E) is two, so (E) can be eliminated, and (C) is the correct answer.

4. D

The question asks for "how much," but looking at the answer choices you see that you are not being asked for an exact amount. This is an estimation question. You need to compare the relative values of the two amounts. If the amounts were simply 1 cup and 3 cups, it would clearly be 2 cups. But now you have to determine the relationship between $\frac{2}{3}$ and $\frac{3}{4}$.

Because 3 is two more than 1 and $\frac{3}{4}$ is a little more than $\frac{2}{3}$, a little more than 2 cups must be added to go from $1\frac{2}{3}$ to $3\frac{3}{4}$. This can done by converting both fractions to a common denominator: $\frac{2}{3} = \frac{8}{12}$ and $\frac{3}{4} = \frac{9}{12}$. $\frac{2}{3}$ is slightly smaller than $\frac{3}{4}$, so to get from $1\frac{2}{3}$ to $3\frac{3}{4}$ you will need a little more than 2 cups.

5. D

This problem requires you to determine a scale factor and to apply that to a given measurement. Because 2 scaled inches on the diagram equal 8 inches in reality, a scale factor of $8 \div 2 = 4$ is being used. If the speakers measure 6 inches in the diagram, we can multiply this by the scale factor to find their height in reality: $6 \times 4 = 24$. Because the answer choices are in feet and inches, convert 24 inches to feet by dividing 24 inches by 12 inches per foot to calculate that the speakers have an actual height of $24 \div 12 = 2$ feet, choice (D).

6. E

In this problem you are given a bar graph that displays information about the weight (in pounds) of certain ingredients required to make 50 loaves of bread. You are then asked to use this information to calculate the weight of an ingredient required to make 100 loaves of bread. The ingredient whose weight you are asked to calculate to make 100 loaves of bread is sugar. From the graph you can see that it takes 5 lbs of sugar to make 50 loaves. You can now set up the following proportion, letting *x* stand for the unknown number of pounds of sugar in the 100 loaves: $\frac{5}{50} = \frac{x}{100}$.

Simply cross multiply and solve for *x* as follows:

$$50x = 500$$
$$x = 10$$

It will take 10 lbs of sugar to make 100 loaves of bread, so choice (E) is correct. You do not need to use the information provided about the amount of flour per 50 loaves to solve this problem.

7. D

$1,600 \div 4 = 400$ sales representatives who work at the company's corporate headquarters. Because 62.5 percent of these met or exceeded their sales goals last year, 100 percent − 62.5 percent = 37.5 percent who failed to meet their goals. Convert 37.5 percent into a decimal by dividing by 100: $37.5 \div 100 = 0.375$. The number of sales representatives who work at the corporate headquarters who failed to meet their sales goals last year can thus be found by multiplying 0.375 by 400, choice (D).

8. D

The temperature given for May 1996 in the graph is 65° F. Because the temperature is recorded as 52° F in August 1996 and 71° F in December 1996, choice (D) is correct.

9. C

The pie chart provided with this problem does not give the fraction of expenditure represented by savings, but it does give the fraction of expenditure represented by everything else. If $\frac{1}{3}$ is spent on mortgage payments, $\frac{1}{6}$ is spent on groceries, $\frac{1}{6}$ is spent on loan repayments, and $\frac{1}{6}$ represents miscellaneous spending, then these fractions can be subtracted from the whole to find the fraction saved:

$$1 - \frac{1}{3} - \frac{1}{6} - \frac{1}{6} - \frac{1}{6} = 1 - \frac{5}{6} = \frac{1}{6} \text{ saved}$$

Because the Petersons' annual income was $42,000 and $\frac{1}{6}$ of this was saved, $42,000 \div 6 = 7,000$ in savings.

10. D

This question requires two steps, one working backwards and one working forward. In order to find the perimeter of a polygon, you must know the length of each side. Here only one is marked. The opposite side is easy to determine because the figure is a rectangle; it will also be 3. The other two sides will also be equal to each other but must be found using the other information given: the rectangle has an area of 15. This is where you must work backwards. Because the area of a rectangle is determined as $A = lw$, you know that $15 = 3l$. Solve for l. $l = 5$. You now know that the rectangle has two sides of length 3 and two sides of length 5. To find the perimeter, simply add them all together: $3 + 3 + 5 + 5 = 16$

11. D

Begin by combining like terms:

$$26 - y = 2x + 14 + y$$
$$26 - 14 = 2x + y + y$$
$$12 = 2x + 2y$$

Now it is possible to divide both sides by the common factor of 2:

$$\frac{12}{2} = \frac{2x + 2y}{2} =$$
$$6 = x + y$$

12. B

This question asks you to analyze the information in the graph to determine how many stores sold at least twice as many bottles of shampoo X as shampoo Z. Only Store 2 fits, with 19 bottles of shampoo X sold and only 8 of shampoo Z.

13. A

In order to find the fraction of the total number of Shampoo bottles sold at Store 3 represented by Shampoo Y, first find the total number of bottles sold and then find the number of bottles of Shampoo Y sold. Store 3 sold 12 bottles of

Shampoo X, 10 bottles of Shampoo Y, and 18 bottles of Shampoo Z. Thus, the fraction will be $\dfrac{10}{12 + 10 + 18} = \dfrac{10}{40} = \dfrac{1}{4}$.

14. C

Store 2 sold 8 bottles of Shampoo Z, whereas Store 4 sold only 5. Therefore, Store 2 sold $8 - 5 = 3$ more bottles of Shampoo Z than Store 4.

15. D

This question can easily be solved by creating an equation using x to represent the unknown number of times that 0.15 is being multiplied:

$$525 = 0.15x$$
$$\frac{525}{0.15} = x$$
$$\frac{525 \times 100}{0.15 \times 100} = x$$
$$\frac{52{,}500}{15} = x$$
$$3{,}500 = x$$

16. A

This problem can most easily be solved by process of elimination. Start with the figure that appears in the greatest number of answer choices: II. Because it has an area of $\frac{1}{2} \times 3.5 \times 4 = 7$, it does not work, and answer choices (B), (C), and (E) can be eliminated. In order to choose between (A) and (D), try figure III next. It has an area of $\pi(2^2) = 4\pi$, so it does not work, and choice (A) is correct.

17. B

Perform the instructed operations on R after substituting 5 for R.

R is 5
$5 \times 5 = 25$
$25 - 29 = -4$
$-4 + 2 = -2$

18. A

When multiplying by powers of ten, simply move the decimal point the number of places indicated in the exponent of ten to the left if the exponent is negative and to the right if the exponent is positive. Convert all three values this way:

I. $0.76 \times 10^5 = 76{,}000$

II. $7{,}600 \times 10^{-4} = 0.76$

Eliminate choices (B) and (E) since these values are not the same.

Finally,

III. $7.6 \times 10^2 = 760$

Because none of the values are the same, (A) is correct.

19. A

If a number leaves a remainder of 5 when divided into 137, then two things must be true. The number must be greater than 5, and the number must divide evenly into $(137 - 5)$, or 132. Only (A), 12, is greater than 5 and divides evenly into 132.

20. B

In order to compare values easily, they must be in the same form. Convert all values into decimals or percentages in order to solve this problem. (B) is correct because $\frac{3}{2}$, or 1.5, is greater than 1.25. (A) is 1.25, (C) is 0.125, (D) is 0.125, and (E) is $0.\overline{66}$.

21. C

This question asks you to identify the correct part-to-whole ratio from among the answer choices. In this case, the fraction will have the number of seventh graders, 18, as the numerator and the total number of students on the bus, $15 + 18 + 12 = 45$, as the denominator. Because $\frac{18}{45}$ is not an answer choice, it must be simplified:

$$\frac{18}{45} = \frac{18 \div 9}{45 \div 9} = \frac{2}{5}$$

22. C

This problem can easily be solved if translated into an algebraic equation with x as the number of times by which 12 must be multiplied:

$$36 \times 4 = 12x$$

$$\frac{36 \times 4}{12} = \frac{12x}{12}$$

$$3 \times 4 = x$$

$$12 = x$$

23. C

If T is 40% of 900, then

$$T = 900 \times 40\%$$

$$T = 900 \times \frac{4}{10}$$

$$T = \frac{900 \times 4}{10}$$

$$T = 90 \times 4$$

$$T = 360$$

24. E

This question requires that you consider the various possible ways in which a rectangle and a circle lying on a plane could overlap and determine the maximum number of points of intersection. Various possibilities can be sketched if useful. If the rectangle is placed so that one side is tangent to the circle, there will be 1 point of intersection. However, if the rectangle is placed so that each of the four corners overlaps the circumference of the circle, there will be 8 points of intersection. It is impossible to sketch a scenario in which they share more than 8 points of intersection, so choice (E) is correct.

25. C

In order to find the median of a list of values, begin by ordering the values from least to greatest. Thus ordered, this list becomes {3, 5, 6, 8, 12, 13, 15, 15, 24}. Because there are an odd number of values in the list, the median is simply the middle value, which in this case is 12.

26. D

According to the graph, 7 barrels of solvent were sold in January 1993, choice (D).

27. C

Locate on the graph the number of barrels of solvent sold in June 1993, 12, and then locate the number of barrels sold in July 1993, 11. The combined number of barrels sold was 12 + 11 = 23 barrels.

28. D

This question asks you to find the area of a given triangle, so you will need the area formula for a triangle: $A = \frac{1}{2} \times$ base $\times$ height. Because this is a right isosceles triangle, we know that the height is equal to the base, which measures 3, because they are opposite the congruent angles. Now plug the measurements of the base and height into the area formula:

$$A = \frac{1}{2} \times 3 \times 3 = 1.5 \times 3 = 4.5$$

29. D

Solve the equation

$$J + 2 = \frac{K}{4}, \text{ then}$$

$$J = \frac{K}{4} - 2$$

30. E

In order to determine which answer choice is not equivalent to the rest, evaluate each after simplifying by dividing all by their common factor of 4:

(A) 48×8

(B) 8×48

(C) $4 \times 12 \times 8$, or 48×8

(D) $16 \times 12 \times 2 = 4 \times 4 \times 12 \times 2 = 48 \times 8$

(E) $16 \times 3 \times 2 = 4 \times 4 \times 3 \times 2 = 12 \times 8$

It is now clear that choice (E) is different.

31. B

If each of 7 runners runs 1.27 kilometers, then the total distance run by the 7 runners is 8.89 kilometers (1.27 × 7). This is closest to 9. Choice (B) is correct.

32. B

The question states that each seat on the Ferris wheel can hold 3 people and that all but 3 of the 12 cars are full. Therefore, the 9 full cars containing 3 people each contain a total of 27 people. In addition, we are told that 1 car is empty and 2 cars contain 2 people each, adding 4 people to the 27 in the full cars for a total of 31 people on the Ferris wheel.

33. E

This type of question always boils down to substitution. Determine which numbers correspond to which letters and then plug them into the equation. Then, follow the order of operations and solve. In this case $H = -3$, $J = 6$, and $K = 2$. Plugging into the defining equation you get $6 - [2 \times -(3)] = 6 - (-6) = 6 + 6 = 12$.

34. B

Because each figure is composed of identical equilateral triangles, we can call the length of any side of any triangle x. By counting the number of sides that form the perimeter of each figure, we can establish algebraic expressions for the perimeter of each figure.

(A) has a perimeter of $6x$

(B) has a perimeter of $5x$

(C) has a perimeter of $6x$

(D) has a perimeter of $6x$

Thus, choice (B) has the least perimeter.

35. E

The easiest way to solve this problem is to count in increments of four hours until the ninth reading, starting at 12:00 P.M.: 12:00 P.M., 4:00 P.M., 8:00 P.M., 12:00 A.M., 4:00 A.M., 8:00 A.M., 12:00 P.M., 4:00 P.M., 8:00 P.M. Thus, the ninth reading is taken at 8:00 P.M.

36. C

Calculate the area and perimeter of each figure.

(A) Area = 3 × 3 = 9, Perimeter = 4 × 3 = 12. Eliminate.

(B) Area = 2 × 3 = 6, Perimeter = 2(2 + 3) = 10. Eliminate.

(C) Area = 4 × 4 = 16, Perimeter = 4 × 4 = 16. Correct.

(D) Area = $\frac{1}{2}$ × 3 × 4 = 6. Because this is a 3-4-5 right triangle, Perimeter = 3 + 4 + 5 = 12.

37. C

When the length of a rectangle, x, is doubled, it becomes $2x$. When its width, y, is divided by 3, it becomes $\frac{y}{3}$. The area formula for a rectangle can now be applied to these new dimensions:

$A = \text{length} \times \text{width} = 2x \times \frac{y}{3} = \frac{2xy}{3}$, choice (C).

38. C

By asking on how many days both apple pie and ice cream will be served in February, this question is asking how many days have numbers that satisfy both the first statement by being even and the second statement by being a multiple of three. To answer it, simply count the number of dates in February that are even multiples of three, or multiples of 2 × 3 = 6: the 6th, the 12th, the 18th, and the 24th. Regardless of whether it is a leap year, there are never 30 days in February, and so only four dates satisfy both statements.

39. D

In order to find the average (arithmetic mean) of a set of values, divide the sum of the values by the number of values in the set. In this case, a common denominator must be found before $\frac{3}{5}$ and $\frac{9}{2}$ can be added; the lowest common denominator is 10:

$$\frac{3}{5} = \frac{6}{10} \text{ and } \frac{9}{2} = \frac{45}{10}$$

The average is

$$\frac{\frac{51}{10}}{2} = \frac{51}{10} \times \frac{1}{2} = \frac{51}{20}$$

40. D

Scientific notation is correctly represented by a value with digits only in the ones place and to the right of the decimal multiplied by a power of 10. The exponent that 10 is raised to represents the number of places the decimal has been moved in order to leave a value with digits only in the ones place and to the right of the decimal. Only choice (D) is in proper scientific notation, so no calculations need to be made.

WRITING EXPLANATIONS

Usage

1. C

Bleeding, the gerund, is the subject of the verb *to be considered*, so you need to change the sentence to read *bleeding...was considered*.

2. C

The verb *improved* needs to be modified by an adverb. Change *dramatic* to *dramatically*.

3. D

This sentence has a word choice problem. *Respectively* is used when you consider one or more members of a group separately. In this case, the author is probably looking for the word *respectfully*, because the counselors are standing below the king's throne, showing their respect.

4. B

The second clause in this sentence lacks a verb. You could change *have agreement* to *have reached an agreement* or *have agreed*.

5. A

Have you ever heard "people aren't whiches" in your English class? That old grammar saying applies here: the delegates are people, so the sentence requires *who* instead of *which*.

6. E

This sentence contains no error.

7. B

The effort is the subject of the verb *to result*, and because *effort* is singular, the verb should be changed to *results*.

8. A

Every one is the subject of the verb *to be closed*. *Every one* takes the singular form of the verb, so it should read *was closed*.

9. D

Should not hardly just sounds wrong. There's no need for the word *hardly*, so you should omit it.

10. A

This question focuses on word choice. *Imaginary* refers to something that is not real, and the paper in question is surely real. *Imaginative* is a better choice here.

11. C

The *memoirs* are the subject of the verb *to promise*. Because *memoirs* are plural, you need the singular form, *promise*.

12. A

The point on issue just sounds wrong. The correct idiom is *point at issue*.

13. A

Raising is a form of the active verb "to raise." Because no one is performing an action, the passive verb "to rise" works better here to describe *rising living costs*.

14. E

This sentence contains no error.

15. C

Capable for just sounds wrong. The diver was *capable of collecting...specimens* works better.

16. B

There's no need for the future tense in this sentence, which describes how a round robin works. *Has to* is a good replacement for *will have to*.

17. B

The pronoun *him* should be changed to the possessive *his* to correct this sentence. *Retiring* could be changed to *retirement* to make the sentence even clearer.

18. B

The gerund *Having* is the subject of the verb *to assure*. *Having...assures* is the correct verb form.

19. B

Was, a form of the verb "to be," needs to be modified by an adverb. Replace *frequent* with *frequently*.

Sentence Correction

20. A

The original sentence is best.

21. E

Choices (A), (B), and (D) contain *that* or *who*. These words seem to introduce an additional clause that never appears. Choice (E) uses the correct verb form *commuters believe* and is correct.

22. C

Ask yourself: what was developed? As it stands, the sentence tells us that the president himself was developed by a scientific team (a scary thought!). Only choice (C) corrects the problem by providing a phrase that logically modifies *the president*.

23. D

The second part of the sentence describes regions that have certain characteristics. *Only* is the correct linking word to set those regions apart. Choice (C) doesn't make sense, so (D) is correct.

34. B

Choice (B) most clearly shows the connection between the first part of the sentence, the lingering political death, and the second part, the attempts of groups and individuals to prevent this demise. A conjunction like *although* is needed to show contrast and to link the two clauses.

25. A

This is a complex sentence, but (A), the original, says it best.

26. E

Choice (E) is the most clear and concise, omitting the unnecessary *when you are* from the original sentence.

27. B

Choices (A) and (C) use the passive voice, which is awkward. Choices (D) and (E) use incorrect forms of the conditional. (B) is the clearest choice.

28. E

The company is singular, so the use of the pronoun *they* in choices (A) and (C) is incorrect. Choices (B) and (D) awkwardly use the passive voice. (E) is the most clear and concise choice.

29. E

When comparing two people, *better* should be used instead of *best*. Only choice (E) does this correctly.

30. A

The original sentence is best.

31. B

The original sentence compares *the variety...of services* with *low-cost programs*, which doesn't make much sense. Choices (B) and (D) clarify the sentence by inserting *the number of* and making a more appropriate comparison. However, choice (D) uses the wrong verb form, making choice (B) the best choice.

32. C

Choices (B), (C), and (E) all correctly use a semicolon to join the two independent clauses. Only choice (C), however, makes sense of the sentence by using *he* to refer to the politician.

33. B

Choice (B) is the clearest and most concise choice. All the other choices use overly wordy and imprecise constructions.

34. D

A parallelism problem. The idea in this sentence is best expressed with the *not only...but also* formula. When this formula is used, the two items connected by it have to be in the same grammatical form. Because what are described are *ambitions*, it's idiomatic to use infinitives.

35. E

The original sentence doesn't have any verb because an "-ing" word without a helping verb isn't a verb. Choices (C) and (E) supply verbs, but choice (C) introduces an incorrect pronoun. The pronoun must refer to *government,* which is singular. So, the pronoun must be *its.*

36. D

Again, the original sentence doesn't have a verb. Choices (B) and (D) supply the missing verb, but (B) makes other changes that introduce new mistakes.

37. A

The original sentence is best. This sentence describes a two-step process. It's a bit like a very short list. Therefore, both steps must be given in parallel forms. The first step is *working* (with no pronoun), so the second step should be simply *sleeping* (with no pronoun).

38. E

Strolling hand in hand is a modifying phrase that modifies the noun *couple.* Only (E) places the modifying phrase next to *couple.*

WRITTEN ASSIGNMENT SAMPLE RESPONSE

The following is an example of a strong response to the written assignment.

I believe that some security measures in a school are important. If the idea of the security is actually to keep children safe while at school, it is a very good thing. If the idea has no safety value but infringes on the rights of the students, I would not be in favor of them. Let me explain my position with examples.

Security guards in the school, and even a local police precinct located in a school, can be a very positive thing for all involved. In this way, students and police generally get to know each other on a more personal basis and can begin to trust and respect each other. If a police-person knew the students on a personal, informal basis, it might help him or her not to jump to conclusions based on a student's appearance or perceived behavior. It also might afford the students the opportunity to talk to the police when they thought trouble might be coming.

Since it is easy to hide a weapon in a backpack, another safeguard that might be helpful is not allowing students to carry backpacks to class. The backpacks can be kept in the lockers and only books carried to class. Schools might need to adjust the time allowed for changing between classes so students have the time to go to their lockers to exchange their books. This would be a minor modification and could mean a big difference in the safety of all the students.

An example that I believe is not a good safety measure would be requiring students to wear uniforms. Granted, in some schools, certain dress may have the appearance of gang clothing, but I think this is a limited argument. Dress, as long as it does not contain obscene material and sufficiently covers the student, is a matter of personal style. I do not believe it is the school's job to try to make everyone alike. Schools attempt to create individuals who can think critically and take a stand on an issue. By making everyone look alike, they tend to send the message that everyone should think alike. I do not believe that this is the job of school.

In summary, I believe that there are measures that can be taken to improve safety in schools. They should be well thought-out and not unduly infringe on the rights of students in the school. In other words, the measures taken should have the sole purpose of improving safety of everyone in the school.

Practice Test Two
Answer Sheet

**Remove (or photocopy) this answer sheet and use it to complete the practice test.
(See answer key following the test when finished.)**

If a section has fewer questions than answer spaces, leave the extra spaces blank.

Reading—60 minutes

1 Ⓐ Ⓑ Ⓒ Ⓓ Ⓔ   11 Ⓐ Ⓑ Ⓒ Ⓓ Ⓔ   21 Ⓐ Ⓑ Ⓒ Ⓓ Ⓔ   31 Ⓐ Ⓑ Ⓒ Ⓓ Ⓔ
2 Ⓐ Ⓑ Ⓒ Ⓓ Ⓔ   12 Ⓐ Ⓑ Ⓒ Ⓓ Ⓔ   22 Ⓐ Ⓑ Ⓒ Ⓓ Ⓔ   32 Ⓐ Ⓑ Ⓒ Ⓓ Ⓔ
3 Ⓐ Ⓑ Ⓒ Ⓓ Ⓔ   13 Ⓐ Ⓑ Ⓒ Ⓓ Ⓔ   23 Ⓐ Ⓑ Ⓒ Ⓓ Ⓔ   33 Ⓐ Ⓑ Ⓒ Ⓓ Ⓔ
4 Ⓐ Ⓑ Ⓒ Ⓓ Ⓔ   14 Ⓐ Ⓑ Ⓒ Ⓓ Ⓔ   24 Ⓐ Ⓑ Ⓒ Ⓓ Ⓔ   34 Ⓐ Ⓑ Ⓒ Ⓓ Ⓔ
5 Ⓐ Ⓑ Ⓒ Ⓓ Ⓔ   15 Ⓐ Ⓑ Ⓒ Ⓓ Ⓔ   25 Ⓐ Ⓑ Ⓒ Ⓓ Ⓔ   35 Ⓐ Ⓑ Ⓒ Ⓓ Ⓔ
6 Ⓐ Ⓑ Ⓒ Ⓓ Ⓔ   16 Ⓐ Ⓑ Ⓒ Ⓓ Ⓔ   26 Ⓐ Ⓑ Ⓒ Ⓓ Ⓔ   36 Ⓐ Ⓑ Ⓒ Ⓓ Ⓔ
7 Ⓐ Ⓑ Ⓒ Ⓓ Ⓔ   17 Ⓐ Ⓑ Ⓒ Ⓓ Ⓔ   27 Ⓐ Ⓑ Ⓒ Ⓓ Ⓔ   37 Ⓐ Ⓑ Ⓒ Ⓓ Ⓔ
8 Ⓐ Ⓑ Ⓒ Ⓓ Ⓔ   18 Ⓐ Ⓑ Ⓒ Ⓓ Ⓔ   28 Ⓐ Ⓑ Ⓒ Ⓓ Ⓔ   38 Ⓐ Ⓑ Ⓒ Ⓓ Ⓔ
9 Ⓐ Ⓑ Ⓒ Ⓓ Ⓔ   19 Ⓐ Ⓑ Ⓒ Ⓓ Ⓔ   29 Ⓐ Ⓑ Ⓒ Ⓓ Ⓔ   39 Ⓐ Ⓑ Ⓒ Ⓓ Ⓔ
10 Ⓐ Ⓑ Ⓒ Ⓓ Ⓔ   20 Ⓐ Ⓑ Ⓒ Ⓓ Ⓔ   30 Ⓐ Ⓑ Ⓒ Ⓓ Ⓔ   40 Ⓐ Ⓑ Ⓒ Ⓓ Ⓔ

Math—60 minutes

1 Ⓐ Ⓑ Ⓒ Ⓓ Ⓔ   11 Ⓐ Ⓑ Ⓒ Ⓓ Ⓔ   21 Ⓐ Ⓑ Ⓒ Ⓓ Ⓔ   31 Ⓐ Ⓑ Ⓒ Ⓓ Ⓔ
2 Ⓐ Ⓑ Ⓒ Ⓓ Ⓔ   12 Ⓐ Ⓑ Ⓒ Ⓓ Ⓔ   22 Ⓐ Ⓑ Ⓒ Ⓓ Ⓔ   32 Ⓐ Ⓑ Ⓒ Ⓓ Ⓔ
3 Ⓐ Ⓑ Ⓒ Ⓓ Ⓔ   13 Ⓐ Ⓑ Ⓒ Ⓓ Ⓔ   23 Ⓐ Ⓑ Ⓒ Ⓓ Ⓔ   33 Ⓐ Ⓑ Ⓒ Ⓓ Ⓔ
4 Ⓐ Ⓑ Ⓒ Ⓓ Ⓔ   14 Ⓐ Ⓑ Ⓒ Ⓓ Ⓔ   24 Ⓐ Ⓑ Ⓒ Ⓓ Ⓔ   34 Ⓐ Ⓑ Ⓒ Ⓓ Ⓔ
5 Ⓐ Ⓑ Ⓒ Ⓓ Ⓔ   15 Ⓐ Ⓑ Ⓒ Ⓓ Ⓔ   25 Ⓐ Ⓑ Ⓒ Ⓓ Ⓔ   35 Ⓐ Ⓑ Ⓒ Ⓓ Ⓔ
6 Ⓐ Ⓑ Ⓒ Ⓓ Ⓔ   16 Ⓐ Ⓑ Ⓒ Ⓓ Ⓔ   26 Ⓐ Ⓑ Ⓒ Ⓓ Ⓔ   36 Ⓐ Ⓑ Ⓒ Ⓓ Ⓔ
7 Ⓐ Ⓑ Ⓒ Ⓓ Ⓔ   17 Ⓐ Ⓑ Ⓒ Ⓓ Ⓔ   27 Ⓐ Ⓑ Ⓒ Ⓓ Ⓔ   37 Ⓐ Ⓑ Ⓒ Ⓓ Ⓔ
8 Ⓐ Ⓑ Ⓒ Ⓓ Ⓔ   18 Ⓐ Ⓑ Ⓒ Ⓓ Ⓔ   28 Ⓐ Ⓑ Ⓒ Ⓓ Ⓕ   38 Ⓐ Ⓑ Ⓒ Ⓓ Ⓔ
9 Ⓐ Ⓑ Ⓒ Ⓓ Ⓔ   19 Ⓐ Ⓑ Ⓒ Ⓓ Ⓔ   29 Ⓐ Ⓑ Ⓒ Ⓓ Ⓔ   39 Ⓐ Ⓑ Ⓒ Ⓓ Ⓔ
10 Ⓐ Ⓑ Ⓒ Ⓓ Ⓔ   20 Ⓐ Ⓑ Ⓒ Ⓓ Ⓔ   30 Ⓐ Ⓑ Ⓒ Ⓓ Ⓔ   40 Ⓐ Ⓑ Ⓒ Ⓓ Ⓔ

Writing—60 minutes

1 Ⓐ Ⓑ Ⓒ Ⓓ Ⓔ   11 Ⓐ Ⓑ Ⓒ Ⓓ Ⓔ   21 Ⓐ Ⓑ Ⓒ Ⓓ Ⓔ   31 Ⓐ Ⓑ Ⓒ Ⓓ Ⓔ
2 Ⓐ Ⓑ Ⓒ Ⓓ Ⓔ   12 Ⓐ Ⓑ Ⓒ Ⓓ Ⓔ   22 Ⓐ Ⓑ Ⓒ Ⓓ Ⓔ   32 Ⓐ Ⓑ Ⓒ Ⓓ Ⓔ
3 Ⓐ Ⓑ Ⓒ Ⓓ Ⓔ   13 Ⓐ Ⓑ Ⓒ Ⓓ Ⓔ   23 Ⓐ Ⓑ Ⓒ Ⓓ Ⓔ   33 Ⓐ Ⓑ Ⓒ Ⓓ Ⓔ
4 Ⓐ Ⓑ Ⓒ Ⓓ Ⓔ   14 Ⓐ Ⓑ Ⓒ Ⓓ Ⓔ   24 Ⓐ Ⓑ Ⓒ Ⓓ Ⓔ   34 Ⓐ Ⓑ Ⓒ Ⓓ Ⓔ
5 Ⓐ Ⓑ Ⓒ Ⓓ Ⓔ   15 Ⓐ Ⓑ Ⓒ Ⓓ Ⓔ   25 Ⓐ Ⓑ Ⓒ Ⓓ Ⓔ   35 Ⓐ Ⓑ Ⓒ Ⓓ Ⓔ
6 Ⓐ Ⓑ Ⓒ Ⓓ Ⓔ   16 Ⓐ Ⓑ Ⓒ Ⓓ Ⓔ   26 Ⓐ Ⓑ Ⓒ Ⓓ Ⓔ   36 Ⓐ Ⓑ Ⓒ Ⓓ Ⓔ
7 Ⓐ Ⓑ Ⓒ Ⓓ Ⓔ   17 Ⓐ Ⓑ Ⓒ Ⓓ Ⓔ   27 Ⓐ Ⓑ Ⓒ Ⓓ Ⓔ   37 Ⓐ Ⓑ Ⓒ Ⓓ Ⓔ
8 Ⓐ Ⓑ Ⓒ Ⓓ Ⓔ   18 Ⓐ Ⓑ Ⓒ Ⓓ Ⓔ   28 Ⓐ Ⓑ Ⓒ Ⓓ Ⓔ   38 Ⓐ Ⓑ Ⓒ Ⓓ Ⓔ
9 Ⓐ Ⓑ Ⓒ Ⓓ Ⓔ   19 Ⓐ Ⓑ Ⓒ Ⓓ Ⓔ   29 Ⓐ Ⓑ Ⓒ Ⓓ Ⓔ
10 Ⓐ Ⓑ Ⓒ Ⓓ Ⓔ   20 Ⓐ Ⓑ Ⓒ Ⓓ Ⓔ   30 Ⓐ Ⓑ Ⓒ Ⓓ Ⓔ

Practice Test Two
Pre-Professional Skills
Test (PPST)

This timed practice serves as a diagnostic tool. It provides an opportunity for you to apply, in a test-like setting, what you already know, and identify areas of weakness.

Reading

Time—60 Minutes
40 Questions

Directions: Each statement or passage in this test is followed by a question or questions based on its content. After reading a statement or passage, choose the best answer to each question from among the five choices given. Answer all questions following a statement or passage on the basis of what is stated or implied in that statement or passage; you are not expected to have any previous knowledge of the topics treated in the statements and passages.

Be sure to mark all your answers on your answer sheet, and fill in completely the lettered space with a heavy, dark mark so that you cannot see the letter.

Remember, try to answer every question.

Questions 1–2

Cats were first domesticated 4,000 years ago by the ancient Egyptians, who revered them as household gods. By the third century B.C., the domestic cat was widely distributed across Europe thanks to seafaring Greek merchants and colonizers who associated cats with the goddess Artemis and used them to protect their grain supplies.

After millions of the creatures were slaughtered alongside the hundreds of thousands of pagans, heretics, and Jews with whom they were associated during the Middle Ages, cats may have gotten their revenge. The absence of cats in Europe probably contributed to the spread and the severity of the bubonic plague that devastated the continent in the 14th century.

1. An appropriate title for this passage would be

(A) Ancient Egyptian Deities
(B) From Gods to Outcasts: The Early History of the Domestic Cat
(C) Cats and the Bubonic Plague
(D) Cats and Dogs from Antiquity through the Middle Ages
(E) The Goddess Artemis and the Domestic House Cat

2. It can be inferred from this passage that

(A) after cats were slaughtered in the Middle Ages, the rodent population in Europe increased
(B) cats are a vengeful species
(C) Greek merchants sold domestic cats for large sums of money
(D) the bubonic plague could be spread through cats
(E) cats were especially popular house pets among pagans, heretics, and Jews

3. The number of chronically hungry people in the world is expected to decrease by nearly one half by 2030 according to recent computer models. Whereas this estimate is encouraging, it falls short of previous estimates that anticipated world hunger to be halved by 2015. The model concludes that global grain production will need to increase by 1.2 percent every year to meet demands for food and feed.

   The tone of this passage is best described as

   (A) pessimistic
   (B) discouraged
   (C) critical
   (D) passionate
   (E) guardedly optimistic

4. A human body can survive without water for several days and without food for as long as several weeks. However, if breathing stops for as little as three to six minutes, death is likely. All animals require a constant supply of oxygen to the body tissues and especially to the heart or brain. In the human body, the respiratory and circulatory systems perform this function by delivering oxygen to the blood, which then transports it to tissues throughout the body. Respiration in large animals involves more than just breathing in oxygen. It is a complex process that delivers oxygen while eliminating carbon dioxide produced by cells.

   Which bodily function, according to the passage, is least essential to the immediate survival of the average human being?

   (A) eating
   (B) drinking
   (C) breathing
   (D) blood circulation
   (E) sleeping

GO ON TO THE NEXT PAGE

Questions 5–7

The following passage presents a scientific discussion of the human ability to use language.

It is the use of language that sets apart humans from the animals. Language is what enables us to reveal our conscious selves, to
Line transmit knowledge to each other and to
(5) succeeding generations, to discuss and debate ideas, and to build and maintain the framework of civilization.

Is a human born with the innate capacity for language, or is language a complex form
(10) of behavior that one learns as a child? Although this question is still unanswered, it is clear from the work of neuroscientists that once a human possesses language, certain structures and areas of the brain do control
(15) its use.

Nineteenth-century scientist Pierre Paul Broca, for example, discovered the specific region of the brain that controls the flow of words from brain to mouth: he did the
(20) autopsy of a brain-damaged patient who had been incapable of speaking for over 20 years and found the lesion in the brain tissue that had caused the problem. The area of the brain that enables us to comprehend
(25) speech was located by Broca's contemporary Carl Wernicke in a similar way.

5. The author's statement about what "language" entails (lines 2–7) is made primarily by using

   (A) quotations
   (B) scientific data
   (C) generalizations
   (D) analogies
   (E) inferences

6. The question in the second paragraph chiefly serves to

   (A) present a scientific dilemma that has been resolved
   (B) suggest that there are some questions not being addressed by scientists
   (C) summarize an issue that is the subject of continued debate
   (D) outline the position of the author
   (E) introduce a topic that will be discussed for the rest of the passage

7. The author discusses the work of Broca and Wernicke in the third paragraph to illustrate the

   (A) method by which early discoveries were made about the brain and language
   (B) imprecision of the techniques of 19th-century scientists
   (C) extent to which the localization of speech in the brain is understood
   (D) study of language processing in the brain of normal patients
   (E) range of early neuroscientific ideas about where language is processed in the brain

8. Scientists are able to predict the occurrence of earthquakes with a reasonable degree of accuracy using a device called a seismograph. In 1990, scientists used a seismograph to predict that city X would experience a major earthquake in 1994. However, no major earthquake actually occurred.

Based only on the information above, which of the following statements is a valid conclusion?

(A) City X will probably experience a major earthquake in the next few years.

(B) Natural disasters are impossible for scientists to predict.

(C) Scientists are currently researching other ways of predicting earthquakes.

(D) Seismographic predictions are not always reliable.

(E) City X actually experienced a minor earthquake in 1994.

9. The media is really out of control. When the press gets a story, it seems that within minutes they have produced flashy moving graphics and sound effects to entice viewers and garner ratings. Real facts and unbiased coverage of an issue are totally abandoned in exchange for an overly sentimental or one-sided story that too often distorts the truth. Viewers need to learn to recognize real reporting from the junk on nearly every television channel these days.

The author would be most likely to agree with which of the following?

(A) newspapers should have more editorials

(B) flashy graphics add substance to television news reporting

(C) objective news reporting is a dying art

(D) television news anchors are valuable sources of information

(E) television news needs more human interest stories

GO ON TO THE NEXT PAGE

10. In computer design, the effectiveness of a program generally depends on the ability of the programmer. Still, remarkable progress has been made in the development of artificial intelligence. This progress has scientists wondering whether it will eventually be possible to develop a computer capable of intelligent thought. When a computer defeated Garry Kasparov, considered by many the greatest chess player of all time, it was taken to be a vindication of the claims of the strongest supporters of artificial intelligence. Despite this accomplishment, others argue that whereas computers may imitate the human mind, they will never possess the capacity for true intelligence.

The main idea of this passage is

(A) Computers can never learn to think.
(B) Chess is a game in which computers are superior.
(C) Great strides have been made in artificial intelligence.
(D) Artificial intelligence is a scientific miracle.
(E) Garry Kasparov is a great chess player.

Questions 11–12

Desert plants have evolved very special adaptations for living in extremely dry conditions. Most have small thick leaves, an *Line* adaptation that limits water loss by reducing (5) surface area relative to volume. During the driest months, some desert plants shed their leaves. Others, such as cacti, subsist on water the plant stores in its fleshy stems during the rainy season. Some send out long, deep (10) taproots in order to reach underlying water. Others have developed shallow, widespread root systems, which allow them to take advantage of very occasional but heavy rainfalls. Some plants have ways of actively (15) protecting their water supplies. The creosote bush, for instance, produces a powerful poison that discourages the growth of competing root systems.

11. Which of the following best tells what the passage is about?

(A) the discovery of stomates
(B) the process of photosynthesis
(C) how desert plants adapt to survive
(D) competition between plants in the desert
(E) the shortage of water in the desert

12. Which of the following weather conditions would most benefit plants with wide, shallow root systems?

(A) a prolonged drought
(B) a windstorm
(C) a light spring rain
(D) a winter snowfall
(E) a flash flood

GO ON TO THE NEXT PAGE

13. The actor who played the Tin Man in the movie "The Wizard of Oz" was not the first choice to play that role. Another actor was cast for the role but had to be replaced because he was allergic to the make-up for the role.

According to the given information, which statement must be true?

(A) The originally cast actor was generally considered a better actor than his replacement.

(B) Actors can be allergic to the make-up used in films.

(C) It is very unusual for actors to be allergic to make-up.

(D) The originally cast actor had to give up his acting career because of his unusual illness.

(E) The actor originally cast as the Tin Man would be rich and famous now if he had played that role.

14. When Babe Ruth was sold from the Boston Red Sox to the New York Yankees in 1920 for $100,000, most thought it was a bad trade. Few could have predicted that the Yankees, who had never before won a World Series, would go on to become the most successful franchise in sports history or that, inversely, the Red Sox, who had won the World Series five times before the Ruth trade, would never again win a World Series title. This change of luck, now often called "The Curse of the Bambino," is one of baseball's most colorful stories and one that is bound to continue until the Red Sox break the curse and win their first World Series title in over 80 years.

According to the passage, the Red Sox have won how many World Series titles?

(A) five
(B) seven
(C) two
(D) one
(E) none

GO ON TO THE NEXT PAGE

15. Local elementary schools have changed considerably over the past 50 years. Where once we had schools in every small town, now students bus for miles to attend larger, more advanced schools. Whereas most parents see this as a positive step for progress and education, some worry about their children losing touch with the simple things around them. A few have even decided to home school their children instead of sending them to nearby towns.

The author's tone in this passage is

(A) embittered
(B) informative
(C) biased
(D) ambivalent
(E) accusatory

Questions 16–19

Alchemy is the name given to the attempt to change lead, copper, and other metals into silver or gold. Today, alchemy is regarded as a
Line pseudoscience. Its associations with astrology
(5) and the occult suggest primitive superstition to the modern mind, and the alchemist is generally portrayed as a charlatan obsessed by dreams of impossible wealth. However, for many centuries, alchemy was a highly
(10) respected art. In the search for the elusive secret to making gold, alchemists helped to develop many of the apparatuses and procedures that are used in laboratories today. Moreover, the results of their experiments laid
(15) the basic conceptual framework of the modern science of chemistry.

The philosophy underlying the practice of alchemy emerged in similar forms in ancient China, India, and Greece. They
(20) regarded gold as the "purest" and "noblest" of all metals and believed that "base" metals such as copper and lead were only imperfectly developed forms of gold. With purification, the alchemists believed that
(25) base metals attained a state of perfection, just as human souls attained a perfect state in heaven.

In the 12th century, translations of Arabic works on alchemy started to become
(30) available in Europe, generating a new wave of European interest in the art. Ultimately, the possibility of making gold was conclusively disproved in the 19th century. Yet, this belief provided the basis for some of
(35) the most fascinating chapters in the history of science.

GO ON TO THE NEXT PAGE

16. Why are the alchemists not favorably regarded today?

    (A) Their secret techniques have mostly been forgotten.
    (B) The results of all their experiments were disproved.
    (C) The Europeans were not interested in an Eastern art form.
    (D) Their use of astrology seems superstitious to scientists.
    (E) Many of their apparatuses and procedures are out of date.

17. What did the alchemists believe about metals such as copper and lead?

    (A) They were imperfect forms of gold.
    (B) They were the noblest of all metals.
    (C) They consisted primarily of air and water.
    (D) They were heavier than other metals.
    (E) They originated in China, India, and Greece.

18. What does the passage imply about the process of "purifying" metals?

    (A) It was perfected by the Europeans.
    (B) It was distorted in translations of Arabic works.
    (C) The alchemists regarded it as a spiritual experience.
    (D) It was discovered in the 12th century.
    (E) Few people realized its commercial value.

19. With which of the following statements about alchemy would the author most likely agree?

    (A) Belief in alchemy delayed scientific progress for centuries.
    (B) Some of the principles of alchemy are still valid today.
    (C) Modern chemistry owes nothing to the achievements of the alchemists.
    (D) Though not a science, alchemy is an important part of scientific history.
    (E) Most alchemists wanted to produce gold only for their own financial benefit.

GO ON TO THE NEXT PAGE

20. For do-it-yourself types, the cost of getting regular oil changes seems unnecessary. After all, the steps are fairly easy as long as you are safe. First, make sure that the car is stationary and on a level surface. Always use the emergency brake to ensure that the car does not roll on top of you. Next, locate the drain plug for the oil under the engine. Remember to place the oil drain pan under the plug before you start. When it is drained fully, wipe off the drain plug and the plug opening, and then replace the drain plug. Next, simply place your funnel in the engine and pour in new oil. Be sure to return the oil cap when you're done. Finally, run the engine for a minute, and then check the dipstick to see if you need more oil in your engine.

According to the passage, immediately after draining the old oil from the engine, you should

(A) replace the oil cap

(B) run the engine for a moment, and check the dipstick

(C) wipe off and replace the drain plug

(D) engage the emergency brake

(E) make sure the car is stationary and on a level surface

Questions 21–22

Most people think that the Hula Hoop was a fad born in the 1950s, but in fact, people were doing much the same thing
Line with circular hoops made from grape vines
(5) and stiff grasses all over the ancient world. More than 3,000 years ago, children in Egypt played with large hoops of dried grapevines. The toy was propelled along the ground with a stick or swung around at the
(10) waist. During the 14th century, a "hooping" craze swept England and was as popular among adults as kids.

The word hula became associated with the toy in the early 1800s when British sailors
(15) visited the Hawaiian Islands and noted the similarity between hooping and hula dancing. In 1957, an Australian company began making wood rings for sale in retail stores. The item attracted the attention of
(20) Wham-O, a fledgling California toy manufacturer. The plastic Hula Hoop was introduced in 1958 and was an instant hit.

21. According to the passage, all of the following statements are true EXCEPT

(A) most people do not appreciate the ancient origins of the Hula Hoop

(B) the earliest prototypes of the Hula Hoop were made of grape leaves and stiff grasses

(C) early precursors of the Hula Hoop were only used by children

(D) the Hula Hoop was an early success for the toy company Wham-O

(E) the name of the Hula Hoop was partly inspired by a popular dance of the Hawaiian Islands

GO ON TO THE NEXT PAGE

22. The author's primary purpose in this passage is to

    (A) describe the way that fads like the Hula Hoop come and go
    (B) discuss the historical origins of the Hula Hoop
    (C) explain how the Hula Hoop got its name
    (D) question the reasons for the Hula Hoop's popularity
    (E) use the example of the Hula Hoop to illustrate a point about fads

23. According to a recent school survey, the number of students who regularly play after-school sports has increased by 50 percent in the last 10 years. It must be the increased interest in health and physical fitness among the students in our school that has massively reduced the amount of pizza purchased in the cafeteria.

    Which of the following, if true, most significantly weakens the inference above?

    (A) Most of the students who now play after-school sports do so only for social reasons.
    (B) School health teachers have time and again spoken about the importance of a low-fat diet.
    (C) Fifteen years ago, the school switched from requiring physical education to an optional program.
    (D) Not all students responded to the survey.
    (E) Pizza was never very popular in the cafeteria.

24. One of the most frequently used of all meters is iambic pentameter. An iamb is the name for a piece in two syllables with the stress on the second syllable. Pentameter refers to the number of feet or groupings of syllables. In this case, the foot is an iamb. William Shakespeare is perhaps the most famous writer of the iambic pentameter, having composed hundred of poems in this meter, popularizing it for the masses.

    According to the passage, a foot is

    (A) a grouping of syllables
    (B) similar to a meter
    (C) named after William Shakespeare
    (D) rarely used in poetry
    (E) none of the above

GO ON TO THE NEXT PAGE

Questions 25–26

Most life is fundamentally dependent on photosynthetic organisms that store radiant energy from the sun. The existence of
Line organisms that are not dependent on the
(5) sun's light has long been established, but until recently, they were regarded as anomalies. However, over the last 20 years, research in deep sea areas has revealed the existence of entire ecosystems in which the
(10) primary producers are bacteria that are dependent on energy from within the earth itself. Indeed, growing evidence suggests that these unique chemosynthetic ecosystems model the way in which life first came about
(15) on this planet.

25. This passage suggests that most life is ultimately dependent on what?

    (A) deep-sea hot springs
    (B) the world's oceans
    (C) bacterial microorganisms
    (D) light from the sun
    (E) chemosynthesis

26. Why is the ecosystem described in this passage called "unique"?

    (A) It has no need for an environmental source of energy.
    (B) It thrives in the absence of sunlight.
    (C) It exists in airless, waterless surroundings.
    (D) It is infested by dangerous octopods.
    (E) It is the only ecosystem found in deep ocean water.

27. It is often said that American involvement in World War I would not have begun in earnest were it not for the German sinking of the passenger ship the *Lusitania* on February 18, 1915. America had remained neutral before this incident. Until that time, America was offering only financial and tactical support for Britain and France against Germany and Austria-Hungary. However, the sinking of the huge passenger ship altered public opinion about U.S. involvement and subsequently led to military escalation, truly making the war a matter for the whole world.

The main idea of the passage is that

    (A) The Germans sank the *Lusitania* because of America's financial and tactical support for Britain and France.
    (B) Austria-Hungary and Germany were allies in World War I.
    (C) American involvement in World War I was minimal.
    (D) The sinking of the *Lusitania* prompted increased American involvement in World War I.
    (E) The German government was justified in sinking the *Lusitania*.

GO ON TO THE NEXT PAGE

28. It was without a sense of humor that the foreign ambassador responded to allegations that his driver had over 2,000 unpaid parking tickets. For a moment, it seemed as if he would perhaps go item by item to discount the allegation. Not only did he demand an apology for the way the story had been handled by the press, but he also insinuated that the incident might actually affect the two countries' relations in the future. One thing that was never addressed was the fact that the tickets have still not been paid.

The foreign ambassador would be most likely to

(A) support a resolution to grant diplomats immunity from parking tickets

(B) support a call for more police on the beat

(C) admit involvement in parking scams around the city

(D) return to his country if the tickets were paid

(E) use mass transit instead of his car

Questions 29–31

The dancer and choreographer Martha Graham is regarded as one of the outstanding innovators in the history of
Line dance. Trained in a variety of different
(5) international styles of dance, she set out in the mid-1920s to break away from the rigid traditions of classical ballet. She wanted to create new dance forms and movements that would reflect the changed atmosphere
(10) of the postwar period. Her early dances reflect this spirit.

She avoided decorative sets and costumes and used an all-female dance troupe. In fact, Graham's early work was so stark and severe
(15) that it was described by one critic as "uncompromisingly ugly." As the decades passed, Graham's work found wider acceptance. By the 1940s, it had already become the tradition against which a new
(20) avant-garde was rebelling; this is a fate common to all artistic revolutions.

29. Martha Graham introduced new dance techniques in order to

(A) attract attention to her all-female troupe

(B) visually dramatize the ugliness of life

(C) express the changed mood of her time

(D) strike a blow at the traditions of classical ballet

(E) emphasize the rigidity of conventional dance movement

GO ON TO THE NEXT PAGE

30. It can be inferred that classical ballet of the early 20th century generally

    (A) was loose and formless
    (B) was disliked by critics and the public
    (C) sought to dramatize ugliness
    (D) reflected the changing times
    (E) employed elaborate sets and costumes

31. The "fate common to all artistic revolutions" (lines 20–21) is best illustrated by which of the following?

    (A) a revolutionary method of painting that is eventually accepted but later rejected by innovative artists
    (B) a style of musical composition that ignores the rules of harmony and emphasizes dissonance and ugly sounds
    (C) a movement in fiction that focuses on the gritty aspects of everyday life rather than its beautiful aspects
    (D) a new trend in theatrical performance that becomes immensely popular but is soon forgotten
    (E) a technical innovation in cinematography that makes moviemaking much less expensive

32. Professional basketball will soon overtake Major League Baseball as America's favorite sport. Whereas baseball salaries skyrocket because of owners' willingness to overpay for top players, NBA salaries follow a system of paying players based on the number of years they have been in the league. This system rewards veterans and keeps players happy. The most recent infusion of international talent to the NBA has only broadened its marketability overseas. Previously untapped markets in places as far away as China, Japan, Russia, and Australia are now opening up to the NBA, thus giving NBA players even more leverage at the bargaining tables.

    According to the passage, the NBA's marketability will increase because

    (A) players are getting more money from owners
    (B) Major League Baseball is losing fans
    (C) international markets are opening up to the game
    (D) its system rewards veteran players
    (E) basketball owners do not overpay their top players

33. Despite a steady stream of pessimistic forecasts, our economy continues to grow and prosper. Over the last 15 years, the service sector of our economy has greatly expanded. Last year alone, 500,000 Americans found employment in the service sector. In the face of evidence such as this, one cannot argue that our economy is wilting.

Which of the following, if true, would most seriously undermine the conclusion drawn above?

(A) Many Americans who took jobs in the service sector last year were also offered jobs in other sectors of the economy.

(B) Most of the job growth in the service sector can be attributed to people forced out of the declining manufacturing sector.

(C) American society has developed many programs that greatly offset the consequences of a sluggish economy.

(D) Forty years ago, the American economy experienced a period of prosperity far greater than that of today.

(E) The importance of the service sector in determining the well-being of the overall American economy has decreased somewhat in the past 10 years.

Questions 34–38

All telescopes use curved lenses to focus the light from distant objects, such as stars. Generally, the larger a telescope is, the
Line greater its magnifying power. Two different
(5) kinds of lenses can be used. The first telescopes, made during the 16th century, were refractors. However, their perfectly round lenses did not focus light sharply. Lenses made of a single piece of glass also
(10) bent light of different colors differently, producing color distortions.

Meanwhile, the problems of refractors led some telescope makers to experiment with reflectors. They used mirrors that were
(15) not perfectly round so that light was sharply focused. Moreover, mirrors did not produce color distortions. But these early reflectors had other problems. They were made of polished metal, which did not reflect light
(20) well. Also, metal mirrors often cracked as they cooled after being cast.

For two hundred years, opticians worked to perfect both kinds of telescopes. Finally, in 1851, two Englishmen, Varnish and
(25) Mellish, found a way to cover glass with a very thin sheet of silver. This made it possible to build reflecting telescopes using a large curved mirror made of silver-covered glass. These telescopes reflected much more
(30) light than earlier reflectors and did not crack so easily. Today, nearly all large optical telescopes are built on this basic design.

GO ON TO THE NEXT PAGE

34. Which of the following best tells what this passage is about?

    (A) the design of modern telescopes
    (B) how the telescope was developed
    (C) the problems of early telescopes
    (D) the experiments of Varnish and Mellish
    (E) how lenses are made

35. The passage suggests that there is usually a relationship between the size of a telescope and its

    (A) ability to reflect light
    (B) magnifying power
    (C) resistance to cracking
    (D) accuracy in focusing light
    (E) ability to bend light of different colors equally

36. Which of the following was a problem of early refracting telescopes?

    (A) They did not transmit colored light.
    (B) They produced blurred images.
    (C) Their glass lenses cracked frequently.
    (D) They could not be used to view the stars.
    (E) They were made of colored glass.

37. Some early telescope makers experimented with reflecting telescopes because

    (A) refractors had not yet been invented
    (B) they did not need telescopes with great magnifying power
    (C) opticians had stopped working to build better refractors
    (D) early refractors produced distorted images
    (E) opticians had found a way to coat glass with silver

38. Telescope makers probably want to construct larger telescopes in order to

    (A) avoid the blurred images produced by small telescopes
    (B) be able to view a wider range of colors
    (C) enlarge the focused image for easier viewing
    (D) create a more polished metal surface
    (E) see farther into the universe

39. The jaguarundi is a species of cat native to Central and South America. Often referred to as the "otter cat," these creatures have short weasel-like ears and range in color from dark grey to brown. Jaguarundis are most often found in lowland habitats with good cover. They are solitary hunters who tend to roam the floor of the rainforest. As deforestation continues, these animals are in danger of losing their natural habitat. There has been some debate as to when the jaguarundis hunt. Although the bulk of data points to a diurnal, or daytime, hunting schedule, there is evidence that some jaguarundis adopt a crepuscular hunting schedule. These jaguarundis emerge to hunt in the twilight of dusk and dawn.

Which of the following can be inferred from the passage?

(A) Jaguarundis hunt only during dusk and dawn

(B) The vegetation on the floor of the rainforest aids jaguarundis in hunting

(C) Jaguarundis are distant cousins of otters

(D) Most jaguarundis are diurnal hunters who hunt at night

(E) Some jaguarundis are herbivorous

40. Louis "Satchmo" Armstrong was born in New Orleans in 1901. In his childhood, he earned money singing and playing music on street corners. He also worked on a junk wagon, cleaned graves, and sold coal—anything to make ends meet. As a self-taught cornet player entertaining on the streets of New Orleans, Armstrong caught the eye of Joe "King" Oliver, an established trumpet player in Kid Ory's band. Soon after he began to study with Oliver, Armstrong found a place in Ory's band and continued as a professional performer for the rest of his life. He popularized jazz and scat singing and influenced numerous musicians who came after him. His nickname "Satchmo" is short for "Satchelmouth." Apparently, Armstrong's mouth was nearly as big as his impact on jazz.

According to the passage, Armstrong was first noticed by an established musician

(A) selling coal as a youngster

(B) scat singing in Kid Ory's band

(C) playing the cornet on street corners

(D) earning the nickname "Satchmo"

(E) popularizing jazz with Joe "King" Oliver

STOP!

If you finish before time is up, you may go back and check your work.

Mathematics

Time—60 Minutes
40 Questions

Directions: Each of the questions below is followed by five answer choices. Select the choice that best answers the question and fill the corresponding oval on your answer sheet. Remember, try to answer every question. Note: Figures are drawn to scale unless otherwise indicated. All figures can be assumed to lie in a plane, and all lines can be assumed to be straight unless otherwise indicated.

1. Jackie puts 50 slips of paper into a hat. The slips of paper are numbered 1 through 50. If Jackie pulls a slip of paper out at random, what is the probability that the number on the slip will be a factor of 20?

   (A) $\frac{6}{50}$

   (B) $\frac{20}{50}$

   (C) $\frac{2}{50}$

   (D) $\frac{40}{50}$

   (E) $\frac{15}{50}$

2. You are packing boxes of shoes into crates. Each crate can hold 15 boxes. If you are packing the 63rd box, which crate are you currently filling?

   (A) third
   (B) fourth
   (C) fifth
   (D) sixth
   (E) seventh

3. Which of the following is LEAST?

   (A) $\frac{5}{8}$

   (B) $\frac{9}{16}$

   (C) $\frac{17}{32}$

   (D) $\frac{33}{64}$

   (E) $\frac{65}{128}$

4. If $\frac{2x}{3} - 1 = 11$, what does x equal?

   (A) 17
   (B) 18
   (C) 19
   (D) 20
   (E) 21

GO ON TO THE NEXT PAGE

5. The town of Spartaville is 500 km away from the town of Pleasantville. A map is drawn of the county to a scale of 1 cm = 2.5 km. How many centimeters apart are the two towns on the map?

   (A)   200
   (B)   500
   (C)   50
   (D) 1,000
   (E) 1,250

Budget for the Town of Magnolia

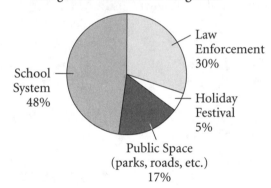

School System 48%
Law Enforcement 30%
Holiday Festival 5%
Public Space (parks, roads, etc.) 17%

6. The pie chart above shows the budget for the town of Magnolia this year. If the town spends $5,400 on Law Enforcement, what was the total budget?

   (A) $11,000
   (B) $16,000
   (C) $18,000
   (D) $30,000
   (E) $108,000

7. The average (arithmetic mean) of 9 numbers is 12. What is the sum of those numbers?

   (A)   18
   (B)   27
   (C)   108
   (D)   120
   (E)   1,008

a	b
$\frac{41}{70}$	$\frac{1}{3}$
$\frac{401}{700}$	$\frac{2}{9}$
$\frac{4,001}{7,000}$	$\frac{3}{27}$
$\frac{40,001}{70,000}$	$\frac{4}{81}$
$\frac{400,001}{700,000}$	$\frac{5}{243}$

8. Which of the following is true about the data shown above?

   (A) As a decreases, b decreases.
   (B) As a decreases, b increases.
   (C) As a decreases, b does not change.
   (D) As a increases, b does not change.
   (E) As a increases, b decreases.

9. Which of the following is equivalent to $8n - 15 > 49$?

   (A) $n > 15$
   (B) $8n > 34$
   (C) $n < 4$
   (D) $8n > 32$
   (E) $n > 8$

GO ON TO THE NEXT PAGE

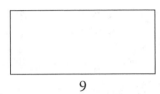

9

10. If the area of the rectangle above is 36, what is the perimeter?

(A)   4
(B)   13
(C)   18
(D) 26
(E)   81

11. If $3x + 3 = 6(y + 2)$, then $x - 2y =$

(A) $-\dfrac{1}{3}$
(B)   0
(C)   3
(D)   5
(E)   9

Questions 12–13 refer to the graph below.

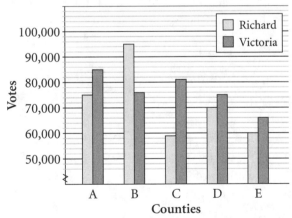

12. Based on the graph above, what is the ratio of counties Victoria won to the counties that Richard won?

(A)   1:4
(B) 20:17
(C)   4:5
(D)   4:1
(E) 17:20

13. Which two counties were won by the smallest difference in the number of votes?

(A) A and D
(B) A and E
(C) D and E
(D) C and D
(E) A and C

14. Bill has c cards in his baseball card collection. Jason has 25 more baseball cards than Bill. Charlie has one-fifth the number of baseball cards that Jason has. Which of the following represents the number of baseball cards that Charlie has?

(A) $\dfrac{c}{5} + 25$

(B) $c + 25 - 5$

(C) $(c + 25) \times 5$

(D) $\dfrac{c}{5} + 5$

(E) $25(c - 5)$

GO ON TO THE NEXT PAGE

15. Which of the following shows a right triangle whose area is 8 and whose right angle has a vertex that is located at (3, 4)?

(A)   (B)

(C)   (D)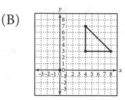

(E)

16.

> Peggy washes cars for 10 weeks during her summer vacation. It takes her about 1 hour to wash a car. She washes a total of 123 cars during her vacation. She earns $8 for every car that she washes.

Which of the following numbers are needed to calculate the total amount of money Peggy earns washing cars during her vacation?

(A) 10, 123, and 1
(B) 10, 123, and $8
(C) 10, 1, and $8
(D) 10, 1, 123, and $8
(E) 123 and $8

17. A vendor who only takes five-dollar bills is selling pizzas for $10 and sodas at 3 for $5. Nabila wants to buy 2 pizzas and 9 sodas for her friends. How many five-dollar bills will she need?

(A) 5
(B) 7
(C) 11
(D) 22
(E) 35

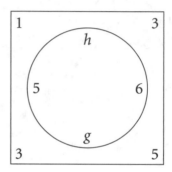

18. If the product of the numbers outside of the circle equals the sum of the numbers inside the circle, what does $g + h$ equal?

(A) 45
(B) 36
(C) 34
(D) 28
(E) 9

19. Which of the following does not have a remainder of 7 when divided into 163?

(A) 6
(B) 12
(C) 13
(D) 26
(E) 52

GO ON TO THE NEXT PAGE

20. Which of the following is greater than $\frac{13}{20}$?

    (A) 58%

    (B) $\frac{3}{5}$

    (C) 0.655

    (D) $\frac{5}{8}$

    (E) 0.074

21. Miguel cleaned $\frac{1}{4}$ of his room Saturday morning and $\frac{1}{6}$ of the room on Sunday. What is the ratio of the amount of the room he has cleaned to the amount that he has not cleaned?

    (A) 5:12
    (B) 5:7
    (C) 7:12
    (D) 7:5
    (E) 12:5

22. 1,400 divided by 70 is the same as 2 times

    (A)   1
    (B)   10
    (C)   100
    (D)   1,000
    (E)   10,000

23. Eighty percent of G is 352. What is G?

    (A)   44
    (B) 281.6
    (C) 428
    (D) 440
    (E) 633.6

24. If a, b, and c are all positive numbers, which of the following is always true?

    (A) $(a + b) \times c = a + (b \times c)$
    (B) $a - b - c = c - b - a$
    (C) $(a + b) + c = a + (c + b)$
    (D) $(a - b) + c = (b - a) + c$
    (E) $bc + a = ac + b$

25. The median of an odd list of numbers is the number that falls in the middle when the values are arranged in increasing order. In an even list, the median is the average of the two middle numbers. The mode of a list of numbers is the number that occurs the most number of times.

    $$\{25, 27, 27, 27, 32, 32, 42, 46, 46\}$$

    In the above set of numbers, what is the average of the median and mode?

    (A) 27
    (B) 29.5
    (C) 28.25
    (D) 35.5
    (E) 37

26. Approximately 19 percent of the voters voted for the independent candidate. If 212,822 people voted, which of the following could be the number of people who voted for the independent candidate?

    (A)   210
    (B)   2,200
    (C)   4,100
    (D)   41,000
    (E)   62,000

GO ON TO THE NEXT PAGE

27. Bruno and Mitch both run hotdog stands. On Friday afternoon, Bruno sold t hotdogs and received $20 in tips. Mitch sold $\frac{4}{5}$ as many hotdogs as Bruno and received $6 less in tips. If each man charges $2 for a hotdog, which of the following represents the number of dollars Mitch earned?

    (A) $\frac{4t}{5} - 6$

    (B) $\frac{4t}{5} + 6$

    (C) $\frac{8t}{5} + 14$

    (D) $\frac{8t}{5} + 26$

    (E) $\frac{t}{10} - 14$

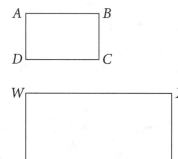

28. If rectangle $ABCD$ has an area of 12 square feet, which of the following is most likely the area of rectangle $WXYZ$?

    (A) 20
    (B) 24
    (C) 36
    (D) 48
    (E) 96

29. If $G = \frac{3}{H} + 4$, then $H =$

    (A) $\frac{G-4}{3}$

    (B) $\frac{G}{3-4}$

    (C) $\frac{3}{G-4}$

    (D) $\frac{G}{3} - 4$

    (E) $3(G-4)$

30. Which of the following is NOT equivalent to the others?

    (A) $18 \times 6 \times 7 \times 10$
    (B) $6^2 \times 70$
    (C) $2^2 \times 9 \times 7 \times 10$
    (D) $70 \times 12 \times 3$
    (E) $7 \times 10 \times 3^2 \times 4$

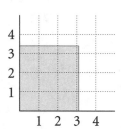

31. What is the approximate area of the shaded region in the figure shown above?

    (A) 9 square units
    (B) 9.5 square units
    (C) 10.5 square units
    (D) 11.75 square units
    (E) 12.5 square units

GO ON TO THE NEXT PAGE

32. A survey is taken of 25 people. Five people say that they own both a VCR and a DVD player, whereas 6 people say that they own neither. If 17 people own a VCR, how many own a DVD player?

    (A) 7
    (B) 9
    (C) 11
    (D) 15
    (E) 17

33. If $\boxed{\begin{smallmatrix}a\\b\end{smallmatrix}} = ab + \dfrac{b}{4}$, then $\boxed{\begin{smallmatrix}6\\8\end{smallmatrix}}$ is equal to

    (A) 14
    (B) 16
    (C) 24
    (D) 32
    (E) 50

34. On the first week of the year 2000, the twelfth week of the year, and every eleventh week thereafter, John washed his car. On the first week of the year 2000, the tenth week, and every ninth week thereafter, John went camping. How many weeks in 2000 did John both wash his car and go camping?

    (A) 0
    (B) 1
    (C) 2
    (D) 3
    (E) 4

35. A coat of paint is supposed to dry for 34 hours and 25 minutes, according to Marie's calculations. She finished painting at 8:36 P.M. At what time of day will the paint be dry?

    (A) 6:01 A.M.
    (B) 6:11 A.M.
    (C) 7:01 A.M.
    (D) 7:11 A.M.
    (E) 8:11 A.M.

36. Which of the following disproves the statement "If a number x is prime, $x + 1$ will not be prime"?

    (A) $x = 0$
    (B) $x = 1$
    (C) $x = 2$
    (D) $x = 3$
    (E) $x = 4$

37. $1, 1\frac{1}{2}, 2, 2\frac{1}{2}, 3, 3\frac{1}{2}, \ldots$

    In the sequence above, every number is $\frac{1}{2}$ more than the previous number. What is the difference between 42nd and 48th terms?

    (A) $1\frac{1}{2}$
    (B) $2\frac{1}{2}$
    (C) 3
    (D) 5
    (E) 6

38. All of John's cats are purebred.
Some of his cats like tuna fish.
Some of his cats like chicken.

Based on the above information, which of the following must be true?

(A) All cats like tuna fish.
(B) Some of John's cats like both tuna fish and chicken.
(C) All cats that like tuna fish are purebred.
(D) Some purebred cats like chicken.
(E) All of John's cats like either tuna fish or chicken.

39. What number is halfway between $\frac{2}{9}$ and $\frac{4}{5}$?

(A) $\frac{1}{4}$

(B) $\frac{13}{45}$

(C) $\frac{3}{7}$

(D) $\frac{23}{45}$

(E) $\frac{26}{45}$

40. How is 4,345,000,000 written in scientific notation?

(A) 0.4345×10^{10}
(B) 4.345×10^6
(C) 4.345×10^9
(D) 43.45×10^9
(E) $4,345 \times 10^6$

STOP!

If you finish before time is up, you may go back and check your work.

Writing

Time—60 Minutes
38 Questions and Essay

<u>Directions:</u> For each of the following questions, choose the best answer from the given choices and darken the corresponding oval.

The following sentences contain problems in grammar, usage, diction (choice of words), and idiom. Some sentences are correct. None of the sentences contains more than one error. The error, if there is one in the sentence, is underlined and lettered. Parts of the sentence that are not underlined are correct and cannot be changed. In selecting answers, follow the requirements of standard written English. If there is an error, choose the <u>one underlined part</u> that must be changed to make the sentence correct and fill in the corresponding oval on your answer grid.

If there is no error, fill in oval E.

1. <u>Squandering</u> his inheritance, the prodigal son
     A
   <u>felt no compunction</u> in <u>wasting</u> his <u>father's</u>
        B   C   D
   hard-earned fortune. <u>No error</u>
                    E

2. Although the piano <u>as we know it today</u> did
                   A
   not exist in his time, Bach <u>was writing</u>
                    B
   many pieces <u>that are</u> now frequently played
            C
   <u>on that instrument.</u> <u>No error</u>
      D   E

3. The chemist Sir Humphrey Davy was a friend
   <u>of the poet</u> William Wordsworth; <u>he</u> <u>would visit</u>
     A   B   C
   with several other guests <u>at</u> a tiny cottage in
                    D
   the English Lake District. <u>No error</u>
                    E

4. <u>Grading</u> research papers <u>over the years</u>, the
     A   B
   professor became expert <u>at recognizing</u>
                    C
   submissions that <u>have been plagiarized</u> or
                D
   inadequately documented. <u>No error</u>
                  E

5. <u>During</u> the military coup, the deposed prime
    A

    minister's property was <u>put up</u> for sale without
                      B

    <u>him</u> <u>having</u> any opportunity to object. <u>No error</u>
     C   D   E

6. The primary difference <u>between</u> the two
                       A

    positions advertised <u>is</u> <u>that</u> one is exciting;
                       B C

    <u>the other, boring.</u> <u>No error</u>
         D   E

7. <u>To conserve calories</u>, to promote digestion,
        A

    <u>or so that they are</u> less vulnerable to predators,
        B

    wild animals <u>rest</u> during <u>many of</u> their waking
               C   D

    hours. <u>No error</u>
         E

8. <u>It</u> did not occur to the interviewer <u>to ask</u> either
   A   B

    the job applicant <u>nor</u> his reference <u>whether</u>
                  C   D

    the applicant had completed the project he

    initiated. <u>No error</u>
           E

9. The Ivorian students <u>considered it</u> more
                    A

    disrespectful <u>to look</u> <u>directly into</u> an elder's eyes
                B   C

    than to refuse <u>to answer</u> a teacher's question.
                  D

    <u>No error</u>
      E

10. <u>Having</u> little concern for others, <u>as well as</u>
    A   B

    <u>a lack of</u> curiosity about the unknown,
      C

    <u>the woman</u> made an ineffectual teacher.
        D

    <u>No error</u>
      E

11. There <u>was</u> a huge public outcry <u>over</u> the cruel
       A   B

    methods <u>employed at</u> the animal pound, but
              C

    in the end, nothing came of <u>them</u>. <u>No error</u>
                         D   E

12. A pioneering scholar <u>of</u> anthropology, Ruth
                 A

    Benedict <u>was also</u> a spokesperson <u>against</u>
            B   C

    ethnic bigotry <u>which</u> recognized that cultures
              D

    influence ideas about gender. <u>No error</u>
                     E

13. <u>Not far from</u> the finest <u>remaining</u> examples of
    A   B

    Federal architecture <u>stands</u> a geometric
                 C

    structure <u>of</u> glass, steel, and chrome. <u>No error</u>
         D   E

GO ON TO THE NEXT PAGE

14. <u>Virtually</u> all of the members <u>who</u> attended the
      A   B
    meeting <u>agreed to</u> the president's viewpoint
              C
    on <u>the issue</u> of budgetary restraints. <u>No error</u>
          D   E

15. <u>Fewer</u> U.S. citizens are visiting Europe <u>as</u>
     A   B
    American currency dwindles in exchange

    value and prices <u>raise</u> <u>in</u> several European
                      C D
    countries. <u>No error</u>
              E

16. The first public school in North America,

    Boston Latin School, <u>begun</u> <u>teaching</u> <u>its</u>
                         A   B
    classical curriculum in 1635, one year <u>before</u>
                                       C
    Harvard University <u>was founded</u>. <u>No error</u>
                   D   E

17. <u>Of all</u> the disasters that occurred during the
      A
    movie's production, the death of the two stars

    <u>who</u> performed their own stunts <u>were</u> surely
     B   C
    <u>the worst</u>. <u>No error</u>
      D   E

18. There is no sense <u>in continuing</u> the research,
                        A
    now that the assumptions <u>on which</u> it
                             B
    <u>was based</u> <u>had been</u> disproved. <u>No error</u>
      C   D   E

19. The councilwoman could not understand

    how the mayor <u>could declare</u> that the city
                  A
    <u>is thriving</u> <u>when</u> the number of firms
      B   C
    declaring bankruptcy <u>increase</u> every month.
                      D
    <u>No error</u>
     E

GO ON TO THE NEXT PAGE

Directions: The following sentences test accuracy and effectiveness of expression. In selecting answers, follow the rules of standard written English; in other words, consider grammar, choice of words, sentence construction, and punctuation.

In each of the following sentences, a portion or all of the sentence is underlined. Under each sentence you will find five ways of phrasing the underlined portion. Choice A repeats the original underlined portion; the other four choices provide alternative phrasings.

Select the choice that best expresses the meaning of the original sentence. If the original sentence is better than any of the alternative phrasings, choose A; otherwise, select one of the alternatives. Your selection should construct the most effective sentence—clear and precise with no awkwardness or ambiguity.

20. Samuel Johnson's Dictionary, published in 1755, was neither the first in English nor the largest, but its quotations illustrating definitions made it the best for many decades.

    (A) was neither the first in English nor the largest
    (B) neither was it the first in English nor the largest
    (C) neither was the first in English nor the largest
    (D) neither was the first in English, and it was not the largest either
    (E) was neither the first in English, nor was it the largest

21. In the Middle Ages, when astronomical phenomena were poorly understood, the comets that seemed to portend military conflicts or other social crises.

    (A) the comets that seemed to portend
    (B) the comets seeming to portend
    (C) the comets seemed to portend
    (D) the comets apparently portending
    (E) and when the comets seemed to portend

22. Unusual numbers of playwrights and artists flourishing in the England of Shakespeare's time and the Italy of Michelangelo's day, when cultural conditions were particularly conducive to creativity.

    (A) flourishing in the England of Shakespeare's time
    (B) by flourishing in the England of Shakespeare's time
    (C) while flourishing in Shakespeare's England
    (D) flourished in the England of Shakespeare's time
    (E) having flourished in Shakespeare's England

23. During World War I, United States Army psychologists administered a forerunner of today's I.Q. tests, where it had directions that were given orally in acoustically poor and crowded rooms.

    (A) where it had directions that
    (B) whereby there were directions that
    (C) whose directions
    (D) and for it they had directions which
    (E) and it had directions which

GO ON TO THE NEXT PAGE

24. A dispute arose between Rimland and Heartland over the eastern provinces from which 20 years before a great many people <u>had emigrated</u>.

    (A) had emigrated
    (B) emigrated
    (C) had immigrated
    (D) immigrated
    (E) migrated

25. In an effort to sound like an expert, <u>the director's speech which was riddled with esoteric references</u> and specialized terms.

    (A) the director's speech which was riddled with esoteric references
    (B) the director's speech was riddled with esoteric references
    (C) the director delivered a speech riddled with esoteric references
    (D) his speech which was riddled with esoteric references
    (E) the speech of the director was riddled with esoteric references

26. <u>If the construction strike has not occurred,</u> the contractor would have had no difficulty in finishing the renovation of the restaurant on time.

    (A) If the construction strike has not occurred
    (B) If the construction strike would not have occurred
    (C) Had the construction strike not of occurred
    (D) Had it not been that the construction strike had occurred
    (E) Had it not been for the construction strike

27. Even though the senators on the committee <u>were reluctant to schedule</u> a formal inquiry, they went on record as favoring one.

    (A) were reluctant to schedule
    (B) were reluctant as far as scheduling
    (C) were reluctant in scheduling
    (D) have been reluctant at scheduling
    (E) have had reluctance to schedule

28. Mary Cassatt, an American painter strongly influenced by French <u>impressionism, she also responded</u> to Japanese paintings exhibited in Paris in the 1890s.

    (A) impressionism, she also responded
    (B) impressionism, also responded
    (C) impressionism, also responding
    (D) impressionism, nevertheless, she responded
    (E) impressionism before responding

29. The choreographer Katherine Dunham <u>having trained as an anthropologist, she studied</u> dance in Jamaica, Haiti, and Senegal and developed a distinctive dance method.

    (A) having trained as an anthropologist, she studied
    (B) was a trained anthropologist, having studied
    (C) was a trained anthropologist and a student of
    (D) was a trained anthropologist who studied
    (E) training as an anthropologist, she studied

30. The few surviving writings of Greek philosophers before Plato <u>are not only brief and obscure but also figurative</u> at times.

    (A) are not only brief and obscure but also figurative

    (B) are not only brief and obscure, they can be figurative too,

    (C) not only are brief and obscure but also figurative

    (D) while not only brief and obscure, they also are figurative

    (E) being not only brief and obscure, are also figurative

31. <u>In 1891, the Chace Copyright Act began protecting British authors, until then</u> American publishers could reprint British books without paying their writers.

    (A) In 1891, the Chace Copyright Act began protecting British authors, until then

    (B) The Chace Copyright Act began, in 1891, protecting British authors, whom, until then

    (C) Although the Chace Copyright Act began to protect British authors in 1891, until which time

    (D) Before 1891, when the Chace Copyright Act began protecting British authors,

    (E) Finally, the Chace Copyright Act began protecting British authors in 1891, however, until then

32. Theorists of extraterrestrial intelligence depend on astronomical observations, chemical research, <u>and they draw inferences about nonhuman biology</u>.

    (A) and they draw inferences about nonhuman biology

    (B) while they infer biologically about nonhuman life

    (C) and biologically infer about nonhuman life

    (D) as well as drawing inferences biologically about nonhuman life

    (E) and biological inferences about nonhuman life

33. Even after becoming blind, <u>the poet John Milton's daughters took dictation of his epic poem *Paradise Lost*</u>.

    (A) the poet John Milton's daughters took dictation of his epic poem *Paradise Lost*

    (B) the poet John Milton's daughters taking dictation, his epic poem *Paradise Lost* was written

    (C) the epic poem *Paradise Lost* was dictated by the poet John Milton to his daughters

    (D) the epic poem *Paradise Lost* was dictated to his daughters by the poet John Milton

    (E) the poet John Milton dictated his epic poem *Paradise Lost* to his daughters

GO ON TO THE NEXT PAGE

34. Initiated in 1975, <u>sandhill cranes must unwittingly cooperate in the conservationists' project to raise</u> endangered whooping crane chicks.

    (A) sandhill cranes must unwittingly cooperate in the conservationists' project to raise

    (B) sandhill cranes' unwitting cooperation is required in the conservationists' project to raise

    (C) the conservationists require that sandhill cranes unwittingly cooperate in their project of raising

    (D) the conservationists require sandhill cranes to cooperate unwittingly in their project to raise

    (E) the conservationists' project requires the unwitting cooperation of sandhill cranes in raising

35. <u>The journalist lived and conversed with the guerrilla rebels and he</u> was finally accepted as an informed interpreter of their cause.

    (A) The journalist lived and conversed with the guerrilla rebels and he

    (B) The journalist living and conversing with the guerrilla rebels, and he

    (C) The journalist, who lived and conversed with the guerrilla rebels,

    (D) The journalist's having lived and conversed with the guerrilla rebels,

    (E) While living and conversing with the guerrilla rebels, the journalist

36. Modern dance and classical ballet help strengthen concentration, tone muscles, <u>and for creating a sense of poise</u>.

    (A) and for creating a sense of poise

    (B) thereby creating a sense of poise

    (C) and the creation of a sense of poise

    (D) and create a sense of poise

    (E) so that a sense of poise is created

37. Historians of literacy encounter a fundamental <u>obstacle, no one can know for certain</u> how many people could read in earlier centuries.

    (A) obstacle, no one can know for certain

    (B) obstacle; no one can know for certain

    (C) obstacle; no one being able to know for certain

    (D) obstacle; none of whom can know with certainty

    (E) obstacle and no one can know for certain

38. With his plays, George Bernard Shaw tested the limits of British <u>censorship; the purpose being to</u> make audiences aware of social inequities.

    (A) censorship; the purpose being to

    (B) censorship and the purpose was to

    (C) censorship, with the purpose to

    (D) censorship; so that he could

    (E) censorship to

GO ON TO THE NEXT PAGE

SAMPLE DIRECTIONS FOR THE WRITTEN ASSIGNMENT

This section of the test consists of a written assignment. You are asked to prepare a written response of about 300–600 words on the assigned topic. *The assignment can be found on the next page.* You should use your time to plan, write, review, and edit what you have written for the assignment.

Read the assignment carefully before you begin to write. Think about how you will organize what you plan to write. You may use any blank space provided on the following pages to make notes, write an outline, or otherwise prepare your response. *However, your score will be based solely on the response you write in the space provided on pages 3, 4, 5, and 6 in the answer document.*

Your response to the written assignment will be evaluated based on your demonstrated ability to:

- Comprehend and focus on a unified, controlling topic
- Select and use a strategy of expression that is appropriate for the intended audience and purpose
- Present a reasoned, organized argument or exposition
- Use support and evidence to develop and bolster your ideas and account for the views of others
- Express yourself clearly and without distractions caused by inattention to sentence and paragraph structure, choice and use of words, and mechanics (i.e., spelling, punctuation, and capitalization)

Your response will be evaluated based on your demonstrated ability to express and support opinions, not on the nature or content of the opinions expressed. The final version of the response should conform to the conventions of edited American English. This should be your original work, written in your own words, and not copied or paraphrased from some other work.

Be sure to write about the assigned topic and use multiple paragraphs. Please write legibly. You may not use any reference materials during the test. Remember to review what you have written and make any changes you think will improve your response.

GO ON TO THE NEXT PAGE

WRITTEN ASSIGNMENT

There has been much research and evidence presented that schools are not providing an equal eduction for boys and girls. Among other things, it has been shown that teachers call on boys more often, allow boys to call out answers while requiring girls to raise their hands, allow boys more time to respond to questions, and give boys more feedback.

You do not need to agree or disagree with the above statements, but do elaborate with examples on both sides of the issue (equal versus unequal treatment of girls and boys), and state examples of things teachers can do to alter this situation.

STOP!

If you finish before time is up, you may go back and check your work.

Practice Test Two (PPST)
Answers and Explanations

READING		MATHEMATICS		WRITING		
1. B	21. C	1. A	21. B	1. E	14. C	27. A
2. A	22. B	2. C	22. B	2. B	15. C	28. B
3. E	23. A	3. E	23. D	3. B	16. A	29. D
4. A	24. A	4. B	24. C	4. D	17. C	30. A
5. C	25. D	5. A	25. B	5. C	18. D	31. D
6. C	26. B	6. C	26. D	6. D	19. D	32. E
7. A	27. D	7. C	27. C	7. B	20. A	33. E
8. D	28. A	8. A	28. D	8. C	21. C	34. E
9. C	29. C	9. E	29. C	9. E	22. D	35. C
10. C	30. E	10. D	30. A	10. E	23. C	36. D
11. C	31. A	11. C	31. C	11. D	24. A	37. B
12. E	32. C	12. D	32. A	12. D	25. C	38. E
13. B	33. B	13. C	33. E	13. E	26. E	
14. A	34. B	14. D	34. B			
15. B	35. B	15. A	35. C			
16. D	36. B	16. E	36. C			
17. A	37. D	17. B	37. C			
18. C	38. C	18. C	38. D			
19. D	39. B	19. A	39. D			
20. C	40. C	20. C	40. C			

READING EXPLANATIONS

Cat Passage: Questions 1–2

1. B

The correct answer choice to this main idea question is (B). The passage briefly touches on the history of domestic cats, from the time of ancient Egypt when they were viewed as household gods through to the Middle Ages when they were slaughtered by superstitious Christians along with pagans, heretics, and Jews. Thus, the title, "From Gods to Outcasts: The Early History of the Domestic Cat" covers all of these areas. If the correct answer does not jump out at you, you can always eliminate wrong answer choices. (A) is wrong because the passage is clearly about domestic cats not ancient Egyptian deities. Choice (C) is too narrow, given that the passage begins in ancient Egypt. Choice (D) is out because dogs are never mentioned in the passage. Finally, (E) is out because the goddess Artemis is only briefly mentioned in the passage.

2. A

This inference question requires a little more inferring than most. You are told that after cats were slaughtered in the Middle Ages, the absence of cats probably "contributed to the spread and the severity of the bubonic plague that devastated the continent." Why would this be the case? The logical inference is that the rodent population must have increased, and rodents helped to spread the bubonic plague.

You could also have eliminated wrong answer choices. It certainly does not make sense that cats are a vengeful species (B)—whatever revenge cats wrought was not deliberate on their part. There's nothing in the passage to indicate that Greek merchants sold domestic cats "for large sums of money," (C), and it doesn't follow that the bubonic plague could be spread through cats, given that their absence, not their presence, precipitated the

plague. Finally, just because cats were slaughtered along with pagans, heretics, and Jews, that does not necessarily mean that they were "especially popular house pets" with these groups, as (E) states.

3. E

The tone of this passage is guardedly optimistic, or (E). Frequently, the correct answer on tone questions is qualified. PRAXIS passages tend to steer clear of overly negative or positive tones. In this passage, the numbers of hungry people are going down but not as quickly as initially anticipated. Also, for things to proceed in that positive direction, global grain production will have to continue to increase over the years. All of this inspires a tone of guarded optimism.

4. A

This problem is a great example for why you should read the question before the passage. If you knew to only look for the bodily function least essential to immediate survival, you would have noticed the answer in the first sentence and only skimmed the rest of the passage and saved a lot of time. Because the body can survive without food longer than it can survive without drinking, (B), or breathing, (C), eating is the least essential to survival. Choice (A) is correct. (D) is incorrect because blood circulation is mentioned in regards to breathing, which is more essential to survival than eating. (E) is incorrect because sleeping is never mentioned in the passage. It's essential that you answer questions based entirely on what you see in the passage. Never rely on outside knowledge to answer a question.

Language Ability Passage: Questions 5–7

This science passage shouldn't present too many difficulties for the reader who knows better than to get bogged down in the wealth of information presented in a typical science passage. When you first read the passage, instead of trying to take it all in, you should work on just getting a general sense of the structure of the passage and the broad themes under discussion.

The first paragraph introduces the main idea of the passage, which is that language separates humans from animals.

5. C

This is a line reference question, so reread the sentence in question. It's easy to see that the author here is not using *quotations* (A) or *scientific data* (B). Nor is she using *analogies* (D) or *inferences* (E). Phrases such as "to discuss and debate ideas" arc *generalizations* (C), however.

6. C

The question that begins paragraph two serves to introduce and summarize the debate that is unsettled and therefore continuing. (A), (B), and (D) are flat out wrong, and (E) is off because the topic shifts in the middle of the next paragraph.

7. A

Scan for the reference to Broca and Wernicke in the third paragraph, and reread this portion to figure out its relevance to the passage. As the passage notes, much of the information about the brain's acquisition of language comes from their studies. In other words, the author discusses the work of Broca and Wernicke to illustrate the method by which early discoveries were made about the brain and language (A).

8. D

There isn't much that you can conclude from the information in the question stem except that the earthquake that was predicted by seismograph didn't occur, which shows that seismographs aren't always correct in their predictions. This makes (D) the correct answer. There is no reason to think, at least as far as you know, that the earthquake is still coming (A) or that there was a minor earthquake instead of

the predicted major one (E), although both are of course possible. (B) is far too harsh an indictment of scientists based on the failure of one prediction, and there is no evidence to support (C).

9. C

For inference questions, you should read the entire passage, and it is often best to attack each answer choice and eliminate those that do not follow from the passage. (A) clearly contradicts the author's words. The author is not likely to agree that news anchors are valuable sources of information, choice (D), but that only "real reporters" are. (A) goes beyond the scope of the passage and may or may not be true based on what you have read. The correct answer will be something that must be true based on what's given, like choice (C).

10. C

The correct choice for a main idea question will express what the author believes. The passage states that remarkable progress has been made in artificial intelligence, so choice (C) is correct. Whereas the author discusses the difference of opinion between those who believe that there will eventually be a computer capable of intelligent thought and those who do not, he does not assert the truth of either statement, so choice (A) is incorrect. Be wary of answers such as (D) that use extreme language. Chess is not the main focus of the passage, so (B) and (E) are incorrect.

Desert Plants Passage: Questions 11–12

This passage is a science passage about desert plants and how they adapt to their environment. It also describes a variety of different ways in which plants adapt to the shortage of water in the desert.

11. C

The first sentence of the passage indicates what it's about—the "special adaptations" that desert plants have made for "living in extremely dry conditions."

(A) and (B) are topics pertaining to plants but are not mentioned in the passage. Competition (D) is only one aspect of how plants survive, and shortage of water in the desert (E) is only discussed in reference to desert plants.

12. E

Once again, we're told that wide, shallow root systems help plants adjust to "occasional, but heavy rainfalls" (lines 13–14). Choice (E), a flash flood, fits this description best.

13. B

Let's review the facts. The original Tin Man couldn't play the part because he was allergic to makeup, so he was replaced by another actor. The only conclusion you can draw from this is that it is possible for an actor to be allergic to the makeup used in films (B). We don't know which actor was better, how unusual this allergy is, what subsequently happened to the original actor, or what would have happened had he played the role, so none of the other choices has to be true.

14. A

This is a very straightforward detail question, so just be careful to locate the information to answer the question. The question asks how many World Series titles have been won by the Red Sox, and the passage states that before the Ruth trade, the Red Sox had won the series five times but never won another title since. So the Red Sox won a total of five World Series titles, choice (A).

15. B

Remember that in tone questions, the answers tend to be from the less extreme of the choices. Choice (B) is correct because the passage merely conveys relevant facts about an issue. Whereas the author does describe two opposing reactions that parents have had to the changes in elementary schools, no preference is implied. Therefore, choices (A), (C), and (E) are incorrect. Be cautious with choices such as these that use extreme language.

Alchemy Passage: Questions 17–19

This is a social studies passage about alchemy, the ancient science of trying to turn various different metals into gold. Paragraph 1 emphasizes the historical importance of alchemy—even though it seems ridiculous to the modern mind, we're told that alchemy helped lay the basic framework for the science of chemistry. Paragraph 2 describes the philosophy behind alchemy—the idea was that "base" metals such as copper and lead were just "imperfect" and could somehow be "purified" and turned into gold. Paragraph 3 gives us some more history—Europeans were interested in alchemy as early as the 12th century.

16. D

Lines 3–6 describe the reputation of alchemists today—we're told that alchemy's associations with astrology suggest "primitive superstition" to the modern mind. (A) goes against the gist of the passage, which suggests overall that historians know a lot about alchemy. (B) is a detail from paragraph 3 where we're told that the alchemists' idea of making gold was disproved. That just stopped people from trying to make gold—it wasn't responsible for the unfavorable reputation of alchemists today. (C) is contradicted in paragraph 3. (E) distorts paragraph 1 where it's stated that alchemists helped develop modern "apparatuses and procedures."

17. A

Copper and lead are discussed in paragraph 2. Lines 21–23 indicate that the alchemists believed they were "only imperfectly developed forms of gold."

18. C

The "purification" process is described in paragraph 2; toward the end of the paragraph, we're told that "metals attained a state of perfection just as souls attained perfection in heaven."

You can infer from this that the alchemists regarded the process as a spiritual experience—

choice (C). Europeans (A) are not mentioned in connection with purification. No distortion of Arabic works (B) is stated or implied. The 12th century (D) is described as the time when alchemy became widespread in Europe, so presumably the purification process was first attempted earlier. (E) is a big distortion—alchemists were clearly aware that they were trying to make gold, the most valuable of metals.

19. D

The author sums up his point of view on alchemy at the end of the passage—although not practiced today, alchemy "provided the basis for some of the most fascinating chapters in the history of science." (A) and (C) are wrong because the passage argues that alchemy did contribute to the development of science. (E) is a point of view that the author contradicts in paragraph 1. (B) distorts the points; sure, the alchemists left us some valuable apparatuses and procedures, but their basic principles have been disproved.

20. C

For sequence questions, look up the answer in the text. According to the passage, when the engine is fully drained, you should wipe off the drain plug and replace it, choice (C).

Hula Hoop Passage: Questions 21–22

21. C

This is an EXCEPT question focusing on the explicit details of the passage. Each of the incorrect answers will include a fact or point made during the passage. The correct answer will be the one choice that distorts or contradicts the facts described in the passage.

(A) and (B) are both discussed in the first sentence of the first paragraph. Choice (D) is discussed in the last two sentences of the second paragraph. Choice (E) is discussed in the first sentence of the second paragraph where "British sailors visited the Hawaiian Islands and noted the similarity between 'hooping' and hula dancing."

Only choice (C) is not discussed in the passage. In fact, (C) is contradicted in the last sentence of the first paragraph where the popularity of "hooping" among adults in the 14th century is described.

22. B

This question asks you to determine why the author wrote this passage. Only choice (B) is right in line with the scope and topic of the passage, which are the historical origins of the Hula-Hoop.

(A) and (E) are too broad in scope for this passage. It is about the Hula-Hoop, not about fads in general. Choice (C) is discussed in the passage, but it is too narrow in focus to address the passage as a whole. Last, (D) misses the mark because the Hula-Hoops popularity is never questioned in the passage.

23. A

Two assumptions hold this argument together. First, the author decides that the survey means that that the student body has become more interested in physical fitness. Then she decides that this is what has reduced the buying of pizza in the cafeteria. So, we'll look for a choice that suggests that either increased participation in after-school sports or reduced purchasing of pizza could be attributed to factors other than these. We get the former in (A). If most students join intramural sports for social reasons, then this majority isn't playing sports because of increased interest in physical fitness, and this destroys the author's primary assumption. (B) would strengthen the author's argument because it sums up her second assumption. If the students had really become more interested in physical fitness due to their health teachers' influence, the author would be justified in asserting that such interest was a factor in the decrease in pizza sales. (C) lists the change in physical education guidelines made 15 years ago. The survey compares the number of students playing intramural sports in the last 10 years, and the author is implicitly speaking of the last decade. (D) tries to attack the author's evidence, positing that not all students responded to the survey, but a survey only needs a sufficient representative sample. (E) takes us way out of the ballpark—who said pizza was ever very popular? All we know is its sales have been massively reduced. The answer is (A).

24. A

To answer this detail question, scan the passage for a reference to foot or feet. The first such mention is in the third sentence, which states: "Pentameter refers to the number of feet or groupings of syllables." Clearly, then, a foot is just that, a grouping of syllables, choice (A).

Underwater Ecosystems Passage: Questions 25–26

This is a science passage about underwater ecosystems that explains that most ecosystems on our planet depend on the light of the sun. Through the process of photosynthesis, the sun provides energy for plants and algae, which in turn provide energy for animals higher up the food chain. However, toward the end of the paragraph, we're told that a new type of ecosystem has been discovered in deep sea areas where the first link in the food chain is provided by bacteria that are dependent on energy from within the earth itself.

25. D

Lines 1–3 provide the answer here; we're told that "most life is fundamentally dependent on photosynthetic organisms that store radiant energy from the sun." So, it's light from the sun (D), not bacterial microorganisms (C), that powers most life on earth.

26. B

The paragraph describes the contrast that makes the chemosynthetic ecosystems "unique"—most life on earth depends on the sun's energy, but chemosynthetic ecosystems depend on energy provided from within the earth itself. Choice (B) expresses this idea best. (A) distorts the passage—it's not that chemosynthetic ecosystems have no need for a source of energy. (C) is illogical—these deep sea ecosystems are plainly not airless and waterless. (D) is not mentioned as a feature that

makes chemosynthetic ecosystems unique, and we're not told if these are the only ecosystems found at these depths (E).

27. D

This is a main idea question, so reading the passage for details is not necessary, although paying attention to the overall effect of those details is. The author notes that public opinion on the war was swayed when the *Lusitania* was attacked, prompting increased military involvement from the U.S. Choice (D) is a paraphrase of this main idea. Of the wrong answer choices, (A) is out because it distorts a detail found in the passage, implying a causal link between America's support for Britain and France and Germany's sinking of the *Lusitania* that is not supported by the passage. Choice (B) refers to a minor detail in the passage, and choice (C) is simply not true according to the passage, particularly after the sinking of the *Lusitania*. Whether the German government was justified in sinking the *Lusitania* is never discussed within the passage, so (E) is out as well.

28. A

This question asks you to infer what the foreign ambassador might do in a given situation. From the details given, one can see the ambassador as a man who expects certain favors and protests loudly when those favors are not granted. Thus, of the choices given, (A) makes the most sense because the ambassador clearly does not feel parking tickets should apply to diplomats.

Martha Graham Passage: Questions 29–31

This is a humanities passage about the great American dancer Martha Graham. Paragraph 1 gives us some background on Graham's approach—we're told she wanted to break away from the conventions of classical ballet and create new dance forms for the postwar period. Paragraph 2 describes her characteristic style—stark and severe to some, "uncompromisingly ugly" to others.

29. C

Paragraph 1 puts Graham's approach in context—we're told that she wanted to create "new dance forms and movements that would reflect the changed atmosphere of the postwar period." (C) fits the bill here. (A) and (B) touch on minor elements of Graham's style. Choices (D) and (E) exaggerate Graham's reaction against classical ballet; Graham was fed up with classical ballet, so she decided to invent a new dance form that she felt was more appropriate for the period, but she didn't set out to destroy the ballet tradition (D) or just parody it (E).

30. E

Paragraph 2 contrasts classical ballet with Graham's new style of dance. We're told that she avoided "decorative sets and costumes" and using an "all-female dance troupe." You can infer from this that classical ballet of the time did use elaborate sets and costumes. Choices (A) through (D) all describe Graham's style and how it was received.

31. A

The line "The tradition against which a new avant-garde was rebelling" is the fate the author's referring to. In other words, whereas Graham's work was revolutionary in the twenties, it had become quite acceptable by the forties, with the result that younger dancers and choreographers were rebelling against it. Choice (A) describes this chain of events.

32. C

Don't try to overanalyze on a detail question. They are straightforward, and to find the answer, you need only to check the text, which says, "the recent infusion of international talent has ... broadened its marketability overseas," which is paraphrased in choice (C). Whereas (A), (D), and (E) are mentioned in the passage, they are used as evidence for the assertion that basketball will overtake baseball as America's favorite sport. (B) is not mentioned.

33. B

The conclusion here is that the U.S. economy continues to grow and prosper. As evidence, the author cites the expansion over the last 15 years of the service sector, where last year alone 500,000 Americans found employment. She assumes that this growth correlates to growth in the economy. What if declines in other sectors offset the growth in service? If, as correct choice (B) says, growth in the service sector can be at least partly attributed to a decline in the manufacturing and heavy industry sectors, then growth in the service sector can't be a reliable indicator of growth in the overall economy.

(A) tends to support the conclusion—job offers imply health, contributing to a sense that the economy isn't in bad shape. (C) doesn't do much to affect the author's conclusion. Just because the American economy isn't sluggish, doesn't mean it's growing and prospering. (D) can be eliminated because the author is claiming that the American economy is prospering—she isn't claiming that it's prospering more than ever. Finally, (E) weakens the argument a bit, suggesting that some of the evidence for the claim of economic growth and health isn't as central as the author believes. However, using the service sector as a barometer of economic growth may be valid, regardless of the doubt (E) casts on how much of that growth is caused by the service sector. Because (E)'s ability to weaken the argument is dubious while (B)'s is certain, it's (B) for this question.

Telescope Passage: Questions 34–38

This passage is a science passage about telescopes. Paragraph 1 describes how telescopes work and tells us about the first refractor telescopes and the problems scientists had in producing a focused image. Paragraph 2 describes the first reflectors developed and details their problems. Paragraph 3 talks about how the basic telescope design used today was finally developed.

34. B

The passage describes several stages in the development of the modern telescope. So really the passage is about how the telescope was developed—choice (B). (A) and (D) describe paragraph 3 only. (C) describes paragraphs 1 and 2 only. How lenses are made (E) isn't really discussed anywhere in the passage.

35. B

The second sentence of the passage states that, "Generally, the larger a telescope is, the greater its magnifying power." Lines 19–20 suggest that both a telescope's ability to reflect light (A) and its resistance to cracking (C) are related to the quality of its mirror, not the mirror's size. Lines 14–16 show that accuracy in focusing light (D) was achieved, regardless of the telescope's size, by "using mirrors that were not perfectly round." Paragraph 1 states that color distortions—bending different colors of light differently (E)—were caused by single layers of glass, not the size.

36. B

Paragraph 1 describes the problems of refractors—they didn't "focus light sharply," and they produced "color distortions." Choice (B) hits on the first problem. (A) is an exaggeration—the passage doesn't say that the refractors didn't transmit colored light at all. (C) describes a reflector problem. There's no evidence for (D), and (E) is not presented in the passage as a problem.

37. D

Lines 9–11 describe why scientists moved on to experimenting with reflectors—there were too many problems with refractors. Refractors produced distorted images (a major problem in a telescope), as correct choice (D) suggests. (A) is wrong because refractors had been invented—it's just that they didn't work. Lack of magnifying power (B) is not mentioned as a problem. (C) is nonsense, and silver-coating (E) wasn't invented until later in 1851.

38. C

Lines 1–3 indicate the advantages of building large telescopes; "generally, the larger a telescope is, the greater its magnifying power." You can infer from this that larger telescopes are produced in order to enlarge the focused image for easier viewing—choice (C).

39. B

The passage states that jaguarundis are hunters who use the cover provided by the rainforest to hunt. The passage also states that as deforestation continues, these animals are in danger of losing their natural habitat. These two facts lead to the inference that the vegetation on the floor of the rainforest aids the jaguarundi in hunting, (B). (A) is a distortion. There is evidence that some jaguarundi hunt during the dusk and dawn, but it also states that the majority of data suggests that they hunt during the day. (C) is off target. Although they are called "otter cats," that does not imply that they are related to otters. (D) contradicts the passage that defines diurnal as hunting during the day. (E) is far afield. There is no mention of jaguarundis eating plants, and they are only described as hunters in the passage.

40. C

According to the passage, Armstrong caught the eye of Joe "King" Oliver while playing the cornet on the streets of New Orleans, so (C) is correct. Whereas he did sell coal as a youngster, (A), no established musician took note of him doing so. He joined Kid Ory's band after he was noticed by Oliver, so (B) is out. (D) is a distractor that focuses on the side note about Armstrong's nickname. (E) is out because it was Oliver who noticed Armstrong. By the time Armstrong was playing with Oliver, he had already been noticed.

MATHEMATICS EXPLANATIONS

1. A

This question tests probability, as well as factors. The factors of 20 are 1, 2, 4, 5, 10, and 20. There are six factors. Probability is determined as the ratio of desired outcomes to the number of total possible outcomes. Because the desired outcomes are the factors of 20 and the total possible outcomes are all numbers from 1 to 50, the probability is $\frac{6}{50}$.

2. C

The question asks for the number of the crate that is currently being filled. This is equal to the number of crates that are completely filled plus one. Because each crate holds 15 boxes of shoes, the 60th box completes the fourth crate. This means that the 63rd box is going into the fifth crate.

3. E

This question requires you to compare fractions whose denominators are different and determine which one is least. Compare the fractions one by one using a common denominator. For instance, to compare $\frac{5}{8}$ to $\frac{9}{16}$, use the common denominator of 16. Thus, we compare $\frac{10}{16}$ to $\frac{9}{16}$ and determine that (B) is smaller. Then, compare (B) to (C), $\frac{9}{16}$ to $\frac{17}{32}$, or $\frac{18}{32}$ to $\frac{17}{32}$. So (C) is smaller. (D) $\frac{33}{64}$ is smaller than (C) $\frac{34}{64}$. Finally, (E) $\frac{65}{128}$ is smaller than (D) $\frac{66}{128}$.

4. B

This is a basic one variable algebra problem. Your task is to isolate the variable. The first step is to add 1 to each side. This operation yields $\frac{2x}{3} = 12$. Next, multiply both sides by 3: $2x = 36$. Finally, divide both sides by 2: $x = 18$.

5. A

Use a proportion to determine the distance on the map. The relationship between map and actual kilometers is given in the scale 1 cm = 2.5 km. The ratio is always the same. So $\frac{1 \text{ cm}}{2.5 \text{ km}} = \frac{x \text{ cm}}{500 \text{ km}}$. Cross-multiply and solve for the number of centimeters, 200.

6. C

This pie chart shows part\whole relationships by percent. The budget for Law Enforcement is 30% of the whole budget. Therefore, $5,400 is 30% of the whole budget. Set up the proportion $\frac{30}{100} = \frac{\$5,400}{?}$. Cross-multiply and solve for the whole budget, $18,000.

7. C

This question requires you to think in terms of rearranging the average formula reverse. Sometimes you are given a set of numbers and asked to find the average. In that case you would add up all the numbers and divide by the number of items. In this question you are given the average and the number of items. To find the sum of those numbers, you simply have to multiply the average by the number of items: $12 \times 9 = 108$.

8. A

Going from top to bottom, compare the fractions in *a*'s column to determine whether these fractions are increasing or decreasing. Use common denominators to compare just the first two fractions. The whole set must follow the same pattern as any two. To compare $\frac{41}{70}$ and $\frac{401}{700}$, use the common denominator of 700. $\frac{410}{700}$ is larger than $\frac{401}{700}$, so comparing the other consecutive pairs of fractions, we find that *a* must be decreasing as it goes down the chart. Now evaluate *b*'s column from top to bottom. To compare $\frac{1}{3}$ and $\frac{2}{9}$, use the common denominator of 9. $\frac{3}{9}$ is larger than $\frac{2}{9}$, so the fractions in *b*'s column are also decreasing from top to bottom. So (A) is correct, as *a* decreases, *b* decreases. Notice though that the question does not specify going from top to bottom. If you went from bottom to top, you get as *a* increases, *b* increases. This is also correct, but not in our answer choices.

9. E

Don't let the inequality sign throw you. This is just like solving any one variable equation. You are trying to isolate the variable. First isolate $8n$. This yields $8n > 64$. Now all you have to do is divide by 8, which gives you $n > 8$.

10. D

The area of a rectangle is length times width. The area of this rectangle is 36 and the length is 9. So, $36 = 9 \times$ width, and the width is $\frac{36}{9} = 4$. The perimeter of a rectangle with a length *L* and a width *W* is $2L + 2W$. The perimeter of this rectangle is $2(9) + 2(4) = 18 + 8 = 26$.

11. C

This question requires you to rearrange the equation until you have $x - 2y$ isolated on one side. Start with the parentheses, and use the distributive property. $3x + 3 = 6y + 12$. Now, get all the numbers on the right side by subtracting 3 from both sides. $3x = 6y + 9$. Then you need the *y*'s on the same side as the *x*'s, so subtract $6y$ from both sides. $3x - 6y = 9$. Lastly, because you want to know what $x - 2y$ is equal to, divide both sides of the equation by 3. $x - 2y = 3$.

12. D

Victoria won 4 counties, whereas Richard only won 1, County B. The ratio is therefore 4:1. Remember, the question is not asking for the ratio of votes, nor is it asking for the ratio of counties Victoria won to total counties.

13. C

The two counties with the least difference in votes between Richard and Victoria are D and E.

14. D

You must follow the information one step at a time to build up the expression for which you are asked. The variable *c* represents the number of cards that Bill owns. Use this to write an expression for Jason. Because Jason has 25 more cards than Bill, the number of cards that Jason has can be expressed as $c + 25$. Now look at what it says about Charlie: he has $\frac{1}{5}$ as many cards as Jason. This means you have to divide the expression representing the number of cards that Jason has by 5.

$$\frac{c + 25}{5} = \frac{c}{5} + \frac{25}{5} = \frac{c}{5} + 5$$

15. A

A coordinate is written in the form (x, y) where x is the number of spaces left or right of the origin, and y is the number of spaces up or down from the origin. Only (A) and (C) have a vertex at $(3, 4)$, 3 to the right, and 4 up from the origin. (A) is the one that has its right angle at that point. (C)'s right angle is at $(3, 0)$, with a different corner at $(3, 4)$. Note that you do not have to consider area at all.

16. E

The question asks you to identify which of the numbers given are needed to determine how much money Peggy earns washing cars. There are four numbers: 10 weeks, 1 hour, 123 cars, and $8 per car. You only need to know the number of cars and the rate she earns per car to determine the total amount she earns: 123 and $8.

17. B

Nabila needs 2 five-dollar bills for every pizza she buys, and since she buys two, she needs 4 five-dollar bills for pizza. Similarly, for soda she needs 1 five-dollar bill for every 3 she buys, and since she buys 9, she needs 3 five-dollar bills for soda. Four bills for pizza plus 3 bills for soda means Nabila needs 7 five-dollar bills in total.

18. C

You can set this up as an equation. According to the question stem, $1 \times 3 \times 5 \times 3 = 5 + 6 + g + h$. To solve the problem you need to isolate $g + h$ as a unit.

$$1 \times 3 \times 5 \times 3 = 5 + 6 + g + h$$
$$45 = 11 + g + h$$
$$45 - 11 = 11 - 11 + g + h$$
$$34 = g + h$$

19. A

Be careful. One helpful way to solve these problems if often to subtract the remainder (7) from the larger number (163), which leaves 156. Then you would test each answer choice to see which one did not go evenly into 156. However, in this case every answer choice goes into 156 evenly. Six, though, could not leave a remainder of 7, because 7 is larger than it is. Six goes into 163 twenty-seven times and leave a remainder of 1.

20. C

This question requires that you compare a few numbers in different formats, so the first thing you should do is convert them to the same format. For instance, $\frac{13}{20}$ as a decimal is 0.65. The only one bigger is (C) 0.655.

21. B

To determine the ratio of the amount cleaned to the amount not cleaned, you must first determine the amount cleaned. If Miguel cleaned $\frac{1}{4}$ and then $\frac{1}{6}$ of his room, add those fractions together to get $\frac{5}{12}$. If he has cleaned $\frac{5}{12}$, that leaves $\frac{7}{12}$ not clean. So the ratio of clean to not clean is $\frac{5}{12}$ to $\frac{7}{12}$. Just like a fraction, a ratio can be simplified to 5:7.

22. B

Fourteen hundred can be rewritten as 14×100, and 70 as 7×10. To quickly determine 1400 divided by 70, you can divide 14 by 7, resulting in 2, and 100 by 10, resulting in 10. $\frac{1400}{70}$ is 20, or 2 times 10.

23. D

Set up a proportion. $\frac{80}{100} = \frac{352}{G}$ (Remember, G is the whole, and 352 is the 80%.) Cross-multiply and solve for G. Or remember that $\frac{1}{8}$ of 80% is 10%, so $\frac{1}{8}$ of 352, which is 44, is 10% of G. Multiply by 10 to determine that G is 44×10 or 440 is 100%.

24. C

This question is really just an indirect test of knowledge of some basic arithmetic rules. You should know that the order or grouping of a set of numbers does not matter when there is only addition. That is why (C) is correct. Notice that the question asks for something that is *always* true. The other answers *could* be true with certain sets of numbers but are not always true. Let's test each with 1, 2, and 3 as the values of *a*, *b*, and *c*.

(A) $(1 + 2) \times 3 = 1 + (2 \times 3)$
$$3 \times 3 = 1 + 6$$
$$9 = 7 \quad \text{No!}$$

(B) $1 - 2 - 3 = 3 - 2 - 1$
$$-4 = 0 \quad \text{No!}$$

(D) $(1 - 2) + 3 = (2 - 1) + 3$
$$-1 + 3 = 1 + 3$$
$$2 = 4 \quad \text{No!}$$

(E) $2(3) + 1 = 1(3) + 2$
$$6 + 1 = 3 + 2$$
$$7 = 5 \quad \text{No!}$$

25. B

The mode of the set is 27, which shows up three times, more often than any other number. The median is 32, the middle number of the set. The average of 27 and 32 is determined by adding the two numbers and dividing by 2, resulting in 29.5.

26. D

This is an estimation problem. You do not need to calculate the exact value of 19 percent of 212,822. Rather, you need only determine the general range of where that value would fall. Think of it this way: 19 percent is a little less than 20 percent, and 20 percent is twice 10 percent. Round 212,822 to 210,000. Ten percent of that figure is 21,000, so 20 percent is 42,000. Nineteen percent of 212,822 will be a little less than 42,000. There is only one answer choice that is even close to that figure.

27. C

To solve this type problem, you must begin with the information about the first element and apply what you learn about the second. We know that Bruno sold *t* hotdogs and received $20 in tips. Mitch sold $\frac{4}{5}$ as many hotdogs. This can be expressed by $\frac{4t}{5}$. We also learn that he received $6 less in tips, which means that he received $14 in tips. The last piece of information allows you to express the whole thing in terms of dollars. Because each hotdog sells for $2, the money earned by Mitch from hotdogs equals $2 \times$ number of hotdogs. Mitch earned $2 \times \frac{4t}{5} + 14 = \frac{8t}{5} + 14$ dollars.

28. D

The rectangle *WXYZ* looks like its length is twice that of the smaller rectangle, and its width also looks like twice the width of the smaller rectangle. If you were to draw the smaller rectangle *ABCD* inside the larger rectangle *WXYZ*, you would be able to fit four of them inside, thus the area of the larger rectangle must be approximately 4 times the area of the smaller, or 4 times 12, resulting in 48.

29. C

This question asks you to rearrange the equation to isolate *H*. The first step is to subtract 4 from both sides, resulting in $G - 4 = \frac{3}{H}$. Now we can multiply both sides by *H* to get $H(G - 4) = 3$. Now divide each side by $(G - 4)$ to get $H = \frac{3}{G - 4}$.

30. A

Each expression contains either 70 or 7×10, so you can ignore those and look at the other numbers. (A) and (B) are clearly not equal because 6^2 means 6×6, and (A) contains 18×6. Looking at (C) you can determine that $2^2 \times 9$ equals 36, which is equal to 6^2. Once you know that (B) and (C) are equivalent, you know that (A) has to be the correct answer.

31. C

By reading the markings on the figure, we see that the rectangular figure has dimensions of approximately 3.1 and 3.4. Because you are only asked for the approximate area, you can round these figures to 3 and 3.5. Calculating the approximate area yields $3 \times 3.5 = 10.5$.

32. A

Solving this type of problem requires three steps. First, subtract the number of people that have neither a VCR nor a DVD player from the total. This leaves you with 19. From this number, subtract the number that own a VCR, 17. This gives you 2 for the number of people that own *only* a DVD player. Finally, add 5 (the number of people who own both) to 2 to get the total number of people who own a DVD player. The figure below may help to understand how these numbers are related.

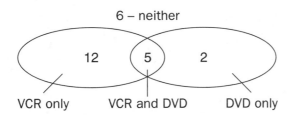

6 – neither

VCR only   VCR and DVD   DVD only

33. E

This is essentially a substitution problem. Substitute into the expression $ab + \dfrac{b}{4}$, $a = 6$ and $b = 8$. Therefore $(6 \times 8) + \dfrac{8}{4}$, which equals $48 + \dfrac{8}{4}$, which equals $48 + 2$, which equals 50.

34. B

This type of question requires you to write out two sequences. You cannot solve these in your head.

The first sequence is: 1, 12, 23, 34, 45. The second sequence is 1, 10, 19, 28, 37, 46. The two sequences share only one number: 1.

35. C

One good way to approach a problem with this type of long stretch of time is to break it down into chunks. First, 24 hours gets you right back to 8:36 P.M., with 10 hours and 25 minutes left to go. Another four hours takes you to 12:36 A.M., with 6 hours and 25 minutes left. The last six hours gets you to 6:36 A.M., with 25 minutes left to go, which takes you to 7:01 A.M.

36. C

Two is prime (it is the smallest, and it is the only even prime), and $2 + 1 = 3$, which is also prime. (B) $1 + 1 = 2$, which is prime, but 1 is not prime. Neither is 0. The only prime number choices are (C) and (D), 2 and 3, but $3 + 1 = 4$, which is also NOT prime.

37. C

Because the interval between terms is constant $\left(\dfrac{1}{2}\right)$, the difference between the 42nd and 48th terms will be equal to the difference between the largest and the smallest of *any* seven consecutive terms. So just begin with 1, and write the sequence out to six more terms, then subtract 1 from the value of that term: 1, $1\dfrac{1}{2}$, 2, $2\dfrac{1}{2}$, 3, $3\dfrac{1}{2}$, 4. $4 - 1 = 3$

38. D

Use a Venn diagram to map out the information given to you. All of John's cats are within a larger circle of purebred cats. Some of his cats like chicken, and some like tuna fish, but there is no indication that those two circles overlap. So (B) is out. Also, there may be space in the circle of John's cats that is not covered by either the chicken or the tuna fish circle, i.e., John's cats that like neither, so (E) is out. But some of John's cats DEFINITELY like chicken, and all of John's cats are purebreds, so there are some cats that are both purebred AND like chicken, (D). There is no indication about the behaviors of ALL cats (A), and there may well be cats that like tuna fish that are not purebreds (C), if the tuna fish circle extends past the box for purebreds.

Purebreds

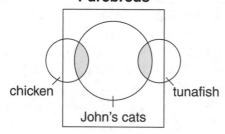

39. **D**

First, change these fractions to a form that can be easily compared. Use a common denominator of $45\left(\dfrac{2}{9}=\dfrac{10}{45}\text{ and }\dfrac{4}{5}=\dfrac{36}{45}\right)$. Halfway between 10 and 36 is $\dfrac{10+36}{2}=\dfrac{46}{2}=23$. So $\dfrac{23}{45}$ is halfway between $\dfrac{10}{45}$ and $\dfrac{36}{45}$.

40. **C**

Scientific notation must be written as a number between 1 and 10 multiplied by 10 to a power. That knocks out (A), (D), and (E). Count the number of decimal places from after the first 4 until the end and you get nine. So 4.345 must be multiplied by 10 raised to the ninth power.

WRITING EXPLANATIONS

Usage

1. E

This sentence contains no error. The verb forms are correct, and the preposition *in* is used idiomatically with *compunction.*

2. B

The past participle—*was writing*—is used to describe an ongoing action contemporary with another action. In this case, the simple past tense, *wrote,* should be used.

3. B

He could refer to either *Davy* or *Wordsworth;* this pronoun has no clear antecedent.

4. D

To indicate that plagiarism or documentation came before both the recognition and the becoming expert, this sentence needs the past perfect tense: *had been plagiarized* or inadequately documented.

5. C

The gerund, not the pronoun, should be the object of the preposition *without,* and the pronoun *him* should be changed to the possessive *his.*

6. D

A semicolon is used to separate two independent clauses. The second half of the sentence should read something like "the other is boring."

7. B

Items in a list need to be parallel. The underlined portion should read something like "or to be less vulnerable to predators."

8. C

The construction *either ... or* requires *or,* not *nor.*

9. E

This sentence contains no error.

10. E

This sentence contains no error.

11. D

The pronoun *them* refers to the singular noun *outcry,* so it should be corrected to *it.*

12. D

The antecedent of *which* is *Ruth Benedict,* but it's incorrect to use *which* to refer to a person. *Who* is correct here.

13. E

This sentence contains no error.

14. C

Agreed to and *agreed with* are both perfectly good idioms, but they mean different things. This context calls for *agreed with.*

15. C

Unlike *rise, raise* requires a direct object. Prices can't *raise* by themselves; something or someone has to raise them.

16. A

Even if you didn't know that a past participle can't stand alone, *begun* should still have "sounded" wrong to you.

17. C

The subject isn't *stunts, stars,* or *disasters,* but *death,* a singular noun. Therefore, the verb must be singular. *Was* is correct here.

18. D

Temporarily ignoring the clause *on which it was based*, the phrase *now that* strongly suggests that the disproving has happened relatively recently. The verb should be *have been*—the present perfect, used to represent a present state as the outcome of recent past events or to express actions occurring in the past and continuing in the present.

19. D

The subject of the clause is *number*, not *firms*. Thus, a singular verb, *increases*, is needed.

Sentence Correction

20. A

The original sentence is the most clear and concise.

21. C

The original sentence has no independent clause. This problem is corrected by getting rid of *that*. Choices (B) and (D) have no independent clauses either; they contain "-ing" forms of verbs that can't function as main verbs.

22. D

Only (D) corrects the problem with the sentence by turning *flourishing* into *flourished*—a main verb in the past tense.

23. C

Choice (C) most clearly shows the connection between the first clause of the sentence, which identifies a kind of test, and the second clause of the sentence, which asserts something about the directions of the test. *Whose directions* compactly states the relation between these clauses.

24. A

The original sentence is best. The past perfect tense is correct because it describes an action that occurred prior to the main action of the sentence, which is in the past tense (*arose*). Note that *emigrated*, not *immigrated*, is the correct word here: you *emigrate* from a place and *immigrate* to a place.

25. C

Logically, the introductory phrase should refer to the director himself, not to his speech. Therefore, the correct answer has to begin with *the director*.

26. E

Only (E) formulates the conditional mood correctly.

27. A

The original sentence is best.

28. B

The subject of the sentence is *Mary Cassatt*; the noun phrase *an American painter strongly influenced by French impressionism* is an appositive. The pronoun *she*, therefore, is an extra subject and completely superfluous in (A) and (D). (B) correctly omits this pronoun. (C) and (E) also omit the pronoun, but they change the present tense verb into a present participle, which can't act as a verb by itself.

29. D

The original sentence turns the whole first part of the sentence into an elliptical clause. It's awkward, and the chronology becomes muddled. (B), (C), and (E) all start the same but then diverge after *anthropologist*. (B) implies that Dunham's development of *a distinctive dance method* was part of her training as an anthropologist, but that's not very likely. (C) links so many ideas with *and* that it's hard to follow the direction of the sentence. (E) muddies the chronology and other links among various parts of the sentence.

30. A

The original sentence is best. The parallelism of the construction *not only ... but also* goes awry in the revisions.

31. D

(A) and (E) are comma splices. *Whom* is unnecessary in (B). (C) is a fragment.

32. E

Items in a list joined by *and* or *or* should be grammatically parallel. This sentence lists two noun phrases and an independent clause. (E) provides a third noun phrase.

33. E

John Milton has to be the subject of the sentence. The introductory phrase in this sentence can't modify anything else.

34. E

An introductory modifying phrase must modify the subject of the sentence. Because the introductory phrase isn't underlined, the subject must be changed. It's the *project*, not the *cranes* or the *conservationists*, that was initiated in 1975. (E) gets it right.

35. C

The original sentence is a run-on in which two independent clauses are improperly coordinated without linking punctuation. (C) corrects this problem by transforming one clause into a dependent clause.

36. D

Items in a list must be parallel. In this sentence, neither of the first two items is underlined. Each is a predicate consisting of a verb and direct object, so the third item must also be a predicate, not a prepositional phrase.

37. B

A semicolon separates two complete, but related, sentences.

38. E

The preposition *to* conveys the meaning of *purpose* perfectly well.

WRITTEN ASSIGNMENT SAMPLE RESPONSE

The following is an example of a strong response to the written assignment.

In my 16 years as a student in the public schools, I have witnessed education favoring boys at certain times and girls at other times. This has been true from elementary school through college. I will give an example at each level: elementary school, high school, and college.

In elementary school, we were divided into reading groups. The high group was always mostly girls. Once you were put into a group (high, medium, or low), you were almost never moved, so it was difficult for boys to achieve the high group. Boys were often more active in elementary school, so they would get into trouble for being loud or getting out of their seats.

In high school, it seemed that the education had pretty much evened out. I went to a school where girls were encouraged to take math and science courses, although there were more boys in chemistry, physics, and precalculus. When we did group work, the girls talked a lot but didn't usually get into trouble. The teacher probably thought they were talking about the project. Boys got into trouble for talking, because they usually yelled across the room. Sometimes the girls didn't get to participate as much in class because boys called out answers, and the teachers accepted them. If a girl tried to just call out an answer, she was usually told to hush and raise her hand.

In college, I am majoring in elementary education, and there are very few males in the program. It is hard to say if this is unequal. Were they discouraged from going into elementary education because the little kids are for women and the high school content areas are for men? It is hard for me to say if this is true, but it seems a likely idea. Elementary schools need more male teachers so the reading groups even out and the boisterous boys don't lose their playfulness. It might even help some girls find their inner playfulness.

In summary, based on my experiences, I believe there have been unequal opportunities for boys and girls in school. My hope, though, is that in the end it all evens out, and everyone has gained equal knowledge.

Section Three

PRAXIS II: PRINCIPLES OF LEARNING AND TEACHING

Introducing the PRAXIS II: Principles of Learning and Teaching (PLT)

This section of the book is dedicated to the Principles of Learning and Teaching (PLT) test, which is part of the PRAXIS II. You should refer to the requirements for the state in which you plan on teaching to determine which of these tests you will need to take. See the Appendix table for more information.

WHAT IS THE PLT?

The PLT focuses on the basic principles of learning and teaching that are essential for running a classroom. These principles are drawn from the theoretical foundations provided by key educational theorists and developmental psychologists.

Chapter four provides a review of the main names and theories that appear on the PLT tests. Although the PLT tests are divided up according to grade levels, the review is designed to address the universal concerns and theories relevant to learning and teaching. These same principles are tested in each of four PLT tests (for Early Education and grades K–6, 5–9, and 7–12) and in several elementary education subject assessments covered in the next section.

Consequently, chapter four applies to you if you are required to take any of the following exams—(test codes are included in parentheses after the test name):

- PLT: Early Education (0521) and Grades K–6 (0522); PLT: Grades 5–9 (0523); and PLT Grades 7–12 (0524)
- Elementary Education: Curriculum, Instruction, and Assessment (0011)
- Elementary Education: Curriculum, Instruction, and Assessment K–5 (0016)
- Elementary Education: Content Area Exercises (0012)
- Elementary Education: Content Knowledge (0014)

Please note that, in this book, a single test is used to prepare for all four PLT tests. This sample test includes scenarios from each of the grade ranges. All four tests reference the same PLT concepts and vary only slightly from each other.

If you are taking any of these PLT tests, Elementary Education: Curriculum, Instruction, and Assessment (0011)/(0016), or Elementary Education: Content Area Exercises (0012), begin by working through the review in chapter four. Then conclude your preparation with the sample practice tests and explanations. A practice test for the PLT can be found in this section, and the other practice tests can be found in the next section.

If you are taking the Elementary Education: Content Knowledge (0014) test, then the review in chapter four is less relevant, and your focus should shift to an overall review of content on the test. If you are preparing for this test, heading directly to the practice test and explanations in the next section would be your best bet.

Good luck in your preparation for the PRAXIS II series of tests!

CHAPTER FOUR

REVIEW OF THE PRINCIPLES OF LEARNING AND TEACHING (PLT)

ORGANIZING CONTENT KNOWLEDGE FOR STUDENT LEARNING (35%)

Human Development

As a teacher, it is important to know how children develop. Over the years, the role of teacher has expanded not only to teaching their minds, but also to providing learning opportunities that support their physical, social, emotional, linguistic, cognitive, and aesthetic development. Children differ in their development and approaches to learning. You will need to support the development and learning levels of individual children with different teaching strategies and instructional methods. The students' periods of relatively rapid growth (spurts) may appear between periods of slower growth (plateaus). Their heredity, their environments, and their interactions will all affect their developments. This is frequently referred to as "nature versus nurture."

In your teaching, you must learn how to apply the factors of cultural, linguistic, socio-economic, and family diversity that influence the development and learning of your students. By recognizing that children are best understood in the contexts of family, culture, language, and society, you will understand the many influences on personal, social, and moral development including parents, guardians, peers, teachers, media, and church.

Knowing the difference between **self-concept** and **self-esteem** is important in teaching. Self-concept is a general idea concerning how we think about ourselves. It is developed through actions, reflection, and interactions with others, especially with respect to expectations of self and others. Self-concept is influenced by our previous behaviors and performances and expectations of others toward ourselves. Self-esteem is how we feel about or value ourselves. It measures the components of self-concept.

When you, the teacher, have high self-esteem and a positive self-concept, you will guide your students in becoming more confident in accepting challenges and in being flexible in responding to new ideas.

In your teaching, you will need to create an atmosphere that fosters positive self-esteem. You will also need to provide the students with:

- Acceptance—identifying and accepting their strengths and weaknesses
- Help—setting realistic goals for them
- Time—encouraging alone time (regularly) with personal thoughts and feelings and activities (learning to enjoy their own company)
- Trust—acting on what students think is right and doing what makes them feel happy and fulfilled
- Respect—being proud of who they think they are and exploring and appreciating their own special talents
- Love—learning to love the unique students they are and accepting their own successes and failures
- Praise and encouragement—taking pride in all their achievements, offering them encouragement along the way, and emphasizing a "can-do" attitude

By giving positive feedback for students' accomplishments, you can communicate a genuine interest in their well being and be aware of their personal issues.

Theories of Development

You must have knowledge of the basic theorists' views on developmental stages, ways of learning, social development, and moral and reasoning development to plan instruction. The following list contains the theorists and their theories that are widely acknowledged as stages of development.

Piaget

Jean Piaget was a theorist who worked on the development of thinking. He observed infants and found that as they explored the objects in their environment, they gained knowledge of the world around them. Piaget called these skills **schemas**. When the infant used the schemas to observe a new object, Piaget called this **assimilation**, or interpreting an experience in terms of current ways of understanding. When the infant tried the old schema on a new object and molded it to fit the new object and be recategorized, Piaget called this **accommodation**, or a change in cognitive structures that produces a corresponding behavioral change.

Piaget developed four stages of cognitive development:

- **Sensorimotor Level:** Children from birth to age 2 base their thoughts primarily on their senses and motor abilities.

- **Preoperational Stage**: Children from ages 2–7 think mainly in symbolic terms—manipulating symbols used in creative play in the absence of the actual objects involved.

- **Concrete Operational Stage**: Children from ages 7–11 think in logical terms. They are not very abstract. At this stage, children need hands on, concrete experiences to manipulate symbols logically. They must perform these operations within the context of concrete situations.

- **Formal Operational Stage**: Children from 11–15 years of age develop abstract and hypothetical thinking. They use logical operations in the abstract rather than the concrete.

Piaget believed in cognitive **constructivism**, where students construct their own knowledge when they interact in social ways. Learning involves risk taking and mistakes, but over time, students develop greater moral and intellectual capacities.

Piaget, Vygotsky, and Dewey define learning as the creation of meaning that occurs when an individual links new knowledge within the context of existing knowledge.

Kohlberg

Lawrence Kohlberg expanded Piaget's work and presented six stages of **moral development**, based on **cognitive reasoning**, through which each person passes in unvarying and irreversible order. Everyone begins at Stage 1 and progresses through the stages in order. According to Kohlberg, few people reach Stages 5 and 6. Stages 1 and 2 in the **Preconventional level** involve an "egocentric point of view" and a "concrete individualistic perspective." Children from ages 4–10 respond mainly to reward and punishment. Stages 3 and 4 of the **Conventional level** involve the maintenance of positive relations and the rules of society. Children conform to the rules and wishes of society to preserve the social order. Stages 5 and 6 of the **Postconventional level** involve reasoning from an abstract point of view and possessing ideals where precedence takes over particular societal laws. Individuals act according to an enlightened conscience at this level.

Montessori

Maria Montessori believed that childhood is divided into four stages: Birth to age 2, ages 2–5, ages 5 and 6, and ages 7–12. Adolescence is in two levels: ages 12–15 and ages 16–18. Age ranges are approximate and refer to stages of the cognitive and emotional development common to most children. The process of learning is divided into three stages: (1) introduction to a concept by means of a lesson, something read in a book, or some other outside source, (2) processing the information and developing an understanding of the concept through work, experimentation, and creation, and (3) knowing the information or possessing an understanding of it, demonstrated by the ability to pass a test with confidence, teach another, or express it with ease. Children learn directly from the environment and from other children more than from the teacher. The teacher prepares the environment and facilitates learning. The environment nurtures all **multiple intelligences** and **styles of**

learning. Education of movement and of character comes before education of the mind. Children learn to take care of themselves, their environment, and each other and learn to speak politely, be considerate, and be helpful. Learning experiences provided for the children during their absorbent mind years are particularly designed to promote cognitive and emotional development.

Dewey

John Dewey established the progressive education practice that fosters individuality, free activity, and learning through experience. **Cooperative learning** among peers, the individual needs of the students, and the introductions of art, music, dancing, etc. in education were all cornerstones of Dewey's educational approach. He believed that the school should prepare the child for active participation in the life of the community. He thought that education should break down, rather than reinforce, the gap between the experience of schooling and the needs of a truly participatory democracy. He felt that the school was primarily a social institution, and education was a social process and a process of living, not a preparation for future living. His *Pedagogic Creed*, published in 1897, explained his views on education. This was a guide for teaching.

Bruner

Jerome Bruner considered learning to be an active process in which learners construct new ideas or concepts based on their current and past knowledge. Within this **constructivist** theory, the learner selects and transforms information, constructs hypotheses, and makes decisions, relying on a cognitive structure to do so. This allows students to go beyond the information given to them and encourages them to discover principles by themselves, or **discovery learning**. Teachers and students should engage in an active dialogue. The curriculum should be organized in a spiral manner so that the students continually build upon what they have already learned. This is known as **inquiry teaching**, where the students are active partners in the search for knowledge.

Vygotsky

Lev Semenovich Vygotsky's social development theory is based on the principle that social interaction plays a fundamental role in the development of cognition. Every function in the child's cultural development appears twice: first, on the social level, and second, on the individual level. The potential for cognitive development is limited to a certain time span called the **zone of proximal development** where full development depends on full social interaction either with teacher guidance or peer collaboration, as in **cooperative learning**. Cognitive development is limited to a certain range at any given age. The development of thought and language and their interrelationships led Vygotsky to explain consciousness as the end product of socialization. The learning of language begins with thought, undergoes changes, and turns into speech. Children's learning development is affected by their culture, including the culture of the family environment, in which they are enmeshed. The language used by the adults transmits to the child. Children's language serves as their primary tool of intellectual adaptation. Eventually, children can use their internal language to direct their own behavior.

Vygotsky also introduced an instructional technique called **scaffolding** in which the teacher breaks a complex task into smaller tasks, models the desired learning strategy or task, provides support as students learn to do the task, and then gradually shifts responsibility to the students. In this manner, a teacher enables students to accomplish as much of a task as possible without adult assistance. The skills, in essence, are gradually transferred to the learner.

Teachers should know the above theorist's views on students' learning and have a general idea about each theory and its stages. Knowing the theory's implications for children and what, in turn, you will need to know and do as a result in planning, teaching, assessment, motivation, and management will enhance your teaching.

Diversity

Common teacher expectations and understanding of the diversity of their students include: dialect, immigrant status, low socio-economic backgrounds, discipline problems, ethnicity, race, creed/religion, language, culture, social styles, learning or thinking styles, scholastic abilities, challenges, and lifestyles.

Effective schools provide many ways to adapt to their diverse school population. Positive teachers with high expectations are hired. Parents/guardians are encouraged to be involved in the school activities and daily routines. The academic objectives of the school are clear and are presented by the teachers with good planning for the diversity in the classrooms.

Understand how the influence of the students' culture, language, and experiences are related to the students' success in the classroom. Learn the culture, language, and the traditions and environment of the family to the best of your ability. Have general considerations about ethnicity, race, and sex and their implications for teachers in planning, teaching, assessing, motivating, managing, and communicating.

Regarding bilingual education, understand the differences among **English-immersion instruction, English as a second language instruction, transitional bilingual education, and two-way bilingual education**.

English immersion instruction is entirely in English. Teachers deliver lessons in simplified English so that students learn English and academic subjects. English as a second language instruction may be the same as immersion but also may have some support for individuals using their native languages. These students may have a special class each day to work strictly on their English skills. Transitional bilingual education instruction is in the students' native language, but there is also instruction each day on developing English skills. Finally, two-way bilingual education instruction is given in two languages to the students. The goal of this instruction is having students' become proficient in both languages. In this case, teachers team teach. This approach is sometimes called dual-immersion or dual-language instruction.

Remember that students who are diverse learners because of their language barriers have differences in the ways they learn and perform.

Learning Styles

Learning styles are different approaches or ways of learning. The four types of learning styles are: **Visual Learning**, **Auditory Learning**, **Tactile Learning**, and **Kinesthetic Learning**.

- Visual learners learn through seeing. These students watch the teacher's body language and facial expressions to understand the content of the lessons. They learn best from visual displays, diagrams, illustrated books, overhead transparencies, videos, flipcharts, and handouts. The visual learners take detailed notes to absorb the information.

- Auditory learners learn through listening. Verbal lectures, class discussions, and listening to what others have to say is how they learn best. Written information has little meaning for them unless it is read aloud. Auditory learners learn well by listening to a tape recorder or audio program on a computer.

- Tactile learners learn through touching. They have to actively explore the physical world around them. These tactile learning students learn best through a hands-on approach.

- Kinesthetic learners learn through moving and doing. These students find it difficult to sit still for long periods of time and need activity and exploration.

Another approach comes from Kolb's theory of learning styles and includes **concrete experiences** (being involved in a new experience), **reflective observation** (watching others or developing observations about their own experience), **abstract conceptualization** (creating theories to explain their observations), and **active experimentation** (using theories to solve problems and make decisions). Each of these learning styles requires teachers to offer different methods for students to learn the lessons.

The concrete experiencer learns well through activities such as field trips, lab work, or interactive computer programs. Writing in journals or learning logs is an effective means of helping the reflective observer learn because it forces them to concentrate on the content of the lesson and target their learning style. Students who learn through abstract conceptualization will work well with lectures, papers, and text work because these activities emphasize their learning style. Simulations, case studies, and active homework are the most helpful activities for students who are active experimenters.

Knowing and being aware of the learning styles of the students will aid the teacher in preparing instruction, materials, and activities for the lessons. There are many ways to teach, as there are many ways to learn. The instructional strategies and methods can be designed to meet the variety of learning styles of the students.

Multiple Intelligences

Dr. Howard Gardner, the John H. and Elizabeth A. Hobbs Professor of Cognition and Education at Harvard University, developed this theory of **multiple intelligences** in 1983. Rather than accept the traditional and limited idea of intelligence, based on I.Q. testing of mathematics and reading skills, Dr. Gardner proposed that there are eight different levels of intelligence.

These **eight multiple intelligences** are as follows:

- Verbal/linguistic intelligence or word smart: These students demonstrate highly developed auditory skills and sensitivity to the meaning and order of words. They learn best by saying, hearing, and seeing words. Motivate them by talking with them, providing them with books, recordings, and opportunities to use their writing abilities.

- Logical-mathematical intelligence or number-reasoning smart: These students demonstrate the ability to handle chains of reasoning and to recognize patterns and order. They are conceptual thinkers who explore relationships, patterns, and experimenting with things in an orderly and controlled manner. They typically compute arithmetic in their heads and reason out other problems. Provide them with time and concrete materials for their experiments such as science kits, games like chess, brainteasers, and a computer.

- Visual/spatial intelligence or picture smart: These students think in mental pictures and images. They have the ability to perceive the world accurately and to re-create or transform aspects of that world. These students learn visually. Teach these students with images, pictures, and color. Films, videos, diagrams, maps, and charts motivate them. Provide them with cameras, telescopes, 3D building supplies, and art supplies.

- Bodily-kinesthetic intelligence or body smart: These students are athletically gifted and pick up knowledge through bodily sensations. They communicate by using gestures and body language. They like to act out their thoughts and are clever mimics. Their learning comes with touching and moving. Motivate them through role play, dramatic improvisation, creative movement, and all kinds of physical activity. These students require hands-on activities for their learning opportunities.

- Musical intelligence or music smart: These students have sensitivity to pitch, melody, rhythm, and tones. They often sing, hum, or whistle melodies to themselves. They may play musical instruments or want to. They are also sensitive to nonverbal sounds that others overlook, such as crickets chirping or a bird singing. These students learn through rhythm and melody. They can memorize easily when they sing it out. They study effectively with music in the background. Motivate them with records, tapes, and musical instruments.

- Interpersonal intelligence or people smart: These students have the ability to understand people and relationships. They are "people people" who often become leaders of the classroom, playground, and neighborhood children. These students know how to organize, communicate, mediate, and manipulate. They have many friends. Provide them with opportunities in peer-group dynamics, school, and community activities that open learning doors for them.

- Intrapersonal intelligence or self smart: These students have the ability to assess their own emotional life as a means to understand themselves and others. They have a powerful sense of self and shy away from groups to work alone, even isolated. Their inner life is rich and filled with dreams, intuition, feelings, and ideas. They write diaries. They learn best by themselves. Provide them with their own private space where they can work and spend time in quiet introspection. Respect their privacy and acknowledge to them that it's all right to be independent.

- Naturalist intelligence or nature smart: These students have the ability to observe nature and discern patterns and trends. They recognize species of plants or animals in their environment. They learn the many characteristics of different birds. They are aware of changes in their local or global environment. They enjoy collecting and cataloging natural material. They learn best in the outdoors. Provide them with opportunities to explore the outdoors regularly and bring the outdoors indoors. Supply them with many books, visuals, and props related to the natural world. Have them create observation notebooks of natural phenomena. Have them draw or photograph natural objects. Provide them with binoculars, telescopes, or microscopes in their observational work.

According to Dr. Gardner, teachers should place equal attention on linguistic and logical-mathematical intelligence, along with incorporating strategies that include individuals who show gifts in the other intelligences. If teachers are trained to present their lessons in a wide variety of ways using music, cooperative learning, art activities, role play, multimedia, field trips, and inner reflection rather than lectures and worksheets, the children will have an opportunity to learn in ways harmonious with their unique multiple intelligences.

By incorporating factors of the multiple intelligence theory into the instruction, learning may be facilitated more effectively. Teachers will not have the same level of difficulty reaching the students. Teachers do not have to teach all the lessons in all eight intelligences, but they should include the appropriate multiple intelligence for the lesson content.

Differences Between Sexes

Learning strategies differ by sex. Girls tend to emphasize memorization. Boys learn more by elaboration strategies. Girls evaluate their own learning during the learning process. They use control strategies more often than boys. Boys need more assistance in planning, organizing, and structuring their learning activities. Students who lack self-confidence in their ability to learn are often exposed to failure. Self-concept plays an important part in studying reading and mathematics. Girls perform well in reading activities but often lack the self-confidence in mathematics. The opposite is true for boys.

Boys and girls differ in their physical, emotional, and intellectual development, but there is no evidence that their educational success is explained by these biological differences. Differences have been observed regarding emotions. Girls tend to express emotions with words, whereas boys express emotions through action.

Teachers must be aware of motivation and self-esteem differences among boys and girls and use appropriate teaching strategies in instruction. Classroom variables to consider when viewing the gender differences are the grouping of the students, management of the class, the use of time on tasks, assessment standards, and expectations of the students. Differences in teacher's expectations for girls and boys may be one factor contributing to the differences in mathematics between the sexes. There is a tendency to encourage boys to work harder at more complex math problems, whereas girls are expected to do well with routing problems. Teachers tend to attribute boys' failures to effort; therefore, they receive more feedback from teachers on the intellectual quality of their work than girls do. Girls are more associated with reading and social studies.

4MAT

Bernice McCarthy developed the **4MAT** Curriculum Development Model that allows teachers to create approaches that reflect the four different learning styles, eight multiple intelligences, and the individual differences of the students. This model works in a cyclical manner, starting by proposing **Why** questions to the students. These types of questions initiate discussion, thought, and motivation. Elements that should be reinforced in this step are brainstorming, speaking, understanding and listening to other ideas, and building off of those ideas.

The next phase is to engage in **What** activities. These activities should foster adapting the ideas and observations of the previous discussion into concepts through analytical thinking. Elements to reinforce are classification, conceptualization, and development of patterns and connections.

Third is encouraging the students to ask **How**. This type of thinking will lead to reasoning and, in turn, building common sense and practicing with trial and error. Elements to reinforce are manipulation of ideas into concrete proposals, experimentation, and association of concepts with realistic entities.

The final stage is answering the **If** question. Through the development and deduction of "if" questions, students will become more aware of their thought process and their ability to teach others. Elements of this stage are collaboration, adaptation of ideas with other ideas, and exploration of their intuition.

The classroom environment should be one that incorporates aspects of different cultures so that the students feel respected and are more open to learning. Each student should be equally challenged by the classroom activities, but the differences in the approaches to learning that may be found with diverse students should always be appreciated. The curriculum is designed so that all individual differences are addressed, providing something for everyone—each student not only finds the learning styles of greatest comfort, but also they are challenged to adapt to other, less comfortable but equally valuable styles.

Cultural Expectations

Activities are needed where students can actively begin to reflect on their own culture and how that culture is projected onto others. An activity that students engage in to define *culture* and *multicultural* will help deal with misconceptions that students have. Teachers can encourage students to define *culture* both in terms of a dictionary definition and what it means to them individually. Allow the students to give their own definitions, including surface-level cultural aspects such as music, food, religion, language, etc. With older students, teachers can then group the list of definitions given by the students using Hidalgo's three levels of culture: concrete, behavioral, and symbolic. This can be followed with a discussion about relatedness, importance, and the consistency of how the students define themselves and others. This strategy of having students themselves define what is culturally important to them will help teachers use those definitions as a starting point in the development of multicultural education curricula.

By understanding the differences in thinking about other cultures that students have, the teacher is able to plan appropriate lessons to meet the various student needs. Having a clear understanding of the students, their families, and their community will help to provide meaningful instruction and also help enhance your teaching methods and strategies.

Family expectations placed on a student—based on cultural influences such as tradition, religion, or future advancement—may differ from the expectations of the teacher. A match between the cultural expectations for literacy and the teacher's expectations for literacy is vital in the successful acquisition of reading skills. Positive connections between home life and culture and the school help to ensure the success of each student.

Having a diverse group of students means having numerous sets of expectations regarding teacher relationships and behaviors that most likely were set in their home countries, their former schools, or their families. If these students expect more traditional teaching like they had in their previous schools, they may be offended or upset if their new teacher is more informal. They may be used to a clear, ordered pattern of their classroom activities. In certain cultures, students expect the teacher to be the only one to present knowledge. These students have difficulty working in groups and doing cooperative learning activities. They may have difficulty respecting other students' ideas, and they may be uncomfortable in classroom situations that disagree with their cultural understanding of how to learn. These are the types of circumstances that a teacher must look out for when learning how to adapt lessons and teaching strategies to include every student and make each one feel comfortable.

In schools where migration is common, understanding that such movements often affect the student's learning, self-esteem, and behavior is important because teachers must create an exceptional learning environment that enables all students to meet high academic standards plus meet their other needs, such as health and nutrition. The needs of these students are often exacerbated as their families move around the states. Many of these students lose quite a lot of schooling over the course of a year and benefit from the careful guidance of their new teachers.

Accelerating the curriculum, using innovation in instruction, positive use of time and other resources, and involving parents more centrally in planning, decision-making, and instructional support roles will upgrade the effectiveness of the instruction and the academic achievement of the migratory students. Teachers need to create lessons that use the previous knowledge of the students so that connections are made. Effective use of technology will help students learn in active ways. Teachers should try to create an accepting, comfortable climate in the classroom so that the students don't feel isolated.

Using appropriate topics for discussion and study in the classroom requires the teacher to know the cultural as well as personal sensitivity of the students and use discretion when presenting discussion topics. In a high-achieving classroom environment, teachers can have students explore ideas and issues by drawing on their own and other students' cultures, experiences, and knowledge. At-risk students need classroom environments that provide them with authentic tasks, many opportunities, and many ways to learn and succeed.

Teachers must remember that their own cultural values may not be the same as those of their students. Cultural values are formed from experiences in different social, historical, and economic environments. Cultural values are also formed with contact with other cultural groups.

Understanding the age-appropriate knowledge and behavior, and working with the student culture at the school will help teachers differentiate instruction for the diverse students. Knowing the family backgrounds, the linguistic patterns and differences, the cognitive patterns and differences, and the social and emotional issues the diverse students bring with them to the classroom is also important for classroom instruction.

Students with Special Needs

Areas of exceptionality in students' learning vary when the students are eligible for special education. Regular classroom teachers must know how to accommodate the diversity of learning abilities in the classroom when special education students are mainstreamed into the regular classroom. Special education students can have visual and perceptual difficulties, special physical or sensory challenges, learning disabilities, Attention Deficit Disorder (ADD), Attention Deficit Hyperactive Disorder (ADHA), Fetal Alcohol Syndrome, functional mental retardation, or giftedness.

When teachers assume the responsibility for teaching each student in their classroom, it becomes challenging because of the increasing number of students with special needs. The task becomes determining which strategies will help these students succeed not only in the classroom, but also in the environment in which they will live. Teachers must have an open mind, an understanding of what exceptionalities are, and a willingness to accept the challenge of teaching students who have them. Having an extensive repertoire of teaching methods and strategies and knowing that there is no one solution to meeting special education students' needs will allow you to be creative in developing new strategies to help your students succeed. Teachers should always try to use strategies that rely on the students' strengths.

CREATING AN ENVIRONMENT FOR STUDENT LEARNING (35%)

Choosing Objectives, Writing Objectives, and Modifying Objectives

Objectives should answer the question, "What are students supposed to know or be able to do once the lesson is completed?" They should not describe what the teacher does during the lesson. They should not be overly specific, involved, or complicated. The objectives need to address behaviors and knowledge so that teachers can determine whether they are met. They must be observable, detectable, and measurable/assessable. Include more than knowledge and comprehension taxonomy levels in your objectives.

You need to know and use national and state standards for all content areas plus local curriculum guidelines and scope and sequence guides in writing your lesson plan objectives. Always design learning activities that are in line with the appropriate standards, and include appropriate assessment criteria.

When writing specific behavioral objectives, consider what is worth knowing, what is important to know and do, and what will present the students with lasting understanding. At the beginning of the lesson, incorporate a way to activate the students' previous knowledge of the lesson. Build the new information based on what the students already know.

Incorporate various multimedia/technology resources/materials in your lesson planning, and apply these resources specifically to the objectives of your lesson. Write adaptations of the objectives for individual students. Use the eight multiple intelligences, various learning styles, learning modalities, and specific accommodations for children with special needs (include gifted, low-achiever, and disabled students).

Vary teaching strategies. Use teacher-directed learning activities such as demonstrations, guided practice, mastery learning, independent practice, questioning, study skills, modeling, whole group discussion, and transitions. Use the work of **Hunter** and **Ausubel**.

Madeline Hunter developed a **direct instruction** model for effective instruction. Her outline of a lesson consists of: the objectives, standards of performance and expectations, anticipatory set or advance organizer, the teaching (input, modeling and demo, direction giving, and checking for understanding), guided practice and monitoring, closure, and independent practice. This model is generally referred to as the Madeline Hunter Method.

David Ausubel proposed an instructional technique called the **advance organizer**. These organizers are introduced before the learning begins and are also presented at a higher level of abstraction. They are selected on the basis of suitability for explaining, integrating, and interrelating the material to be presented to the class. These are not overviews or summaries but rather act as bridges for the students between the new learning material and their previous knowledge. Making a semantic web with the students before the lesson or unit begins is an example of an advance organizer.

Use student-centered, involved learning activities, such as collaborative learning, cooperative learning groups (CLG), concept development, discovery learning, independent study, inquiry, interdisciplinary and integrated study, project-based learning, simulations, and units. When creating lessons and teaching strategies, involve some of the following concepts: creative thinking, concept mapping, higher-order thinking, induction, deductive reasoning, problem solving, and recall.

Taxonomy of Objectives

Benjamin Bloom created a taxonomy or classification system for categorizing the level of abstraction questions and behavior for educational settings. With the help of others, he established a hierarchy of educational objectives, which is often known as **Bloom's Taxonomy**. They identified three domains, or types of learning of educational activities. The **Cognitive Domain** involves knowledge and development of intellectual attitudes and skills. The other domains are the **Affective Domain**, which deals with growth in feelings or emotional areas and attitudes, and the **Psychomotor Domain**, which deals with manual or physical skills. Teachers mainly use Bloom's Taxonomy of Educational Objectives in the cognitive domain to write lesson plan objectives, to formulate questions, and to use methods and teaching strategies from the simplest to the most complex. If the lesson requires manual or physical skills, teachers use the psychomotor domain to plan.

Bloom's Taxonomy of the Cognitive Domain

- **Knowledge**: lowest level of learning outcomes; recall of specific facts and terms from the materials.
- **Comprehension**: understands facts and principles and can interpret the meaning of the material.
- **Application**: ability to use learned material concepts and principles in new and concrete situations.
- **Analysis**: ability to break down material into its component parts so that the organizational structure may be understood.
- **Synthesis**: ability to put parts together to create a new whole; uses creative behaviors to formulate new patterns and structure.
- **Evaluation**: ability to judge the value of the material for a given purpose; value judgments are based on either internal or external definite criteria.

Planning to Teach the Lesson

You should use techniques for planning instruction that will meet curriculum goals, including the incorporation of learning theory, subject matter, curriculum development, and student development. Create effective bridges, like advance organizers, between curriculum goals and students' experiences. Include **modeling** and use **guided** and **independent practice**. By using **transitions**, activating students' **previous knowledge**, encouraging exploration and **problem solving**, and building new skills, your lessons will be successful.

Questions to ask yourself:

1. How will you group the students for instruction? Be specific about why you have chosen the grouping and how it will help to achieve the desired objectives. Will you use small groups, whole groups, cooperative learning groups, or independent learning?

2. What teaching method(s) will you use for the lesson? Is this lesson teacher-directed only? Is there a holistic question/activity? Do the methods incorporate the **learning styles**, **learning modalities**, and **multiple intelligences** of your students?

3. Have you considered all the instructional strategies you could use? **Cooperative learning? Direct instruction? Discovery learning? Whole-group discussion? Independent study? Interdisciplinary instruction? Concept mapping? Inquiry method?** Will any of these help to attain your educational goals?

4. What specific activities have been planned? What will the students do to accomplish learning the objectives? Do these activities incorporate learning styles, modalities, and multiple intelligences? Has sufficient time been allocated for the activities?

5. What instructional and curricular materials are planned for use? Include multimedia technology (Internet) as well as email and websites. Curriculum materials include the textbooks, teacher guides, kits, models, visuals, and any innovative ways used to help deliver the curriculum. A variety of resources to use in instructional planning may also include local experts, field trips, and library research.

6. Will the accommodations for specific students be included in the lesson and meet the objectives? Can you provide instructional support for students who are exceptional, gifted, ADD or ADHA, mentally retarded, learning disabled, visually or perceptually challenged, specially, physically, or sensory challenged, or second-language learners?

7. Is there a plan for evaluation and assessment of each student learning style? How will you know whether students learned the material? Is there a plan for follow-up of this lesson? Can you use the knowledge the students gained for future lessons?

Assessment

Know how to select and use culturally unbiased, informal, and formal assessment strategies to plan and individualize curriculum and teaching practices.

Knowing how to make **accommodations** for the various learning styles, the multiple intelligences, and the exceptionalities of the students will lead to your students being successful in your classroom. This does not mean that you should lower your expectations of student learning, but it does mean some students will learn and express their knowledge in different ways. The advantages of reasonable accommodations are academic success, better motivation, and more confidence for the students. Some of the more common accommodations include having the student take an untimed test, providing a tape of your test, and having other test-taking alternatives and modifications.

Provide **alternative or authentic assessment** options in which students originate a response to a task or question. Such responses could include demonstrations, exhibits, portfolios, oral presentations, or essays. You can then obtain information about the students' successes or failures on meaningful and significant tasks. There is a performance component where the students actually show what they can do, unlike a paper and pencil objective type of test, which is called **traditional assessment**.

Traditional assessment is a means of securing information about what the students know in which the students select responses from a multiple-choice list, a true or false list, or a matching list. Assessment of students' learning will assist you in planning and in communicating with the students and with their parents/guardians. Remember to correlate your method of assessment with the objectives of your lesson.

Standardized tests are assessments that are administered and scored in exactly the same manner for all students. Traditional standardized tests are typically mass produced and machine scored. They are designed to measure skills and knowledge that are thought to be taught to all students following the state standards provided to school districts. Standardized tests can be **norm-referenced**, which indicates that the performance results of the students who take this test are compared with the performance results of other students taking the test. Standardized tests that are **criterion-referenced** compare students' knowledge and achievement in an academic area to those objectives of the curriculum established by the state standards. Students are not compared to each other, but results are given that show a student's mastery of particular content areas.

Performance assessments can also be standardized if they are administered and scored in the same way for all students. This is accomplished with systematic and direct observation of student performance, or examples of student performance. These assessments are ranked according to pre-established performance criteria or guidelines that are listed on **rubrics**.

Know how to communicate assessment results and integrate them for others as an active participant of the school team in the development and implementation of **Individual Education Plan (IEP)** goals. These IEP plans are made for specific students based on their individual abilities.

Know how to develop and use formative and summative program evaluations to ensure comprehensive quality of the total environment for children. **Formative assessment** is intended to aid learning by providing feedback about what has been learned so far and what remains to be learned. An example would be a quiz over the material covered in a particular lesson or homework assignment. Students and teachers can use this type of assessment as a diagnostic tool to identify and improve areas of weakness and as a means of practicing a skill.

Summative assessment is a measure of the students' achievement at the completion of a block of work. The students' learning is summarized at a specific point in time. Examples include an end-of-the-chapter test or a unit test.

Be aware of the key issues related to state testing programs and curriculum alignment. How well does the state test correlate to match the state standards? Teachers receive materials from their districts that aid them in correlating the subjects tested on the state test with those outlined in their state standards. Preparing students for the state testing programs is vital to teachers because teachers, districts, and states are using these assessment instruments as a means of interpreting effectiveness. Teachers are affected by state-testing relative to their curriculum planning and instructional practices, the pressure to improve test scores, and the time spent in preparing students for the tests. Federal funding for the states is now predicated on the results of individual state testing results.

Informal assessments are supplemental to the standardized testing formats and are used by teachers to optimally understand students' learning strengths and weaknesses. These assessments show the teacher the why and how of their students' learning. Such assessments include learning logs, journals, observations, checklists, teacher-made classroom tests, and anecdotal records of student work and behavior. Teachers use **holistic scoring**, where each element of a student's work is used to assess the total quality of the student's work and receives one score. This is in opposition to **analytic scoring**, where one score is given after separate grades are recorded for each element of the student's work based on whether the elements are correct or not, and quality is not considered. Teachers can create detailed rubrics to use in holistic scoring of the students' work. Students receive these rubrics beforehand so that they know the quality expectations of the work to be done.

Motivation and Successful Learning

Motivation can be **intrinsic** (from within) or **extrinsic** (from without). Intrinsic motivation comes from self-determination, where the student is in control of her own destiny and can make choices. With intrinsic motivation, students themselves want to learn and do not need external incentives, such as stickers or candy. Motivation is what energizes, drives, and directs students' behaviors. Children are intrinsically motivated to learn. Teachers can stimulate this motivation through appropriate lesson planning and diverse teaching strategies.

Skinner and other behavior theorists suggest that teachers first identify the behavior they are trying to change, then reward positive behavior and provide consequences for negative behavior. This approach controls students' behaviors with immediate, extrinsic rewards. This works for short-term behavior changes but impairs learning and does not provide for long-term changes. Teachers can create celebrations of learning. Anything spontaneous that acknowledges accomplishments by the students is long lasting and more motivating. Students are eager to learn when teachers provide a positive learning environment.

Using a mixture of teaching and learning methods, engaging emotions and natural curiosity, providing high expectations, and showing students how to manage their own states of learning will spark intrinsic motivation. Teachers need to provide safe and optimal learning environments by ensuring the opportunity for intrinsic motivation as opposed to extrinsic motivation, which is often considered to be manipulative and a promotion of negative learning outcomes.

Using appropriate grouping in the classroom, correct curriculum and assessment systems, and providing for few distractions, teachers can influence the motivation of students to learn. Teachers must consider the learning strategies used because these activate the motivational issues of the students.

There are many approaches to motivation. The **Humanistic** approach to motivation uses **Maslow's Hierarchy of Needs**. Maslow introduced the term "self-actualization" as one of these needs. The underlying assumption of self-actualization is that man is basically good and has within himself all he needs to develop his full potential to be a worthwhile individual. Maslow's hierarchy of five motivational needs includes security, social, esteem, physiological, and self-actualization. The **Behavioral** approach to motivation uses reinforcement or extrinsic rewards, as exemplified by Skinner. The **Cognitive** approach is based on the learning-goal theory, self-monitoring and reflective behaviors, and self-evaluation. The **Attribution Theory** approach is centered on the social cognitive needs of the students. This theory allows students to blame or credit their own performance or nonperformance.

Attributions can influence cognition and behavior. This would include the emotional reactions to success and failure plus the expectations for future successes and failures. Teachers should observe the classroom performance of the students after assessment results are presented to the students. Motivation will be affected if the students are influenced by the attribution factors.

Teachers can promote better learning motivation if they capitalize on students' interests and communicate the belief that all students can learn. Teachers can develop appropriate strategies to focus students on learning rather than performance. Allow students to have failure, and model what to do.

Increased learning can take place if teachers provide **positive reinforcement** (or **operant conditioning**) for the responses students make. This often leads to students repeating successful learning responses. Teachers should not use put-downs or phrases that discourage students in their learning. Phrases such as, "Who has a better answer?" discourage students.

Adapting Instruction and Cultural and Linguistic Diversity

Know how to plan and implement **developmentally appropriate programs (DAP)** based on knowledge of the individual development levels of the students. Teachers plan their teaching strategies and methods based on the needs of their students in the areas of cognition, physical activity, emotional growth, and social adjustment.

Instruction should be amended or changed to meet the unique learning or social needs of the students. All factors of individual differences are considered in planning the instruction. This includes cultural diversity, exceptionalities, and the developmental levels of the students.

TEACHING FOR STUDENT LEARNING (COMMUNICATING WITH OTHERS) (15%)

Managing the Instructional Environment

You, the teacher, should always be well prepared before you begin teaching. Have all your necessary materials ready and be prompt for class. When you respect your students, they will respect you. You will need to communicate expectations clearly, and with understanding of your students. Effective verbal and nonverbal communication is a part of teaching. You need to have methods to stimulate discussion and responses in your classroom. Always consider the effect of cultural and sex differences on communication in your classroom. By using various types of questions that will stimulate discussion in different ways, you will increase communication and make students feel more comfortable participating.

Specific Management Techniques

Having some general knowledge about limited English proficiency for students and parents/guardians and the implications for teachers in planning, teaching, assessment, motivation, management, and communicating will allow you to better serve your students. Know how to use both verbal and nonverbal communication, and understand the various questioning techniques.

For effective **classroom management**:

1. Have expectations written down. Give one to each student and to each parent/guardian. This may require a signature from the student and parent/guardian for more effect.

2. An expectation list or contract that the teacher makes for himself creates a positive working environment.

3. Be consistent. Relaxing on the expectations could cause misbehavior.

4. The lesson model should include 15–20 minutes of "teacher talk" followed by student work.

5. Have more than one activity per lesson. Activities should build on each other.

6. During student presentations, involve the other students (taking notes or evaluating).

7. Discipline a student's misbehavior in private. Never reprimand in front of the entire class; this can be embarrassing for both you and the student.

8. Always keep your sense of humor.

9. If you need help in management of the class, ask for it.

10. Take the attendance/roll while students are engaged in work. Do not "call out" the roll because this can lead to misbehavior.

Know the principles of effective classroom management and strategies to promote positive relationships, cooperation, and purposeful learning:

1. Establish daily procedures and routines.

2. Establish classroom rules, rewards, and consequences.

3. Give timely feedback.

4. Maintain accurate records.

5. Communicate with parents, guardians, and caregivers.

6. Use objective behavior descriptions.

7. Respond to student misbehavior.

8. Arrange the classroom physical environment.

9. Pace and structure the lessons.

CHANGING BEHAVIOR

Know the pluses and minuses of using the **Assertive Discipline Model** (**Canter**) and **Kounin's** management plan.

With the assertive discipline model, names of students showing inappropriate behavior are now written in a book, not on the chalkboard, because it avoids public shame. Assertive discipline teaches desired behaviors, gives positive reinforcement, and invokes a discipline plan if necessary. The Canter model is based on the following principles: (1) teachers should insist on responsible behavior; (2) when teachers fail, it is typically because of poor class control; (3) using firm but humane control is liberating; (4) teachers have basic rights as educators; (5) students have basic rights as learners; (6) a discipline plan clearly stated by the teacher meets the needs and rights of both the students and the teacher; and (7) the assertive teacher is more effective than the nonassertive or the hostile teacher. The assertive teacher is able to maintain a positive, caring, supporting, and productive climate in the classroom.

The five steps to assertive discipline according to Canter are as follows: (1) recognize and remove roadblocks—negative expectations about the students, (2) practice the use of assertive response styles—nonassertive, hostile, and assertive, (3) learn to set limits for every activity—what you want and need from the students, (4) learn to follow through on limits—the positive demands you have made on the students, and (5) implement a system of positive assertions—when systematic attention is given to students who behave appropriately, the amount of problem behavior decreases, and the classroom climate becomes more positive.

Extrinsic rewards to use with the assertive discipline model are positive notes or calls to parents, special privileges, personal attention from the teacher—such as greetings, compliments, smiles, and friendly eye contact—and group rewards (preferred activities).

Effective classroom management techniques according to **Kounin** are as follows: (1) showing your students that you are "with it" (with-it-ness), (2) learning to cope with overlapping situations, (3) striving to maintain smoothness and momentum in the class activities, (4) trying to keep the whole class involved, even when you're dealing with individual students, (5) introducing variety and being enthusiastic, and (6) being aware of the ripple effect. Focus on behavior rather than on personalities, and avoid angry outbursts.

Classroom management and management of student behavior are skills that teachers acquire and perfect over time. Effective classroom management skills are central to teaching and require consistency, a sense of fairness, courage, and common sense. Some very basic factors recommended for effective classroom management are (1) know what you want and what you don't want, (2) show and tell your students what you want, (3) when you get what you want, acknowledge it, don't praise it, and (4) when you get something else, act quickly and appropriately. By greeting each student at the door with a friendly greeting, many minor problems can be handled before they become public classroom confrontations.

For effective management, teachers should also do the following:

1. Keep eye contact with the students.

2. Move around the room; being near the students can extinguish potential problems.

3. Establish a quiet signal, e.g. clap hands, a bell, or a hand signal.

4. Let the students work. Do not interrupt anyone's learning unless it's an emergency.

5. Use humor, smiles, choices, and positive reinforcements.

6. Remember, learning is a social activity. Let the students talk during their work time. A totally quiet classroom is not always a good learning environment.

Create a **climate for learning**. Become a student of the students; learn how they learn. Providing options for learning will reduce behavior problems. If you adapt the lessons to the exceptionalities, the learning styles, modalities, or multiple intelligences of the students, you'll find that many behavior problems disappear.

Some specific questions for you to consider when creating your classroom management plan are: How many behavior plans are in your room? How do you monitor noise level in your classroom? Do your students yell out in class? Do your students have extra activities to do when they finish their work? Do you have specific procedures for them when they finish their work? What do you expect of your students during instruction from you? What do you expect of your students during their independent work? Where is your desk located in the room? Is your desk barricaded with things all around it? Have you learned and used any behavior modification training techniques? These questions will assist you in creating a learning climate for all your students to be successful. When you believe that your students are capable of learning and that you are capable of teaching them successfully, a climate for learning will be established. Maximize the degree to which students are engaged in ongoing academic activities. Minimize the time spent on getting organized, making transitions, or dealing with behavior problems.

Know the basics of the these approaches to classroom management styles: **Authoritarian**, **Laissez-faire**, and **Authoritative**. Authoritarian teachers establish rules and expect students to obey them. These teachers use reward and punishments that are administered for following and breaking rules, respectively. The motto of the authoritarian teacher is, "Do as I say because I say so."

The Laissez-faire teacher establishes no rules, and students can do what they want. These teachers provide advice only when directly asked by a student. Their motto is, "Do as I say because you like and respect my judgment."

The Authoritative teacher provides rules and discusses the reasons for the rules with the students. These teachers teach the students how to meet the goals, reward the students for demonstrating self-control, and as the students show more responsibility, reward them with more self-governance. This approach to classroom management leads to intrinsic motivation by the students. The students can use this at home and in the future. These teachers have the motto, "Do what I say because doing so will help you learn more."

Know the basics of **conflict resolution technique** and the **behavior modification techniques** and how they can be used in the classroom.

Conflict resolution is a constructive approach to interpersonal and intergroup conflicts that helps students with opposing positions work together to arrive at mutually acceptable compromise. The main theme is active listening, where each student can meet and summarize verbally what each other's differences are. Initially, teachers serve as facilitators and coaches and may use role playing to model the mediation process to the students. Afterwards, the teacher sets up an area in the classroom for students themselves to use for mediating their conflicts.

The basis of conflict resolution is to teach students strategies about affirmation, cooperation, and communication. With these foundations in place, problem-solving techniques are taught and are successful. Students are able to handle conflicts peacefully and cooperatively outside the traditional disciplinary procedures. Peer mediation is a specific form of conflict resolution where students are used as neutral third parties in resolving disputes among other students.

The purposes of conflict resolution are to provide an environment in which "each student can feel physically and psychologically free from threats and danger." Students can find opportunities to work and learn with other students for the mutual achievement of all. Most students have positive self-concepts and work cooperatively with their classmates. Conflict is understood, and students respect each other. Conflict resolution techniques are given to the students so they can use them in the classroom and later throughout their lives. Both aggressive students and shy students profit from this technique because they can choose how to respond, without resorting to violence. The diversity of a classroom population is respected and celebrated. Peaceful classrooms result when the values and skills of cooperation, communication, tolerance, positive emotional expression, and conflict resolution are taught and supported by the teacher, the school, and the parents/guardians.

Teachers who use the conflict resolution technique with their classes appreciate the fact that their students have responsibilities, interests, and needs just like adults. Understanding the developmental tasks of social cooperation and problem-solving skills of students enables these teachers to provide help in responding to the conflicts the students meet. Conflict resolution skills work well in developmentally appropriate curricula for early childhood, elementary, and secondary classroom.

Behavior modification originated from Skinner's modern behavior modification techniques and Pavlov's classical conditioning techniques. Behavior modification is the application of the principles of conditioning and is used to promote or to discourage behaviors—change the behavior from being undesired to one that is more acceptable or appropriate and it will be long lasting. Behavior modification is used to change observable and measurable behaviors. All behavior is maintained, changed, or shaped by the consequences of that behavior. Students function more effectively under the right set of consequences or reinforcers that strengthen behavior and punishments that weaken behavior.

Steps a teacher can take to apply the behavior modification techniques are as follows: (1) identify the problem, (2) design a way to change the behavior, (3) identify an effective positive reinforcer, and use it often when the behavior is positive, and (4) apply the reinforcer consistently to shape or change the behavior. Some methods of positive reinforcement can be social, token, edible, or tangible reinforcers. Teachers can determine which positive reinforcers will work well with individual students, especially students with exceptionalities.

Controlling and correcting behavior through behavior modification can be accomplished by the teacher through direct instruction, reinforcement techniques, including social praise, punishment-oriented techniques, including verbal reprimand or time out, and behavioral contracting.

Effective teachers use behavior modification techniques to maintain an attractive, well-organized classroom, establishing clear rules and consequences for following them and breaking them, presenting well-prepared lessons, and setting forth a continuum of consequences for inappropriate behavior that everyone understands. These teachers also demonstrate an expectation for good behavior, understand the learning characteristics of their students, and plan for appropriate instruction. They make certain that all the students understand the rules and consequences and emphasize success rather than failure. Modeling appropriate behavior and communicating with students in positive, sensitive, and assertive ways are other techniques effective teachers use with the behavior modification approach.

TEACHER PROFESSIONALISM (15%)

The School and Society

Dewey suggested that teachers understand the factors in their students' environments outside of school that may influence their lives and learning (family circumstances, community environments, health, or economics). Teachers must be aware of ways to involve community personnel in the school setting. Develop ways to include the parents and guardians in the classroom lessons. Develop basic strategies for involving leaders in the community in the educational process. Remember that teachers and schools are a resource to the entire community.

Have knowledge of professional literature and associations within your field of education. Be able to share the titles of periodicals from specific professional associations, and know what the current views of specific professional associations are and how they are related to best teaching practices in your area. Understand the purpose of professional development requirements as required by the state and local agencies. Know types of resources available for professional development and learning in your field. Seek out opportunities to grow professionally.

Know the value of reflection as it pertains to you in the teaching profession. Understand that being a **reflective practitioner** in your teaching practices is critical. Truly effective teachers are those who evaluate their teaching strategies at all times to become the most effective educator possible. Teachers must reflect on their methods and strategies continuously to ensure that they are reaching all students. Continually evaluating the effects of their choices and actions on students, parents, and other professionals in the learning community is part of the reflective process.

These teachers use reflective statements that include clear descriptions of sources of information they have used to evaluate their teaching and the students' learning. These teachers use methods of self-evaluation and problem-solving strategies for reflecting on their practice and to make changes in their teaching. They also describe how they used specific resources such as readings and professional relationships with colleagues and others to learn and grow as teachers.

Legal, Legislative, and Political Influences

Understand the basics of the *No Child Left Behind Act*. How does this act affect the Title I schools? Children at risk? Parental involvement? Private schools? What grants are available for at-risk schools? What is **Reading First**? How does it affect schools? Know that Title VI establishes the rights of children with limited English proficiency. Title VI is based on the Civil Rights Act of 1964 and the court decisions interpreting it.

Your State Board of Education and your State Department of Education can also influence your teaching methods and strategies. Know what types of teaching responsibilities and curricula they can influence. There may be certain management or academic areas that are not allowed to be taught in your school. There are certain political groups, special interest groups (nongovernmental), teachers unions, corporate foundations, and courts that have an influence in shaping educational policies and programs.

Know the changes that states can make using the state testing programs as a benchmark for decision-making and education changes. Some states will graduate or promote students based solely on the student's performance on one multiple-choice, norm-referenced test.

Know the basics of the **Americans with Disabilities Act (1990) (ADA)**. This act establishes a clear and comprehensive prohibition of discrimination on the basis of disability. It provides a national mandate for the clear, strong, consistent, and enforceable standards addressing discrimination against individuals with disabilities. It ensures that the Federal Government plays a central role in enforcing the standards established in this act. This act further invokes the sweep of congressional authority, including the power to enforce the 14th Amendment and to regulate commerce, to address the major areas of discrimination faced by people with disabilities.

Know the basics of the **Individuals with Disabilities Education Act (IDEA)**. This act became Public Law 105-17 in 1997 and ensures that children with disabilities and the families of such children have access to a free appropriate public education. This act further provides incentives for whole-school approaches and prereferral interventions to reduce the need to label children as disabled to address their learning needs. It focuses resources on teaching and learning, whereas reducing paperwork and requirements that do not assist in improving educational results. The Federal Government has a role in assisting state and local efforts to educate children with disabilities to improve results for such children and ensure equal protection of the law.

There are specific regulations related to students' rights and teachers' responsibilities within your own state and school district. Understand these laws as they relate to confidentiality and privacy, appropriate treatment of students, and how to report situations related to possible child abuse. Check your handbook for specific regulations within your school and school district.

Know that the **Individualized Education Plan (IEP)** describes the special education and related services specifically designed to meet the unique educational needs of special needs students. The IEP covers all deficit areas, related services, and needed accommodations in both general (regular and vocational) and special education. The goals and short-term instructional objectives in an IEP must be stated in measurable, observable behaviors and fit the student's current level of functioning and probable growth rate. A sequence of skills must be indicated. A statement of related specific services, special education placement, and time and duration of services must be included. The language of the IEP must be written to be understandable to both parents/guardians and professionals. A consensus among parents/guardians, the students, and school personnel must be represented. The law requires an annual meeting to review progress and goals, but many states now use "benchmarks" as often as four times a year to let parents/guardians know the progress being made. If the goals need to be adjusted, parents/guardians must be called in for an IEP update meeting. A list of the individuals who are responsible for implementation of the IEP must be included.

The IDEA law requires a "least restrictive environment" to enable special education students to function effectively. Specifics when considering the special education student for regular classroom activities must be stated in the IEP indicating exactly what would be necessary to enable the student to receive satisfactory benefits in the regular environment with typical students. This may include receiving assistance in other areas of the school, away from the regular classroom.

Historical and Philosophical Foundations

Understand the major elements of the *Brown v. Board of Education* legal case, 1954. Know that this landmark decision struck down the "separate but equal" doctrine. The Supreme Court unanimously concluded that state-imposed segregated schools were inherently unequal and must be abolished.

Know the changes made in the *Brown v. Board of Education* case of 1955. The Supreme Court decision was that desegregation should occur with "all deliberate speed" and plans were developed in federal district courts. This decision caused a delay for desegregation in many southern states and districts.

Understand the relationship between philosophical theories and educational policy, including the formulation of educational goals, teaching methods, and curricula. Know some of the major philosophical influences on public elementary and secondary education in the United States.

Know the various periods in American education:

Colonial Period, 1600–1776

Early National Period, 1776–1840

Common School Period, 1840–1880

Progressive Period, 1880–1920

Modern Period, 1920–Present

Have an understanding of the changes in the history of American education including the colonial period, the rise of the common (public elementary) schools, antebellum and postbellum periods, the history of special and vocational education, the 20th century, the rise of the public high school, and the effects of the civil rights movement on schools and cultural centers. Understand the cultural influences from abroad.

History of American Education

The Puritans in the New England Colonies presented a stern and austere Puritan worship service. They placed an emphasis on death. The New England Primer, the Hornbook, the Dame School, and the Latin Grammar School were all part of the Colonial Period education influences.

The Normal Schools (state-funded public education) were widespread in the eastern and middle colonies but were not seen in the southern states until well after the Civil War.

Horace Mann was the first secretary of the first State Board of Education in Massachusetts in 1837. Among his various written articles, he supported the Southern ideas about education. He helped in bringing about the denouncement of the New England Colonies' education system as being "autocratic."

Others who influenced American education include Benjamin Franklin, Thomas Jefferson, Noah Webster, and Benjamin Rush.

The Land Ordinance of 1785 enacted by the United States Congress helped to consolidate schools and make education mandatory. By allotting certain areas in the townships for education and other areas for religion, the separation of church and state began. Public schools were now organized as training places for public leaders. The Northwest Ordinance of 1787 also cited the purpose of education without religion as specifically being a part of the curriculum.

The **McGuffey Readers**, 1841, introduced children to Rev. William Holmes McGuffey's ethical code. The themes of the lessons in the first reader were honesty, truthfulness, promptness, and being good and kind. The second reader used the same theme but added spelling, outlines of history and sciences, table etiquette, and behaviors and attitudes with family, teachers, God, and the poor. The "Eclectic Readers" included literature from British writers and the Bible. These readers were very moralistic in tone.

Massachusetts enacted the first law about mandatory school attendance in 1852. All children between the ages of 8 and 14 were required to spend at least three months in school. Six of the weeks in school had to be consecutive. This law was revised in 1873 where the age limit was reduced to 12 and the required attendance increased to 20 weeks per year. Hours for children working were specified, as was the monetary fine for not attending school. By 1918, all states had passed a compulsory attendance law.

Influences and changes to American education were made by G. Stanley Hall, founder of the American Psychological Association, who helped perpetrate the testing movement in the schools.

In the 19th century, there were also controversial issues that affected higher education in America. The issues included (1) the Church versus state control, (2) the value of the college versus the university, and (3) the issue of classical curriculum versus the principle of election. Should the curriculum be relevant to commerce, industry, and agriculture or should it be the traditional curriculum?

Practice Test Three
Answer Sheet

Remove (or photocopy) this answer sheet and use it to complete the practice test.
(See answer key following the test when finished.)

If a section has fewer questions than answer spaces, leave the extra spaces blank.

PLT Multiple-Choice Questions I

1 (A) (B) (C) (D)   7 (A) (B) (C) (D)
2 (A) (B) (C) (D)   8 (A) (B) (C) (D)
3 (A) (B) (C) (D)   9 (A) (B) (C) (D)
4 (A) (B) (C) (D)   10 (A) (B) (C) (D)
5 (A) (B) (C) (D)   11 (A) (B) (C) (D)
6 (A) (B) (C) (D)   12 (A) (B) (C) (D)

PLT Multiple-Choice Questions II

1 (A) (B) (C) (D)   7 (A) (B) (C) (D)
2 (A) (B) (C) (D)   8 (A) (B) (C) (D)
3 (A) (B) (C) (D)   9 (A) (B) (C) (D)
4 (A) (B) (C) (D)   10 (A) (B) (C) (D)
5 (A) (B) (C) (D)   11 (A) (B) (C) (D)
6 (A) (B) (C) (D)   12 (A) (B) (C) (D)

Practice Test Three
Principles of Learning and Teaching (PLT)

Time—2 Hours

PLT SCENARIO #1: K–6

Suzanne Carter is a second-year teacher at the Hudson Elementary K–6 school. Approximately 430 of the 750 students at Hudson are ESL children. There are 10 languages represented in the school plus many dialects of each language. Suzanne has 18 ESL students in her class of 35 fourth graders. These ESL students speak Arabic, Farsi, Spanish, Vietnamese, Lao, and Mandarin Chinese. Many of the children are not literate in their own language and have little or no formal educational experience.

The school has always worked with limited-English-proficient children. Besides classroom teachers, the staff includes many ESL resource teachers who spend time with the students for English instruction. Paraprofessionals were also hired for each of the regular classroom teachers and for the resource teachers. Many of these paraprofessionals speak other languages besides English.

Suzanne speaks fluent Spanish, holds a standard teaching credential for grades 3–6, and has a college minor in Special Education. She traveled to China the summer after graduating from college. While she was there, she visited a few of the elementary schools that were in session and saw the type of programs they were presenting. She spent her time in the cities of Beijing and Hong Kong and never visited the smaller cities. She had learned a few of the common, daily phrases in Chinese, but is not fluent.

The schedule in Suzanne's class was pretty set. Students spent time with her or her paraprofessional in class and spent time with the ESL resource teachers learning English. Suzanne chatted in Spanish with her

Mexican-American students and shared her limited knowledge of Chinese with her Chinese students. The students taught her some phrases from their own language. The rapport was good, and the students enjoyed school. Suzanne could see good, academic progress in most of her students, but she was concerned about a few who were in the Special Education program. The State Testing program would begin next month, and some of her students still had difficulty reading fourth grade material.

There were two students in particular who worried Suzanne. One student spoke a limited amount of English yet could still read at a third-grade level. Unfortunately, she was diagnosed with ADHD. Although she was on medication, she was unable to concentrate and was extremely hyperactive. Suzanne thought that separating her from the rest of the class would help her pass the state exams, but the other students were jealous of the special treatment being shown to her, which caused even more of a distraction.

The other student who concerned Suzanne was a ten-year-old boy who could not speak English and was not even literate in his own language. He had little in the way of formal schooling and didn't even like school. He had few classroom skills; he didn't know how to sit at his desk. He was constantly up and walking around the room, talking to himself, and disturbing the rest of the class. The paraprofessional in Suzanne's room would often escort him out and take him down to the ESL resource room where there was someone who spoke his language. This took him out of class very often.

Suzanne decided to schedule an IEP meeting for both students and approach the state testing concerns she had.

At the IEP meeting for the girl, it was decided that her IEP would be amended to allow her to take her state tests in the ESL resource room so that she would not distract the other students in Suzanne's class. Her parents signed the revised IEP program plan and were very appreciative for all the help the school was providing for their daughter. "She loves going to school, and she loves Ms. Carter," they said.

The boy's parents didn't make it to the first scheduled IEP meeting or the second rescheduled meeting. Finally, they showed up for the third meeting, and, through a translator, Suzanne learned that her student enjoyed his time in the ESL room. His parents wanted to know if he could spend all of his time there. The IEP team tried to explain that he needed to attend his regular class, but the parents were adamant. They also did not think it was important for their son to take the state tests because he couldn't read them. They refused to sign the IEP papers. Suzanne knew that she should intervene, but how?

PLT SCENARIO #1: K–6 QUESTIONS

1. Is the regular classroom the best placement for non-English-speaking students new to this country? Base your response on the principles of planning for students as diverse learners.

2. Explain how Ms. Carter can deal sensitively yet firmly with the language differences disrupting her classroom. Be specific as to the difficulty with the male student.

3. Explain the requirements of the "Least Restrictive Environment" and what, by law, must be included in each IEP.

_____

_____

_____

_____

_____

_____

_____

_____

_____

_____

_____

_____

_____

_____

_____

_____

_____

_____

_____

PLT SCENARIO #2: 5–9

Every fifth-grade student at Diamond Junior High School hoped that he or she would be assigned to Ms. Julia Ross for sixth grade math. Ms. Ross was young and hip. She wore the latest fashionable clothing and even had a tiny little tattoo on her neck. She knew the latest music and always seemed to know who was winning and who was losing in every pro and college sport. More important, she really made math fun. She was always creating new projects and games, usually relating functions, graphs, and long division to things that happened in her students' lives. The young girls in Ms. Ross' class worshipped her and tried to emulate her dress and speech. The young boys all harbored huge crushes.

Ms. Ross knew of her students' devotion and didn't take it lightly. She believed that student-teacher relationships were based on mutual respect and trust. She prided herself on the fact that many of her students would come by during lunch or after school just to say, "Hi." Sometimes they would stay and chat. Whereas she never pried, some students really opened up to Ms. Ross, telling her about their families, siblings, friends, and other events in their lives.

Of course, there were exceptions to the students' adoration of Ms. Ross. Some students never really warmed to Ms. Ross' style. Often it was the popular students who were confident enough to approach and befriend Ms. Ross, whereas others felt more intimidated. Thomas Williams was a prime example. A quiet boy, Thomas' most defining characteristic, and consequently the basis of his identity, was his weight. He was enough overweight that he was considered obese, and he had been this way for as long as anyone could remember.

The other students made fun of Thomas outside of class, calling him "Tom Tub" or "The Whale." For several reasons, Ms. Ross had never gotten involved in the students' teasing. It occurred in class sometimes, but she ignored it. She didn't know what would be the most effective way to stop it. After all, she thought, teasing and name-calling were simply part of the world of a sixth grader. As far as Ms. Ross could tell, Thomas took a lot of taunting, but he had a few friends, and his work, while often sloppy and inconsistent, was not a major concern.

Ms. Ross felt badly for Thomas. She decided to talk to his guidance counselor, Mr. Perry. He told her about Thomas's home life and his struggle with obesity.

"It's a combination of things," he said. "Poor diet, poor adult supervision, and very little physical activity. It's actually one of the biggest problems facing students, but no one seems to be talking about it. In fact, our school board wants to cut the health and PE budget almost in half for next year."

Ms. Ross was thankful for Mr. Perry's input. Now she had gained a deeper understanding of Thomas and made up her mind to see if she could help him out a little.

Unfortunately, the opposite happened. The other students noticed that Ms. Ross was spending time at lunch with Thomas. They started to make fun of Thomas right in front of Ms. Ross. It was worse than before, so she decided to discuss the problem with the class. This did not work either because it sounded like she was acknowledging that Thomas was different and had a weight problem.

Many of the students giggled throughout her talk. Thomas just glared at her for bringing even more attention to him. He finally put his head down on his desk. It was one of those moments in teaching that Ms. Ross wished she could just rewind and start all over again. What was she to do?

PLT SCENARIO #2: 5–9 QUESTIONS

1. Teachers have acquired their own attitudes, experiences, and prejudices about obesity and many other issues that affect students. Where do teachers have opportunities to examine their own attitudes? Explain how these biases could affect teaching.

2. Should Ms. Ross have been involved in managing the students' teasing and bickering? Discuss two management strategies Ms. Ross could use for behavior management.

3. Explain: Is obesity—and other personal health problems—the responsibility, or within the domain of, the classroom teacher? The guidance counselor? The school community?

_____

_____

_____

_____

_____

_____

_____

_____

_____

_____

_____

_____

_____

_____

_____

_____

_____

_____

PLT SCENARIO #3: 7–12

Tom Hallett was a first-year science teacher at the Roberto Garcia Junior High School. Somehow, he'd made it to the first day of the spring semester and was feeling pretty good about his career choice, his classes, and his students. After all, teaching middle school students wasn't an easy assignment. Like many first-year teachers, Tom found teaching much more exhausting than he had anticipated. He frequently found himself frustrated by the resistance and lack of attention of some of his students. It just wasn't "cool" to like science, let alone show some enthusiasm for it. What did seem to matter, and matter too much in his opinion, were music, clothes, and dating. Tom certainly had many opportunities to observe what and who were "in" because he had some 128 students in his five classes: two academically talented eighth grades, two average seventh grades, and one remedial ninth grade general science class.

Roberto Garcia Junior High was one of two junior highs in a working class community. Tom found the school administration a bit rigid, especially when he tried to bring a little creativity into the curriculum. For example, when he went to Principal Brown to discuss his plan to engage his academically talented classes in an investigation of the impurities in the community's water supply, he got a clear and direct message, "Don't rock the boat." Principal Brown wagged a finger at Tom when he said, "Mr. Hallett, it is hard enough to control these students when they're in the building. If you take them off school property, there is no telling what might happen!"

Tom had adapted fairly well to the environment that encouraged an unwavering focus on teaching and learning. He felt especially successful with his academically talented students, with whom he was able to transmit knowledge and an appetite for science. Although he knew he was less successful with his seventh grade classes, he was happy that they at least did the worksheets he assigned in class and attempted to answer the questions from the back of the text that Tom assigned for homework each night.

With his remedial ninth grade students, Tom felt totally incompetent. Nothing he tried was working. He spent most of his time policing the class, leaving little time for actual science teaching. The students in this class were more interested in socializing than learning about science. They barely completed his in-class worksheets, and rarely did the homework questions from the text. He was tired of reprimanding them for not doing their work.

Tom had four months before the state testing began. He needed to revise his teaching strategies and methods for this remedial class or they would score at the bottom of the state tests, and this would certainly affect his own teaching evaluations. He needed some ideas to get this remedial class involved in learning science. He needed to put their socializing into a positive use, and he needed to do it quickly! What was he to do?

PLT SCENARIO #3: 7–12 QUESTIONS

1. Tom needs to understand that it is critical for him to be reflective in his teaching practices. What specific teaching strategies and methods would you suggest that Tom evaluate and reflect about? Name three, and provide reasons for your suggestions to Tom.

2. How can Tom effectively use the remedial students' social skills in his classroom environment? What two effective strategies for helping these students work cooperatively and productively in groups can you recommend to Tom?

3. What three strategies can you recommend to Tom for classroom and individual behavior management that would help the students develop self control and manage their own behavior?

_____

_____

_____

_____

_____

_____

_____

_____

_____

_____

_____

_____

_____

_____

_____

_____

PLT SCENARIO #4: K–6

Leticia Jackson was a second grade teacher at the East Hill Elementary School, a well-run suburban school that had a sizeable low-income community. This was her first year of teaching and was definitely not at the school she had pictured herself in when she decided to become a teacher. In fact, all of her practice and student teaching experiences were in very tough neighborhoods. She had wanted to be a role model for children who needed to see people like themselves at the front of the room. So, what was she doing in East Hill?

The teacher-placement advisor at her college told her that East Hill was "a place where someone like you could make the mistakes of a beginning teacher and come out a better teacher on the other end." She focused on classroom management and on creating a structured and disciplined academic environment. In her effort to gain authority, she was concerned that she was missing out on the mentoring role of teaching.

As a minority, one of the most difficult realities of being at East Hill was seeing the contrasts between the middle-income children who were mostly white and the lower-income children who were often part of a minority group. Academically, it seemed to be the white students who were always excelling and the minority students who needed extra help. It bothered Leticia to see the parade of African American boys sent to the principal's office on a daily basis. She hoped that the discipline was deserved and not based on prejudice. Leticia was aware of how critical she could be of problems imposed upon the African American community, such as drug and alcohol abuse and teenage sexual activity. She had grown up in the same kind of community and knew the problems. She had made a conscious decision to keep her expectations high. In her classroom, there would be no excuse for behavior that disrupted learning or fell short on effort.

William Baker, one of the few white students in her class, was one student who had sorely tested Leticia's resolve. All year she had struggled to control William's aggressive, disruptive behavior. Even when she had finally been able to quiet him down, he showed no interest in learning and was one of the few students who had trouble in reading. Leticia had been trying to conduct a reading group with the 10 slowest readers in the class, including William. Last year's standardized test placed him at the lowest level in reading. He had been absent for 35 days last year and had spent a good amount of his school days in the principal's office, many times missing the reading lessons in his first grade classroom.

When the 10 members of the reading group met, the rest of the class worked on workbook assignments at their desks. However, each time the reading group met, William would start an argument, and most of the children at their desks would snap to attention to watch the scene William was making. The chemistry in the reading group—and in the class in general—had been explosive since August. Leticia knew that the progress of the rest of the class was hindered by William's behavior. She had to do something.

PLT SCENARIO #4: K–6 QUESTIONS

1. Ms. Jackson knows that the progress of the class in reading is being slowed down by external disturbances. Explain two instructional strategies that she could use in teaching reading to the class to improve progress.

2. There are many measures Ms. Jackson could take regarding William's conduct and behavior in the reading group. Explain two behavior management techniques she could use.

3. Explain three issues Ms. Jackson can discuss with William's parents in a parent-teacher conference.

_____

_____

_____

_____

_____

_____

_____

_____

_____

_____

_____

_____

_____

_____

_____

_____

_____

_____

_____

PLT MULTIPLE-CHOICE QUESTIONS I

1. At the age of 5 or 6, children typically begin to experience a significant change in regard to their social development. Which of the following statements BEST describes the developmental progression that occurs at this time?

    (A) At the beginning of this period, most children prefer to work cooperatively in groups to solve problems; by the end of this period, most prefer to work independently.

    (B) At the beginning of this period, the desire to please peers tends to be most important; by the end of this period, the desire to please adults is foremost.

    (C) At the beginning of this period, children tend to seek mainly same-sex friends; by the end of this period, most children have roughly equal numbers of male and female friends.

    (D) At the beginning of this period, children value relationships with adults above all others; by the end of this period, friends have become increasingly important.

2. Which of the following kinds of instruction is often cited as the opposite of discovery learning?

    (A) mastery learning
    (B) expository teaching
    (C) constructivist learning
    (D) schema training

3. According to Maslow, a child who often comes to school hungry, tired, and dressed in dirty clothing has which of the following unmet needs?

    (A) self-esteem
    (B) love and a sense of belonging
    (C) physiological
    (D) safety and security

GO ON TO THE NEXT PAGE

4. Which line on the table below correctly matches a major learning theory with the view of learning associated with that theory?

Line	Learning Theory	Description of Theory
A	Behaviorism (B.F. Skinner)	Learning occurs through connections established between stimulus inputs and responses; desirable learning strategies and behaviors in children can be increased with reinforcers.
B	Cognitive-Developmental Theory (Jean Piaget)	Learning occurs through observation and imitation of models; as children become older, they become more selective in the behaviors they imitate.
C	Social Learning Theory (Albert Bandura)	Learning occurs in eight distinct stages of psychosocial development as children use new skills and attitudes to resolve conflicts related to psychological needs.
D	Sociocultural Theory (Lev Vygotsky)	Learning occurs in stages characterized by particular ways of thinking; children acquire knowledge through active construction and multiple opportunities to connect new ideas to previous experiences.

GO ON TO THE NEXT PAGE

5. In the "Guidelines for Developmentally Appropriate Practice," the National Association for the Education of Young Children (NAEYC) advocates that teachers have the following parent-teacher relationship:

   (A) Clarify the limits on parents' access to their children's classrooms.

   (B) View parents as partners in the educational process.

   (C) Contact parents about every developmental change their children undergo.

   (D) Encourage parents to accept teachers as experts who know what is best academically for their children.

6. Which of the following is something teachers should almost always discuss when students are given a new type of assignment?

   (A) how the assignment will be graded

   (B) what they can expect to learn from doing the assignment

   (C) what experience the teacher has had with this type of assignment

   (D) if the material on the assignment will be tested

7. Piaget's term that refers to a change in cognitive structures that produces corresponding behavioral changes is known as

   (A) assimilation

   (B) accommodation

   (C) centration

   (D) egocentrism

8. The instructional strategy in which a teacher places students of varying abilities and interests to work together in small groups to solve a problem, complete a project, or achieve a common goal is known as

   (A) constructivism

   (B) cognitively guided instruction

   (C) interdisciplinary curriculum

   (D) collaborative learning

9. Which of the following defines formative assessment?

   (A) An assessment attempt used to summarize student learning at some point in time

   (B) A means of securing information about a student's success or failure on meaningful and significant tasks

   (C) An assessment in which students originate a response to a task or question

   (D) A means used to give students an indication of how they are progressing in terms of their skills and understanding

10. What is the main reason a teacher uses an advance organizer?

    (A) The teacher can easily measure whether the objectives are met.

    (B) The teacher can have authority over the students *In loco parentis.*

    (C) The teacher can introduce what is to come in a lesson.

    (D) The teacher can seek appropriate goals and insist on student responsibility.

11. The difference between English immersion instruction and English as a second language instruction is

   (A) English immersion instruction is entirely in English

   (B) English as a second language instruction is entirely in English

   (C) English immersion instruction is entirely in the native language of the students

   (D) English as a second language instruction is entirely in the native language of the students

12. The four types of learning styles are

   (A) Visual learners, Perceptual learners, Auditory learners, Accelerated learners

   (B) Visual learners, Tactile learners, Adaptive learners, Heuristic learners

   (C) Visual learners, Kinesthetic learners, Auditory learners, Naturalistic learners

   (D) Visual learners, Auditory learners, Tactile learners, Kinesthetic learners

GO ON TO THE NEXT PAGE

PLT MULTIPLE-CHOICE QUESTIONS II

1. The *No Child Left Behind Act* of 2001 contains four basic education reform principles. One of these is

    (A) decreased local control of school systems
    (B) emphasis on teaching methods that have been proven to work
    (C) states will make monthly reports on the progress of meeting the state standards
    (D) progress by racial or ethnic minority groups will not be reported in the state reports

2. When working with students of diverse cultures, it is important to have "accommodation without assimilation." This means that a teacher must

    (A) adapt to the dominant culture without losing that cultural identity
    (B) accept and value the differences of the students
    (C) use the individual and competitive norms of the students
    (D) learn the language of the students

3. Different children develop at different rates. This development is affected by

    (A) socioeconomic levels
    (B) self-esteem
    (C) heredity and environment and their interaction
    (D) beginning school at an early age

4. The practice of inclusion means that the classroom teacher must teach lessons that accommodate which of the following groups of students?

    (A) gifted, physically disabled, learning disabled, and emotional and behavioral disorders
    (B) students with all multiple intelligent levels of learning
    (C) only those students with academic difficulties
    (D) those students identified by the principal

5. Culturally responsive teaching includes acknowledging cultural diversity in the classroom. It means that the teacher must accommodate the diversity and differences in daily instruction. Which of the following are potential differences of students that teachers must accommodate?

    (A) language, dialect, and economic levels
    (B) eye contact, family relationships, and expectations
    (C) clothing, eye color, and diet
    (D) personal questions, family income, and level of academics

6. Jean Piaget's theory on the stages of development for children could be classified as

    (A) Psychometric
    (B) Triarchic Theory
    (C) Developmental Cognitive
    (D) Social Development

GO ON TO THE NEXT PAGE

7. Which of the following is a misuse of Gardner's Multiple Intelligence Theory?

    (A) cultivation of desired capabilities
    (B) personalization of education
    (C) approaching a discipline in a variety of ways
    (D) grading without regard to context

8. The level of Bloom's Taxonomy that allows a student to use learned material concepts and principles in new and concrete situations is

    (A) synthesis
    (B) evaluation
    (C) comprehension
    (D) application

9. When the teacher models the desired learning strategy or task and then gradually shifts responsibility to the students, this is known as

    (A) reversibility
    (B) direct instruction
    (C) holistic teaching
    (D) scaffolding

10. The first stage of Piaget's theory of cognitive development is

    (A) preoperational
    (B) sensorimotor
    (C) concrete operational
    (D) socialization

11. Locus of control refers to

    (A) various kinds of support or assistance provided by an adult to help children perform activities they cannot do independently
    (B) a classroom situation that provides necessary support for a disabled student's continuing educational progress while also minimizing the time the student is removed from a normal educational environment
    (C) teachers' ability to handle two or more classroom issues simultaneously
    (D) some individuals' belief that the causes of behavior reside within themselves, whereas others believe their behaviors are caused by other people

12. Which one of the following is an example of extrinsic motivation?

    (A) The child is given a sticker for good work.
    (B) The child is happy about his work.
    (C) The child is not given a sticker for good work.
    (D) The child continues to do good work.

STOP!

If you finish before time is up, you may go back and check your work.

Practice Test Three (PLT) Answers and Explanations

PLT Scenario #1: K–6
Sample Responses to Questions

1.

Principals and teachers must consider the influence of the students' culture, language, and experiences when placing non-English-speaking students new to this country in regular classrooms. Information obtained from the student's parent/guardian will help the school understand the student's previous school organization. If the student's previous classroom in a foreign country had a traditional, structured, teacher-directed environment, then the placement for the student should be in a classroom as close to a traditional, structured, teacher-directed environment as possible and not in a classroom where activities are more student-centered. The differences in the approach to learning should always be appreciated and considered. Immersion in the English-speaking classroom will help the student learn English from the teacher and the other children; however, the student could attend special classes each day to work strictly on her English skills. If the student had no or little schooling in her previous country, then placement in a transitional bilingual education program where she received instruction in her native language and in English would be appropriate, followed by a slow transition to a regular classroom after the student has learned English skills.

2.

Ms. Carter has a multicultural classroom environment. To ensure that non-English-speaking students do not feel different and left out, she could incorporate aspects of the different cultures and languages in her teaching so that all the students are learning and feel respected. She could also structure her lesson plan to include activities for the entire class that incorporate the ESL teachers and paraprofessionals to promote equality. She could have a class discussion on culture using a concept web and have the students present their own definitions of culture and write them on the web. When all responses are written down, the students might see how different they all are and how different their responses were.

In working with the male student, Ms. Carter might make a home visit with a translator and try to explore the reasons why the parents are not involved and are not supportive of their son receiving a well-rounded education. She could let him continue his successes in the ESL resource room because this seems to be a positive experience for him, but she needs to make sure he is included in the activities of his class. When he learns some English, he may feel more comfortable being in a regular, English-speaking classroom full time.

3.

The "Least Restrictive Environment" on the Individual Education Plan (IEP) is required by the Individuals with Disabilities Education Act (IDEA). It states that for special education students to function effectively, they must be placed in an environment that fosters diversity and has resources that cater to different learning and other disabilities. This is spelled out in detail on the IEP and may require the student to receive assistance in other areas of the school like a resource room or ESL room for certain portions of the day without penalties from their regular instructors.

PLT Scenario #2: 5–9
Sample Responses to Questions

1.

Teachers have opportunities to examine their own attitudes by being reflective practitioners. By looking back and considering the many dimensions of an event, such as influencing factors, identifying controlling factors, and adjustments that might be made the next time, teachers can continue to grow as authoritative figures and empathetic beings. The goal of reflection is moving forward. Reflections can be explored through many ways, including written reflections through journals, peer coaching with another teacher, networking with other teachers, or performing action research for a more formalized reflective process.

The benefit of engaging in personal reflection is that a person's beliefs, judgments, and biases may be exposed and thus dissected. In teaching, it is necessary to be able to recognize the influence of these personal beliefs on your behavior in the classroom because of the vast amounts of students and lifestyles you are shaping. If you are not treating students equally because of a personal feeling toward their lifestyles, then you are not fulfilling your duty as an instructor. By serious reflection, teachers can see whether changing their old ways can make advantageous adjustments in their instruction.

2.

In the classroom, the teacher is the disciplinarian and plays the role of guardian when the students are in her care. It was the responsibility of Ms. Ross to manage the behavior of the other students toward Thomas because he could not defend himself. One management technique Ms. Ross could have used with her class is the Assertive Discipline method where she would insist on responsible behavior based on a list of rules with specific consequences for misbehavior and positive assertions for appropriate behavior spelled out. Using this technique, Ms. Ross would be more effective because she could maintain a positive, caring, supporting, and productive climate in her classroom. If she sets limits for every classroom activity (what she wants and needs from the students), the amount of problem behavior will decrease. "We do not tease others," could be one of the assertive discipline rules that Ms. Ross enforces.

Another management technique Ms. Ross could have used with her class is Kounin's technique of teacher with-it-ness. In this scenario, the teacher is the effective manager of lessons and is able to cope with overlapping situations. Ms. Ross needs to strive to maintain smoothness and momentum in the class activities as well as keeping the whole class involved, even when she deals with individual students. Ms. Ross should focus on behavior rather than on personalities and always avoid angry outbursts with her students. If Ms. Ross had been clearer about not tolerating the teasing behavior and had been firmer originally when the teasing began, the students would have known that she was in control.

3.

Obesity and other personal health problems related to students are not the responsibility of the schools, the school boards, the community, and the teachers. The parents/guardians are the people inevitably responsible for their children. However, schools are identified as a key setting for public health strategies to prevent and educate their students about poor health. Most students spend a large portion of time in school where they should have opportunities to engage in healthy eating and physical activity.

Teachers, staff, and parents/guardians should be educated about the importance of physical activity and nutrition programs and policies in schools. They should also know the importance they hold as role models for healthy eating and regular physical activity for the students. Schools should ensure that the meals offered through the school breakfast and lunch programs meet nutritional standards. They should also ensure that the snacks and foods provided in vending machines, school stores, and other places within the school's control are healthy. Schools and districts should provide daily physical education programs for the students. However, teachers should not approach students individually about their health problems. This is a sensitive issue and could lead to a lawsuit. Rather, teachers should relate their concerns to the parents and suggest a meeting with the school principal, school counselor, and perhaps the health education instructor.

PLT Scenario #3: 7–12
Sample Responses to Questions

1.

(1) Tom needs to evaluate and reflect about his homework assignments. If he wants the students to prepare for the State tests, he should make certain the homework questions pertain to the standards tested. (2) Tom needs to evaluate and reflect about his methods and strategies in teaching the remedial students. What he's doing now is not working. Perhaps he needs to use other teaching strategies with these students, not the same ones he's using with his academically talented classes. (3) Tom needs to evaluate and reflect about why he's waited until the spring semester to worry about the State tests and what to do about his remedial class' lack of science knowledge. These tests should be discussed with the classes at the beginning of the year, and perhaps then the students would work harder toward the goal of succeeding.

2.

Tom can effectively use his remedial students' social skills by having them work in cooperative learning groups of four on the worksheets he wants them to do. If each group works on one worksheet together, they can use their social skills and learning skills at the same time. Tom can have them do this within in a specific time and then follow with each group's contribution in a class discussion. He could also ask his students to pair up to work on the homework. Tom wants his remedial students to learn the science content. If he gives the students a list of chapter concepts he wants them to know before they do their homework, the students will understand that Tom is serious about what he wants them to know for the State tests.

3.

Tom needs to demonstrate his understanding of the basic principles and theories of classroom management. He needs to create a learning environment in which his students assume responsibility for themselves and for each other. He could use conflict resolution where the students can discuss their conflicts peacefully between themselves and arrive at a mutually acceptable compromise. He could set up rules for the classroom and use the assertive discipline model of behavior management where he lists consequences and rewards for appropriate and inappropriate behavior by the students. He could use role-play techniques where his concerns about lack of homework and the socializing are acted out. The students could then create their own rules for the classroom with Tom's help. In the future, Tom could also write down the expectations he wants from his students at the beginning of the year. He may also look at the physical arrangement of the classroom and check whether it is set up for effective teaching and learning.

PLT Scenario #4: K–6
Sample Responses to Questions

1.

One strategy that Ms. Jackson could use would be to teach reading using the phonetics approach and basal readers. The students in her class are attempting to learn in a volatile environment, and breaking down the reading lessons to form a narrow learning path will help her to gauge the success of individual students and the lessons better than if the class was trying to intake a broader curriculum. Ms. Jackson could also use writing as a strategy to enhance her students' focus and reading levels. Writing assignments based on reading passages that focus on correct spelling and grammar force the students to understand the individual words rather than attempting to decipher the meaning of an entire passage. If the students are busy working on these assignments, it is less likely that they will be so easily distracted by William's behavior.

2.

Ms. Jackson should sit down and have a personal conversation with William where she discusses his behaviors that must be changed. She can provide him with a list of positive and negative reinforcements that will come with certain types of behaviors. For instance, if he continues to disrupt the class, he will have to accept the consequences of that action. The list must be specific so that William's negative behavior will be shaped into a positive state. A contract designed by William and Ms. Jackson together to actually set goals not only for completed work, but also for practiced behavior would also be useful. There should be an incentive for reaching these goals.

3.

(1) In a parent/teacher conference with William's parents or guardians, Ms. Jackson can discuss the areas in which William shows strengths and her concerns about William's weaknesses in his performance in class. She needs to share with William's parents the positive growth and development William is making and how much more he can make. (2) Ms. Jackson should find out where William reads in the home and make suggestions as to how William's parents can help him succeed. (3) Ms. Jackson can share the reinforcement guidelines she is using to help with behavior modification in the classroom and ask the parents/guardians to do similar things at home so that William's behavior modification will be complete.

MULTIPLE-CHOICE QUESTIONS I

1. D
2. B
3. C
4. A
5. B
6. B
7. B
8. D
9. D
10. C
11. A
12. D

MULTIPLE-CHOICE QUESTIONS II

1. B
2. A
3. C
4. A
5. B
6. C
7. D
8. D
9. D
10. B
11. D
12. A

MULTIPLE-CHOICE I EXPLANATIONS

1. D

At the age of 5 or 6, a child's social development and patterns of affiliation begin to change. At the beginning of this period, children value relationships with adults above all others. By the end of this period, children place increasing importance on friends and peers, choice (D). This transition generally coincides with a student's involvement in more formalized schooling.

2. B

Discovery learning is a phrase to associate with Bruner. It centers around the notion that teachers and students should engage in active dialogue and that students should be allowed to go beyond the information they are given and to discover more. By contrast, expository teaching, (B), emphasizes that teachers engage in straight lecture or exposition to give students only the information they deem necessary. Interaction and discovery are not essential components to expository teaching.

3. C

Abraham Maslow should be associated with the Hierarchy of Needs. Maslow conceptualized this hierarchy as a pyramid in which the most basic needs such as food, water, and shelter would comprise the lowest level of the pyramid. Higher-order needs like love and sense of belonging would appear higher up in the pyramid. In the example cited in this question, a student who is hungry, tired, and dirty is not meeting the most basic physiological needs, choice (C).

4. A

Behaviorism (B.F. Skinner) is correctly paired with learning occurring through connections between stimulus inputs and responses, choice (A). According to a behaviorist perspective, reinforcers can be used to encourage desirable behaviors.

Cognitive-Developmental Theory (Piaget) should be paired with the idea that learning occurs in stages characterized by particular ways of thinking. Social Learning Theory (Bandura) claims that learning occurs through observation and imitation of models. Finally, Sociocultural Theory (Vygotsky) emphasizes the zone of proximal development and the importance of cooperative learning and the social environment to the learning process.

5. B

According to the NAEYC, the parent-teacher relationship is a central component in a child's education and parents and teachers are seen as partners in the educational process, choice (B). Each of the incorrect answers for this question places unnecessary limits on the involvement of parents in the parent-teacher relationship.

6. B

Teachers should always tell their students what they can expect to learn from doing an assignment, so (B) is correct. This information allows a student to become an active participant in their learning process. Each of the incorrect answer choices focuses too narrowly on the grading process or on the teacher's experience.

7. B

Piaget used the term accommodation to refer to a change in cognitive structures that produces a corresponding behavioral change, (B). Assimilation, (A), is the term Piaget used to describe interpreting an experience in terms of current ways of understanding. Centration, (C), and egocentrism, (D), refer to terms Piaget used in reference to the preoperational stage of cognitive development.

8. D

Placing students of varying abilities and interests into small groups to solve problems or achieve a common goal is an example of collaborative learning, choice (D). Constructivism, (A), refers to the approach in which learning is understood as an active process wherein learners construct new ideas based on their current and past knowledge. Cognitively guided instruction, (B), refers to a type of curriculum design for K–6 science and mathematics. Interdisciplinary curriculum, (C), refers to a curriculum that teaches content across multiple disciplines at the same time. For example, a teacher may address math, science, and social studies concepts in a lesson on space travel.

9. D

Formative assessment is a means used to give students an indication of how they are progressing in terms of their skills and understanding. Formative assessments emphasize developing an individual understanding of one's strengths, weaknesses, and learning processes. None of the other answer choices emphasizes a student's awareness of his own skills and learning.

10. C

The advanced organizer prepares students for material they have not seen yet, so choice (C) best describes this. *In loco parentis* refers to when a teacher, administrator, or school acts in the position or place of a parent.

11. A

English immersion instruction refers to instruction that takes place entirely in English, choice (A). This is in contrast to English as a second language (ESL) instruction, which allows for some use of a student's native language.

12. D

Learning styles refer to the different approaches or styles that work best with a given student. The four types of learning styles are visual learners, auditory learners, tactile learners, and kinesthetic learners, choice (D).

MULTIPLE-CHOICE II EXPLANATIONS

1. B

One of the key aspects of the *No Child Left Behind Act* is that educational reform should place an emphasis on teaching methods that have been proven to work, choice (B). Decreased local control of schools, (A), monthly reports on meeting standards, (C), and progress reports based on race or ethnicity, (D), are not discussed in the NCLB Act.

2. A

Accommodation without assimilation refers to the importance of encouraging students to adapt to the dominant culture (accommodation) while maintaining a sense of their cultural identity, choice (A). Encouraging students to lose their cultural identity would be assimilation and would not demonstrate tolerance and understanding of diversity and multiculturalism. Choice (B) is incorrect because it fails to consider how accommodating to the dominant culture is an important component in "accommodation without assimilation."

3. C

The main components that affect the developmental process and the rate at which a child develops are heredity (nature) and the environment (nurture), choice (C). It is important to remember that a child's development is also affected by the interplay and interaction between the two. Socioeconomic levels, self-esteem, and age at the beginning of school are less influential on development.

4. A

The practice of inclusion requires classrooms to be prepared for a wide range of students. These groups can include gifted students, physically disabled students, learning disabled students, and students with emotional and behavioral disorders,

choice (A). Choices (B), (C), and (D) focus too narrowly on individual groups of students. Only (A) addresses the larger groups discussed in relation to inclusion.

5. B

Economic issues and physical qualities and dress cannot be accommodated in terms of daily instruction. Cultural differences in behavior patterns like eye contact and family relationships and expectations can be dealt with in terms of a teacher's daily instruction. Consequently, (B) is correct.

6. C

Piaget's theory about development is based on the idea of learning through active involvement in the child's environment. Children develop by discerning ideas about the physical nature of things, also described as action and logic versus perception. He believed that children developed in four stages, going from birth to understanding concepts based on reason. This type of learning is classified as cognitive, so (C) is correct.

7. D

Cultivation of desired capabilities, (A), personalization of education, (B), and approaching a discipline from a variety of ways, (C), all respond to the idea that there are multiple intelligences and that students strengths should be identified and dealt with accordingly. Choice (D), grading without regard to context, fails to take this sort of sensitivity into account and would be a misuse of Gardner's Multiple Intelligence Theory. Consequently, (D) is correct.

8. D

According to Bloom's Taxonomy, *application* allows a student to use learned material concepts and principals in new and concrete situations. Synthesis, (A), refers to using old ideas to create new ones or connecting or relating knowledge from several areas. Evaluation, (B), refers to assessing value to different ideas. Comprehension, (C), refers to understanding and grasping the meaning of ideas.

9. D

Scaffolding is a concept from Vygotsky's social constructivist approach that emphasizes the social context in which learning takes place. In the case of scaffolding, a behavior is initially modeled by a teacher and then gradually conferred over to the students. This scaffolding or bridging demonstrates the social context or zone of proximal development in which much of learning takes place. (D) is correct.

10. B

Piaget's stages of cognitive development proceed as follows: sensorimotor, preoperational, concrete operations, and formal operations. Therefore, the first stage would be (B), sensorimotor.

11. D

Locus of control refers to the notion that certain people believe that the causes of behavior or events are internal, whereas others believe that these things result from external, environmental factors. (D) is correct.

12. A

The distinction between extrinsic and intrinsic motivation is an important one to understand for the PLT test. Intrinsic motivation is motivation that comes from the enjoyment and engagement inherent in the task itself. Extrinsic motivation is motivation based on external rewards or reinforcers. In the case of this question, a child being given a gold sticker for good work is an example of extrinsic motivation, choice (A).

Section Four

ELEMENTARY EDUCATION PRACTICE TESTS AND EXPLANTATIONS

CHAPTER FIVE

REVIEW OF THE CONTENT AREA EXERCISES (0012)

INTRODUCTION

To effectively use the Reading, Language Arts, Mathematics, Science, and Social Studies teaching strategies and activities for students, the teacher needs to understand how students learn and develop. Teachers also need to provide learning experiences that support all students' intellectual, social, and personal growth. This includes students who have special needs and those who are second language learners. By using a variety of instructional and assessment strategies for academic development, you will encourage students to actively participate in their learning. You should also encourage home-school partnerships to achieve the common goals for the student's education. Most importantly, you will be able to create a cooperative and supportive classroom environment that addresses the needs of individual students and where all students can grow and learn.

READING/LANGUAGE ARTS (25%)

Instruction

You will need to provide a balanced reading, writing, speaking, and listening program and recognize the importance of Reading/Language Arts competence for learning across the content areas. Know how to apply language arts strategies and concepts in relation to content in a variety of subjects. Understand that learning across the content areas requires mastery of Reading/Language Arts competencies. Provide instruction that promotes students' transfer of skills developed in a Reading/Language Arts context to other content areas. For example, using prereading, during-reading, and postreading activities in the study of social studies will increase comprehension.

Recognize the interrelationships of reading, writing, listening, and speaking. Phonological awareness, knowledge of the alphabetic principle, and spelling skills are all linked and are important for success in reading and writing. Incorporate all aspects of students' language development based on their previous language experiences and strengths. Creating an environment in which students come to understand the importance of the development of literacy will empower them to direct their own language learning and make literacy meaningful to them.

The reading process is an interaction between the reader, text, and context to construct meaning. Recognize how reading competence emerges, and apply this knowledge in instructional contexts. Know the interrelationships between decoding and the comprehension processes. The competencies needed to develop proficiency in decoding text are phonological and phonemic awareness, application of the alphabetic principle, word analysis skills, phonics, syllabication, structural analysis/morphology, and use of semantic and syntactic clues. Know what role previous knowledge and developmental issues play in the emergence and extension of literacy.

Reading for various purposes requires the use of different reading strategies. Understand the factors that affect comprehension reading fluency, word identification skills, and previous knowledge. Some strategies that help students understand written material are self-questioning, predicting, inferring, and summarizing. Include comprehension skills, such as comparing and contrasting, drawing conclusions, and finding the main idea, in your daily instructions.

Recognize students' difficulties in their development of reading competence. Know how to use appropriate instructional methods and resources to help the students compensate for their difficulties. Certain reading disorders and difficulties that may arise are dyslexia, social-emotional issues, lack of previous educational experience, background knowledge, vocabulary knowledge, lack of phonemic and phonological awareness, and lack of reading fluency. Some ways of dealing with those disorders and difficulties are explicit instruction in needed skills, developing students' background knowledge, and matching instructional methods and materials to the students' developmental levels and learning styles. Know how to plan interventions for specific needs for individual students and for small groups of students.

Apply a variety of methods, materials, approaches, and classroom organization strategies to use in reading and language arts instruction. Provide opportunities for students to apply and extend skills through various approaches and activities such as language experience, thinking aloud, directed reading/thinking, collaborative and individual writing, creative dramatics, independent reading, and conferencing. Know how to select and use appropriate materials, such as big books, decodable texts, trade books, magazines, and computer software, to support instruction. Organize the classroom environment to facilitate learning can be accomplished through heterogeneous grouping, reading centers, and writing centers.

It is important to use a variety of children's literature in the classroom. Understand that using appropriate literature can promote the students' social, emotional, intellectual, and literary development. Familiarity with major types of children's fiction and nonfiction literature, popular books, authors, and themes of children's literature will help in selecting books for students for purposes such as addressing individual student needs and interests, promoting independent reading, and encouraging the appreciation and critical evaluation of literature.

The three parts to reading instruction lessons are prereading, during-reading, and postreading instruction. Understand the importance of prereading activities like word recognition, context clues, and K-W-L charts. Know that during reading, students can work on vocabulary development, graphic organizers, and decoding skills. For postreading activities, include journal writing, reactions, rewriting information, and comprehension and interpretation skills.

Know the similarities and differences between oral and written English-syntax and vocabulary. Be familiar with strategies for helping students transfer their oral language communication skills to writing. Prewriting, Drafting, Revising, Editing, and Publishing are all part of writing instruction. Know the students' stages of writing development and strategies to correct and improve their skills.

Direct instruction and guided practice in the English writing conventions of grammar, capitalization, punctuation, and spelling should be available to students. Know the various stages of spelling development: prephonetic, phonetic, transitional, and conventions. Students will need support to progress from one developmental stage to the next. Know how to provide systematic instruction in common spelling patterns based on phonics skills already taught. Provide opportunities for students to use and develop their understanding of English writing conventions in the context of meaningful written expression.

Listening is an active cognitive process in which the listener constructs meaning from the content and intent of the speaker's message. It is also affected by the students' previous knowledge and their ability to ask appropriate questions. Know how to guide students to improve their listening through instructional activities, such as directed listening/thinking and reading literature.

A student's development of listening, speaking, writing, and reading vocabularies are affected by cognitive maturity, experiential background, cultural and language background, personality characteristics, and social interactions. These factors affect student progress. Identify instructional methods and strategies likely to be effective in working with individual students as well as groups. You must be clear when promoting students' awareness of the sounds (phonemes) of oral language to facilitate their understanding of the alphabetic principle and development of graphophonemic knowledge (letter-sound relationships). Some strategies to promote students' vocabulary development are retelling stories, creating semantic maps or concept maps, using graphophonemic cues, structural analysis, etymology, and context clues to determine word meanings.

Assessment

Assessment of the students in Reading and Language Arts reveals the success of the instructional teaching methods and strategies used. Know how to administer and interpret the results of a variety of informal and formal assessment instruments, both criterion-referenced and norm-referenced. Know how to plan instruction based on these formal assessment results. Understand the characteristics, uses, and limitations of various types of conventional reading assessment instruments and the rationales for selecting particular assessment instruments in given situations.

Using multiple, ongoing assessments and knowledge of grade-level expectations to identify students' reading and language arts strengths assists in the development of specific reading and language arts skills. Monitor student performance, plan appropriate reading and language arts instruction, and determine when a student may be in need of additional help (classroom intervention, individualized instruction, and help beyond the classroom). It is important to recognize when to use intervention before remediation becomes necessary. The instructional applications of diagnostic results are identifying students' reading strengths and selecting instructional methods and materials to respond to students' needs.

Observe the stages of the students' development, and maintain appropriate records of these observations. Know how to analyze and assess student work using informal measures such as observation, informal reading inventories (IRI), running records, miscue analysis, cloze procedure, anecdotal records, conferencing, oral reports, and portfolios.

Understand the basis for using the Frye Readability Index in assessing texts and other reading materials suitable for student use. Try administering the basal reader assessment instruments, interpreting the results, and planning instruction from the results. You should be able to plan and provide learning activities that build on the students' stages of development (what they already know and what they are able to do at their stages of development).

Adapt assessment materials for the students with special needs, including the gifted students. Provide opportunities that use performance and authentic assessment as well as structured assessment situations. There is a big difference between students requiring regular intervention and the instructional needs of students with special needs.

Understand the criteria and procedures for evaluating reading programs and materials. The evaluation results may modify reading programs and materials used.

Reading Glossary

alphabetic principle
anecdotal record
background knowledge
basal reader
cloze procedure

comprehension
concept of print
concept web
conferencing
context clues
decodable text
decoding
developmentally appropriate
during-reading
dyslexia
emergent literacy
expository text
fluency
graphic organizer
informal reading inventory (IRI)
journals
language acquisition
language arts
literacy
linguistically diverse
miscue analysis
morphology
narrative text
orthographic knowledge
phonemic awareness
phonics
phonological awareness
phonology
portfolios
postreading
predictable text
prereading
previous knowledge
print rich environment
readability
reading strategies
retelling stories
running record
scanning

semantic map
semantics
structural analysis
syntactic
trade books
vocabulary development
word analysis

Writing, Spelling, & Listening Glossary

brainstorming
clustering
conventional
drafting
editing
etymology
graphophonemic knowledge
inventive spelling
listening skills
oral language
orthographic knowledge
outlining
phonemes
phonetic
prefix
prephonetic
prewriting
publishing
punctuation
restructuring
revising
spelling skills
structural analysis
suffix
syntax
transitional
webbing
writing conference

MATHEMATICS (25%)

Understand mathematical communication, and use mathematical language and vocabulary, representations, and data to communicate information to the students. Know how to describe and communicate quantitative information using symbolic, verbal, graphic, and concrete representations, such as models, tables, graphs, diagrams, and drawings, to the students. The use of these terms should be emphasized in the classroom to breed familiarity.

Understand the fundamental concepts of number and numeration systems including quantification, notation, and operations, and relate these concepts to real-life situations. Know how to promote students' understanding of number and numeration by using such mathematical activities as measuring, ordering, comparing, and symbolizing. Identify opportunities to integrate mathematical concepts into instruction in other content areas.

How can everyday situations be used to aid students in their exploration of patterns, their understanding of the functional relationships shown in these patterns, their ability to represent patterns they have seen, and their ability to make predictions based on their observations? Use mathematical operations and computations as an instructional technique to answer this question.

Know how to represent geometric figures through a variety of means such as model making and drawing from different perspectives. Be able to communicate to the students an understanding of geometry as a method for exploring the physical world. The principles and conventions of measurement can be used to describe and compare phenomena in the real world. Learn strategies that use nonstandard and standard units of measurement. Be able to instruct students on making conversions within a measurement system.

Provide instruction that aids students in their ability to apply statistics and probability concepts, to collect, organize, and interpret data, construct and interpret charts and graphs, draw conclusions, and make decisions in everyday statistical and probability situations. Explore the use of manipulatives and developmentally appropriate materials to enhance student learning.

There are three ways to organize the classroom for efficient instruction: small group, whole group, or individual work. Create a mathematics atmosphere in the classroom that encourages questions, conjectures, problem solving, and experimentation.

Recognize the role of higher-order thinking and questioning in the mathematics curriculum. Encourage the development of thinking and questioning skills in students by providing opportunities for students to discover and apply mathematical principles in a variety of contexts, including real world applications. Select appropriate strategies from a variety of approaches to problem solving such as acting out problems, making models, using manipulatives, guessing and checking, and working backwards. Know how to guide students in the problem-solving process. Be able to develop the students' ability to solve problems using a variety of strategies and techniques. Know how to use calculators and computers in problem solving and concept development. Encourage the use of computers and calculators in the classroom.

Mathematical concepts and skills within mathematics may be related to other content areas and daily life. Understand the interrelatedness of the various areas of mathematics and use mathematics as a context for extending learning on other curricular areas. Teaching strategies and activities that will aid in the development, delivery, and evaluation of the mathematics curriculum components are scope and sequence of skills and materials, appropriate materials and technology, and learner objectives. Consider the developmental levels of the students when implementing the mathematics instructional program. Understand how to assess previous mathematics knowledge, how to construct knowledge, how to model lessons, how to use informal reasoning, and how to use graphic organizers.

Know how to analyze students' work and correct misconceptions, errors, and what they do incorrectly. Understand the use of rubrics in assessment, when to remediate, and when to accelerate instruction. Know how to use the results of standardized tests as well as informal testing results.

Mathematics Glossary

addition & subtraction relationship

algorithm

arithmetic

attribute

base-ten

basic math facts

calculator

classifying

comparing

composites

computer

computation

conservation of number

constructivist teaching

coordinate geometry

counting

decimals, fractions, percents

equations

equivalence

estimation

expanded notation

factors

geometric concepts

graphing

heuristic

informal geometry

logic

manipulatives

mathematics

measurement

metric units

multiples

multiplication & division relationship

number concepts

number patterns

number theory

numeration systems

odd & even

operations

ordered sets

place value

Polya's problem solving process

primes

probability

problem solving

ratio & proportion

rational counting

rational numbers

remainders

rubrics

sets

statistics

story problems

visual-spatial

whole numbers

SCIENCE OR SOCIAL STUDIES (25%)

Science

Understand the science curriculum components of scope and sequence, appropriate materials, technology, and learner objectives. Provide developmentally appropriate experiences that will promote the students' understanding, skills, and concepts. Students need appropriate opportunities for them to apply their previous knowledge. Understand learning cycles, constructivism, inquiry, and discovery learning. Know how to apply and encourage higher-order thinking skills in the sciences that will provide students with opportunities to develop these skills in meaningful contexts.

Understand basic science concepts and be able to apply these concepts to interpret and analyze phenomena in planning instruction. The techniques and strategies that promote students' understanding of science as inquiry learning are best demonstrated as active construction of ideas and explanations, ability to ask questions, investigate, observe, construct explanations, and communicate results, and problem solving. Understand the unifying concepts and processes in science, such as providing connections between the traditional scientific disciplines of systems, subsystems, models, and conservation.

Recognize procedures for systematically observing the natural and human-made world. Be able to instruct students in locating needed information, organizing science data, identifying similarities and differences, and on how to arrange events and activities in appropriate sequential order to support a scientific investigation. Communicate the appropriate scientific vocabulary and visual representations such as graphs, tables, diagrams, maps, and models required to accurately communicate scientific information.

Be familiar with the basic safety rules required in a scientific laboratory. You should know how to model the correct use of the equipment, technology, and the instructional materials available in science laboratories.

Provide students with meaningful and developmentally appropriate experiences to assist them in developing an understanding of experimental design. Setting up hypotheses, testing hypotheses using control and experimental groups, identifying variables, and recognizing changes, errors, and omissions in experiments are steps frequently required for experimentation.

Know how to analyze students' work. Understand what the student does correctly, what misconceptions and errors are involved, and at what level of development are the concepts being understood. Be able to use the results of rubrics, formal and informal testing, and remediation or enrichment.

Demonstrate to the students an understanding of how the life, earth, space, and physical sciences relate to one another. Understand the interrelatedness of science to other curricular areas. Use opportunities to integrate elements of the science curriculum into other content areas, such as language arts, social studies, and mathematics. The students need to learn how to investigate science and apply scientific principles and skills. Be able to provide developmentally appropriate experiences for the students that will assist them in their skills and concept development. Some of these skills are organizing data, problem solving, comparing and contrasting, model building, planning, forecasting, and decision-making.

Science Glossary

analyze

calculator

computer

concept

conceptualizing

conclusion

constructivism

control group

corrclation

discovery learning

experiment

experimental design

experimental group

higher-order thinking

hypothesis

inquiry

interpretation

investigation

learning cycle

misconception

model

observation

rubric

scientific principle

scientific process

scientific skills

variable

Social Studies

There are many components of the social studies curriculum. Some of the most important ones are scope and sequence, appropriate materials, technology, and learner objectives. Know how to provide developmentally appropriate experiences that will promote the students' understanding of these concepts and skills. Instruct using inquiry based instruction, and assist students in decision-making, forecasting, planning, problem solving, comparing and contrasting, and organizing data. Know how to instruct map and globe skills and the use of models.

Understand, apply, and encourage higher-order thinking skills in students evaluating decisions or having diverse views regarding a historical or contemporary issue. Provide students with opportunities to develop these skills in varied and meaningful contexts. Understand how to use a variety of methods including visual and oral approaches to present and interpret social studies information such as maps, tables, time lines, charts, graphs, Internet sites, and models. Be helpful in instructing students on how to do presentations, demonstrations, dramatizations, exhibits, and debates.

The major characteristics of world civilizations, cultures groups, historical events, social structures, social organizations, and human behavior in society should be emphasized in each lesson. Provide students with opportunities to gain an understanding of past societies and to recognize the connections between the past and the present. Be able to assist the students in understanding the geography, government, and history of the United States and the world. Inform students about the major developments in the history of the United States, including the governmental system, the principles, ideals, rights, and responsibilities of citizenship, and the fundamental principles and concepts of economics. Recognize the major developments in world history, and foster students' understanding of those basic developments.

Incorporate appropriate activities for students to explore the nature and significance of cultural diversity in historical and contemporary contexts, and how culture and cultural diversity have shaped the United States and other societies.

Promote the development of appropriate concepts and skills in organizing data, problem solving, comparing and contrasting, model building, planning, forecasting, and decision-making.

Research skills and methods in social studies are needed to provide students with opportunities to choose topics and develop ideas in varied and meaningful contexts. Adapt skills and methods for the developmental levels of the students in formulating research questions, identifying primary and secondary sources to meet given needs, recognizing the uses of maps, observation, statistical data, and interviews, applying note-taking skills, and evaluating and organizing information gathered from source materials.

Integrating social studies with other areas of the curriculum such as reading, language arts, science, and mathematics will only expand the larger scope of the students' intelligence. Be able to provide instruction using knowledge of the students' learning levels, multiple intelligences, and developmental levels, and adapt instruction for students with special needs.

Create a social studies atmosphere in the classroom that encourages questions, promotes appreciation of and respect for human diversity, and provides opportunities for students to explore and understand social interactions where they can recognize their own personal social responsibilities.

The use of traditional and standardized testing results may assist in instruction. Be able to anticipate and identify common points of confusion in social studies such as factual errors, patterns of error, inaccuracies, and conceptual misconceptions.

Social Studies Glossary

citizenship

concepts

contemporary society

culture

cultural diversity

democratic values

economics

geography

government

history

interrelationships

observation

political science

research

society

statistical data

INTERDISCIPLINARY INSTRUCTION (25%)

Understand the interrelationships among the content areas. Integrate concepts and skills across content areas. Understand how to use a variety of methods and strategies that help students understand the interrelationship and see connections with the different content areas. Know teaching strategies and activities that will aid in the development, delivery, and evaluation of the integrated content areas. Understand that students can read, write, draw, make models and maps, dramatize, use puppets, sing, make exhibits or demonstrations, and perform in debates in all of the content areas: reading, language arts, mathematics, science, and social studies. Be able to provide methods to identify, assess, activate, and build on the previous knowledge, experiences, and skills that a given group of students brings to learning in each content area. Be able to provide justification for instructional activities in integrated content areas.

Know which teaching and learning strategies will help individual students and groups of students understand varied topics and concepts. Adapt instruction for students of special needs, including gifted and second-language learners.

Practice Test Four Content Area Exercises (0012)

QUESTION 1: READING—30 Minutes

Madison is the youngest student in Miss Thompson's first grade class and has repeatedly shown signs of stress at being unable to do things that the older students are able to accomplish with ease. Miss Thompson has become concerned about this situation and is trying to think of ways to help Madison succeed in the daily classroom activities. She has thought about pairing Madison up with an older student during difficult activities or giving Madison alternative work when the other students are doing more difficult activities. However, Miss Thompson is not sure that this would improve Madison's ability to do the first grade curriculum.

Miss Thompson has assessed Madison's reading skills and has found that she makes several errors in her oral reading, especially when she comes across unfamiliar words. Madison substitutes other real words or nonsense words that are structurally similar to the printed words rather than words that are semantically or syntactically correct. Because of Madison's errors (miscues) with unfamiliar words, she has difficulty comprehending reading passages and interpreting the written questions about the passages.

Miss Thompson needs to work on a strategy to help Madison's self-esteem, intrinsic motivation, and strategies to improve Madison's sight word repertoire, her decoding strategies, and other strategies to assure that she is successful in the first grade reading program.

What appropriate instructional approaches should Miss Thompson apply to help Madison gain reading competence? How can Miss Thompson help Madison develop a positive self-concept and improve her self-esteem? How can Miss Thompson help Madison develop a wide range of cognitive skills and abilities for Madison within the classroom environment?

_____

_____

_____

_____

_____

_____

_____

_____

_____

_____

_____

_____

_____

_____

_____

_____

_____

_____

_____

_____

QUESTION 2: INTEGRATED SCIENCE/LANGUAGE ART—30 Minutes

Mr. Garcia's sixth grade class is made up of 10 Mexican-Americans, 8 African-Americans, and 10 white students. Of the 28 students in the class, 8 are in the gifted program, 5 are ADHD, and 1 of the students has a physical disability.

Mr. Garcia always has his sixth grade class use different types of literature and language arts skills in all the content areas. Their first unit in science was a unit on volcanoes. He organized the students into groups of four and gave them a list of questions about volcanoes to work on together. So far, Mr. Garcia's sixth graders have read magazine articles, current news reports, and information books from the school library. They've also performed research on the Internet in the classroom. He also encouraged the groups to think of questions they could ask themselves as they read to help them assess all the materials they were reading. Mr. Garcia has let his students work in groups with the questions and materials for three weeks.

Today, Mr. Garcia plans to meet with the entire class and present other activities for the groups. What activities could Mr. Garcia present to help the students learn more about volcanoes and at the same time use their reading and language arts skills? How can he create learning experiences that are meaningful for the diverse students in his class? What activities could he use that would foster inquiry, critical thinking, problem solving, collaboration, performance skills, and supportive interaction for all the students? Mr. Garcia plans to support the individual students' cognitive, social, and personal development as well as their acquisition of knowledge and motivation.

List and describe in detail four activities that Mr. Garcia could use with his sixth grade class.

_____

_____

_____

_____

_____

_____

_____

_____

_____

_____

QUESTION 3: SOCIAL STUDIES—30 Minutes

Mrs. Palmer, a first year teacher, had her third graders read several folk tales from around the world to help promote her students' multicultural awareness and appreciation of other countries. After the students read a folk tale, they drew a map of each folk tale's country, showing the cities and landforms. Mrs. Palmer has planned on having the students write a report comparing any two folk tales and describe the cultural characteristics of each country. She plans on having the students present their reports to the class. She is concerned about how meaningful these assignments would be for Maria. Maria's family moved to the United States from Venezuela four months ago. Her speaking skills in English are improving, but her reading comprehension tends to vary from selection to selection. Mrs. Palmer believes this may be related to Maria's degree of familiarity with the topic of a selection and her English reading ability.

Mrs. Palmer recognizes the importance of language competence for learning across the content areas, but she is uncertain how to apply meaningful strategies and concepts to help Maria's English speaking and reading comprehension difficulties. Mrs. Palmer wants to promote all her students' cognitive development and their understanding of cultural diversity through active exploration of the social studies concepts and principles.

Instead of having the class only read the folk tales for information for their report, what other methods and approaches can Mrs. Palmer use to present and interpret the social studies information? How can she adapt the assignments for Maria so that she has a meaningful learning experience? How can Mrs. Palmer organize her instructional methods and resources to help Maria compensate for her difficulties?

_____

_____

_____

_____

_____

_____

_____

_____

_____

_____

QUESTION 4: MATHEMATICS—30 Minutes

Ms. Lowden has a combination class of 12 first and 12 second graders. She is planning a five-day unit on number patterns for the students and hopes her lessons will reinforce their understanding of the concept of patterns. She wants them to recognize, predict, compare, manipulate, create, and repeat patterns in a hands-on environment. She also wants them to recognize the patterns they meet every day in the real world. She wants all of her students to achieve high mathematical standards. Her goal is that by working with patterns and their relationships, the students will learn that mathematics is really a type of science. She knows that she must consider the individual developmental levels of her students and plan learning experiences for them that are chronologically age-appropriate and relevant to her students' previous knowledge. She would like to plan methods and strategies in this unit that incorporate the learning styles and modalities as well as the multiple intelligences.

Ms. Lowden has the following materials available in her classroom to use with her patterns unit:

Linking cubes (Unifix)	Shoelaces
Pattern blocks	Blocks, tiles
Cuisenaire rods	Popsicle sticks
Large box of buttons	Calculators
Box of stickers	Graph paper
Boxes of colored toothpicks	Colored pencils
Colored beads	Colored paper
Blank paper	

Miss Lowden's lesson plan for the unit on patterns begins with her objectives:

- The students will recognize how everyday situations may be used to aid them in their exploration of patterns and functional relationships shown in these patterns.
- The students will demonstrate an understanding of number patterns by drawing patterns they have seen, making predictions based on their observations, creating their own patterns, and demonstrating an understanding of the relationship of these patterns.

Introduction

1. Discuss with the students what a pattern is. Write their responses on a web. Remind them that patterns can be found in many places, and they also include numbers.

2. Ask the students to name some number patterns they know. Write these on the board.

3. Write a number pattern on the board (2,3,4,5, __). Ask the students what would come next.

4. Write a letter pattern on the board (AA, BB, ABA, AA, BB, __). Ask the students what would come next.

5. Write a color pattern on the board (red, blue, yellow, red, blue, __). Ask the students what would come next.

6. Write an object pattern on the board (rock, stick, seed, rock, stick, seed, __). Ask the students what would come next.

Day 1 Activity

Have the students write three of their own number patterns, three color patterns, and three object patterns on a piece of blank paper. Remind them to be creative in their patterns.

When the students have completed their pattern papers, have them share them with the class.

Day 2 Activity

Review what a pattern is. Ask for volunteers to come to the board to write a pattern. It can be a number, letter, color, or object pattern.

Give each child a small paper bag and take the class on a nature walk around the school grounds. Have them collect small objects that they could use to make patterns (pebbles, leaves, pinecones, feathers, grass, seeds, etc.) and put them in their paper bags. Return to the classroom, and have the students work in groups of two to four to move their objects into a patterned form. Hand out blank paper for this. When they finish, have them share their patterns with the class.

Activities for Days 3–5

This is where Ms. Lowden needs your help. She needs activities for day 3, day 4, and day 5 that will allow the students to accomplish her learning goals about patterns. She wants these activities to incorporate learning styles and modalities as well as the multiple intelligences. What activities can you suggest to Ms. Lowden. Use as many of the materials she has in her classroom that you can for this unit.

Practice Test Four
Content Area Exercises
Sample Responses

1.

Miss Thompson understands the indicators that are causing Madison's problem in reading competence. By using her knowledge of reading as a process, Miss Thompson should apply appropriate instructional approaches and intervention in relation to these indicators. She can provide books or computer software reading programs for Madison that have the vocabulary of regular and irregular sight words so she can begin improving her sight reading vocabulary. Miss Thompson can prepare sets of flash cards of the words that Madison's miscues so that she can work with these in the classroom and at home. She can also provide Madison with a tape recorder so that she can tape her own oral reading and make a self-evaluation of what she read aloud. In this manner, Madison could hear her nonsense words and understand that they do not fit in the content or context of the reading passage. Miss Thompson could help Madison understand the use of context clues in figuring out difficult words if she and Madison both listened to the tapes. Miss Thompson should also help Madison with her decoding skills and confirm that Madison knows the phonemes linked to the letter symbols. She should also review the basic phonics skills that Madison needs. This should help Madison improve her comprehension skills. If Miss Thompson provides a print-rich classroom environment where everything in the room is labeled, Madison will be immersed in the environment and can learn more sight words.

Miss Thompson could address the issue of Madison's poor self-concept and self-esteem by creating a developmentally appropriate learning environment that provides opportunities for Madison to develop a sense of achievement and competence within her own stage of development and learning domains. Once Miss Thompson has figured out where Madison is developmentally on Piaget's cognitive levels of development, she can provide opportunities for Madison to develop a wide range of cognitive skills and abilities that Madison can perform with success thus increasing a positive self-concept.

2.

Mr. Garcia should create a list of various developmentally appropriate activities for his diverse class and create a rubric for assessment of each activity. He should give copies of both of these to the students. Because Mr. Garcia has culturally diverse as well as special needs students in his classroom, the activities should further develop the students' scientific knowledge about volcanoes and be adaptable to all his students. The activities should incorporate all the learning styles, learning modalities, and the eight multiple intelligences.

These are four activities that Mr. Garcia could use with his sixth grade class:

1. Each group is to make a model of a volcano out of paper-maché. From their previous three weeks of research, the students should understand that there are three types of volcanoes, and each type has a distinct shape. The students are to make their model in one of the types and shapes. They are to write a detailed description of their volcano and tell how their type of volcano was formed. They are to also create a poem or song about their volcano. This activity meets the needs of the students who have bodily kinesthetic, verbal/linguistic, musical, or visual/spatial intelligences. They will present their model, description, and song/poem to the class.

2. Each group is to make a working model of a volcano that has a chemical reaction—they will be provided with the directions by Mr. Garcia. Each group will receive different directions for making a volcano that Mr. Garcia has found. They will do this in the school's science lab. They will write a science lab report that explains in scientific terms what actually happens when their model volcano "erupts." This activity will support the individual students' cognitive, social, and personal development as well as their acquisition of knowledge about volcanoes and motivation.

3. Mr. Garcia will present a written scenario to the class about the year 2005 when a large Indonesian volcano has erupted. It is the worst eruption in recorded history. To make matters worse, four of the other major volcanoes in the world are also erupting, all violently. Have each group act as teams of volcanologists assigned as aides to the president of the United States. Each group's assignment is to give the president a report on what can be expected to happen and what steps can be taken to help people cope with the disaster. The students can use the Internet or other research materials to locate the largest volcanoes in the world and learn some background material about them. They should answer questions such as "What kind of volcanic eruption are we dealing with in each case?" and "How fast is the lava or ash flowing?" Have each group make a logbook of its findings and recommendations. Who is in danger? What are the recommendations to save people and towns? How will each eruption affect the environment? How long will the effects last? Have each group present its findings to the class. This activity will provide students the opportunity to use their previous knowledge, use basic science concepts, use higher-order thinking skills, and allow them to use their inquiry and discovery skills.

4. Live from the Kalapana Volcano! Mr. Garcia can have the students write news accounts as if they were reporters covering the eruption in Kalapana, Hawaii, detailing the sights and sounds of the city's destruction. They can use the Internet or other resources to research the eruption. Have them prepare visuals to support their news stories and report their stories "live" from the scene. They should include mock interviews with Kalapana citizens and volcanologists on site. Mr. Garcia can have the students plan out their articles using a computer and display their work around the classroom.

   This higher-level thinking activity will allow the students to use their writing skills, computer skills, and will appeal to those who display visual/spatial, verbal/linguistic, and interpersonal intelligences.

Adaptations for the gifted students

1. Have each student research a famous volcanic eruption in history and describe the eruption scientifically, explaining the type of eruption and its long-term effects on the environment and its effects on human life.

2. Have each student create a front-page newspaper story on the computer describing an important volcano eruption.

Adaptation for special needs students

Have each student research and make a list of all the volcanoes in the world sorted by country/area: Africa, Australia, Europe, West Asia, North America, North Asia, South America, and Southeast Asia. Have them create their list on the computer.

3.

Instead of having the class only read the folk tales for information, also have them use the Internet for more information on the countries and the cultures and on the folk tales themselves. They can also listen to tapes of the stories that Mrs. Palmer can get from the school media center, or make herself, or they can read the folk tales aloud to each other.

If the students are paired up to read to each other, Mrs. Palmer can choose a student who reads well to read to Maria so that she hears the story read aloud as she follows along in her own copy of the folk tale. This will help her with her English language skills.

If Mrs. Palmer puts her students into groups of four, she can have each group work on a required research project list that she prepares and do this research project report together. Mrs. Palmer can give each group copies of a rubric with the requirements for the report. She would discuss the rubric with the class. She can also give them a list of many different activities that incorporate the different learning styles and different modalities as well as the eight multiple intelligences. This list would have activities appropriate for the lowest learners and the gifted or talented students. Mrs. Palmer can have each group choose any five to work on (or whatever number she decides). In this way, Maria can work on activities that are at her language development level, as well as cognitive level, and have success in working on meaningful learning experiences.

When the groups finish their reports, they can present them to the class. In this way, Mrs. Palmer can use the rubric she created to assess their performance (performance assessment). Maria can join her group in presenting their report and share her work. If Mrs. Palmer had the students read a folk tale from Venezuela, Maria could be placed in the group that used this folk tale in their report. Then Maria could share more of her culture, family traditions, and perhaps another Venezuelan folk tale.

The more Maria is immersed in the English language, the more she'll improve in speaking English. Working with a group of students will help her very much in speaking English and with her self-concept as a second language learner.

If Mrs. Palmer establishes a classroom climate that emphasizes collaboration and supportive interactions, the students will learn to respect diversity and individual differences while they engage in their active learning activities. The students will also increase their acceptance and respect for Maria and her diverse background and needs.

4.

Because Ms. Lowden has a mixed class of first and second graders, she needs to be aware of the cognitive development levels of her students and use age appropriate teaching methods and strategies so that all her students will have successful and meaningful experiences. At this age, mathematics should involve many hands-on activities and the use of manipulatives so that the students experience lessons that meet their preoperational needs.

She should begin each day's lesson with a review of what they have learned so far. Having students share in this will allow Ms. Lowden to informally assess what the students are learning. She needs to plan lessons so that activities progress in a logical sequence and support her instructional goals.

On day 3, I'd have the students make a patterned display by combining their collection from the previous day with another student's collection. When they are done creating patterns on their own, I'd give them direct instruction by comparing and contrasting patterns that they have discovered. Then I'd explain the linear patterns in terms of letters—ABAB, ABB, ABBAABB, etc. on the board. I'd also write the patterns in words: pebble, grass, pebble, grass, etc.

I'd give them a piece of blank paper to record their patterns using both letters and pictures. Afterwards, I'd display them all on a bulletin board.

On day 4, I would suggest another student involvement activity in learning more about identifying, analyzing, and extending patterns by taking another walk around the inside and outside of the school. Have the students look for patterns. Stop and discuss any patterns that the students notice. When the class returns to the classroom, have the students draw the pattern they liked the best. Have them make a model of the pattern using the pattern blocks, Unifix cubes, or other materials Ms. Lowden has in the classroom.

Also on day 4, I would have a group lesson on the board. I'd call the lesson, "Guess my rule." I'd write a sequence of four or five numbers on the board and ask the students what numbers would come next. After the students have correctly added two or three numbers, I'd ask them what rule they're using to figure out the next number in the sequence. I'd remind them that the rule must work for every number in the sequence.

I'd use the following numbers for this exercise:

   1,3,5,7

   1,4,7,10

   1,2,3,7,11

   2,4,6,8

   5,10, 15, 20

   10, 20, 30, 40

   1,3,6,10

   1,2,3,5,8

I'd accept all suggested rules the students present and I would try to apply them to the patterns. I would avoid labeling ideas as right and wrong because I want them to take risks in giving their ideas for this higher-level activity.

I'd then hand out slips of papers with number patterns written on them and have the students use any manipulatives of their choice to build the number patterns. For example, 1 3 1 3 (number pattern)

   O O O O

   O O (manipulatives)

   O O

I'd prepare many different levels of difficulty of these number patterns to assure success by even the slowest learner.

On day 5, I'd have the entire class use the same manipulatives. Ms. Lowden has an ample supply of popsicle sticks. I'd demonstrate on the board how to make a fence pattern with the sticks. Picket fence - IIII – AAAA or a fence post with one wire - I-I-I - ABABA. I'd have the students build their own fence patterns with the popsicle sticks, glue them to paper, and have them label them with the AB patterns and name them. I'd let them be as creative as they wanted to be, remembering that the developmental levels are very different in this class.

When the students finished building their fence patterns, we'd have a class circle meeting and share our work. I'd have each student pick one of their fence patterns and tell why the letter pattern fit the fence they made.

Practice Test Five
Answer Sheet

Remove (or photocopy) this answer sheet and use it to complete the practice test.
(See answer key following the test when finished.)

If a section has fewer questions than answer spaces, leave the extra spaces blank.

Reading and Language Arts

1 Ⓐ Ⓑ Ⓒ Ⓓ	11 Ⓐ Ⓑ Ⓒ Ⓓ	21 Ⓐ Ⓑ Ⓒ Ⓓ	31 Ⓐ Ⓑ Ⓒ Ⓓ
2 Ⓐ Ⓑ Ⓒ Ⓓ	12 Ⓐ Ⓑ Ⓒ Ⓓ	22 Ⓐ Ⓑ Ⓒ Ⓓ	32 Ⓐ Ⓑ Ⓒ Ⓓ
3 Ⓐ Ⓑ Ⓒ Ⓓ	13 Ⓐ Ⓑ Ⓒ Ⓓ	23 Ⓐ Ⓑ Ⓒ Ⓓ	33 Ⓐ Ⓑ Ⓒ Ⓓ
4 Ⓐ Ⓑ Ⓒ Ⓓ	14 Ⓐ Ⓑ Ⓒ Ⓓ	24 Ⓐ Ⓑ Ⓒ Ⓓ	34 Ⓐ Ⓑ Ⓒ Ⓓ
5 Ⓐ Ⓑ Ⓒ Ⓓ	15 Ⓐ Ⓑ Ⓒ Ⓓ	25 Ⓐ Ⓑ Ⓒ Ⓓ	35 Ⓐ Ⓑ Ⓒ Ⓓ
6 Ⓐ Ⓑ Ⓒ Ⓓ	16 Ⓐ Ⓑ Ⓒ Ⓓ	26 Ⓐ Ⓑ Ⓒ Ⓓ	36 Ⓐ Ⓑ Ⓒ Ⓓ
7 Ⓐ Ⓑ Ⓒ Ⓓ	17 Ⓐ Ⓑ Ⓒ Ⓓ	27 Ⓐ Ⓑ Ⓒ Ⓓ	37 Ⓐ Ⓑ Ⓒ Ⓓ
8 Ⓐ Ⓑ Ⓒ Ⓓ	18 Ⓐ Ⓑ Ⓒ Ⓓ	28 Ⓐ Ⓑ Ⓒ Ⓓ	38 Ⓐ Ⓑ Ⓒ Ⓓ
9 Ⓐ Ⓑ Ⓒ Ⓓ	19 Ⓐ Ⓑ Ⓒ Ⓓ	29 Ⓐ Ⓑ Ⓒ Ⓓ	
10 Ⓐ Ⓑ Ⓒ Ⓓ	20 Ⓐ Ⓑ Ⓒ Ⓓ	30 Ⓐ Ⓑ Ⓒ Ⓓ	

Mathematics   ## Science

39 Ⓐ Ⓑ Ⓒ Ⓓ	50 Ⓐ Ⓑ Ⓒ Ⓓ	61 Ⓐ Ⓑ Ⓒ Ⓓ
40 Ⓐ Ⓑ Ⓒ Ⓓ	51 Ⓐ Ⓑ Ⓒ Ⓓ	62 Ⓐ Ⓑ Ⓒ Ⓓ
41 Ⓐ Ⓑ Ⓒ Ⓓ	52 Ⓐ Ⓑ Ⓒ Ⓓ	63 Ⓐ Ⓑ Ⓒ Ⓓ
42 Ⓐ Ⓑ Ⓒ Ⓓ	53 Ⓐ Ⓑ Ⓒ Ⓓ	64 Ⓐ Ⓑ Ⓒ Ⓓ
43 Ⓐ Ⓑ Ⓒ Ⓓ	54 Ⓐ Ⓑ Ⓒ Ⓓ	65 Ⓐ Ⓑ Ⓒ Ⓓ
44 Ⓐ Ⓑ Ⓒ Ⓓ	55 Ⓐ Ⓑ Ⓒ Ⓓ	66 Ⓐ Ⓑ Ⓒ Ⓓ
45 Ⓐ Ⓑ Ⓒ Ⓓ	56 Ⓐ Ⓑ Ⓒ Ⓓ	67 Ⓐ Ⓑ Ⓒ Ⓓ
46 Ⓐ Ⓑ Ⓒ Ⓓ	57 Ⓐ Ⓑ Ⓒ Ⓓ	68 Ⓐ Ⓑ Ⓒ Ⓓ
47 Ⓐ Ⓑ Ⓒ Ⓓ	58 Ⓐ Ⓑ Ⓒ Ⓓ	69 Ⓐ Ⓑ Ⓒ Ⓓ
48 Ⓐ Ⓑ Ⓒ Ⓓ	59 Ⓐ Ⓑ Ⓒ Ⓓ	70 Ⓐ Ⓑ Ⓒ Ⓓ
49 Ⓐ Ⓑ Ⓒ Ⓓ	60 Ⓐ Ⓑ Ⓒ Ⓓ	71 Ⓐ Ⓑ Ⓒ Ⓓ

Social Studies   ## Arts & Physical Education   ## General Information

72 Ⓐ Ⓑ Ⓒ Ⓓ	83 Ⓐ Ⓑ Ⓒ Ⓓ	94 Ⓐ Ⓑ Ⓒ Ⓓ	104 Ⓐ Ⓑ Ⓒ Ⓓ
73 Ⓐ Ⓑ Ⓒ Ⓓ	84 Ⓐ Ⓑ Ⓒ Ⓓ	95 Ⓐ Ⓑ Ⓒ Ⓓ	105 Ⓐ Ⓑ Ⓒ Ⓓ
74 Ⓐ Ⓑ Ⓒ Ⓓ	85 Ⓐ Ⓑ Ⓒ Ⓓ	96 Ⓐ Ⓑ Ⓒ Ⓓ	106 Ⓐ Ⓑ Ⓒ Ⓓ
75 Ⓐ Ⓑ Ⓒ Ⓓ	86 Ⓐ Ⓑ Ⓒ Ⓓ	97 Ⓐ Ⓑ Ⓒ Ⓓ	107 Ⓐ Ⓑ Ⓒ Ⓓ
76 Ⓐ Ⓑ Ⓒ Ⓓ	87 Ⓐ Ⓑ Ⓒ Ⓓ	98 Ⓐ Ⓑ Ⓒ Ⓓ	108 Ⓐ Ⓑ Ⓒ Ⓓ
77 Ⓐ Ⓑ Ⓒ Ⓓ	88 Ⓐ Ⓑ Ⓒ Ⓓ	99 Ⓐ Ⓑ Ⓒ Ⓓ	109 Ⓐ Ⓑ Ⓒ Ⓓ
78 Ⓐ Ⓑ Ⓒ Ⓓ	89 Ⓐ Ⓑ Ⓒ Ⓓ	100 Ⓐ Ⓑ Ⓒ Ⓓ	110 Ⓐ Ⓑ Ⓒ Ⓓ
79 Ⓐ Ⓑ Ⓒ Ⓓ	90 Ⓐ Ⓑ Ⓒ Ⓓ	101 Ⓐ Ⓑ Ⓒ Ⓓ	
80 Ⓐ Ⓑ Ⓒ Ⓓ	91 Ⓐ Ⓑ Ⓒ Ⓓ	102 Ⓐ Ⓑ Ⓒ Ⓓ	
81 Ⓐ Ⓑ Ⓒ Ⓓ	92 Ⓐ Ⓑ Ⓒ Ⓓ	103 Ⓐ Ⓑ Ⓒ Ⓓ	
82 Ⓐ Ⓑ Ⓒ Ⓓ	93 Ⓐ Ⓑ Ⓒ Ⓓ		

Practice Test Five
Curriculum, Instruction, and Assessment
(0011/0016)

Time—2 Hours
110 Questions

Reading and Language Arts

Questions 1–3

A fourth-grade teacher has her students get into a reading circle three times a day to read short stories, or sections of stories, for 15 minutes each. While in the reading circle, the students take turns reading two paragraphs each. When difficult words are encountered, the more capable students help the other students with them. In one story, a student has trouble with the word "glistened." When the story is completed, the teacher asks the group to describe how the dew on the leaves looked.

1. By asking the question at the end, the teacher is helping her students to use the word-attack strategy of

    (A) phonic clues
    (B) morphemic clues
    (C) context clues
    (D) sight-word clues

2. What is a limitation of the word-attack strategy the teacher is using?

    (A) This strategy is only useful when reading narratives or stories, not other literature forms.
    (B) The strategy can only be used when a text is written below the student's reading level.
    (C) The text may not contain the necessary information to supply the definition being sought.
    (D) There are irregular pronunciations of consonant blends.

3. By choosing the time and frequency she has chosen (having the students read orally three times a day for fifteen minutes each), the teacher is using

    (A) distributed practice
    (B) massed practice
    (C) guided practice
    (D) independent practice

4. A third-grade teacher wishes to do an appropriate prereading activity that will encourage the students to want to read the story. Which of the following prereading activities would be most likely to accomplish that?

    (A) Telling the students about the author and the period in which the story was written

    (B) Giving the students a list of literary devices they will find employed in the story

    (C) Telling the children that there is a surprise ending and that they will be required to draw a picture showing that ending

    (D) Telling the children the main plot of the story

5. The actual term *phonics* refers to the study of the relationship between

    (A) sounds and symbols

    (B) words and meaning

    (C) reading and writing

    (D) various components across the curriculum

6. A major distinction between the terms *phonics* and *phonemic awareness* is that

    (A) phonemic awareness involves the activities done in student practice books (workbooks), but phonics does not

    (B) phonics involves the written word, and phonemic awareness does not necessarily

    (C) phonemic awareness includes reading, but phonics does not

    (D) neither involves reading for meaning

7. Which of the following is an example showing Vygotsky's Zone of Proximal Development?

    (A) A child knows the short vowel sounds, so he is able to learn the long vowel sounds.

    (B) A class "reads" the words under a picture as the teacher guides them while she points and says the word.

    (C) Children read in groups based on their abilities.

    (D) A teacher pairs students with other students of unlike ability and has them do their worksheets together.

> My dog, Joey, likes to roam the hills. Everyday, he walks with me to the bus, then he heads out through the fields. One day, as he ran toward the hills, he saw a rabbit going toward a barn. Joey ran after the rabbit and into the barn.

8. After having a child read the above paragraph, the teacher asks the child, "Where did the dog go?" In this case, the teacher is assessing the child's ability in

    (A) phonics

    (B) phonemic awareness

    (C) fluency

    (D) comprehension

9. The ability to read a text accurately and fluidly, showing comprehension through use of proper word inflections, is

    (A) decoding

    (B) phonemic awareness

    (C) alliteracy

    (D) fluency

GO ON TO THE NEXT PAGE

| dog | shed | fur |

10. In comparing the phonemes in the words above

(A) two have three, and one has four

(B) they each have three

(C) one had one, one has two, and one has three

(D) it cannot be determined unless one hears how each person pronounces the words

11. If a child can spell and write his name at home but fails to do so in front of the teacher, he

(A) is displaying both spelling competence and performance

(B) has spelling competence but does not display spelling performance

(C) cannot actually spell

(D) is showing spelling performance but not competence

12 If a teacher uses only basal readers for teaching her students to read, she most likely believes in

(A) primarily a whole language approach

(B) primarily a phonics approach

(C) a mixture of whole language and phonics

(D) individualized reading instruction

| **Original Sentence:** |
| The girl was <u>cold</u>, so she put on her coat. |
| **Student Response:** |
| The girl was hot so she put on a swimsuit. |

13. In the above exercise, the students were asked to rewrite the sentence replacing the underlined word with a synonym. The student's response indicates that she

(A) has a good understanding of the concepts of synonyms and homophones

(B) is confusing homophones with synonyms

(C) has mastered the concepts of antonyms and synonyms

(D) has not mastered the concept of synonym usage

14. Reading requires that a person recognize that there is a relationship between

(A) the page numbers and the book order

(B) the symbols on the page and the language that we speak

(C) things adults read and children read

(D) various subjects in school

15. Which of the following is NOT an example of a dichotomy?

(A) A person's ideas about a subject involve two polarizing aspects.

(B) One group of teachers believes phonics is the best method of teaching; another group believes whole language is the better method.

(C) A word has two different meanings, with each representing a nuance.

(D) Some children in a teacher's classroom become good readers and others continue to be nonreaders.

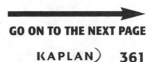

> *Tough Coughs As He Ploughs the Dough*

16. In the title in the box above, the problem with a particular type of reading approach is demonstrated. Which approach?

    (A) Phonics-based approach
    (B) Whole language approach
    (C) Literature-based approach
    (D) Guided reading approach

17. A parent walks into a classroom and sees the children in groups, each gathered around a poster board. The children are writing ideas on the poster board in what looks like graffiti to the parent. When the parent asks the teacher what the children are doing, the teacher is likely to explain that

    (A) this is playtime, and the children need playtime because recess has been taken out of the program
    (B) the children are involved in brainstorming, which is part of the prewriting stage of the writing process
    (C) invented spelling and graffiti type expression is important to the child's development
    (D) the children are creating final versions of posters to be displayed in the school fair

18. If a child is simply sounding out the words in a book using phonics he has learned but does not comprehend what the words are expressing, he is

    (A) reading, but below grade level
    (B) doing meaningless decoding
    (C) pretending to read
    (D) well on his way to becoming literate

19. Each person's vocabulary is a continuum. On the one end of the continuum are words the person knows very well and for which he has a full rich understanding of their various meanings. On the other end of the continuum are

    (A) words he enjoys using regularly
    (B) new words that he's learned both the spelling and meaning for
    (C) words he doesn't recognize
    (D) words he can recognize and figure out the meaning of based on context

20. When a person knows a part of a word because he has encountered the word before or has encountered words that are similar to it, this is called

    (A) partial recognition
    (B) decoding
    (C) cloze activity
    (D) using context

21. Reflection journals in which students are encouraged to write their feelings about a particular literary work and their perceptions of how the work applies to their belief system primarily address assessment in which domain?

    (A) Cognitive
    (B) Social
    (C) Psychomotor
    (D) Affective

GO ON TO THE NEXT PAGE

22. Many teachers teach vocabulary by having students write a word, look it up in the dictionary and copy its definition, and then use the word in a sentence. Research has found that this is

    (A) ineffective for developing a student's vocabulary
    (B) promoted among principals because of its effectiveness
    (C) a good way to teach vocabulary
    (D) effective in preparing students to take college admissions exams

23. If a second-grade teacher has a child who, in early March, is still not reading, she should

    (A) not worry about it, eventually the child will catch up
    (B) be concerned and consider sending the child for remediation so he can learn to read
    (C) figure the child is normal because most children don't really read well until the third grade
    (D) decide that retention is the only option

24. The reason teachers use *guided reading* in the classroom is to give students

    (A) the chance to apply reading strategies with support from the teacher
    (B) books they can take home and read
    (C) the chance to show the whole class they can read aloud
    (D) the chance to read aloud in unison

25. The ultimate goal of using *guided reading* groups in the classroom is for the student to become a(n)

    (A) good group reader
    (B) independent silent reader
    (C) friend to other students in the class
    (D) team player in his group

26. *Reflections* in a reflection journal are described as

    (A) the events that occur in the classroom
    (B) a listing of curriculum used in the classroom
    (C) descriptions of relationships in the classroom
    (D) the author's opinions about what he has seen

27. In terms of working with the children, the first step in *guided reading* is for the teacher to

    (A) place the children in heterogeneous ability groups
    (B) give the students support when they are struggling with words
    (C) give the students a question to answer when they are reading the book
    (D) diagnose the students' reading levels

Questions 28–30

> A teacher pulls a passage out of a book, and writes it out on a worksheet with some of the words replaced with blanks. Then she has the students individually figure out what words they think might go in the blanks. Next, the students get in groups and discuss their suggestions. Each group then comes to a consensus about what words should go in the blanks. Later, she reads the paragraph from the book to them.

28. The above activity is called a

    (A) modified cloze activity with narrowed meaning

    (B) first consonant modified cloze

    (C) interactive cloze activity

    (D) guided reading

29. When writing the passage with the blanks, the teacher should

    (A) leave the first and last sentence intact

    (B) allow students to make up the first and last sentence

    (C) spell words wrong to see if the students can catch them

    (D) always use the first paragraph of the book

30. The reason for doing the above activity with the children before reading a book is for the purpose of providing a(n)

    (A) familiarity with the characters in the book

    (B) setting for the book

    (C) anticipatory set that will make the children be curious enough to want to read the book

    (D) worksheet to grade that shows the students' vocabulary development

31. Which of the following is NOT an essential component of the guided reading process?

    (A) Observing the children as they read

    (B) Providing powerful examples of harder words

    (C) Having the students write out book reports on the books they've read

    (D) Giving support to young readers

32. In terms of rereading books in the classroom, the teacher

    (A) should never allow that because it will bore the children

    (B) should never allow that because the students will not progress if not using new books every day

    (C) may allow books to be reread because it allows the students to recognize their progress from when they first read the book

    (D) may allow books to be reread but only by children who have not read them the first time

33. The study of the meaning of words is called

    (A) phonics

    (B) whole language

    (C) sight word recognition

    (D) vocabulary

34. Once children have been exposed to a new word, they will then

    (A) never use it again unless they need to

    (B) try to use it again in a safe environment

    (C) use it everywhere they can

    (D) need to write it in a sentence in order for it to become a true part of their vocabulary

GO ON TO THE NEXT PAGE

35. In terms of using worksheets in the classroom:

    (A) teachers should never use them

    (B) teachers should use them everyday and grade them according to the directions written on them

    (C) teachers should point out things on the worksheets, have the students answer questions about them, and then do the work indicated by the directions

    (D) teachers should set up a system whereby the students do the worksheets in their workbooks regularly without being told

36. The main reason for doing affix study with children is to

    (A) fix reading problems they are experiencing

    (B) expand student vocabulary by adding prefixes and suffixes with meaning to root words they already know

    (C) show the influence of Latin on present-day English

    (D) prepare students to diagram sentences

37. Which of the following would NOT be an appropriately written objective for a kindergarten class?

    (A) The students will be able to learn their letters.

    (B) The students will be able to write lowercase block letters.

    (C) The students will be able to distinguish between short vowel sounds and long vowel sounds.

    (D) The students will be able to identify capital letters.

38. When a teacher creates a bulletin board in the classroom, its primary purpose is to

    (A) provide a bright learning environment

    (B) display the teacher's creativity so that children will be inspired to be creative as well

    (C) serve as a display for parent conferences

    (D) provide information that relates to the material being taught in the classroom

Mathematics

Questions 39–41 refer to the following passage:

When the principal visited a 7th grade math class, he found three students sitting near the window, looking out at a dog that was chasing a squirrel. When the principal ask the three boys if they needed help, they shrugged and said no and that they knew how to do the work. The principal observed a little longer, then took the three students into the hall to ask why they were continuing to look out of the window instead of doing their worksheet. One replied, "The nerds in there that get done fast have to do more work." Another chimed in. "Yeah, if you wait until there's only about 10 minutes left, then do the worksheet, you don't end up with homework."

39. From the conversation, the principal determined that a routine for

    (A) asking for help with the assignment was in place in the classroom

    (B) rewarding students who finish work promptly was not in place

    (C) requiring students to stay on task while in the classroom had been established

    (D) cooperative learning groups had been formulated so students could work more efficiently

40. The principal can assume from the conversation with the boys that the worksheets being used in the class are

    (A) too advanced for the students
    (B) too easy for the students
    (C) too complicated for the students
    (D) difficult for the students to understand

41. The most appropriate way to address the problem of the students spending their time looking out the window would be to

    (A) put black-out shades over the windows
    (B) move the three boys who are looking out the window away from the window to the inside wall
    (C) put a system of rewards in place for students who stay on task and complete their work correctly in a timely manner
    (D) send the students who look out the window to the principal's office to do their work when they get off task

42. NCTM is what type of organization?

    (A) A government agency
    (B) A non-profit professional organization
    (C) A for-profit organization of teachers and principals
    (D) A federal program developed by Congress to promote math education

43. All of the students in an elementary teacher's classroom obtained stanine scores of 4s and 5s on math computation. The teacher can determine from that that her students are

    (A) mostly average with some just below average in computation
    (B) failing in computational abilities
    (C) a little above average in computation
    (D) performing at the fourth and fifth grade levels in computation

Questions 44–46 refer to the following passage:

Students are given base ten blocks to use to demonstrate their understanding of numeration systems. The ones blocks are red. The tens blocks are green. The hundreds blocks are black. The table below shows how four students demonstrated the number 124.

Barbara	4 red, 12 green
Carletta	4 red, 2 green, 1 black
Janice	4 black, 2 green, 1 red
Jeanne	24 red, 1 black

44. Using a strict place value notation, which of the above students was correct?

    (A) Barbara
    (B) Carletta
    (C) Janice
    (D) Jeanne

45. Allowing for different ways to express a single number value, which of the above students displayed a correct demonstration?

    (A) Barbara and Janice
    (B) Carletta and Janice
    (C) Janice only
    (D) Barbara, Carletta, and Jeanne

46. Using these same manipulatives, along with a yellow minus sign, which of the following would be a correct way to display 124?

    (A) 2 black, 1 yellow, 7 green, 6 red
    (B) 3 black, 2 green, 4 red, 1 yellow, 2 red
    (C) 1 black, 5 green, 4 red, 1 yellow, 3 red
    (D) 1 red, 2 black, 3 green, 1 yellow, 1 black, 2 red, 3 green

GO ON TO THE NEXT PAGE

47. While walking around the room, the teacher notices Marquez has completed the following work:

1/2 + 2/3 = 3/5	1/2 + 1/2 = 2/4
3/5 + 2/3 = 5/8	1/2 + 1/6 = _____

If the error pattern continues, Marquez's answer to the next problem will be

(A) 1/3
(B) 4/5
(C) 7/14
(D) 2/8

48. According to research done on children in the primary grades, the mistakes children make in arithmetic

(A) differ greatly from class to class and year to year
(B) are random
(C) are remarkably consistent in nature
(D) cannot be identified

49. The most common mistake an elementary child makes when doing arithmetic problems is

(A) being illogical in their logic
(B) applying the wrong problem-solving method
(C) having trouble applying the answer to real life
(D) performing computational errors

50. When a teacher is drawing conclusions about a primary student's math ability based on standardized test results, she should use caution because

(A) very little research has been done on primary grade children
(B) the population on which these tests are standardized are older children, not primary grade children
(C) the current standardized tests are invalid in the skills they test
(D) children of this age change so rapidly that scores on a single test may not reflect a student's ability

51. When students are given the chance to use manipulatives to do problems instead of doing them on paper, the result is

(A) they are more likely to get the answer wrong
(B) they are more likely to get the answer right
(C) they enjoy the process less
(D) they do not stay on task

52. Current best practices in mathematics instruction affirms which of the following?

(A) Students should be encouraged to work problems in any way that makes sense to them.
(B) Students should learn appropriate algorithms and always show their work to display proficiency.
(C) Mental math is not an important part of math class work.
(D) Pencil-and-paper drills are the most important part of math class.

53. All of the following are the three most common methods of doing arithmetic EXCEPT

    (A) mental estimation
    (B) using a calculator
    (C) written calculation with paper and pencil
    (D) conversion

54. In order for students to truly learn mathematics, the most effective way for the teacher to structure the math period is to

    (A) have students spend all their time on computation
    (B) have students spend all their time on word problems and applications
    (C) have students spend half their time on computation and half their time on application of math in real life
    (D) have students complete every page in their workbooks

55. If a student is told to add 328 to 527, and he answers 845, this is because he

    (A) borrowed incorrectly
    (B) failed to carry properly
    (C) used the wrong operation
    (D) does not know how to do subtraction

56. The most common borrowing problems students have involve

    (A) numbers in the millions
    (B) the numeral zero
    (C) failure to carry properly
    (D) the numerals 6 and 9

57. When students are working on word problems, what is the first step they should be encouraged to do?

    (A) Figure out what information is being sought
    (B) Determine a plan of action
    (C) Write out an equation
    (D) Figure out a similar problem

58. The word *algorithm* means

    (A) higher level algebra
    (B) a plan for solving a problem
    (C) geometric proportions
    (D) using a graphing calculator

59. In order to do mental math, students must have a mastery of

    (A) basic facts and estimation
    (B) the calculator
    (C) pencil-and-paper drills only
    (D) word problems

60. In the phrase PLEASE EXCUSE MY DEAR AUNT SALLY, the P in PLEASE stands for

    (A) paragraph
    (B) parameter
    (C) parenthesis
    (D) product

GO ON TO THE NEXT PAGE

Science

61. A teacher teaches a lesson on the properties of liquids and gases and then proposes an experiment using soap bubbles. As a class, a hypothesis is proposed. In groups, the experiment is carried out. The results obtained by Groups 1, 2, 3, and 4 confirm the hypothesis. The results from Group 5 do not. If the teacher's objective is for the students to be able to apply the scientific process, which of the following responses would be the LEAST helpful?

    (A) Encouragement for the entire class to redo the experiment

    (B) A recommendation that Group 5 compare their results and methods with another group

    (C) An explanation by the teacher of what the group did wrong

    (D) A suggestion that the students reformulate a new hypothesis based on their data, and do a new experiment to test it

62. After working some problems using a scientific formula, several students have answers that are very different than what they expected. These students are then experiencing

    (A) equilibrium
    (B) disequilibrium
    (C) equilibration
    (D) cognitive balance

63. When the students in the last question ultimately see the reality of why the actual answer is true, the student achieves

    (A) equilibrium
    (B) disequilibrium
    (C) confusion
    (D) perception

64. A teacher in a fifth grade classroom has children go out into the schoolyard and collect rocks. She then has them sort them according to igneous, sedimentary, and metamorphic. She is asking the students to classify the rocks according to

    (A) type of mineral content
    (B) how they were formed
    (C) size and shape
    (D) family and genus

65. That same science teacher has a further objective of having the children classify the rocks according to other characteristics. Which cooperative learning activity would meet that objective?

    (A) Have students read in their texts about rocks

    (B) Have students brainstorm about possible characteristics and then as a group create a chart showing the classifications and rocks that fit in each

    (C) Assign a particular rock to a group, and have them write a group report on the qualities of that rock

    (D) Show a video about the volcanic rocks found in Hawaii

GO ON TO THE NEXT PAGE

66. A teacher has several high-achieving students in his class who finish their science work early and make the other students feel inadequate. To prevent this, an appropriate approach would be to

    (A) allow bonus points for all students who wish to do an extra assignment at any time throughout the hour

    (B) allow bonus point activities for only those students who finish their work ahead of schedule

    (C) allow bonus point activities to be done after the assignment is finished or taken home as homework

    (D) point out to all students that if they work diligently, they too may qualify for doing bonus activities

Questions 67–69

A teacher posted the following table and asked the following question.

James	δδδδ
Marcy	δδδδδδ
Dion	δδδ
Trista	δδδδδδδ
Keva	δδ
δ represents 15 bags of trash collected	

Which of the following statements is true?

Statement 1: Marcy collected half as much as Dion

Statement 2: Trista collected twice as much as Marcy

Statement 3: James and Dion collected the same amount together as did Trista

Statement 4: Keva didn't work as hard as the others

Statement 5: James collected more than Marcy

67. Which of the answers above is correct?

    (A) Statement 1
    (B) Statement 2 and 4
    (C) Statement 3
    (D) Statements 1 and 4

68. What scientific skill is the teacher seeking to teach by asking the question?

    (A) Observation of activities
    (B) Comparison of data
    (C) Collection of data
    (D) Computation and summation

69. The teacher then asked the students to determine how many more bags of trash were collected by the person who collected the most as compared with the person who collected the least. A student in the class gave the answer 5. Evaluate his response

    (A) he read the table correctly and gave the proper answer

    (B) he failed to use the units on the table, so his comparison was incorrect

    (C) the table does not give enough information to determine if his answer was correct or not

    (D) he did not subtract correctly

GO ON TO THE NEXT PAGE

Questions 70–71

A teacher constructs the following test question:

Most people with Type II Diabetes have the disease because of a lifetime of abusing their pancreas. When a person digests food, the food is converted into "blood sugar" that the body then uses for energy. If the blood sugar level is too high, the pancreas secretes insulin to go and vacuum up the excess and store it in the fat cells for future use. If the pancreas is overused, it wears out and no longer works.

The author describes diabetes as a disease that:

(A) attacks people randomly
(B) is devastating to the person who has it
(C) is preventable
(D) is contagious
(E) should be treated

70. The teacher is asking the students to read the information and then

(A) make a judgment based on their comprehension
(B) evaluate the writing
(C) synthesize the information into a statement of fact, not opinion
(D) expound upon the information learned

71. In order to use the above information in an integrated curriculum, which of the following activities would NOT suggest true integration?

(A) Reading a literature book about a grandmother with diabetes who loves eating chocolate
(B) Graphing the sugar content of various foods
(C) Having the students write a report on the disease of diabetes and its treatment
(D) Creating a reading center containing many books on hospitals and hospital workers

Social Studies

Questions 72–73

It is customary in many states for students to do a unit on their state during the fifth grade. In one particular class, the teacher is aware that the students did a unit on the state in the previous grade, but the unit was limited in scope. Also, she is aware that many of the students have lived in the state for most of their lives, so they have previous knowledge about the state. The teacher has decided that before beginning the lesson, she has three objectives:

1) To activate the students' previous knowledge about the state
2) To determine the extent of the students' knowledge about the state
3) To encourage the students to have interest in learning more about the state

72. In the above scenario, giving the students a pretest would meet which of the teacher's preunit objectives?

    (A) 1 only
    (B) 1 and 2 only
    (C) 1 and 3 only
    (D) 1, 2, and 3

73. Which of the following activities would be likely to meet all three objectives in a single class period?

    (A) Have each student make a list of important historical events in the state's history.
    (B) Give each student an aspect concerning the state, and have them research it and give an oral report.
    (C) Have the students brainstorm as a group about what they know about the state, then each draw a picture about one of the pieces of information that is mentioned in the brainstorming session.
    (D) Have the students take a pretest, then color a picture of the outline of the state.

Questions 74–75

A middle school teacher has explained the three branches of government to his students, including the primary functions of each and the balance of power between the branches.

74. The teacher hands out a list of current government officials, then asks the students to determine to which branch each government official belongs. Which of the following is the highest level of thinking in Bloom's Taxonomy that is incorporated into this exercise?

    (A) Knowledge
    (B) Comprehension
    (C) Analysis
    (D) Synthesis

75. Later, the teacher has the students read editorials on the web concerning whether the balance of power is truly effective. After reading three different opinions, the students discuss how valid each of the editorials is. The highest level of Bloom's Taxonomy being tested here is

    (A) Application
    (B) Analysis
    (C) Synthesis
    (D) Evaluation

76. Before teaching students about the cause of the "midnight sun" that occurs in the polar regions of the earth, students would need previous learning about

    (A) how the distance of the earth to the sun changes with the seasons
    (B) the importance of sunspot activity during the winter season
    (C) the tilt of the earth's axis
    (D) the international dateline and the time zones' relationships to it

77. A social studies teacher's husband is running for the local school board. Which of the following actions would NOT be appropriate for the teacher to use in the classroom?

    (A) Allow her husband to be a guest speaker in her class and distribute his campaign literature to her students for them to take home to their parents
    (B) Require her students to research the various candidates in the race and write an essay about the differences in their platforms
    (C) Wear a campaign button promoting her husband while announcing to her students that they too may wear campaign buttons of the candidate of their choice
    (D) Hold a forum in her classroom in which all candidates are invited to participate

GO ON TO THE NEXT PAGE

78. A social studies teacher gives his students a broad subject with a list of terms included in the subject. From this list, students are to learn the basic ideas and then determine a topic they wish to further investigate. This list is thus being used as

    (A) an outline
    (B) a scaffold
    (C) an objective
    (D) a goal

79. The difference between global objectives and instructional objectives in a social studies class is that

    (A) global objectives are more specific
    (B) instructional objectives are more specific
    (C) global objectives are used only in geography
    (D) instructional objectives are determined by the school district

80. A social studies teacher in an elementary school that has the students go to different teachers for different core subjects has determined that while her fifth-hour students do well in class discussions, they do not do well on either quizzes over reading assignments or her chapter tests. She has spoken with the Language Arts teacher who has identified that more than half of the students in her class are foreign born and are reading below their grade level. An appropriate way for her to evaluate her students' learning of her content area would be to modify the evaluations to

    (A) account for cultural diversity
    (B) account for different achievement levels
    (C) incorporate multiple assessments
    (D) include various learning styles

81. A social studies teacher is teaching a unit on the three branches of the federal government. Which of the following topics will NOT be a major component of this unit?

    (A) The offices and duties of the Executive Branch
    (B) The various types of judges from district court judges to judges on the Supreme Court
    (C) The legislative duties of Congress
    (D) The National Park Service directors and organization

82. A social studies teacher introduces a unit on democracy by discussing the concept of self-governance. She then allows the students to determine how they would like to have the unit taught, how to organize the material, and what activities they feel would be useful for achieving the objectives of the unit. By doing this, she is

    (A) planning for across the curriculum integration
    (B) assessing the student's previous knowledge of the subject
    (C) teaching the students to brainstorm
    (D) invoking metacognition

Arts and Physical Education

83. When an elementary child tries to throw a softball using a chest pass similar to the one she had learned to throw a basketball, she is following Piaget's concept of

    (A) egocentrism
    (B) reversibility
    (C) assimilation
    (D) cognitive balance

84. When the child mentioned in question 83 is taken aside and taught how to throw the softball using an overhand motion and then subsequently throws it correctly, she is following Piaget's concept of

    (A) preoperational strategy
    (B) accommodation
    (C) disequilibration
    (D) reversibility

85. Elementary students produce many works of art during their elementary school years. Which of the following is the LEAST important ability for them to develop at this age?

    (A) The ability to use various art materials in a safe and effective manner
    (B) An understanding of multiple processes that can be used in creating works of art
    (C) The ability to represent objects and the human form with a high degree of accuracy
    (D) An understanding of how the world and their imagination can be used to trigger artistic interest within themselves

86. Howard Gardner believes that students have various intelligences. A student who has good map-making skills and can draw representationally probably has strong

    (A) verbal-linguistic intelligence
    (B) interpersonal intelligence
    (C) bodily-kinesthetic intelligence
    (D) spatial intelligence

87. An art curriculum that involves tracking would involve classifying students

    (A) according to ethnicity and gender
    (B) in heterogeneous groups in terms of ability and other identifying characteristics
    (C) homogeneous ability groups
    (D) according to alphabetical order

88. Most opponents of tracking, even in the arts classes, object to the practice because

    (A) traditionally students of low SE status end up in the lower tracks
    (B) gifted students are not addressed
    (C) advanced students are required to work at a level below their ability
    (D) students of lesser ability are not allowed the slower pace they need

89. A P.E. teacher has been keeping records of students' achievements on various weight machines. In order to be the most useful to the students, he should give each student a printout containing which of the following?

    (A) The student's raw scores for each machine
    (B) A mean for the student's overall performance
    (C) Z-score and T-scores so the student can compare how he's doing on each machine
    (D) The standard deviation for the class

90. An elementary music teacher has an objective that the students be able to distinguish between the sounds of various musical instruments. What would be an activity that would allow her to assess if that objective is being met?

    (A) Have the students learn about various instruments from around the world
    (B) Have the students draw pictures of the various instruments and write the sound each makes below the instrument
    (C) Have the students choose an instrument and play it along with the other students in a group jam session
    (D) Play a recording of an instrument being played and have students write down the name of the instrument

GO ON TO THE NEXT PAGE

91. A physical education teacher begins a unit on soccer. Of the following possibilities, which concept will be taught last?

    (A) The rules of the game
    (B) The various positions on the team
    (C) Strategies for scoring goals
    (D) The size of the field and its markings

92. A teacher wants to do an interdisciplinary activity in which the concept of decimals she is teaching in math is used in a P.E. class. Which of the following activities would be most appropriate to meet that goal?

    (A) Comparing the students' times for running the 100-yard dash
    (B) Keeping score for a basketball game
    (C) Counting the jumping jacks each person can do in one minute
    (D) Setting up relay teams to run against one another

93. Which of the following is LEAST likely to be a part of a unit on famous world painters?

    (A) Picasso's works
    (B) Roudin's sculptures
    (C) Italian artists
    (D) Impressionists

General Information

94. Rewards as a major factor in explaining behavioral change is a basic tenet of the

    (A) information-processing theory
    (B) operant conditioning theory
    (C) social cognitive theory
    (D) theory of moral development

95. A standardized test was administered to all six classes of fourth grade students in a school district. The test included only multiple-choice answers and used a grid-like answer sheet, which was mechanically scored. Which of the following events would make the test scores biased?

    (A) one class included four gifted students who took the same test as the rest of the students
    (B) the students taking the test had been taught the format of the test during the week before the test
    (C) one class was given an extra 15 minutes to complete the test because that class included six students with learning disabilities
    (D) a test similar to this one, but at a second grade level, had been administered to this cohort of students two years earlier

96. Which of the following would be the most appropriately written instructional objective?

    (A) The students will understand the process of mitosis.
    (B) The students will learn the state capitols.
    (C) The students will be able to convert fractions to decimals.
    (D) The students will enjoy reading *A Christmas Carol*.

97. In Maslow's Hierarchy, *self-actualization* means

    (A) a student feels safe and secure with his circumstances
    (B) a student's physical needs are being met
    (C) a student knows what his purpose in life is
    (D) a student has a sense of love and belongingness

GO ON TO THE NEXT PAGE

98. In a teacher-centered first grade classroom, the teacher directs all activity within the classroom. Current research suggests that a negative of a teacher-centered classroom is that

    (A) children will not acquire the enjoyment of learning and interest in ideas that is required for long-term growth

    (B) by the end of the school year, the students will be behind others in their ability to take standardized tests well

    (C) children resent being told what to do at this age

    (D) the children will develop academic interests but will lack social skills or desire to interact with others

99. When children are placed in groups based on how they've done on assessments, this is called

    (A) ability grouping

    (B) homogeneous diversity

    (C) heterogeneous tracking

    (D) grade-level typing

100. If a child is said to be learning something vicariously, this means she is

    (A) learning it by doing

    (B) learning through various modalities

    (C) learning from another's experience

    (D) learning from rote memory

101. Glasser's Control Theory approach to classroom management is best summarized as

    (A) students are left on their own to figure out how they should behave

    (B) students will follow the teacher's rules because she is the authority figure

    (C) students help develop the rules and then accept ownership of the consequences

    (D) the teacher takes every opportunity to show students how their behavior is reflected to the real world

102. According to Gardner, a child who recognizes rhythms and sounds in words and enjoys learning about their origins has a strong intelligence in

    (A) musical intelligence

    (B) mathematical intelligence

    (C) linguistic intelligence

    (D) spatial intelligence

103. If a teacher wishes to create a study guide or note-taking guide for a student, the best structure is one that

    (A) lists the procedures the student should follow when reading the assigned material

    (B) delineates the appropriate ways to decode the material

    (C) summarizes helpful hints on how to study and how to highlight material

    (D) organizes the material to be read by listing major topics with subtopics and space for writing between

104. The word coopetition comes from the combination of

    (A) being fair and being reasonable

    (B) co-op and petition

    (C) cooperation and competition

    (D) coordination and repetition

105. The term *ability tracking* refers to the concept that

    (A) a child's ability should be documented and recorded over time

    (B) children are placed in groups based on how they've done on assessment, and those groups remain stable over time

    (C) all children should be given the chance to learn at the same level

    (D) some children simply cannot achieve and should not prevent others from proceeding

GO ON TO THE NEXT PAGE

106. A principal in an open-minded school approaches the teachers about including at least one objective test in each subject each quarter because of what he terms "the need for accountability." The requirement for this accountability has probably come about because of the school board's concern about

    (A) the depth of the content assessed in performance tasks
    (B) the instructional planning time lost to grading essay tests and projects
    (C) the possibility of teacher bias in evaluating students
    (D) the teachers' skill in creating performance-type assessments

107. Guidelines about what a student should know or be able to do are known as

    (A) outlines
    (B) standards
    (C) tables of contents
    (D) indices

108. When a teacher begins a class with an activity that "hooks" the students' interest into the topic, he is using

    (A) objective interest
    (B) closure
    (C) anticipatory set
    (D) a lesson plan without objectives

109. When using peer grading in the classroom, it is important that

    (A) the components the students will be graded on are given out in advance
    (B) people who do not like each other are not allowed to grade one another
    (C) the teacher leave the classroom and stay out of the process
    (D) peers grade individually, never in groups

110. A researcher asks a teacher for the grades she has given over the last two years. The teacher gives him copies of her gradebooks with the names crossed out for the researcher to use. However, she does indicate to the researcher which students are boys and which are girls. In this case, the teacher is using

    (A) confidentiality
    (B) anonymity
    (C) unethical practices
    (D) lack of compliance with the Buckley Amendment

STOP!

If you finish before time is up, you may go back and check your work.

Practice Test Five (0011/0016)
Answers and Explanations

READING & LANGUAGE ARTS		MATHEMATICS	SCIENCE	ARTS & PHYSICAL EDUCATION	GENERAL KNOWLEDGE
1. C	21. D	39. B	61. C	83. C	94. B
2. C	22. A	40. B	62. B	84. B	95. C
3. B	23. B	41. C	63. A	85. C	96. C
4. C	24. A	42. B	64. B	86. D	97. C
5. A	25. B	43. A	65. B	87. C	98. A
6. B	26. D	44. B	66. C	88. A	99. A
7. B	27. D	45. D	67. C	89. C	100. C
8. D	28. C	46. A	68. B	90. D	101. C
9. D	29. A	47. D	69. B	91. C	102. C
10. B	30. C	48. C	70. A	92. A	103. D
11. B	31. C	49. D	71. D	93. B	104. C
12. B	32. C	50. D			105. B
13. D	33. D	51. B			106. D
14. B	34. B	52. A	**SOCIAL STUDIES**		107. B
15. C	35. C	53. D			108. C
16. A	36. B	54. C	72. B		109. A
17. B	37. A	55. B	73. C		110. A
18. B	38. D	56. B	74. C		
19. D		57. A	75. D		
20. A		58. B	76. C		
		59. A	77. A		
		60. C	78. B		
			79. B		
			80. C		
			81. D		
			82. D		

ANSWERS AND EXPLANATIONS

Reading and Language Arts

1. C

(A) Phonic clues would refer to the student matching the sound with the letter. (B) Morphemes are combinations of letter sounds (i.e., th). (C) is the correct answer because the teacher is asking the students to figure out the meaning of a word based on other words they already know in the text. (D) Sight words are words students have memorized to recognize on sight (without sounding them out).

2. C

(A) The context clue strategy can be used in any literature form. (B) Students can use the context clue strategy for material on, or in some cases, above their reading level. (C) is the correct answer because a student can only use context clues if there are words in the reading that indicate the meaning of the unfamiliar word. (D) Pronunciation has nothing to do with context.

3. B

(A) Distributed practice is sustained practice over time (i.e., doing one hour of spelling a day). (B) is the correct answer because massed practice involves practicing a skill in short intervals several times a day. (C) Guided practice involves the teacher actually leading the student through the practice. (D) Independent practice involves a student working on his own without assistance.

4. C

(A) Whereas giving the students background information is a good thing, it will not necessarily invoke desire on their parts to read the story. (B) Recognizing literary devices (i.e., flashbacks) and understanding their usage will help the students gain depth of understanding, but again, this introduction will not create anticipation of the story. (C) is the correct answer because it works as an anticipatory set and notifies the students that they will be held accountable for the content by having to produce a product at the end. (D) Telling the students the plot (the main events that occur) may actually cause some students to decide NOT to read the story because they already know what is going to happen.

5. A

(A) is the correct answer because phonics is the study of how sounds relate to the letter symbols. (B) The relationship between words and meaning is represented by the term vocabulary. (C) The relationship between reading and writing is a reciprocal one but is not phonics. (D) Various components across the curriculum are represented by the term integration.

6. B

(A) The activities done in workbooks involve both phonics and phonemic awareness. (B) is the correct answer because phonemic awareness is being conscious of the various sounds within a word, whereas phonics involves the relationship between the sounds and letter symbols; one can have phonemic awareness in spoken language as well as in written language, but phonics always involves the written word. (C) Obviously phonics does involve reading; phonemic awareness does not have to involve the written word. (D) Whereas this statement is true, it does not provide a distinction between the two.

7. B

(A) This statement shows transfer, not Vygotsky's ZPD. (B) Vygotsky's ZPD refers to the idea that a child with proper scaffolding can experience doing skills at a level above his actual understanding. (C) Group reading in homogeneous ability groups does not involve Vygotsky's ZPD. (D) Pairing students in heterogeneous ability couples does not involve Vygotsky's ZPD.

8. D

(A) Phonics refers to the relationship between sounds and symbols. (B) Phonemic awareness refers to a person's consciousness of sounds within words. (C) Fluency refers to a person's ability to read text accurately and fluidly. (D) is the correct answer because comprehension refers to a person's ability to understand the meaning of a word in context.

9. D

(A) Decoding is saying the correct sounds for the letter symbols (i.e., duh for the letter d). (B) phonemic awareness refers to a person's consciousness of sounds within words. (C) Aliteracy is the term for having the ability to read but choosing not to read regularly. (D) is the correct answer because it is the full definition of fluency.

10. B

Phonemes are the smallest unit of sound (i.e., duh for the letter d or thuh for the letters th). In this example, dog has three phonemes (duh + oh + guh); shed has three phonemes (shuh + eh + duh); and fur has three phonemes (fuh + uh + rrrr).

11. B

(A) Competence means having the ability to do a task; performance means being able to perform a task in public or in a testing situation. (B) is the correct answer because the child has the ability (competence) but is not able to show performance. (C) The child can spell (competence) but has not yet reached the next level of performance. (D) The child is not showing performance, but he is showing competence.

12. B

(A) Basal readers do not typically include literature from trade books as used in the whole language approach. (B) is the correct answer because most basal readers are phonics-based. (C) To include the whole language approach, literature from trade books would need to be included. (D) Basal readers require all students to read the same stories instead of having individualized instruction.

13. D

(A) Synonyms are words with similar meaning (i.e., good/nice), and homophones are words with the same sound but different meanings (i.e., their/there); obviously the student does not have a good understanding of synonyms because she replaced cold with its antonym hot. (B) The student is not confusing homophones with synonyms; instead, she is confusing synonyms (similar meaning) with antonyms (opposites). (C) The student has not mastered either of the concepts but instead is confusing the two. (D) is the correct answer because the student has not mastered the concept of synonyms (similar meaning).

14. B

(A) Understanding page number and order does indicate reading. (B) is the correct answer because reading is the understanding that the words on the page represents language that is spoken. (C) This is not required for reading. (D) Integration of subjects, whereas a good thing, is not necessary for reading.

15. C

(A), (B), and (D) are examples of dichotomies because a dichotomy represents two things that are far apart (and often opposite) in meaning. (C) is the correct answer because this is NOT a dichotomy since the two variations on meaning of a word are not far apart in meaning.

16. A

(A) is the correct answer because the various sounds made by the ough (i.e., uff in tough; off in cough; ow in plough; and oh in dough) are exceptions to decoding rules of phonics. (B), (C), and (D) are approaches that do not involve sounding out words.

17. B

(A) Although it looks like playtime, the fact that all the children are doing a similar activity indicates it is not. (B) is the correct answer because this scenario describes the prewriting activity of brainstorming. (C) This activity does not necessarily include invented spelling, and graffiti expression is not important to development. (D) Obviously these are not final versions of posters but simply brainstorming ideas.

18. B

(A) This child is not actually reading; he is simply decoding. (B) is the correct answer because the child is decoding the words but it is a meaningless activity because he doesn't understand what he is reading (like someone singing a song phonetically in a foreign language). (C) The child is not pretending; he is decoding, but he is not reading. (D) Meaningless decoding does not lead to literacy.

19. D

(A) These words would not be on the other end; they would be in the mid-range of the continuum. (B) These words would be near the far end but not actually on it. (C) These words are not on the continuum. (D) is the correct answer because these are the words at the opposite end of the continuum from the well-known words.

20. A

(A) is the correct answer because the person has some knowledge of the word and can thus recognize it enough to possibly use it. (B) Decoding is sounding out the various phonemes in the word. (C) A cloze activity is a fill-in-the-blank activity.

(D) Whereas a person may use context to figure out the meaning of a word, the encounter described here is not that activity.

21. D

(A) The cognitive domain is about thinking. (B) The social domain is about interaction between people. (C) The psychomotor domain is about the physical. (D) is the correct answer because the affective domain is about a person's feelings and emotions.

22. A

(A) is the correct answer because whereas many teachers do still use this "busy work" activity, it is not an effective method. (B), (C), and (D) are not effective methods.

23. B

(A) Most children are reading by the end of second grade, so this is cause for concern. (B) is the correct answer because most children are reading by the end of second grade and thus remediation may be necessary for this child. (C) Most children are reading by the end of second grade. (D) Retention should be an option to consider only after all other options have been exhausted.

24. A

(A) is the correct answer because guided reading does involve the teacher giving support to children as they read quietly in small group settings. (B) Guided reading takes place in the classroom. (C) Guided reading does not involve the whole class setting. (D) Reading aloud in unison is not a part of the guided reading process.

25. B

(A) Guided reading does take place in groups, but the goal is for a student to learn to read by himself, not as a part of a group reading in unison. (B) is the correct answer because that is the ultimate goal of guided reading. (C) Whereas a laudable goal for any human being, is not an actual part of the guided reading process. (D) Whereas guided reading is done in groups, the ultimate goal is not about group cooperation but instead is about the student learning to read by himself.

26. D

(A) Whereas reports of events may be recorded in a reflection journal, those reports are not actually "reflections." (B) This is not typically a part of the reflection journal and definitely does not meet the definition of "reflection." (C) Whereas reporting these descriptions may be included in the journal as necessary background, they are not actually "reflections." (D) is the correct answer because this defines what a reflection is.

27. D

(A) Whereas a teacher will need to place students in groups, the guided reading process involves using homogeneous ability groups. (B) This is a part of the process but it is not the first step. (C) This is an anticipatory set but not the first step in the guided reading process. (D) is the correct answer because the first step in the guided reading process is to determine the students' reading levels so books at the proper level can be chosen.

28. C

(A) The teacher did not narrow the meaning for this activity. (B) The teacher did not give the first consonants of the words to be filled in. (C) is the correct answer because the activity is interactive (between students and with the teacher) and is a cloze (fill-in-the-blank) activity. (D) This does not describe the guided reading process.

29. A

(A) is the correct answer because this is the first rule of using an interactive cloze activity. (B), (C), and (D) are not rules that should be included in the interactive cloze activity.

30. C

(A) Characters may or may not show up in this activity, and it is not the purpose of the activity. (B) The setting may or may not show up in this activity, and it is not the purpose of the activity. (C) is the correct answer because the purpose is to get the students interested in the story and thus want to read it. (D) Whereas a student's vocabulary development might show up on the worksheet, it also might not.

31. C

(A), (B), and (D) are all parts of the guided reading process. (C) is the correct answer because it is not a part of the guided reading process.

32. C

(A) Just as adults enjoy reruns on tv, children enjoy rereading books. (B) Children can progress by rereading books because they can increase in fluency and fluidity. (C) is the correct answer because children can actually see their progress in the ease with which they can read the book a second or third time. (D) This is not a necessary rule; children may reread books they have read and enjoyed.

33. D

(A) Phonics is the study of the relationship between sounds and symbols. (B) Whole language involves using literature and the use of text in the environment to teach children to read. (C) Sight word recognition refers to words that children have memorized and can recognize without decoding while reading. (D) is the correct answer because this is the definition of vocabulary.

34. B

(A) Children enjoy using the new words they have learned and will try them out whenever they can. (B) is the correct answer because pride can keep a child from trying to show his new vocabulary if he fears he will be humiliated; if he knows the environment is safe, he will try to use the new word even if he doesn't quite get it right. (C) Experience teaches a child where it is safe to make attempts at using new words and where it is not safe (where he might be humiliated if he uses it incorrectly). (D) Children learn to use many words verbally long before they can write them.

35. C

(A) Some worksheets are very helpful in the learning process, so it would be improper to never use them. (B) Some worksheets do not fit well within a teacher's plans and thus would not be used; also, some days a worksheet would not be appropriate. (C) is the correct answer because worksheets can be valuable and can be adapted to fit objectives. (D) Some worksheets in a workbook will not be necessary for all students.

36. B

(A) Affix study (i.e., learning about prefixes and their meanings or suffixes and their meanings) does not address reading problems. (B) is the correct answer because affix study will help a student expand his vocabulary. (C) Whereas affix study will show Latin's influence, it is not the main reason for doing affix study. (D) Affix study does not prepare students to diagram sentences.

37. A

(A) is the correct answer because the verb *learn* is not measurable. (B), (C), and (D) all contain measurable skills.

38. D

(A), (B), and (C) are all good uses of a bulletin board, but none of them are the primary use. (D) is the correct answer because a bulletin board should serve as reinforcement for material being taught in the classroom.

Mathematics

39. B

(A) Whether this was addressed in the classroom or not was not revealed in this vignette. (B) is the correct answer because the students were indicating to the principal that they had no incentive to finish the work. (C) Obviously there was no routine for requiring students to stay on task. (D) There is no evidence of cooperating groups in this vignette.

40. B

(A), (C), and (D) are wrong because the boys indicated they knew how to do the work. (B) is the correct answer because the students were indicating they could do the work in a shorter time than was allowed.

41. C

(A), (B), and (D) would all address the problem of those boys on a superficial level but would not address the inherent problem. (C) is the correct answer because the system of rewards would encourage the students to stay involved in learning tasks.

42. B

NCTM is the acronym for the National Council for Teachers of Mathematics. (A) It is not a governmental agency, although it has members throughout the country. (B) is the correct answer because it is a non-profit agency for professionals in the field of mathematics. (C) It is non-profit. (D) The misconception is that NCTM is a government program, but it is not.

43. A

(A) is the correct answer because a stanine of 5 is average, and 4 is slightly below average. (B) Stanines are norm references, so we do not know whether the students are failing or passing, only that in comparison to the other students who took the test, they scored average to just below average. (C) Because 5 is average, this answer is not correct. (D) Stanines do not indicate grade level abilities.

44. B

(A) Barbara's manipulatives represent 4 ones and 12 tens; this adds up to 124 but does not indicate place value notation. (B) is the correct answer because she had used 4 ones, 2 tens, and 1 hundred. (C) Janice's manipulatives represent 4 hundreds, 2 tens, and 1 red for a total of 421. (D) Jeanne's manipulatives represent 24 ones and 1 hundred; this adds up to 124 but does not indicate place value notation.

45. D

(A), (B), and (C) are wrong because Janice's manipulatives represent 421. (D) is the correct answer because all three have manipulatives representing 124 (Barbara 4 + 120; Carletta 4 + 20 + 100; Jeanne 24 + 100).

46. A

By doing simple arithmetic, you discover that (A) is the only group of numbers that equals 124.

47. D

(D) is the correct answer because the student is obviously adding the numerators and then adding the denominators.

48. C

(A) Whereas there is some difference between individuals, research shows that there is not a lot of difference between classes or years. (B) Students do not make random mistakes. (C) is the correct answer because students do tend to make very similar mistakes across classes and cultures. (D) Obviously mistakes can be identified and corrected.

49. D

(A) Whereas children can be illogical, it is not the most common mistake. (B) Students do sometimes apply the wrong problem-solving method, but again, it is not the most common mistake. (C) Most arithmetic problems do not require a student to apply it to real life. (D) is the correct answer because computational errors are the most common errors.

50. D

(A) Much research has been done on primary children. (B) Tests are standardized against the populations who take them, so tests for primary children would be standardized and normed based on primary children. (C) Current standardized tests are considered more valid than ever because measures have been taken to increase and test validity through the years. (D) is the correct answer because children at this age do change rapidly and may test very differently on one day as opposed to another.

51. B

(A) Manipulatives allow students to see the amounts clearly, so they do not get the answer wrong, which is why (B) is the correct answer. (C) Students enjoy using manipulatives. (D) Students are more likely to stay on task when working with materials than they are when working simply on written work.

52. A

(A) is the correct answer because knowledge is growing at such a rapid rate, the most we can hope for is to teach students how to figure out what they need to do to solve a problem. (B) Showing work and using the standard way of reaching an answer is no longer considered best practices; students should be encouraged to discover answers in ways they understand. (C) Mental math is an important part of the work done in math class because mental math is a part of everyday life. (D) pencil-and-paper drills are still used but definitely no longer considered the most important part of math class.

53. D

(A), (B), and (C) all represent the three most common methods of doing arithmetic. (D) is the correct answer because conversion is not a method of doing arithmetic.

54. C

(A) Students who spend all their time on computation may not be able to transfer those skills to real-life usage of math. (B) Students must be given a knowledge base and have some practice time as well as doing application. (C) is the correct answer because it addresses the need for a knowledge base and the activation of transfer of that knowledge. (D) Obviously not every page in a workbook is necessary for every student.

55. B

(A) Borrowing is not necessary when doing addition. (B) is the correct answer because the student did fail to carry the "1" to the tens column after he added 8 and 7 to get 15. (C) The student used the correct operation. (D) Subtraction was not needed in this problem.

56. B

(A) Whereas borrowing with large numbers can be problematic, it is not the most common borrowing problem. (B) is the correct answer because students have the most difficulty when borrowing with the numeral zero. (C) Carrying is a process in addition, not in subtraction (where borrowing takes place). (D) Students do not typically have trouble with these particular numbers when borrowing.

57. A

(A) is the correct answer because the student must first figure out what he is seeking before he can proceed. (B) This is the second step. (C) Writing out an equation may be a part of solving the problem, or it may not, but it is definitely not the first step. (D) Figuring out a similar problem may help the student to understand, but it is not the first step in working this new problem.

58. B

(A) Whereas higher-level algebra may involve use of algorithms, the term algorithm does not mean higher-level algebra. (B) is the correct answer because this is the definition of the term. (C) Geometric proportions may involve algorithms, but it is not defined as such. (D) One may use a graphing calculator to do algorithms, but the usage of such is not a definition of the word.

59. A

(A) is the correct answer because mental math requires a knowledge base of facts and the ability to estimate. (B) One can do mental math without being able to use a calculator. (C) Pencil and paper drills will not necessarily give the knowledge base needed to enable students to do mental math. (D) Students can do mental math without having complete mastery of word problems.

60. C

The phrase stands for Parenthesis, Exponents, Multiplication and Division (whichever comes first from left to right), and Addition and Subtractions (whichever comes first from left to right). Thus, (C) is the correct answer.

Science

61. C

(A) This is a plausible suggestion that would indeed meet the objective. (B) This suggestion would help the students apply the scientific method. (C) is the correct answer because this is NOT a good suggestion for helping the students apply the scientific method; having the teacher tell them what they did wrong will not be as beneficial as if they try the experiment again or discuss their findings with one another. (D) Using a new hypothesis and gaining new results would meet the objective and possibly the students would discover what they did wrong as they compared what they did differently the second time.

62. B

(A) Equilibrium means cognitive balance. (B) is the correct answer because disequilibrium means experiencing something that does not fit in one's belief system. (C) Equilibration is the act of bringing one into cognitive balance. (D) Cognitive balance means that a person's experiences are matching his belief system.

63. A

(A) is the correct answer because equilibrium means that a person's belief system matches their experiences. (B) Disequilibrium means experiencing something that does not fit in one's belief system; once he has made the adjustment of his belief system (through learning a new concept), the experience now fits his belief system. (C) Confusion was occurring when he was in disequilibrium; once he has achieved cognitive balance, he is not confused. (D) Perception is one's take on a particular event, and he used perception to make the original judgment, as well as the new one, but it was a tool, not the state he achieved.

64. B

(A) The minerals contained in a rock do not determine this set of classifications. (B) is the correct answer because these classifications are based on how the rock was formed. (C) The size and shape of a rock do not matter in these classifications. (D) Family and genus are classifications used with animals, not rocks.

65. B

(A) Students reading texts is not a cooperative learning activity; also, it probably would not lead to the students meeting the objective. (B) is the correct answer because it is a cooperative learning activity and it would lead to the students classifying using different characteristics. (C) Whereas this is a cooperative learning activity, it is not likely to lead to the objective of doing various classifications because only a single rock is being used for each group. (D) Again, only a single type of rock is being used, and watching a video is not a cooperative learning activity.

66. C

(A) Allowing for bonus work to be done at any time could actually work as an incentive that prevents students from completing the work that is actually assigned. (B) Allowing bonus points to students who finish early gives an unfair advantage for grading purposes in the classroom and should be avoided. (C) is the correct answer because by allowing the bonus points to be available to everyone, the students who work at a slower rate can still have an equal chance by doing the bonus work at home; in addition, the faster students will have an activity to do to keep them busy throughout the hour so they do not distract the other students who are still working on the original assignment. (D) Bonus activities must be available to all students for fairness.

67. C

(A) Marcy collected 90 bags of trash; Dion collected 45 bags of trash. (B) Trista collected 105 bags, and Marcy collected 90; as for Statement 4, how hard a student worked cannot be determined from the table. (C) is the correct answer because James collected 60 bags and Dion collected 45 bags; this is the same amount as Trista who collected 105. (D) Marcy, 90, and Dion, 45, means Statement 1 is not correct; James collected less than Marcy, so Statement 4 is also incorrect.

68. B

(A) The students are not observing the activities although the table is a record of someone having observed the activities. (B) is the correct answer because the question is asking the students to compare the data that is displayed on the table. (C) The students were not expected to collect the data; it was previously collected and placed on the table. (D) The students are not being asked to compute or sum the data, but rather to compare parts of it.

69. B

(A) The person who collected the most was Trista (105) and the person who collected the least was Keva (30); the difference was 75, not 5. (B) is the correct answer because the student recognized that Trista had 7 symbols on the chart and Keva had 2, but the student failed to use the conversion key to calculate the actual number of bags. (C) The table does give the necessary information. (D) The student subtracted the symbols correctly but failed to multiply by the units.

70. A

(A) is the correct answer because the question does ask the student to make a judgment. (B) No evaluation of the writing is called for. (C) The student is not asked to synthesize the material or to state a fact. (D) The student is not asked to expound (give greater explanation about) the information.

71. D

(A), (B), and (C) all represent activities that would integrate other subjects. (D) is the correct answer because whereas the subject of this reading center is tangentially related, it does not represent integration.

Social Studies

72. B

(A), (C), and (D) are incorrect because objectives 1 and 2 only are met. (B) is the correct answer because the test will activate previous knowledge and assess the size of that knowledge.

73. C

(A) This would meet objective 1, but it would not meet objectives 2 or 3. (B) This might meet objective 3 but not the others. (C) is the correct answer because this would meet all three objectives. (D) This would meet the first two objectives, but it is not likely to meet the third one.

74. C

(A) Knowledge involves only recall of facts. (B) Comprehension involves understanding material. (C) is the correct answer because the students are being asked to analyze the material (break it into parts). (D) Synthesis involves taking material, breaking it down, and then putting the various parts back together to form a new product.

75. D

(A) Application involves using concepts or skills in a new situation. (B) Analysis involves breaking the material into its component parts. (C) Synthesis involves taking material, breaking it down, and then putting the various parts back together to form a new product. (D) is the correct answer because evaluation involves judging the value of something.

76. C

(C) is the correct answer. The midnight sun occurs because of the earth's tilt in relation to its orbit around the sun. (A), (B), and (D) are tangential in relationship to the topic.

77. A

(A) is the correct answer because this is considered an unfair use of power and could be considered coercion. (B), (C), and (D) are appropriate activities for the classroom because they allow the students to be exposed to, and make choices about, the various candidates.

78. B

(A) An outline involves inclusion of the major components with their subordinate parts organized to show the relationships. (B) is the correct answer because a scaffold provides support for a student as he seeks to do his own learning. (C) An objective is the behavioral outcome of a lesson. (D) A goal is the global plan for the lesson.

79. B

(A) Instructional objectives are more specific than are global ones; therefore, (B) is the correct answer. (C) Global objectives can be used in any subject. (D) Typically, instructional objectives are determined by the teacher, but actually, either could; if a school district was determining the instructional objectives, they would most likely be determining the global ones as well.

80. C

(A) Cultural diversity will not address this issue. (B) Whereas different achievement levels will show up, for these purposes, she should not modify the evaluations to allow for differences. (C) is the correct answer because by incorporating multiple assessments, she will be able to determine if the students are achieving the objectives despite of their language arts difficulties. (D) Evaluations do not involve learning styles.

81. D

(A), (B), and (C) all represent major components (executive, judicial, and legislative branches). (D) Whereas the National Park Service is a federal agency, it would not be taught as a major component of a unit focusing on the three branches of government.

82. D

(A) This strategy is for a unit within social studies and does not really address integration per se. (B) Assessing previous knowledge is not happening in this activity, at least not on a large scale. (C) This is not a brainstorming activity. (D) is the correct answer because the teacher is teaching the students about democracy, then allowing them to participate in democracy; this is metacognition.

Arts and Physical Education

83. C

(A) Egocentrism refers to the concept of believing that the world centers around oneself and does not apply here. (B) Reversibility refers to the idea that a child learns to understand the relationship between two things and the reverse of that relationship (i.e., the box is under the bed; the bed is over the box). (C) is the correct answer because assimilation is the process of doing a new activity by invoking old skills and using them to attempt a new activity one has seen. (D) Cognitive balance means one's view of the world agrees with one's belief system.

84. B

(A) Preoperational refers to a developmental stage of children but does not apply here. (B) is the correct answer because the child is adjusting his behavior to do the skill and this is considered accommodation. (C) Disequilibration is the concept of someone going from cognitive balance to disequilibrium. (D) Reversibility refers to the idea that a child learns to understand the relationship between two things and the reverse of that relationship (i.e., the box is under the bed; the bed is over the box).

85. C

(A), (B), and (D) are all important goals of an elementary art program. (C) is the correct answer because development of a child's ability to draw accurate representations is not a necessary part.

86. D

(A) The verbal-linguistic intelligence involves a person's ability to communicate orally and with written language. (B) The interpersonal intelligence involves a person's ability to interact with others and be cognizant of another's body language and feelings. (C) The bodily-kinesthetic intelligence involves a person's ability to use his body skillfully and to move easily in response to stimulus. (D) is the correct answer because drawing and map making both involve a person's understanding of where an object is in its space and in relationship to other objects in that space.

87. C

(A) Tracking does not involve ethnicity and gender grouping. (B) Heterogeneous means of varying degree; tracking involves homogeneous ability grouping. (C) is the correct answer because tracking does place students in groups of like ability. (D) Tracking does not use alphabetical order.

88. A

(A) is the correct answer because research shows that students of lower socio-economic status are usually placed in lower tracks than students from higher-income homes. (B) Gifted students are often placed in the higher tracks, and they are addressed. (C) Advanced students can actually work at advanced rates. (D) Slower students are allowed to progress at a slower rate.

89. C

(A) The students' raw scores will not allow for comparison because each machine's units may be different and measure different things. (B) Averaging the students' scores will not give any meaning. (C) is the correct answer because z-scores and T-scores allow scores of different units and even of different measures to be compared to one another. (D) The standard deviation for the class will tell the students nothing about their actual performance.

90. D

(A) Learning about various instruments will not assess the objective of being able to identify the sound of each instrument and how it varies from another. (B) Writing a word representing a sound will not actually assess if the student can make the distinction when listening. (C) Doing a group jam session will not enable the students to show they can distinguish between the sounds. (D) is the

correct answer because the teacher is asking the students to identify the sound when listening to it, thereby displaying their ability to meet, or not meet, the objective.

91. C

(A), (B), and D are all background material that must be taught first. (C) is the correct answer because game strategies will be taught much later in a unit, after the background and initial skills are taught.

92. A

(A) is the correct answer because times for the 100-yard dash are scored to the tenths, hundredths, and sometimes even thousandths places. (B) Basketball scores involve whole numbers, not decimals. (C) Counting repetitions does not involve decimals. (D) Setting up a team does not involve the use of decimals.

93. B

(A) Picasso is a world famous painter and so would be included. (B) is the correct answer because the unit is on painters, not sculptors. (C) Italian artists include many painters and would be an appropriate subheading within the unit. (D) Impressionists are painters and so could be included.

General Knowledge

94. B

(A) Information-processing theory refers to a way that students take in material and work with it and does not apply here. (B) is the correct answer because operant conditioning does work using rewards to change behavior. (C) Social cognitive theory refers to Bandura's work and includes behaviorism, social factors, and cognitive systems; it does not apply here. (D) Kohlberg's Theory of Moral Development involves the various ways students make moral choices as they mature.

95. C

(A) Any testing situation assumes there will be differences in the students taking the test; this does not make it biased. (B) If all students taking the test were taught the format, then all had an equal chance on the test. (C) is the correct answer because giving one set of students more time than the rest of the students biases the test. (D) This is a normal situation and does not in any way indicate bias.

96. C

(A), (B), and (D) are instructional objectives that must include measurable objectives; understand, learn, and enjoy are not measurable. (C) is the correct answer because convert is a measurable objective.

97. C

(A) This would indicate the second level of the hierarchy, safety and security, not self-actualization. (B) This would indicate the lowest level of the hierarchy, physiological. (C) is the correct answer because self-actualization refers to a student finding his place in life. (D) This would indicate the third level of the hierarchy, love and belongingness.

98. A

(A) is the correct answer because the lack of inherent interest is the negative side of this approach. (B) Students being taught with this kind of approach typically do not do any better or any worse on standardized tests than others. (C) First grade children do not typically mind being told what to do. (D) Children always have social interests; they don't have to be taught to desire to interact with others.

99. A

(A) is the correct answer because this is the definition of ability grouping. (B) Homogeneous means same and diversity means different, so this is a nonsense term. (C) Heterogeneous means

different and tracking means to place children on a track and keep them there; again, this answer is a nonsense term. (D) Grade-level typing refers to placing children by chronological age, not by ability.

100. C

(A) Vicarious means experiencing something through observing another's experience, not by doing it oneself. (B) The term does not address various ways of doing things, only that it's done by observation of another's experience. (C) is the correct answer because vicarious means learning from another's experience. (D) Rote memory means to learn something by repeating it over and over again; it does not apply here.

101. C

(C) is the correct answer because Glasser's Control Theory is about students having control of their learning environments. (A), (B), and (D) indicate behaviors that are not included in the theory.

102. C

(A) Although rhythms and sounds are a part of music, this particular definition applies to the rhythms and sounds of words. (B) Whereas this is one of Gardner's intelligences, it does not apply here. (C) is the correct answer because a person with strong linguistic intelligence is interested in all aspects of word. (D) Spatial intelligence refers to a person's understanding of position of items within a particular space.

103. D

(A) This is not a note-taking guide and probably would be ignored by most students. (B) Decoding is sounding out words and does not apply here. (C) Again, this is not a note-taking guide. (D) is the correct answer because this does describe an appropriate note-taking guide.

104. C

(A) Whereas being fair and reasonable is a part of a coopetition activity, it is not the two combining factors to create the concept. (B) Co-op, which comes from the word cooperation or cooperative, works, but petition does not. (C) is the correct answer because coopetition refers to the ideas that children can all have the opportunity to win (i.e., all teams can win a point for each item, without reference to how the other team answers) and can still be in competition because the points at the end are what count; in a typical spelling bee, other students must lose for a student to win. In coopetition students are awarded points based on what they accomplish, irrespective of how others do. (D) These words are not a part of this term.

105. B

(A) Whereas a child's ability is documented and recorded over time in schools that use ability tracking, it is not what the concept means. (B) is the correct answer because this is the definition of the term. (C) In ability tracking, each track is given the chance to learn at different levels. (D) This is not a definition of the concept, although it is a rationale that some people use for the idea of using ability tracking.

106. D

(A), (B), and (C) are all possibilities but probably not the driving force. (D) is the correct answer because the school board is probably concerned that the teachers' assessments are not rigorous enough, and they want to make sure there is a "professional" tool involved.

107. B

(B) is the correct answer because the term standards refers to guidelines about what a student should accomplish. (A), (C), and (D) are distractors that have nothing to do with standards.

108. C

(A) Objective interest is the concept that the person teaching a subject or topic has no motive other than dissemination of information. (B) Closure is the idea of completing a process or concept in such a way that the person can add it to his knowledge base and return to cognitive balance. (C) is the correct answer because an anticipatory set is a hook that gains the students' initial interest, causing them to want to know more. (D) Having an anticipatory set can be a part of a well thought out lesson plan.

109. A

(A) is the correct answer because students do need guidelines when doing peer grading. (B) Teaching students to be fair in grading products is an important part of the process. (C) The teacher should not actually do the grading, but she should definitely stay present and guide students in their work. (D) Peer grading in groups is an excellent way for students to discuss products objectively.

110. A

(A) is the correct answer because confidentiality means the teacher knows the names, but she is not releasing them. (B) Anonymity is what the researcher is using because she does not know the names. (C) This is not an unethical practice. (D) As long as the names are not being used, it is in compliance with the Buckley Amendment.

Practice Test Six
Answer Sheet

Remove (or photocopy) this answer sheet and use it to complete the practice test.
(See answer key following the test when finished.)

If a section has fewer questions than answer spaces, leave the extra spaces blank.

Language Arts

1 Ⓐ Ⓑ Ⓒ Ⓓ   11 Ⓐ Ⓑ Ⓒ Ⓓ   21 Ⓐ Ⓑ Ⓒ Ⓓ
2 Ⓐ Ⓑ Ⓒ Ⓓ   12 Ⓐ Ⓑ Ⓒ Ⓓ   22 Ⓐ Ⓑ Ⓒ Ⓓ
3 Ⓐ Ⓑ Ⓒ Ⓓ   13 Ⓐ Ⓑ Ⓒ Ⓓ   23 Ⓐ Ⓑ Ⓒ Ⓓ
4 Ⓐ Ⓑ Ⓒ Ⓓ   14 Ⓐ Ⓑ Ⓒ Ⓓ   24 Ⓐ Ⓑ Ⓒ Ⓓ
5 Ⓐ Ⓑ Ⓒ Ⓓ   15 Ⓐ Ⓑ Ⓒ Ⓓ   25 Ⓐ Ⓑ Ⓒ Ⓓ
6 Ⓐ Ⓑ Ⓒ Ⓓ   16 Ⓐ Ⓑ Ⓒ Ⓓ   26 Ⓐ Ⓑ Ⓒ Ⓓ
7 Ⓐ Ⓑ Ⓒ Ⓓ   17 Ⓐ Ⓑ Ⓒ Ⓓ   27 Ⓐ Ⓑ Ⓒ Ⓓ
8 Ⓐ Ⓑ Ⓒ Ⓓ   18 Ⓐ Ⓑ Ⓒ Ⓓ   28 Ⓐ Ⓑ Ⓒ Ⓓ
9 Ⓐ Ⓑ Ⓒ Ⓓ   19 Ⓐ Ⓑ Ⓒ Ⓓ   29 Ⓐ Ⓑ Ⓒ Ⓓ
10 Ⓐ Ⓑ Ⓒ Ⓓ   20 Ⓐ Ⓑ Ⓒ Ⓓ   30 Ⓐ Ⓑ Ⓒ Ⓓ

Social Studies

61 Ⓐ Ⓑ Ⓒ Ⓓ   71 Ⓐ Ⓑ Ⓒ Ⓓ   81 Ⓐ Ⓑ Ⓒ Ⓓ
62 Ⓐ Ⓑ Ⓒ Ⓓ   72 Ⓐ Ⓑ Ⓒ Ⓓ   82 Ⓐ Ⓑ Ⓒ Ⓓ
63 Ⓐ Ⓑ Ⓒ Ⓓ   73 Ⓐ Ⓑ Ⓒ Ⓓ   83 Ⓐ Ⓑ Ⓒ Ⓓ
64 Ⓐ Ⓑ Ⓒ Ⓓ   74 Ⓐ Ⓑ Ⓒ Ⓓ   84 Ⓐ Ⓑ Ⓒ Ⓓ
65 Ⓐ Ⓑ Ⓒ Ⓓ   75 Ⓐ Ⓑ Ⓒ Ⓓ   85 Ⓐ Ⓑ Ⓒ Ⓓ
66 Ⓐ Ⓑ Ⓒ Ⓓ   76 Ⓐ Ⓑ Ⓒ Ⓓ   86 Ⓐ Ⓑ Ⓒ Ⓓ
67 Ⓐ Ⓑ Ⓒ Ⓓ   77 Ⓐ Ⓑ Ⓒ Ⓓ   87 Ⓐ Ⓑ Ⓒ Ⓓ
68 Ⓐ Ⓑ Ⓒ Ⓓ   78 Ⓐ Ⓑ Ⓒ Ⓓ   88 Ⓐ Ⓑ Ⓒ Ⓓ
69 Ⓐ Ⓑ Ⓒ Ⓓ   79 Ⓐ Ⓑ Ⓒ Ⓓ   89 Ⓐ Ⓑ Ⓒ Ⓓ
70 Ⓐ Ⓑ Ⓒ Ⓓ   80 Ⓐ Ⓑ Ⓒ Ⓓ   90 Ⓐ Ⓑ Ⓒ Ⓓ

Math

31 Ⓐ Ⓑ Ⓒ Ⓓ   41 Ⓐ Ⓑ Ⓒ Ⓓ   51 Ⓐ Ⓑ Ⓒ Ⓓ
32 Ⓐ Ⓑ Ⓒ Ⓓ   42 Ⓐ Ⓑ Ⓒ Ⓓ   52 Ⓐ Ⓑ Ⓒ Ⓓ
33 Ⓐ Ⓑ Ⓒ Ⓓ   43 Ⓐ Ⓑ Ⓒ Ⓓ   53 Ⓐ Ⓑ Ⓒ Ⓓ
34 Ⓐ Ⓑ Ⓒ Ⓓ   44 Ⓐ Ⓑ Ⓒ Ⓓ   54 Ⓐ Ⓑ Ⓒ Ⓓ
35 Ⓐ Ⓑ Ⓒ Ⓓ   45 Ⓐ Ⓑ Ⓒ Ⓓ   55 Ⓐ Ⓑ Ⓒ Ⓓ
36 Ⓐ Ⓑ Ⓒ Ⓓ   46 Ⓐ Ⓑ Ⓒ Ⓓ   56 Ⓐ Ⓑ Ⓒ Ⓓ
37 Ⓐ Ⓑ Ⓒ Ⓓ   47 Ⓐ Ⓑ Ⓒ Ⓓ   57 Ⓐ Ⓑ Ⓒ Ⓓ
38 Ⓐ Ⓑ Ⓒ Ⓓ   48 Ⓐ Ⓑ Ⓒ Ⓓ   58 Ⓐ Ⓑ Ⓒ Ⓓ
39 Ⓐ Ⓑ Ⓒ Ⓓ   49 Ⓐ Ⓑ Ⓒ Ⓓ   59 Ⓐ Ⓑ Ⓒ Ⓓ
40 Ⓐ Ⓑ Ⓒ Ⓓ   50 Ⓐ Ⓑ Ⓒ Ⓓ   60 Ⓐ Ⓑ Ⓒ Ⓓ

Science

91 Ⓐ Ⓑ Ⓒ Ⓓ   101 Ⓐ Ⓑ Ⓒ Ⓓ   111 Ⓐ Ⓑ Ⓒ Ⓓ
92 Ⓐ Ⓑ Ⓒ Ⓓ   102 Ⓐ Ⓑ Ⓒ Ⓓ   112 Ⓐ Ⓑ Ⓒ Ⓓ
93 Ⓐ Ⓑ Ⓒ Ⓓ   103 Ⓐ Ⓑ Ⓒ Ⓓ   113 Ⓐ Ⓑ Ⓒ Ⓓ
94 Ⓐ Ⓑ Ⓒ Ⓓ   104 Ⓐ Ⓑ Ⓒ Ⓓ   114 Ⓐ Ⓑ Ⓒ Ⓓ
95 Ⓐ Ⓑ Ⓒ Ⓓ   105 Ⓐ Ⓑ Ⓒ Ⓓ   115 Ⓐ Ⓑ Ⓒ Ⓓ
96 Ⓐ Ⓑ Ⓒ Ⓓ   106 Ⓐ Ⓑ Ⓒ Ⓓ   116 Ⓐ Ⓑ Ⓒ Ⓓ
97 Ⓐ Ⓑ Ⓒ Ⓓ   107 Ⓐ Ⓑ Ⓒ Ⓓ   117 Ⓐ Ⓑ Ⓒ Ⓓ
98 Ⓐ Ⓑ Ⓒ Ⓓ   108 Ⓐ Ⓑ Ⓒ Ⓓ   118 Ⓐ Ⓑ Ⓒ Ⓓ
99 Ⓐ Ⓑ Ⓒ Ⓓ   109 Ⓐ Ⓑ Ⓒ Ⓓ   119 Ⓐ Ⓑ Ⓒ Ⓓ
100 Ⓐ Ⓑ Ⓒ Ⓓ   110 Ⓐ Ⓑ Ⓒ Ⓓ   120 Ⓐ Ⓑ Ⓒ Ⓓ

Practice Test Six
Content Knowledge (0014)

Time—2 Hours
120 Questions

Language Arts

1. Which of the following is an example of a simile?

   (A) The moon is made of swiss cheese.
   (B) The moon is a cracked dinner plate.
   (C) The moon smiles down upon us.
   (D) The moon is like a lonely hunter.

2. Which of the following words is derived from a French word?

   (A) Armadillo
   (B) Geography
   (C) Poultry
   (D) Laser

   [1]The themes of liberty and freedom are central to much of American literature, particularly the literature produced during the American Renaissance. [2]As the issues of women's rights and abolition came to the forefront of the American consciousness, writers delved deep into an exploration of the meaning of freedom for the country and for individuals. [3]Three such writers from this time period who focus on issues of freedom are Margaret Fuller, Harriet Beecher Stowe, and Harriet Jacobs. [4]Each of these writers develop an answer to the question posed by Stowe in *Uncle Tom's Cabin*: "Liberty!—electric word! What is it?"

3. Which of the following sentences should be revised in order to correct an error?

   (A) Sentence 1, to correct an error in comma use
   (B) Sentence 2, to correct an error in apostrophe use
   (C) Sentence 3, to correct an error in comma use
   (D) Sentence 4, to correct an error in agreement

Questions 4–5

When the great European movement known as the Renaissance reached England, it found its fullest and most lasting expression in the drama. By a fortunate group of coincidences, this intellectual and artistic impulse affected the people of England at a moment when the country was undergoing a rapid and, on the whole, peaceful expansion—when the national spirit soared high, and when the development of the language and the forms of versification had reached a point that made possible the most triumphant literary achievement that the country has seen.

Throughout the Middle Ages, the English drama, like that of other European countries, was mainly religious and didactic, its chief forms being the Miracle Plays, which presented in crude dialogue stories from the Bible and the lives of the saints, and the Moralities, which taught lessons for the guidance of life through the means of allegorical action and the personification of abstract qualities. Both forms were severely limited in their opportunities for picturing human nature and human life with breadth and variety. With the revival of learning came naturally the study and imitation of the ancient classical drama, and in some countries, this proved the chief influence in determining the prevalent type of drama for generations to come. However, in England, although we can trace important results of the models given by Seneca in tragedy and Plautus in comedy, the main characteristics of the drama of the Elizabethan age were of native origin and reflected the spirit and the interests of the Englishmen of that day.

4. Which of the following ideas from the passage above is the most subjective?

   (A) When the Renaissance reached England, the country was experiencing rapid and relatively peaceful expansion.

   (B) English drama of the Middle Ages was generally religious and didactic.

   (C) Miracle Plays and Moralities provided severely limited depictions of human nature and human life.

   (D) During the Renaissance, ancient forms of drama were studied and imitated.

5. Based on the excerpt, it is most likely that the author would agree with which of the following statements?

   (A) Allegory and personification are literary devices that are limited in their ability to effectively portray human emotion.

   (B) Originality is essential to the lasting literary importance of the great Elizabethan dramas.

   (C) Dramatic works that focus on a retelling of biblical stories are typically limited in their appeal to audiences.

   (D) The success of the writers during the Elizabethan period is responsible for major shifts in the development of the English language.

6. "As a child begins to learn to read and write, these skills develop concurrently and in interrelated ways." This statement is most consistent with the latest research in

   (A) phonics
   (B) emergent literacy
   (C) formal operations
   (D) learning styles

GO ON TO THE NEXT PAGE

My great-grandfather came to America in 1907.

My great-grandfather was a doctor in Poland.

My great-grandfather had to work as a dishwasher in a restaurant.

7. Which is the best combination of the three sentences above?

   (A) My great-grandfather had to work as a dishwasher in a restaurant—when he came to America in 1907 he was a doctor in Poland.

   (B) My great-grandfather was a doctor in Poland, and he came to America in 1907 and then had to work as a dishwasher in a restaurant.

   (C) My great-grandfather came to America in 1907; had been a doctor in Poland; he had to work as a dishwasher in a restaurant.

   (D) My great-grandfather, a doctor in Poland, had to work as a dishwasher in a restaurant when he came to America in 1907.

8. When a reader is decoding a word, he or she is focused on

   I. organizing ideas

   II. generating questions to be researched

   III. listing examples associated with a given topic

   IV. evaluating information

   (A) I and II only

   (B) II and III only

   (C) I, II, and IV only

   (D) I, II, III, and IV

9. Which of the following would NOT be an effective thesis statement in a persuasive essay?

   (A) The United States has no right to intervene in the internal affairs of other nations.

   (B) Year-round schooling is an ill-conceived and simplistic solution to a complicated problem.

   (C) Seventy-five percent of surveyed voters feel the president is doing an adequate job.

   (D) Thoreau was right when he said, "The mass of men lead lives of quiet desperation."

10. Each of the 18 students in a graduate course is required to make a 15-minute presentation on a given topic. The professor has informed students that the use of effective nonverbal communication will make up a portion of the grade received on the presentation. Which of the following is the best example of effective nonverbal communication that a student should use during his or her presentation?

   (A) Maintaining eye contact with the professor

   (B) Using no notes

   (C) Standing still behind a podium

   (D) Establishing eye contact throughout the presentation with all members of the audience

11. Which of the following are key components of brainstorming?

   I. Organizing ideas

   II. Generating questions to be researched

   III. Listing examples associated with a given topic

   IV. Evaluating information

(A) I and II only

(B) II and III only

(C) I, II, and IV only

(D) I, II, III, and IV

We will ponder your proposition and when we decide we will let you know. But should we accept it, I here and now make this condition that we will not be denied the privilege without molestation of visiting at any time the tombs of our ancestors, friends, and children. Every part of this soil is sacred in the estimation of my people. Every hillside, every valley, every plain and grove, has been hallowed by some sad or happy event in days long vanished. Even the rocks, which seem to be dumb and dead as they swelter in the sun along the silent shore, thrill with memories of stirring events connected with the lives of my people, and the very dust upon which you now stand responds more lovingly to their footsteps than yours, because it is rich with the blood of our ancestors, and our bare feet *are conscious of the sympathetic touch...*

From a speech given by Chief Seattle in 1854 as reprinted in the October 29, 1887 *Seattle Sunday Star*.

12. Based on this passage, it is most reasonable to assume that the speaker believed which of the following?

(A) The government of the United States would honor the condition he set forth.

(B) The land of his people was sacred because of the ancestors who lived and died there.

(C) The rights of Native Americans were unimportant to the government of the United States.

(D) Immigrants to the United States would come to see the land as sacred.

The sun sank rapidly; the silvery light had faded from the bare boughs and the watery twilight was settling in when Wilson at last walked down the hill, descending into cooler and cooler depths of grayish shadow. His nostril, long unused to it, was quick to detect the smell of wood smoke in the air, blended with the odor of moist spring earth and the saltiness that came up the river with the tide.

From *Alexander's Bridge* by Willa Cather

13. The passage above contains characteristic elements of which of the following literary genres?

(A) Fable

(B) Autobiography

(C) Folktale

(D) Realistic fiction

GO ON TO THE NEXT PAGE

Hope is the thing with feathers
That perches in the soul
And sings the tune without the words
And never stops at all,

And sweetest in the gale is heard;
And sore must be the storm
That could abash the little bird
That kept so many warm

I've heard it in the chillest land
And on the strangest sea,
Yet never, in extremity,
It asked a crumb of me.

"'Hope' is the Thing with Feathers," by Emily
Dickinson

14. Which of the following is true of the poem
    above?

    (A) It is written in iambic pentameter.
    (B) It includes an extended metaphor.
    (C) It is a sonnet.
    (D) It is an oxymoron.

Questions 15–17

The stars were shining, and the leaves rustled in the woods ever so mournful; and I heard an owl, away off, who-whooing about somebody that was dead, and a whippowill and a dog crying about somebody that was going to die; and the wind was trying to whisper something to me, and I couldn't make out what it was, and so it made the cold shivers run over me.

from *The Adventures of Huckleberry Finn*, by Mark
Twain

15. The style of writing employed in this passage
    can best be described as

    (A) standard English
    (B) formal English
    (C) jargon
    (D) dialect

16. The author's use of language in this passage
    helps to demonstrate the speaker's

    (A) lack of intelligence
    (B) lack of education
    (C) good-heartedness
    (D) confusion

17. The author uses imagery in this section to
    illustrate Huck's

    (A) fear and loneliness
    (B) awareness of his environment
    (C) loss of his father
    (D) moral dilemma

GO ON TO THE NEXT PAGE

18. "You will have 30 minutes to complete the assignment. When you're finished, give it to Ms. Fletcher or myself."

    What is the error in the sentences above?

    (A) "30" should be spelled out as "thirty"
    (B) The clauses should be joined by a semicolon, not a period
    (C) "myself" should be "me"
    (D) "you're" should be "your"

19. To be considered a poem, a work of literature must use which of the following?

    I. Verse
    II. Rhythm
    III.   Rhyme
    IV.   Metaphor

    (A) I and II only
    (B) I and IV only
    (C) II and III only
    (D) I only

Words can have multiple meanings and be used as different parts of speech in different contexts. The word "appropriate", for instance, has two meanings.

appropriate

1   *adj.* fitting; proper
2   *v.* to claim or take for one's own, frequently without permission

20. Which of the following sentences uses "appropriate" as a verb, that is, the second definition in the list above?

    (A) Although he felt overdressed, his attire was appropriate for the cocktail party.
    (B) When learning a new language, it can be difficult to find the appropriate words to express one's thoughts.
    (C) The bank may appropriate the farm if the mortgage payments are not made on time.
    (D) Rough-housing is not appropriate in the workplace.

21. In the phrase, "parting brings such <u>sweet sorrow</u>," the underlined portion of the phrase is an example of

    (A) a simile
    (B) a personification
    (C) a hyperbole
    (D) an oxymoron

GO ON TO THE NEXT PAGE

22. When doing research on the life of an important figure, you would probably give more credence to a biography than you would to an autobiography, due to the memoirist's

    (A) verbosity
    (B) creativity
    (C) subjectivity
    (D) experiences

23. Which of the following nonverbal responses from an audience member indicates attention and interest in a speaker?

    (A) Crossed arms and crossed legs
    (B) Leaning forward
    (C) Eye contact with other audience members
    (D) Leaning backward

24. Which of the following best describes the critical period in language development?

    (A) If a child does not learn to write by a certain age, he or she is likely to never acquire basic writing skills.
    (B) If a child is not exposed to a second language by a certain age, he or she is likely to never fluently read or write a second language.
    (C) If a child is not exposed to regular language use by a certain age, he or she is likely to never fully develop language capabilities.
    (D) If a child does not learn phonetics by a certain age, he or she is likely to never acquire basic reading skills.

25. The branch of linguistics that deals with the study of how language represents meaning is

    (A) morphology
    (B) phonetics
    (C) semantics
    (D) syntax

26. The act of preparing a response while listening to a speaker is referred to as

    (A) forming a clarifying a question
    (B) rehearsing
    (C) active listening
    (D) restating information

27. Which of the following is NOT a phase of writing development?

    (A) Picture writing
    (B) Scribble writing
    (C) Conventional writing
    (D) Haphazard writing

28. A child can connect certain letters with sounds, but has not yet grasped the concept that a number of letter-sound combinations make up most words. Which of the following types of errors would indicate this lack of understanding?

    (A) Representing a word or a group of words by a single letter
    (B) Misspelling words like "cat" or "grace" as "kat" or "grase"
    (C) Making errors with exceptional spelling rules, such as "i" before "e," except after "c"
    (D) Spelling the word "dog" as "qxr"

29. A student has drafted a writing assignment, and read it through one additional time, making revisions as she goes through. She is now ready for which of the following stages of the writing process?

    (A) Outlining
    (B) Revising
    (C) Proofreading
    (D) Publishing

30. Which of the following words have acquired new definitions due to technological advances and developments in the 20th century?

    I. Mouse
    II. Surfing
    III. Cookie
    IV. Desktop

    (A) I and III only
    (B) II and IV only
    (C) I, II, and III only
    (D) I, II, III, and IV

Mathematics

31. Which of the following numbers is the greatest?

    (A) 0.21
    (B) 0.203
    (C) 0.2042
    (D) 0.2005

32. Tom is standing next to a fire hydrant. The hydrant casts a shadow that is 32 inches long. Tom's casts a shadow that is 48 inches long. If the hydrant is 40 inches tall, how tall is Tom?

    (A) 52 inches
    (B) 60 inches
    (C) 72 inches
    (D) 84 inches

33. On a national reading test, 40 percent of the 540 students at Stevens Elementary school scored at or below their grade level. Which of the following computations can be used to determine the number of students who scored at or below their grade level on the test?

    (A) $\frac{1}{40} \times 540$

    (B) $\frac{2}{5} \times 540$

    (C) $540 \div 0.40$

    (D) 40×540

GO ON TO THE NEXT PAGE

34. The owner of a hat shop buys hats at a cost of 5 for $17.50 and sells them for $4.00 each. How many hats must the owner sell in order to make a profit of $100?

    (A) 50
    (B) 100
    (C) 150
    (D) 200

35. All of the following are equivalent to dividing 420 by 21 EXCEPT

    (A) $(420 \div 3) \div 7$

    (B) $420 \div (3 \times 7)$

    (C) $(420 \div 3) + (420 \div 7)$

    (D) $\dfrac{420}{3} \times \dfrac{1}{7}$

T-shirt	$5.95
Jeans	$9.95
Sweatshirt	$12.50
Sweater	$6.25
Legwarmers	$4.95

36. If a shopper gives a $50, the change is closest to?

    (A) $8
    (B) $9
    (C) $10
    (D) $11

37. In a group of 25 students, 16 are female. What percent of the group is female?

    (A) 6%
    (B) 40%
    (C) 60%
    (D) 64%

38. The sum of a certain two numbers is 10 and the product of the two numbers is 24. What is the difference of the two numbers?

    (A) 2
    (B) 4
    (C) 6
    (D) 8

39. There are 64 members of a botany club at a local college. If there are three times as many girls as boys in the club, how many girls are in the club?

    (A) 32
    (B) 36
    (C) 42
    (D) 48

$$7(8 + 5) = 7 \times 8 + 7 \times 5$$

40. The equation above demonstrates which of the following?

    (A) The distributive property of multiplication over addition
    (B) Additive inverse and additive identity
    (C) The commutative property of multiplication
    (D) The associative property of multiplication

GO ON TO THE NEXT PAGE

41. Clinton bowled an average score of 180 over four games. If he bowled 156, 172, and 210 in his first three games, what did he bowl in the final game?

    (A) 178
    (B) 180
    (C) 182
    (D) 188

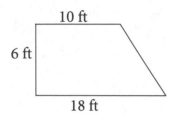

42. What is the perimeter of the following shape?

    (A) 34 ft
    (B) 40 ft
    (C) 44 ft
    (D) 48 ft

43. In a map A, one inch represents 5 miles. In map B, one inch represents 2 miles. What is the difference in square miles between one square inch in map A and one square inch in map B?

    (A) 3
    (B) 10
    (C) 21
    (D) 25

44. In triangle ABC, the measure of angle A is 35° and the measure of angle B is 92°. What is the measure of angle C?

    (A) 53°
    (B) 55°
    (C) 88°
    (D) 145°

45. Monica arrived at work at 8:42 A.M. and worked straight through the day with no breaks. She left work at 4:15 P.M. How long was she at work?

    (A) 7 hours and 27 minutes
    (B) 7 hours and 33 minutes
    (C) 8 hours and 27 minutes
    (D) 8 hours and 33 minutes

46. A high school band is composed of 13 freshmen, 20 sophomores, 16 juniors, and 15 seniors. What is the probability that a band member chosen from random will be a sophomore?

    (A) $\frac{2}{5}$

    (B) $\frac{1}{3}$

    (C) $\frac{4}{13}$

    (D) $\frac{5}{16}$

GO ON TO THE NEXT PAGE

47. Which of the following is closest in value to the decimal 0.40?

    (A) $\frac{1}{3}$

    (B) $\frac{4}{7}$

    (C) $\frac{3}{8}$

    (D) $\frac{1}{2}$

48. A class of 40 students is to be divided into smaller groups. If each group is to contain 3, 4, or 5 people, what is the largest number of groups possible?

    (A) 10
    (B) 12
    (C) 13
    (D) 14

49. If 48 of the 60 seats on a bus were occupied, what percent of the seats were not occupied?

    (A) 12%
    (B) 15%
    (C) 20%
    (D) 25%

50. A full box contains 24 pieces of chocolate. If Doris starts out with 200 pieces of chocolate, how many pieces will she have left over if she fills as many boxes as she can?

    (A) 4
    (B) 8
    (C) 10
    (D) 16

51. Joyce baked 42 biscuits for her 12 guests. If 6 biscuits remain uneaten, what is the average number of biscuits that the guests ate?

    (A) 2
    (B) 3
    (C) 4
    (D) 6

52. In a certain class, 3 out of 24 students are in student organizations. What is the ratio of students in student organizations to students not in student organizations?

    (A) $\frac{1}{8}$

    (B) $\frac{1}{7}$

    (C) $\frac{1}{6}$

    (D) $\frac{1}{4}$

53. A machine labels 150 bottles in 20 minutes. At this rate, how many minutes does it take to label 60 bottles?

    (A) 2
    (B) 4
    (C) 6
    (D) 8

GO ON TO THE NEXT PAGE

54. A subway car passes 3 stations every 10 minutes. At this rate, how many stations will it pass in one hour?

    (A) 15
    (B) 18
    (C) 20
    (D) 30

55. What is the fifth term in the following series?

    6.5; 13.75; 21; 28.25; _____?

    (A) 35.25
    (B) 35.50
    (C) 36.50
    (D) 36.75

56. After eating 25 percent of the jelly beans, Brett had 72 left. How many jelly beans did Brett have originally?

    (A) 90
    (B) 94
    (C) 95
    (D) 96

57. A student finishes the first half of an exam in $\frac{2}{3}$ the time it takes him to finish the second half. If the entire exam takes him an hour, how many minutes does he spend on the first half of the exam?

    (A) 20
    (B) 24
    (C) 27
    (D) 36

58. Marty has exactly 5 blue pens, 6 black pens, and 4 red pens in his knapsack. If he pulls out one pen at random from his knapsack, what is the probability that the pen is either red or black?

    (A) $\frac{2}{3}$

    (B) $\frac{3}{5}$

    (C) $\frac{2}{5}$

    (D) $\frac{1}{3}$

Name	Weight in pounds
Chris	150
Anne	153
Malcolm	154
Paul	157
Sam	151

59. What is the average weight, in pounds, of the five people whose weights are listed in the table above?

    (A) 153
    (B) $153\frac{1}{2}$
    (C) 154
    (D) 155

60. If each digit 5 is replaced with the digit 7, how much will 258,546 be increased?

    (A) 2,020
    (B) 2,200
    (C) 20,020
    (D) 20,200

GO ON TO THE NEXT PAGE

Social Studies

61. The main distinction between weather and climate is that

    (A) weather is more variable and immediate
    (B) climate is more variable and immediate
    (C) climate is a product of current conditions
    (D) weather is more focused on long term, regional conditions

62. Taiga is a type of

    (A) vegetation
    (B) ecosystem
    (C) rock formation
    (D) body of water

63. All of the following are true of map projections EXCEPT

    (A) map projections are flat
    (B) map projections are the most accurate representations of the surface of the Earth
    (C) map projections create distortions
    (D) map projections use grid lines of longitude and latitude

64. Which of the following is generally NOT considered a serious threat to the global environment?

    (A) Global warming
    (B) Deforestation
    (C) Plate tectonics
    (D) Ozone-layer depletion

65. The Agricultural Revolution has been called "the dawn of civilization" because

    (A) it allowed hunter-gatherers to travel further from their homes in search of food
    (B) it allowed for the development of agrarian societies and food surpluses
    (C) it occurred soon after the founding of the first great civilizations
    (D) it occurred concurrently with significant advances in astronomy and the arts

66. The primary cause of soil depletion in rain forest environments is

    (A) global warming
    (B) deforestation
    (C) erosion
    (D) acid rain

67. Hieroglyphics and the pharoahs are most closely associated with which of the following civilizations?

    (A) Rome
    (B) Egypt
    (C) Greece
    (D) Persia

68. Ferdinand Magellan is best known for which of the following?

    (A) The first successful voyage around the Cape of Good Hope
    (B) The first successful transatlantic flight
    (C) The first successful voyage around the globe
    (D) The discovery of the South Pole

69. Which of the following terms is associated with the class structure of traditional Hindu society

    (A) tao
    (B) caste
    (C) kabuki
    (D) zen

70. Holy scriptures for the Judaic faith are called the

    (A) Upanishads
    (B) Torah
    (C) Koran
    (D) Ramayana

71. Ancient Athens and Sparta are examples of

    I. Greek theocracies.
    II. Greek city-states.
    III.   Greek monarchies.
    IV.   major cities in the Greek Empire.

    (A) I, II, and III only
    (B) II and III only
    (C) II and IV only
    (D) II only

72. Which of the following is most responsible for the spread of Greek art, architecture, and thought throughout the ancient Mediterranean world?

    (A) Hammurabi
    (B) Genghis Khan
    (C) Alexander the Great
    (D) Herodotus

73. Which of the following is NOT a central aspect of the Reformation?

    (A) Martin Luther's 95 theses
    (B) Henry VIII's divorce
    (C) The Catholic church's practice of indulgences
    (D) The works of Shakespeare, Michelangelo, and Da Vinci

74. Which of the following were Abolitionists in the years leading into the United States Civil War?

    (A) Elizabeth Cady Stanton, Carrie Nation, and Susan B. Anthony
    (B) Andrew Carnegie, John D. Rockefeller, and J.P. Morgan
    (C) Frederick Douglas, William Lloyd Garrison, and Harriet Beecher Stowe
    (D) Ulysses S. Grant, William Sherman, and Rutherford B. Hayes

75. Which of the following is NOT a concept central to the Monroe Doctrine?

    (A) American neutrality in wars of the European powers
    (B) Limiting European colonial influence in the Americas
    (C) Handling issues relating to the Americas without European intervention
    (D) Establishing an American sphere of influence in Asia

76. Westward expansion in the United States involved each of the following EXCEPT

    (A) Manifest Destiny
    (B) the Louisiana Purchase
    (C) "Big Stick Diplomacy"
    (D) the Trail of Tears

GO ON TO THE NEXT PAGE

Questions 77–78

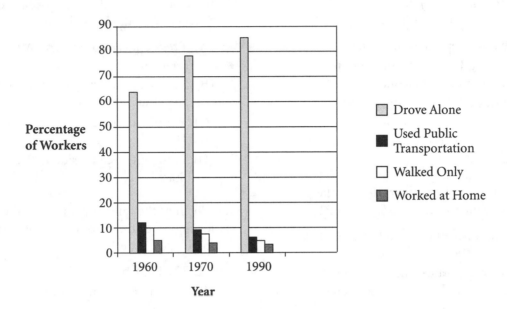

77. In the graph, the percentages of workers who used different modes of transportation to commute to work are shown. The number of workers accounted for in the 1960 Census was approximately 65,000,000. Of these workers, approximately how many walked to work?

    (A) 7,800,000
    (B) 6,500,000
    (C) 5,200,000
    (D) 3,250,000

78. Which of the following statements is best supported by data reported in the graph?

    (A) The number of people who worked at home decreased between the years 1960 and 1990.

    (B) Between 1960 and 1990, the percentage of the population that used public transportation on a daily basis decreased.

    (C) Urban sprawl is a primary factor in the increasing percentage of workers who drive to work.

    (D) In 1970, more than 15% of the working population used public transportation or walked to get to work.

GO ON TO THE NEXT PAGE

79. The Supreme Court case of *Brown v. The Board of Education of Topeka, Kansas* is an important case in that it

    (A) gave women the right to vote
    (B) repealed laws that prohibited the consumption of alcohol
    (C) addressed the constitutionality of segregation in schools
    (D) led directly to the Montgomery bus boycott

80. Each of the following characterizes the Articles of the Confederation EXCEPT?

    (A) It was ratified prior to the United States Constitution.
    (B) It placed greater emphasis on states' rights than did the United States Constitution.
    (C) It was the basis of the Confederacy during the U.S. Civil War.
    (D) It influenced the development of the United States Constitution in the 1780s.

81. The three branches of the U.S. Government are

    (A) the Senate, the House of Representatives, and the President
    (B) Executive, Judicial, and Legislative
    (C) Executive, Defense, and State
    (D) the Supreme Court, the Senate, and the President

82. Which of the following is not guaranteed by the United States Bill of Rights?

    (A) protection from illegal search and seizure
    (B) freedom of speech and religion
    (C) the right to bear arms and keep a well regulated militia
    (D) the right to universal healthcare

83. Which of the following is the correct first three positions in the order of Presidential Succession in the United States?

    (A) President, Vice President, Attorney General
    (B) President, Attorney General, Speaker of the House
    (C) President, Vice President, Speaker of the House
    (D) President, Vice President, Secretary of State

84. Which of the following influenced the formation of the democratic government of the United States?

    I. The French Revolution
    II. The Iroquois Confederacy
    III.   The Magna Carta
    IV.   John Locke

    (A) I and III only
    (B) III and IV only
    (C) II, III, and IV only
    (D) I, II, III, and IV

85. Much of Sigmund Freud's research was dedicated to analyzing dreams. It is most likely that he focused on an individual's dreams in order to

    (A) resolve cognitive dissonances
    (B) interpret symbols connected with the collective unconscious
    (C) analyze aspects of the individual's unconscious mind
    (D) analyze conditioned behavioral responses

GO ON TO THE NEXT PAGE

86. Which pairs the major source of revenue of the federal government with the major source of revenue of local governments in the United States?

    (A) excise taxes—sales taxes
    (B) tariffs—inheritance taxes
    (C) estate taxes—corporate taxes
    (D) income taxes—property taxes

87. In the United States, the development of political parties and the selection of the presidential cabinet are both examples of political practices that are

    (A) sanctioned by the Supreme Court
    (B) carried over from the colonial period
    (C) not written in the Constitution
    (D) developed during John Adams' Administration

88. Appliance stores tend to raise prices of fans and air conditioners as the hottest months of the year approach. This is consistent with which of the following economic principles?

    (A) Deflation
    (B) Supply and demand
    (C) Deficit spending
    (D) Diminishing returns

89. Which of the following does NOT represent a possible negative effect of a laissez-faire economic system, in which government holds little or no control over commerce?

    (A) Trade limitations created by tariffs on imported goods
    (B) The rise of monopolies
    (C) The unrestricted use of immigrant or child labor
    (D) Hazardous working conditions in unregulated factories

90. Which of the following most accurately describes the central goal of the Women's Suffrage Movement in the United States?

    (A) To abolish the practice of slavery
    (B) To ensure equitable salaries for women
    (C) To obtain the right for women to vote
    (D) To prohibit the use of alcohol

Science

91. The process by which plants convert carbon dioxide and water into sugar and oxygen is called

    (A) decomposition
    (B) photosynthesis
    (C) oxidation
    (D) respiration

92. In electricity, a unit of resistance is called an

    (A) ampere
    (B) ohm
    (C) volt
    (D) watt

93. Which of the following depicts a chemical process?

    (A) Helium is combined with neon
    (B) Iron forms rust
    (C) Water causes soil erosion
    (D) Ice melts

94. Blood enters the right atrium of the heart from the

    (A) aorta
    (B) left ventricle
    (C) pulmonary vein
    (D) vena cava

95. Which of the following substances has the highest pH?

    (A) Ammonia
    (B) Battery acid
    (C) Isopropyl alcohol
    (D) Water

96. Insulin is created in the body's

    (A) adrenal glands
    (B) kidneys
    (C) pancreas
    (D) thymus

97. If two brown-eyed parents have a blue-eyed child, the probability that their next child will have blue eyes is

    (A) zero
    (B) 1 in 2
    (C) 1 in 3
    (D) 1 in 4

Use this chart for Question 98

Type of bread	Temperature (°F)	Day 5	Day 10	Day 15	Day 20
White	37	0 cm^2	0 cm^2	1 cm^2	4 cm^2
White	71	0 cm^2	2 cm^2	8 cm^2	18 cm^2
Sourdough	37	0 cm^2	0 cm^2	0 cm^2	1 cm^2
Sourdough	71	0 cm^2	0 cm^2	2 cm^2	7 cm^2

98. It is most reasonable to predict that if the experiment were conducted for an additional five days, the amount of mold found on the sourdough loaf kept at 71°F would be

    (A) 7 cm^2
    (B) 8 cm^2
    (C) 16 cm^2
    (D) 40 cm^2

99. The process by which the sun heats the earth is known as

    (A) conduction
    (B) convection
    (C) radiation
    (D) refraction

GO ON TO THE NEXT PAGE

100. During a lunar eclipse,

    (A) the moon lies between the earth and sun
    (B) the sun lies between the moon and earth
    (C) the earth lies between the moon and sun
    (D) none of the above

101. The climate with the shortest growing season would be in the

    (A) grasslands
    (B) deciduous forest
    (C) tropical forest
    (D) taiga

102. The major portion of an atom's mass consists of

    (A) neutrons and protons
    (B) electrons and protons
    (C) electrons and neutrons
    (D) neutrons and positrons

103. Over the course of 24 hours

    (A) the earth rotates 360 degrees around the sun
    (B) the moon rotates 360 degrees around the earth
    (C) the earth rotates 360 degrees about its axis
    (D) the moon rotates 360 degrees about its axis

104. Which of the following kingdoms is considered the most primitive?

    (A) Fungi
    (B) Protista
    (C) Moneran
    (D) Plant

105. Orbiting around the nucleus of an atom are

    (A) anions
    (B) electrons
    (C) positrons
    (D) photons

106. Fungi are organisms that break down dead matter and return the organic material back into the environment for reuse. They are examples of

    (A) producers
    (B) decomposers
    (C) consumers
    (D) mutualism

107. In degrees Kelvin, the freezing pointing of water is

    (A) −273°
    (B)   0°
    (C) 100°
    (D) 273°

108. Tough elastic tissues found in the joints the connect bones to bones are called

    (A) ligaments
    (B) tendons
    (C) cartilage
    (D) muscles

109. A straw placed in a glass of water appears to be bent or broken. The property of light responsible for the straw appearing to be bent is called

    (A) refraction
    (B) diffraction
    (C) reflection
    (D) interference

GO ON TO THE NEXT PAGE

110. Animals that consume plants are called

(A) saprophytes

(B) herbivores

(C) carnivores

(D) omnivores

111. Rods and cones are light-sensitive cells inside the eye's

(A) cornea

(B) iris

(C) pupil

(D) retina

112. A boulder that begins to roll down a hill is an example of an energy conversion from

(A) potential to thermal

(B) potential to kinetic

(C) kinetic to thermal

(D) kinetic to potential

113. The lowest layer of the earth's atmosphere is called the

(A) ionosphere

(B) mesosphere

(C) stratosphere

(D) troposphere

Four specimens of three species of plants were exposed to different amounts of sunlight over the period of a week. At the end of the week, the number of new leaves on each plant was recorded.

Hours of sunlight per day	New leaves on Species A	New leaves on Species B	New leaves on Species C
0	0	0	0
1	0	1	4
3	0	4	8
6	4	7	5

114. Which of the following conclusions is best supported by information in the table above?

(A) Species A requires 6 hours of sunlight per day to produce new leaves.

(B) No plants can grow without exposure to sunlight.

(C) To optimize growth, Species B should be exposed to more than 6 hours of sunlight per day.

(D) To optimize growth, Species C should be exposed to between 2 and 5 hours of sunlight per day.

GO ON TO THE NEXT PAGE

KAPLAN

115. One major cause of species depletion is the introduction of a new (sometimes called "exotic") species to an established ecosystem. One such example is the Kudzu vine, a Japanese species that was introduced to the United States in 1876 to shade porches on southern mansions. It was also widely planted in the 1940s to control erosion. This vine grows so rapidly that it can kill native trees and shrubs by entirely covering them. Which of the following does NOT explain why introduced species such as the Kudzu vine can cause the depletion or even extinction of species already established in an ecosystem?

(A) The introduced species may not have a natural predator in the new ecosystem.

(B) The introduced species may have adapted more successful defense mechanisms than native species.

(C) Native species may be resistant to diseases present in the established ecosystem.

(D) Native species may not successfully compete with the introduced species for resources.

116. Which of the following muscles are controlled by conscious thought?

(A) Smooth

(B) Striated

(C) Cardiac

(D) All of the above

117. Which of the following is most responsible for oceanic tides?

(A) The orbit of the earth around its own axis

(B) The magnetic polarity of the earth

(C) The orbit of the moon around the earth

(D) The orbit of the earth around the sun

118. A substance that hastens a chemical reaction without undergoing chemical change itself is called a

(A) bromide

(B) catalyst

(C) oxidizing agent

(D) reactant

119. Lack of iron is associated with which of the following diseases?

(A) Anemia

(B) Hemophilia

(C) Goiter

(D) Rickets

120. Which of the following subatomic particles has the largest mass?

(A) Proton

(B) Electron

(C) Positron

(D) Neutrino

STOP!

If you finish before time is up, you may go back and check your work.

Practice Test Six (0014)
Answers and Explanations

LANGUAGE ARTS		MATHEMATICS		SOCIAL STUDIES		SCIENCE	
1. D	21. D	31. A	51. B	61. A	81. B	91. B	111. D
2. C	22. C	32. B	52. B	62. B	82. D	92. B	112. B
3. D	23. B	33. B	53. D	63. B	83. C	93. B	113. D
4. C	24. C	34. D	54. B	64. C	84. C	94. D	114. D
5. B	25. C	35. C	55. B	65. B	85. C	95. A	115. C
6. B	26. B	36. C	56. D	66. B	86. D	96. C	116. B
7. D	27. D	37. D	57. B	67. B	87. C	97. D	117. C
8. A	28. A	38. A	58. A	68. C	88. B	98. C	118. B
9. C	29. C	39. D	59. A	69. B	89. A	99. C	119. A
10. D	30. D	40. A	60. D	70. B	90. C	100. C	120. A
11. B		41. C		71. D		101. D	
12. B		42. C		72. C		102. A	
13. D		43. C		73. D		103. C	
14. B		44. A		74. C		104. C	
15. D		45. B		75. D		105. B	
16. B		46. D		76. C		106. B	
17. A		47. C		77. B		107. D	
18. C		48. C		78. D		108. A	
19. D		49. C		79. C		109. A	
20. C		50. B		80. C		110. B	

ANSWERS AND EXPLANATIONS

Language Arts (1–30)

1. D

A simile is a figure of speech that compares two unlike things using the words *like* or *as*. Only (D) does this comparing the moon and a lonely hunter using the word like. (B) is an example of a metaphor, not a simile, since it compares two unlike things without using either like or as. (C) is an example of personification, wherein an inanimate or inhuman thing is given human-like qualities. (A) fails to use like or as, and may be figurative language or may simply be a confused statement.

2. C

The word "poultry" is derived from the French word "poulet," so (C) is correct. "Geography" is derived from the Greek language. "Laser" is a modern word which is in fact an acronym for light amplified by stimulated emission of radiation. Armadillo is derived from the Spanish language.

3. D

Only sentence 4 contains an error. The single pronoun "each" is the subject of the sentence, so the verb "develop" should be the singular "develops." The comma in sentence 1 is used correctly to separate nonessential descriptive information from the rest of the sentence. The apostrophe in sentence two is correctly used to show possession. All of the commas in sentence 3 are used correctly to separate items in a series.

4. C

This question asks you to identify the most subjective, or opinionated, idea from the passage. In other words, which statement could not be proved by facts? (C) states the author's opinion— that the Miracle Plays and Moralities of the Middle Ages only showed a limited picture of humanity.

The word "severely" is a clue that this is a subjective statement. All of the other statements could be proved through research. A study of history would show that England experienced rapid expansion during the Renaissance (A). A survey of English drama in the Middle Ages would show that most of the plays of this time were indeed religious and didactic (B). A survey of drama from the Renaissance would show the influence of ancient forms of drama (D).

5. B

This inference question asks you to draw a logical conclusion based on information presented in the passage. In the first paragraph, the author refers to the Elizabethan dramas as "the most triumphant literary achievement which that country has seen." In the second paragraph, the author says that, unlike the Renaissance literature of other countries, "the main characteristics of the drama of the Elizabethan age were of native origin." From these two points, it is most logical to assume that originality is important to the literary achievement of the Elizabethan dramas. (A) can be eliminated because the author claims that Mystery Plays and Moralities, not allegory and personification, are limited in their ability to portray human life. (C) can be eliminated because the author does not discuss the appeal of Mystery Plays and Moralities to audiences. In fact, these types of drama were extremely popular with medieval audiences. (D) reverses a cause-effect relationship identified in the passage. The author states that the development of the language made the literary achievement of the Elizabethan drama possible.

6. B

The statement discusses the interrelationship between the development of reading and writing skills. This is consistent with research in emergent literacy, choice (B). Phonics, choice (A), refers to a method of teaching beginning readers to read by learning the phonetic values of letters, letter groups, and syllables. Formal operations, choice (C), refers to the latest stage in Piaget's developmental stages. Learning styles, choice (D), refers to the different modalities through which different types of learners acquire knowledge.

7. D

Combining three sentences into one will require a semicolon, a dash, or commas without the overuse of "and." To eliminate wrong answer choices, look for fragments and run-ons first. Then select the answer choice that best keeps the original meaning of the sentences. (A) is grammatically correct, but garbles the sense of the sentences. (B) sounds tempting and keeps the sense of the three sentences. In fact, it might be the way a real person would speak the sentences. However, it is a run-on sentence, and is awkward and choppy compared to (D). (C) misuses semicolons. The first one is acceptable, but the second one is wrong.

8. A

Decoding refers to making the connection between a written word and the idea or thing it explicitly represents.

9. C

Carefully reading the question stem is essential to selecting the best answer here. A thesis statement is the place where the main point or argument of an essay is put forth. This question asks for you to find the sentence that is NOT an effective thesis statement. (C) would be an ineffective thesis statement for a persuasive essay because it does not clearly state an opinion or position that will be proved in the course of the essay. Each of the other answer choices states a clear opinion.

10. D

In a small group setting such as this, establishing eye contact with several or all members of the audience is an effective way of maintaining the audience's focus on the presentation. Maintaining eye contact with only the professor (A) will not encourage the other students to focus on the presentation. Although eye contact is important, it is not necessary to give a presentation of this length without the use of brief notes (B). In fact, it is usually a good idea for a speaker to have brief notes to refer to in order to convey all of the information planned for a presentation. Standing behind a podium can provide a focal point for the audience, but hand gestures should be used as an additional method of nonverbal communication.

11. B

Brainstorming and freewriting are steps taken at the very beginning of the writing process. In this step, the goal is to generate as many ideas or questions related to a given topic as possible. During brainstorming and freewriting, it is important to focus only on generating ideas, not evaluating or organizing those ideas. These steps come later in the writing process.

12. B

In this excerpt, the speaker clearly believes that Native Americans have a deep connection to the land. He states that "every part of this soil is sacred in the estimation of my people." One reason that the land is viewed as sacred is that "it is rich with the blood of our ancestors." Choice (B) is correct.

13. D

This passage appears to be telling a story about a character named Wilson. The story is told in the third person and appears to use the standard devices of realistic fiction, (D). A fable, choice (A), is an fictitious story usually involving animals that attempts to illustrate a universal truth or moral. An autobiography, choice (B), is a biography in which the author is also the subject of the biography.

Consequently, autobiographies are always in the first person, and (B) can be eliminated. A folktale, choice (C), is a characteristically anonymous, timeless, and placeless tale that is normally communicated orally.

14. B

This poem centers on an extended metaphor in which the abstract concept, hope, is compared with a birdlike creature. So (B) is correct. Iambic pentameter, choice (A), refers to a specific type of meter in which the first syllable is not stressed and the second syllable is stressed. Each stressed, unstressed combination is referred to as an iamb. In iambic pentameter, each line consists of five iambs. A sonnet is a fourteen line poem. This poem is twelve lines long, so it cannot be a sonnet and (C) is out. An oxymoron, choice (D), is a pair of words which are in apparent contrast with one another. The question refers to the poem as a whole, so (D) cannot be correct since it only refers to two words.

15. D

Once again, you should scan the question stems before digging into the passage to find out what, exactly, you will need to know. For questions 15 and 16, you need only have a general sense of the language being used, which in this case is a regional dialect, (D). (A) is incorrect. There is nothing standard about Huck's use of English. (B) is certainly incorrect. Huck is far from formal. (C) may be confusing if test takers have forgotten the meaning of the word. Jargon is terminology specific to an occupation or hobby.

16. B

You might be tempted by (A), but there is nothing in the passage to indicate that Huck is stupid. He is, however, uneducated and superstitious, so (B) is correct. (C) may be tempting to test takers thinking about the overall message of the novel. Huck is, indeed, good-hearted. But there is nothing in this particular passage to indicate this, and certainly not his way of speaking. (D) is incorrect. Huck is lonely and scared in the passage, but not confused. Some test takers may think of his superstitions as confusion. However, Huck's way of speaking does not help to illustrate this.

17. A

The imagery in this selection helps to illustrate Huck's isolation and fear, so (A) is correct. The fact that Huck hears and sees these things certainly indicates that he is aware of his environment (B), but the argument is circular: Huck's awareness does not illustrate his awareness. What he sees and hears illustrates something beyond merely hearing and seeing. It shows a state of mind. (C) is tempting to those who remember the rest of the novel. Huck does lose his father in the novel, but that has nothing to do with this selection. (D) is also tempting. Huck does face a moral dilemma in the novel—but again, not in this particular selection.

18. C

The incorrect use of "myself" is rampant in spoken English, and it may escape your notice. You should remember that "myself" is only to be used reflexively—when the speaker is both the subject and the object of the sentence ("I gave myself a raise."). In all other cases, "I" or "me" should be used, so (C) is correct. (A) might be tempting, but the use of numerals instead of words is not necessarily wrong. Typical style guidelines suggest spelling out numbers under ten. (B) is tempting. The sentences could be joined by a semicolon, but they are not incorrect as written. (C), as we already mentioned, is wrong. (D) is not an error. "Your" would be incorrect in that it is possessive while the meaning here is "you are."

19. D

The key word in this question stem is "must." As you know, not all poetry has to rhyme. Therefore, any answer choice that includes option III must be incorrect. That rules out (C). Free verse does not use a set rhythm. This rules out (A). (B) is tempting, but you should look back at the word "must." Do all poems really have to use metaphor? In fact, the only absolute, definitional requirement of poetry is that it be written in verse, so (D) is correct.

20. C

Only choice (C) uses the word appropriate as a verb. In that sentence, the bank may appropriate, or take, the farm if mortgage payments are not made on time. In each of the other sentences, the word appropriate is used as an adjective. That is, the word appropriate modifies or describes a noun in (A), (B), and (D). In (A), appropriate describes someone's attire. In (B), appropriate describes words. In (D), appropriate describes rough-housing.

21. D

An oxymoron is a figure of speech in which two incongruous or contradictory terms are juxtaposed. In this case, sweet and sorrow are contradictory. (D) is correct. A simile, choice (A), is a figure of speech that compares two unlike things using the words like or as. A personification, choice (B), refers to treating an inanimate or inhuman concept or thing as if it were human. Hyperbole, choice (C), refers to overstatement or exaggeration.

22. C

Where is an autobiography most liable to differ from a third-person account of a life? In the subjectivity of the author, choice (C). A third-person life history is usually more reliable as an objective account of events. (A), wordiness, is a problem that could affect biographers as well as autobiographers. (B), creativity, is not necessarily a liability. You may read too much into this answer choice, and think of it as "lying." Remember to read only what is given. (D) is an asset for research, not a liability, and is expected more of a biographer than an autobiographer.

23. B

Visualizing each of the nonverbal responses should help test takers select the best answer. A listener who is leaning forward indicates that he or she is interested in and focused on what a speaker has to say, so (B) is correct. The other answer choices indicate a lack of focus on the speaker. (A) describes a closed-off nonverbal response, suggesting the listener is not listening with an open mind. Eye contact with other audience members (C) suggests that the listener is focused more on other audience members than on the speaker. (D) suggests a detachment from or boredom with the speaker.

24. C

The critical period refers to the time by which an individual must be exposed to language in order to fully develop language capabilities. Although it is easier for young children to learn second languages than it is for adults, adults can learn to fluently use second languages. Choice (C) is most consistent with this line of thinking.

25. C

Semantics involves the study of how language represents and constructs meaning, so (C) is correct. Morphology deals with the shape and structure of letters in words, so (A) is out. Phonetics is the study of sounds and spoken language, so (B) can be eliminated. Lastly, syntax deals with word order and how that affects meaning, so (D) can is out as well.

26. B

Mentally rehearsing responses or arguments is one type of roadblock to effective communication. Choice (B), rehearsing, is the term used to describe this type of ineffective communication. Choices (A), (C), and (D) all refer to techniques associated with active listening. In terms of the exam, active listening should be viewed positively in that it leads to improved communication.

27. D

Be familiar with the phases of writing development. Picture writing, scribble writing, and conventional writing are all phases of writing development. Haphazard writing is a distracter not associated with writing development. So you can eliminate (A), (B), and (C). (D) is correct.

28. A

A child who makes the connection between letters and sounds but has not yet grasped that a number of letter-sound combinations make up most words would be likely to represent a word or group of words with a single letter. (B) and (C) show mastery of the concept of a group of letters representing a word. These errors represent difficulty with higher level spelling concepts. Lastly, (D) shows no correspondence to the sounds of the words and therefore does not match up with the example in the question.

29. C

The stages of the writing process appear occasionally on the PRAXIS exam. The stages proceed from "pre-writing," which involves brainstorming and outlining, to drafting, which involves writing an initial draft, to revising, which involves rereading the draft for organization, logic, and grammar, to proofreading, which involves your final read through prior to publishing. In the example here, the writer has finished revising the document and is entering the proofreading stage.

30. D

Each of the terms has acquired a new meaning in the 20th century. A mouse (I) is a device used to navigate computer screens. Surfing (II) refers to browsing through Internet sites, as in "surfing the web." A cookie (III) is an electronic trail recording web sites visited. The desktop (IV) refers to the files and programs accessible from a computer's initial screen.

Mathematics

31. A

Choice (A) has a "1" in the second decimal place. All the other answer choices have a 0 in the second decimal place. This means that (A) must be the greatest value and is the correct answer. When comparing decimals, begin at the first place to the right of the decimal (the tenths place) and look for the largest number among the answer choices. If values are equal, move one place to the right, and perform the same comparison. Once you find a larger value for a given decimal place, there is no need to continue to compare further decimal places to the right.

32. B

This is a proportion question. The relationship between the hydrant and the hydrant's shadow will be the same as the relationship between Tom and Tom's shadow. So you could set up the following proportion to solve:

$$\frac{\text{hydrant}}{\text{hydrant's shadow}} = \frac{\text{Tom}}{\text{Tom's shadow}}$$

$$\frac{40}{32} = \frac{x}{48}$$

Now it's time to cross-multiply and solve. Keep in mind that you can use a calculator on this test.

$$32x = 40 \times 48$$
$$32x = 1920$$
$$x = \frac{1920}{32} = 60$$

Choice (B) is correct.

33. B

This question is nice in that you do not need to solve, you simply need to determine the correct way to solve it. You are told that 40% of the 540 students scored at or below grade level. Remember the formula Part = Percent × Whole. You can write 40% as either 0.4 or $\frac{40}{100}$. For the purposes of this question, $\frac{40}{100}$ is what does the trick. This means that $\frac{40}{100} \times 540$ is correct. $\frac{40}{100}$ can be reduced to $\frac{2}{5}$, so you can rewrite the equation as $\frac{2}{5} \times 540$, choice (B).

34. D

To find the profit, subtract the cost from the revenue or money taken in. We know that the owner buys the hats at a cost of 5 for $17.50, and sells them for $4.00 each. So for every 5 hats sold, she takes in 5 × $4.00 = $20 and spends $17.50. That yields a profit of $20 − $17.50 = $2.50 for every five hats. To earn a profit of $100, she'd have to sell $\frac{100}{2.50}$ sets of five hats. That's 40 × 5 = 200 hats total, choice (D).

35. C

You are looking for the one choice that is not equivalent to dividing 420 by 21. You can work this out in your head, or use your calculator. Just be careful, pay attention to the order of operations (PEMDAS) and double-check your answers. (A), (B), and (D) all are equivalent to dividing 420 by 21, or 420 ÷ 21 = 20, so they can be eliminated. In (A), dividing 420 by 3 and then by 7 is the same as dividing 420 by 3 × 7 or 21. In (B), you do what's inside the parentheses first, so 420 is divided by (3 × 7) or 21. In (D), you begin by dividing 420 by 3, and then multiply that by $\frac{1}{7}$, which is the same as dividing by 7. Once again, you are dividing 420 by 3 and then dividing that by 7 which is the same as dividing 420 by 21. That leaves (C) as the correct answer since (420 ÷ 3) + (420 ÷ 7) = 140 + 60 = 200 is not equal to 20.

36. C.

The question asks what the change is closest to. You have two options. You can use your calculator and solve, then find the closest value, or you can approximate. If you approximate: $6 + $10 + $12.50 + $6.50 + $5 = $40 (although the actual value is slightly less). From a $50 bill the shopper would expect roughly $10 back, so (C) is correct.

37. D

When faced with a percent problem like this one, remember the following formular: Percent = $\frac{Part}{Whole} \times 100$. In this case, the part is the number of women which is 16, and the whole is the total number of students which is 25. So $\frac{Part}{Whole} \times 100$

$= \dfrac{16}{25} \times 100 = 64\%$ and choice (D) is correct. You can save time on a question like this one by noticing that the denominator is a factor of 100. Multiply 25 by 4 and you get 100, so to quickly convert $\dfrac{16}{25}$ into a percent (which is really a fraction over 100), multiply the fraction by $\dfrac{4}{4} \cdot \dfrac{16}{25} \times \dfrac{4}{4} \quad \dfrac{64}{100} = 64\%$.

38. A

Factor 24 to find the numbers that have it as a product. 1×24, 2×12, 3×8, and 4×6 all equal 24. Of these pairs, only 4 and 6 have a sum of 10. The difference of 4 and 6 is 2, choice (A).

39. D

You can solve this question by using the answer choices, or by using algebra. Let's try using the answer choices or "backsolving." If (C) were correct, there are 42 girls in the club, there would be $(64 - 42)$ or 22 boys in the club. 42 is less than three times as many as 22, so choice (C) is incorrect, and it is too small. Right away, you can eliminate (C) and any choice that is less than (C). So (A), (B), and (C) are out and you know that (D) must be correct. To confirm, if there are 48 girls in the club, there must be $(64 - 48)$ or 16 boys in the club. 48 is three times 16, so (D) is correct.

Solving this algebraically, let x stand for the number of boys in the club. $x + 3x = 64$. So $4x = 64$, and $x = 16$. If x is the number of boys, then $3x$ is the number of girls. $3(16) = 48$, choice (D).

40. A

The distributive property of multiplication over addition refers to the fact that if you have a value outside of a parentheses and inside the parentheses, you have two values added together, you can multiply the outside term by each of the inside terms and then add the inside terms together. This is exactly what happens with $7(8 + 5) = 7 \times 8 + 7 \times 5$. (A) is correct.

41. C

Remember the average formula:
$\dfrac{\text{Sum}}{\text{Number of Terms}}$. If you apply this formula to the question, you know that

$180 = \dfrac{156 + 172 + 210 + x}{4}$ where x is the missing bowling score. Multiply both sides by 4 to simplify: $4 \times 180 = \dfrac{156 + 172 + 210 + x}{4} \times 4$.

So $720 = 156 + 172 + 210 + x$. Here's an excellent time to use your calculator. $720 = 538 + x$. Subtract 538 from both sides to find that the missing score, x, must equal 182, choice (C).

42. C

This is a tricky question that might take some time. Feel free to skip one like this and return to it later. When faced with a strange shape like the one in this question, think about ways to draw a line that will convert the shape into more familiar shapes. This figure is actually a rectangle and a right triangle. Here's how it looks:

So we're dealing with a 6×10 rectangle and a right triangle with legs of lengths 6 and 8. To find the

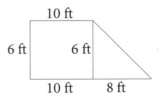

third side of a right triangle, remember the Pythagorean Theorem: $a^2 + b^2 = c^2$. In this case, $a = 6$, and $b = 8$

$$6^2 + 8^2 = c^2$$
$$36 + 64 = c^2$$
$$100 = c^2$$
$$c = 10$$

So the third side of the right triangle has a length of 10. Now the figure looks like this:

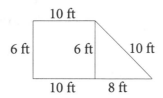

To find the perimeter, add up the lengths of the sides: 6 + 10 + 10 + 18 = 44 ft, choice (C).

43. C

In map A, one inch represents 5 miles, so one square inch would represent 5 × 5 = 25 square miles. In map B, one inch represents 2 miles, so one square inch would represent 2 × 2 = 4 square miles. The difference in square miles would be 25 − 4 = 21 square miles, choice (C).

44. A

The sum of the three interior angles of a triangle is 180 degrees. If two angles are 35 and 92 degrees, the third angle must be the difference between their sum and 180. 35 + 92 = 127. 180 − 127 = 53, choice (A).

45. B

Be careful when calculating time passed, especially when you pass a 12 o'clock along the way. In this case, Monica begins working at 8:42 A.M. In 33 minutes, it would be 9:15 A.M. Then it would be 3 hours to 12:15 P.M., and 4 more hours to 4:15 P.M. That's 7 hours and 33 minutes total, choice (B).

46. D

Remember the probability formula: Probability = $\frac{\text{Number Desired}}{\text{Number Possible}}$. In this case, the number desired would be the number of sophomores, or 20. The number possible would be all the students,

or 13 + 20 + 16 + 15 = 64. So Probability = $\frac{\text{Number Desired}}{\text{Number Possible}} = \frac{20}{64} = \frac{5}{16}$, choice (D).

47. C

It is easier to compare decimals than fractions, so quickly dividing the fractions on your calculator should will this question. $\frac{1}{3} = 0.33$, $\frac{4}{7} = 0.571$, $\frac{3}{8} = 0.375$, and $\frac{1}{2} = 0.50$. (C) is correct since 0.375 is closest to 0.40.

48. C

The largest number of groups will result from the fewest number of students per group. So you want as many groups of 3 as possible. 40 divided by 3 is 13 with a remainder of 1. So you could have 12 groups of 3 and one group of 4. That would be 13 groups total, choice (C).

49. C

Remember the percent formula: Percent = $\frac{\text{Part}}{\text{Whole}} \times 100$. If 48 out of 60 seats are occupied, that means that 12 out of 60 seats are unoccupied. Percent = $\frac{\text{Part}}{\text{Whole}} \times 100 = \frac{12}{60} \times 100 = 20\%$, choice (C)

50. B

This is actually a remainder question. You are asked how many pieces of chocolate will be left over if 200 pieces are put into boxes which contain 24 pieces each. So you are looking for the remainder when 200 is divided by 24. 24 × 8 = 192. So you could fill 8 boxes and you would have 8 pieces left over. (B) is correct.

51. B

If Joyce had 42 biscuits and 6 remained uneaten, that means that $42 - 6 = 36$ biscuits were eaten. To find the average number of biscuits eaten, use the average formula: Average $= \dfrac{\text{Sum}}{\text{Number of Terms}} = \dfrac{36}{12} = 3$, choice (B).

52. B

Be careful here. There are two things to keep in mind on a question like this one. First, a ratio is basically a fraction in which the first term in the ratio is the numerator, and the second term is the denominator. Second, you are looking for a part-to-part ratio, not a part-to-whole ratio. Find the number of students in organizations and put that over the number of students not in organizations, and reduce that fraction to solve. 3 out of 24 students are in organizations, so 21 students are not in organizations. The ration of students in organizations to students not in organizations would be 3:21 or $\dfrac{3}{21} = \dfrac{1}{7}$, choice (B).

53. D

This rate question can be solved by setting up a proportion. $\dfrac{150 \text{ bottles}}{20 \text{ minutes}} = \dfrac{60 \text{ bottles}}{x \text{ minutes}}$. You can cross multiply to get $150x = 1200$. Divide both sides by 150 to solve. $x = \dfrac{1200}{150} = 8$, choice (D).

54. B

There are 60 minutes in one hour. 60 is 6×10. So if a subway car passes 3 stations every 10 minutes, it would pass $6 \times 3 = 18$ stations in one hour. (B) is correct.

55. B

To find the missing term in a series you need to determine how each of the previous terms related to the term that preceded it. Each of the terms in this series is 7.25 greater than the previous term. So the missing term will equal the last term plus 7.25. $28.25 + 7.25 = 35.50$, choice (B)

56. D

Try back solving this one. Brett ate 25% or one-quarter of his jelly beans and was left with 72. Since that is a whole number of jelly beans, you know that the initial value had to be divisible by 4. (A), (B), and (C), are not divisible by 4, so (D), 96, had better work. Let's try it out. $96 - (0.25 \times 96) = 96 - 24 = 72$. Bingo. (D) is correct.

57. B

Be careful. Here we are told that a student takes $\dfrac{2}{3}$ of the time on the first half of the exam that he takes on the second half of the exam. So we are dealing with a 2 to 3 part to part ratio here. The entire exam took him 60 minutes. So if x is the amount of time per unit in this ratio, $2x + 3x = 60$. $5x = 60$, so $x = 12$. If $x = 12$, he spent $2x$ or $2(12) = 24$ minutes taking the first half of the test, choice (B). Keep in mind, you could plug in your answer choices and work backwards here: 24 is of $\dfrac{2}{3}$ 36, and $24 + 36 = 60$, so (B) does work.

58. A

The desired outcome is a red or black pen. The possible outcomes are a red, black, or blue pen. Use the probability formula to solve:

$$\text{Probability} = \frac{\text{Number Desired}}{\text{Number Possible}} = \frac{\#red + \#black}{\#total}$$

$$= \frac{4 + 6}{5 + 6 + 4} = \frac{10}{15} = \frac{2}{3}. \text{ (A) is correct.}$$

59. A

Use the average formula to solve. This question is one where your calculator might come in handy:

$$\text{Average} = \frac{\text{Sum}}{\text{Number of Terms}} =$$

$$\frac{150 + 153 + 154 + 157 + 151}{5} = \frac{765}{5} = 153,$$

choice (A).

60. D

To solve this question, begin by replacing the 5 digits with 7s. The new term is 278,746. The original term was 258,546. Subtract the original term from the new term to solve:

$$278{,}746 - 258{,}546 = 20{,}200, \text{ choice (D)}.$$

Social Studies

61. A

Weather is more variable an immediate than climate, so (A) is correct. Climate is more focused on long term, regional conditions.

62. B

Taiga is a type of ecosystem. It refers to a sub-arctic ecosystem characterized by evergreen coniferous forests dominated by spruce and fir trees. It is an ecosystem that is associated with a slightly warmer climate than tundra.

63. B

Remember on EXCEPT questions that you are looking for the one answer choice that does not apply. In this question about map projections, choice (B) is the exception. Map projections are NOT the most accurate representations of the surface of the Earth. A globe or some other three-dimensional object would be more accurate. Note that map projections are flat, they create distortions due to their attempt to represent three dimensions in a two-dimensional map, and they frequently use grid lines of longitude and latitude.

64. C

Global warming, deforestation, and ozone-layer depletion are all considered serious threats to the global environment, and you should be familiar with them for your exam. Plate tectonics is the term used to describe the movement of the plates of the Earth. While plate tectonics are linked to geological disturbances such as earthquakes and volcanoes, it is not considered a serious threat to the global environment.

65. B

The Agricultural Revolution refers to the development of agricultural tools and techniques like the plow that enabled agrarian societies to flourish. Part of this entailed the creation of food surpluses that allowed for the division of labor, the development of trade, and the "dawn of civilization." (A) is the opposite of what happened with the Agricultural Revolution. Rather than searching further for food, this revolution allowed for settling in one place since food production became reliable. (C) is incorrect since the founding of the first great civilizations followed the Agricultural Revolution, not the other way around. (D) is outside the scope of the Agricultural Revolution.

66. B

Deforestation is the primary cause of soil depletion in rain forest environments. As we've already noted, this is considered by many to be a serious threat to the global environment. Deforestation refers to the removal of trees and other vegetation to make room for development.

67. B

Hieroglyphics refer to the pictographic language associated with ancient Egypt. "Pharaoh" refers to the rulers of ancient Egypt many of whom were treated as gods. The Great Pyramids are thought to be tombs for certain important pharaohs.

68. C

Ferdinand Magellan was an explorer best known for the first successful voyage around the globe. Traveling successfully around the world is also referred to as circumnavigation.

69. B

Traditional Hindu society is associated with a "caste" system in which individuals are born into somewhat rigid levels or castes that are associated with certain types of work. The highest caste is the brahmin which is the caste of priests. Pariahs or "untouchables" are those beneath the lowest caste.

70. B

The Torah is the term used for the holy scriptures of the Judaic faith. The Koran refers to the holy scriptures of the Islamic faith.

71. D

Most participants should recall that Athens was a Greek city-state with a limited form of democracy. In fact, some of our democratic principles come directly from the government of Athens. Because Athens was a limited democracy, (I) theocracy and (III) monarchy can be eliminated. Athens and Sparta were both major powers during the Classical era of Greece, but they were separate city-states. There was not a united Greek Empire. This leaves (II) as the only true statement and (D) as the correct answer.

72. C

Alexander the Great is generally credited as one of the main reasons why elements of the Greek culture spread throughout the Mediterranean world. He was ruler of Macedonia in the 3rd and 4th centuries B.C., and his empire covered much of the Mediterranean world. Hammurabi was a ruler of Ancient Babylon who is credited with establishing a written code of law for his empire. Genghis Khan was a Mongol emperor whose influences stretched across Asia and into the West. Herodotus was a Greek historian who described much of the ancient Mediterranean world.

73. D

The works of Shakespeare, Michaelangelo, and Da Vinci are associated with the Renaissance, not the Reformation, so (D) is correct. Luther's 95 Theses, (A), were what he nailed to the Church door in Wittenburg to signal the beginning of the Reformation and Lutheranism. Henry VIII's divorce, (B), was a key component in the Reformation and led to his founding of the Church of England. The Catholic church's practice of selling indulgences (C), or pardons from sins, was one of the main aspects of its corruption that led to the Reformation.

74. C

Frederick Douglas, William Lloyd Garrison, and Harriet Beecher Stowe were all important figures in the Abolitionist movement in the years leading into the United States Civil War. Elizabeth Cady Stanton and Susan B. Anthony were key member of the Women's Rights movement of the late 19th and early 20th centuries. Primary among their issues was suffrage, the right to vote. Carrie Nation was a member of the Temperance movement that sought to ban consumption of alcohol. Grant, Sherman, and Hayes were all United States generals during the Civil War. Grant and Hayes were also presidents.

75. D

The Monroe Doctrine refers to a speech given by President James Monroe in which he outlined some basic principles for United States foreign policy. Among these principles were the limiting of European influence in the Americas, (B) and (C), and American neutrality in European conflicts (A). At no time does the Monroe Doctrine support the establishment of an American sphere of influence in Asia. So (D) is correct.

76. C

Westward expansion in the United States involved Manifest Destiny, (A), or the belief that it was America's destiny to expand westward to the Pacific. It also involved the Louisiana Purchase, (B), which made much of the land west of the early United States into a vast U.S. territory to be explored and settled. One of the sad legacies of western expansion, however, is the Trail of Tears, (D), which refers to the journey of many Native American tribes from their homelands to government-appointed reservations as westward expansion and settlement led to the expulsion of Native Americans. Only "Big Stick Diplomacy," (C), refers to a concept not associated with westward expansion. "Big Stick Diplomacy" refers to the foreign policy of Teddy Roosevelt who is known for his famous quote, "Talk softly and carry a big stick."

77. B

Based on the chart, approximately 10% of the workers in 1960 walked to work. Ten percent of 65,000,000 is 6,500,000. About 12%, or 7,800,000, of the workers in 1960 used public transportation (A). In that same year, about 5%, or 3,250,000, of the workers worked at home (D). In 1970, about 8% of the workers walked to work (C).

78. D

Only (D) is directly supported by information in this graph. In 1970, about 9% of the workers used public transportation, and about 7% of the workers walked to work. Eliminate (A) because percentages, not total numbers, are reported in the graph. Although the percentage of people working at home decreased, the actual number of people working at home may have increased due to population increase over the 30-year span. Eliminate (B) because only the working population, not the general population, is represented in this graph. Eliminate (C) because the graph does not provide information about factors that caused changes in transportation use. Although it may be true that urban sprawl is responsible for the increase in the percentage of people driving to work, this is not supported by information in the graph.

79. C

The case of *Brown v. The Board of Education, Topeka, Kansas,* was a landmark case that addressed the constitutionality of segregation in public schools. "Separate but equal" education was thrown out as unfair and unconstitutional. Rosa Parks refusal to get up when asked to do so led directly to the Montgomery bus boycott, (D).

80. C

The Articles of the Confederation refers to the initial structure of the United States government prior to the ratification of the Constitution. So (A) and (D) both apply and can be eliminated. The Articles of the Confederation placed a greater emphasis on states' rights than the Constitution, so (B) can be eliminated. (C) is the correct answer since the Articles of the Confederation were not the basis of the Confederacy during the United States Civil War.

81. B

The three branches of the United States government are the Executive, the Judicial, and the Legislative, choice (B). The Executive branch refers primarily to the president and Cabinet, the Judicial refers primarily to the Supreme Court, and the Legislative refers to the two houses of Congress—the Senate and the House of Representatives.

82. D

The Bill of Rights refers to the first ten amendments to the Constitution. Among the rights protected therein are protection from illegal search and seizure, (A), freedom of speech and religion, (B), and the right to bear arms and keep a well regulated milita, (C). Universal healthcare, (D), is not discussed in the Bill of Rights.

83. C

The correct order of Presidential Succession in the United States is President, Vice President, Speaker of the House of Representatives. Choice (C) is correct.

84. C

The French Revolution (I) began in 1789, after the American Revolution. The Constitution of the United States was signed in 1787, so (I) cannot be true. Eliminate (A) and (D). The Constitution of the United States was influenced by The Great Law of the Iroquois Confederacy (II), which was comprised of the Mohawks, Oneidas, Onondagas, Cayugas, Senecas, and Tuscaroras. Eliminate (B). (C) is correct. The Magna Carta (III), written in 1215, guaranteed certain rights to the citizens of England. This document influenced the Bill of Rights. In the late 1600s, John Locke (IV) wrote about the "social contract" between citizens and their government and advocated the separation of powers of government. His influence can be seen in the checks and balances among the three branches of government.

85. C

Participants should remember that Freud was particularly concerned with investigating the unconscious mind. He used the contents of dream to interpret what occurred on an unconscious level in an individual's mind, so (C) is correct. Be careful not to confuse Freud with Jung who was most interested in the idea of the collective unconscious, choice (B).

86. D

The key word is "major." The federal government levies excise taxes on such things as gasoline and alcohol, but it is not its major source of revenue. Tariffs, or taxes on imported goods, are another revenue source, but not a major source. Estate taxes mean the same thing as inheritance taxes. This is not a major source of revenue for the federal government. The major source of revenue for the federal government is income tax. The major source of revenue for local governments is property tax. (D) is correct.

87. C

The selection of a Cabinet of presidential advisors was begun by George Washington. This tradition has remained, and the size of the Cabinet has increased over the last two hundred years. Political parties began at the end of Washington's term when Jefferson and Hamilton, along with their supporters, disagreed over a number of issues. The election that determined the second president was characterized by the competition between two political parties. This tradition remains with us today, and the role of political parties has increased dramatically as well. These two tradition were never a part of the constitution. These elements of our "unwritten constitution" are seen as constitutional and have not been challenged in court. (C) is correct.

88. B

The fact that prices of fans and air conditioners go up during the hottest months of the year is consistent with the principle of supply and demand. When demand is greatest or supply is lowest, prices tend to go up. This is evident in the example given.

89. A

Only choice (A) runs contrary to the basic tenets of the laissez-faire economic system. Trade limitations and tariffs on imported goods are two ways in which government controls commerce. The rise of monopolies, (B), the unrestricted use of immigrant or child labor, (C), and hazardous, unregulated working conditions, (D), are all negative effects of a laissez-faire economic system. Each of these effects was evident in the American economy of the late 19th and early 20th centuries.

90. C

By definition, the suffrage movement was about obtaining the right to vote for women, choice (C). The Abolitionist movement sought to abolish slavery, (A). (B) is a tempting trap, but equal pay for equal work was the focus of supporters of the Equal Rights Amendment, or ERA, in the late 20th century. The Temperance movement sought to prohibit the use of alcohol, (D).

Science

91. B

The process by which plants convert carbon dioxide and water into sugar and oxygen is called photosynthesis. The reverse process, by which animals convert oxygen and sugars into carbon dioxide and water, is called respiration.

92. B

In electricity, a unit of resistance is called an ohm. An ampere is a unit of electric current, a volt is a unit of electro-motive force, and a watt is a unit of power equal to 1 joule per second.

93. B

Iron forms rust when water (or an even better electrolyte) turns iron and oxygen into iron oxide (Fe_2O_3), a chemical process. Helium and neon are both inert, so they do not react chemically. Water causing soil erosion may or may not incur a chemical change, and ice melting does not alter the chemistry of H_2O.

94. D

Blood enters the right atrium of the heart from the vena cava.

95. A

For a substance to have a high pH, it should be a base, or alkaline (a pH of 7 is neutral, like water; a pH of less than 7 is acidic; and a pH of greater than 7 is a base). Of the substance listed, only ammonia is a base.

96. C

Insulin is created in the body's pancreas.

97. D

If two brown-eyed parents have a blue-eyed child, the probability that their next child will have blue eyes is 1 in 4. The blue-eyed gene (b) is recessive to the brown-eyed gene (B), so if both parent have brown eyes and one of the children has blue eyes, both parents carry the recessive blue-eyed gene (Bb), and thus the chances of any more of their children being blue-eyed (bb) is 1 in 4.

98. C

The results shown in the chart suggest that mold grows at an increasingly rapid rate as the days progress. It would be unreasonable to predict that there would be little or no growth, as shown in (A) and (B), between days 20 and 25. There is also nothing in the data that suggests that the surface area covered by the mold would increase almost six times over the course of five days, as represented by (D). An increase of 9 cm² between days 20 and 25 is the only reasonable projection that can be made based on the available data. So (C) is correct.

99. C

The process by which the sun heats the earth is known as radiation.

100. C

A lunar eclipse happens when the Moon passes through the Earth's shadow. During a lunar eclipse, the earth lies between the moon and sun.

101. D

Of the climates listed, the one with the shortest growing season is the taiga, which is characterized by long, severe winters, summers with thawing subsoil, and organisms such as conifers and moose predominating.

102. A

The major portion of an atom's mass consists of neutrons and protons. Electrons, positrons, neutrinos, and other subatomic particles have practically negligible masses.

103. C

Over the course of 24 hours the earth rotates 360 degrees about its axis.

104. C

The Moneran kingdom is considered the most primitive kingdom because its organisms are prokaryotic—that is, their cells lack nuclei.

105. B

Orbiting around the nucleus of an atom are electrons.

106. B

Fungi are decomposers (also known as saprophytes), returning the organic material from dead matter such as leaves, trees and animal remains back into the environment. Producers make their own food, consumers must eat to gain energy, and mutualism is the type of symbiosis whereby organisms living together benefit.

107. D

In degrees Kelvin, the freezing pointing of water is 273°. In the Kelvin temperature scale absolute zero, which is −273° Celsius, is set at 0°, and any temperature in degrees Celsius is 273 degrees less than the same temperature as read in degrees Kelvin. Since the freezing point of water in degrees Celsius is 0°, in degrees Kelvin it is 273°.

108. A

Tough elastic tissues found in the joints the connect bones to bones are called ligaments. Tendons are connective tissue that unite a muscle with some other part, such as a bone. Cartilage is a somewhat elastic tissue (unlike bone) that in adults is found in some joints, respiratory passages, and the external ear. Finally, muscles are body tissue consisting of long cells that contract when stimulated to produce motion.

109. A

The property of light that causes a straw placed in a glass of water to appear bent is called refraction. Refraction is the deflection from a straight path undergone by a light ray or energy wave when passing obliquely from one medium (such as air) into another (such as water) in which its velocity is different.

110. B

Animals that consume plants are called herbivores.

111. D

Rods and cones are light-sensitive cells inside the eye's retina.

112. B

A boulder that begins to roll down a hill is an example of an energy conversion from potential energy to kinetic energy.

113. D

The lowest layer of the earth's atmosphere is called the troposphere. This is the layer in which most weather changes occur and the temperature generally decreases rapidly with altitude and which extends from the surface to the bottom of the stratosphere.

114. D

Only (D) is a valid conclusion. Since Species C had the most new leaves at 3 hours of sunlight and demonstrated a drop off by 6 hours of sunlight, the conclusion that optimal growth occurs for Species C between 2 and 5 hours of sunlight is reasonable. Because the table does not record the number of new leaves produced with exposure to 4 or 5 hours of sunlight, (A) is invalid. (B) is too extreme.

115. C

(C) would give an advantage to native species, not species that are newly introduced to an ecosystem. (A) and (B) each describe ways in which the new species, in this case Kudzu, might grow more rapidly than native species. (D) describes how native species might be at a disadvantage to compete with new species.

116. B

Striated muscles, also known as skeletal muscles, are controlled by conscious thought, unlike cardiac muscles, (C), or the smooth muscles, (A), of the digestive system, which are controlled by the autonomic nervous system.

117. C

The orbit of the moon around the earth, which exerts a gravitational pull on the ocean's waters, is the phenomenon most responsible for oceanic tides.

118. B

A substance that hastens a chemical reaction without undergoing chemical change itself is called a catalyst. The substances involved in such a reaction are generally referred to as reactants, (D).

119. A

Lack of iron is associated with anemia. Hemophilia, (B), is associated with a lack of platelets and difficulty with clotting. Goiter, (C), is associated with iodine deficiencies and the activity of the thyroid. Rickets is linked to a vitamin D deficiency.

120. A

Of the following subatomic particles listed, the proton, (A), has the largest mass. Among subatomic particles, protons and neutrons have the most mass. Electrons, positrons, and neutrinos all have negligible masses, so (B), (C), and (D) are out.

Section Five

PRAXIS II: SUBJECT ASSESSMENTS

Introducing the Subject Overviews and Question Banks

In addition to the reviews and full-length practice tests for the PLT and Elementary Education tests in this book, this section provides you with additional preparation for certain PRAXIS II: Subject Assessments. This additional preparation comes in the form of brief overviews of key English, Science, Social Studies, and Mathematics tests followed by question banks testing content knowledge related to these fields.

If you are required to take any of the tests discussed in this section, these overviews and question banks provide helpful preparatory materials.

Be aware that the question banks that follow are most appropriate for the PRAXIS II Content Knowledge exams. The question banks provide a thorough review of a wide range of content, but they are not designed to resemble any single test. Rather, they test a broad cross-section of each subject area through a series of multiple-choice questions and explanations.

If you are required to take an essay-based exam in one of the subject areas covered in this section, be sure to practice your essay-writing skills in addition to reviewing content that appears in the question banks that follow. As a result, the essay-writing component of the PPST Writing section is useful in preparing for these tests as well.

Good luck!

CHAPTER SIX

SCIENCE

In this section we will cover several key science Subject Assessments. We will begin with a brief summary of the major science subject tests and outlining the content covered on them. The section concludes with three sets of question banks for you to brush up on your content knowledge and test-taking skills in biology, chemistry, physics and earth sciences. Depending on the test you are preparing for, you may need to refer to some or all of these question banks.

PRAXIS II SCIENCE SUBJECT TESTS

This section applies to you if you are taking one of the following tests:

General Science Tests

- General Science (0430)
- General Science: Content Knowledge—Part 1 (0431)
- General Science: Content Knowledge—Part 2 (0432)
- General Science: Content Essays (0433)
- Biology and General Science (0030)
- Chemistry, Physics, and General Science (0070)
- Physical Science: Content Knowledge (0481)
- Physical Science: Content Essays (0482)

Biology Tests

- Biology: Content Knowledge—Part 1 (0231)
- Biology: Content Knowledge—Part 2 (0232)
- Biology: Content Essays (0233)

Chemistry Tests

- Chemistry: Content Knowledge (0241)
- Chemistry: Content Knowledge (0245)
- Chemistry: Content Essays (0242)

Physics Tests

- Physics (0260)
- Physics: Content Knowledge (0261)
- Physics: Content Knowledge (0265)
- Physics: Content Essays (0262)

Earth Science Tests

- Earth Science: Content Knowledge (0571)
- Earth/Space Science (0570)

GENERAL SCIENCE TESTS

Several PRAXIS II Subject tests focus on General Science. These tests pull questions from a wide range of science content areas. Consequently, much of the material covered in the question banks that follow applies to the General Science subject tests.

General Science (0430)

Test Format: 120 multiple-choice questions

Test Length: 2 hours

Content covered:

- Biology: 30 questions, 25 percent of the test
- Chemistry: 30 questions, 25 percent of the test
- Physics: 30 questions, 25 percent of the test
- Earth/Space Science: 30 questions, 25 percent of the test

This test covers the broad range of science concepts covered in all four question banks that follow. Note that the quiz banks contain questions with four answer choices, whereas the actual test has questions with five answer choices. Otherwise, working through the four test banks that follow should give you a good sense of how general science content is tested on this exam.

General Science: Content Knowledge, Part 1 (0431)

Test Format: 60 multiple-choice questions

Test Length: 1 hour

Content covered:

- Methodology/Philosophy; Math/Measurement/Data; Laboratory/Safety: 14 questions, 23 percent of the test
- Basic Principles of Science: 14 questions, 23 percent of the test
- Life Science: 13 questions: 22 percent of the test
- Earth/Space Science; Science, Technology, and Society: 19 questions, 32 percent of the test

This test covers many of the basic concepts addressed in the quiz banks that follow. In particular, the Biology and Earth Science quiz banks address a large percentage of the content that appears on this test.

General Science: Content Knowledge, Part 2 (0432)

Test Format: 60 multiple-choice questions

Test Length: 1 hour

Content Covered:

- Physics: 16 questions, 27 percent of the test
- Chemistry: 16 questions, 27 percent of the test
- Life Science: 11 questions, 18 percent of the test
- Earth/Space Science; Science, Technology, and Society: 17 questions, 28 percent of the test

This test covers many of the concepts addressed in all four of the quiz banks that follow. The General Science: Content Knowledge—Part 2 test references higher-level concepts and a greater level of detailed knowledge than the General Science: Content Knowledge—Part 1 test. It also places a greater emphasis on Physics and Chemistry. As a result, the Physics and Chemistry quiz banks should come more into play in your preparation if you are taking this test.

General Science: Content Essays (0433)

Test Format: 3 short-answer essay questions from each of the three categories below

Test Length: 1 hour

Content Covered:

- Physical Science
- Life Science
- Earth and Space Science

Although this exam is essay-based, the concepts you are expected to discuss with a high level of mastery are the same as those tested in all four of the question banks that follow. One essay will focus on the physical sciences, which are Physics and Chemistry. One essay will focus on Life Science or Biology, and one will focus on Earth and Space Science. Therefore, in preparation for this test, it is worthwhile to review the basic writing skills discussed in the PPST Writing Review in tandem with the content covered in all four question banks that follow.

Biology and General Science (0030)

Test Format: 160 multiple-choice questions

Test Length: 2 hours

Content Covered:

- History, Philosophy, and Methodology of Science; Science, Technology, and Society: 16 questions, 10 percent of the test
- Molecular and Cellular Biology of Prokaryotes and Eukaryotes: 24 questions, 15 percent of the test
- Biology of Plants, Animals, Fungi, and Protists: 32 questions, 20 percent of the test
- Evolution: 19 questions, 12 percent of the test
- Ecology: 21 questions, 13 percent of the test
- Chemistry: 16 questions, 10 percent of the test
- Physics: 16 questions, 10 percent of the test
- Earth and Space Science: 16 questions, 10 percent of the test

Although this test focuses on Biology, 40 percent of the test deals with General Science. Because more than half of this test deals with Biology, it is essential to work through the Biology question bank that follows when preparing for this test. Nonetheless, you can get valuable practice with General Science concepts by working through the Chemistry, Physics, and Earth Science question banks as well. Also, be aware that the question banks contain four answer choices, whereas the actual exam contains questions with five answer choices.

Chemistry, Physics, and General Science (0070)

Test Format: 140 multiple-choice questions

Test Length: 2 hours

Content Covered:

- Major Ideas in Chemistry and Physics: 28 questions, 20 percent of the test
- Chemistry: 42 questions, 30 percent of the test
- Physics: 42 questions, 30 percent of the test
- Earth and Space Science: 14 questions, 10 percent of the test
- Life Science: 14 questions, 10 percent of the test

This test covers General Science content with special emphasis on Chemistry and Physics. Consequently, all four of the question banks that follow are useful in preparation for this exam. Special attention should be placed on the Chemistry and Physics question banks, however.

Physical Science: Content Knowledge (0481)

Test Format: 60 multiple-choice questions

Test Length: 1 hour

Content Covered:

- Methodology; Math, Measurement, Data; Science, Technology, and Society: 20 questions, 33 percent of the test
- Laboratory Procedures and Safety; Matter and Energy: 22 questions, 37 percent of the test
- Heat and Thermodynamics; Atomic and Nuclear Structure: 18 questions, 30 percent of the test

This test focuses on the physical sciences, or Physics and Chemistry. Special attention is paid to laboratory procedures and safety. The Physics and Chemistry question banks that follow cover many of the concepts that appear on this test. Working through both of these question banks and explanations is recommended.

Physical Science: Content Essays (0482)

Test Format: 3 short-answer essay questions from the topics covered in Chemistry Content Knowledge (0241), Physics Content Knowledge (0261), and Physical Science Content Knowledge (0481)

Test Length: 1 hour

Although this exam is essay-based, the concepts you are expected to discuss with a high level of mastery are the same as those tested in the Physics and Chemistry question banks that follow. In preparation for this test, it is worthwhile to review the basic writing skills discussed in the PPST Writing Review in tandem with the content covered in the Physics and Chemistry question banks that follow.

BIOLOGY TESTS

The tests described in the section focus on Biology and Life Sciences. If you are required to take one of the tests in this section, be sure to work through the Biology Question bank that follows.

Biology: Content Knowledge—Part 1 (0231)

Test Format: 75 multiple-choice questions
Test Length: 1 hour

Content Covered:
- Basic Principles of Science: 13 questions, 17 percent of the test
- Molecular and Cellular Biology: 12 questions, 16 percent of the test
- Classical Genetics and Evolution: 11 questions, 15 percent of the test
- Diversity of Life, Plants, and Animals: 19 questions, 26 percent of the test
- Ecology: 10 questions, 13 percent of the test
- Science, Technology, and Society: 10 questions, 13 percent of the test

Biology: Content Knowledge—Part 2 (0232)

Test Format: 75 multiple-choice questions
Test Length: 1 hour

Content Covered:
- Molecular and Cellular Biology: 16 questions, 21 percent of the test
- Classical Genetics and Evolution: 18 questions, 24 percent of the test
- Diversity of Life, Plants, and Animals: 28 questions, 37 percent of the test
- Ecology: 13 questions, 18 percent of the test

The Biology Content Knowledge—Part 1 test covers more basic biology content knowledge than the Biology Content Knowledge—Part 2 test. Biology Content Knowledge—Part 2 covers more difficult concepts with a higher level of detail. The question bank will give you a good sense of kinds of questions you will encounter on test day on both exams.

Biology: Content Essays (0233)

Test Format: 3 short-answer essay questions from each of the three categories below
Test Length: 1 hour

Content Covered:

- Molecular and Cellular Biology
- Classical Genetics and Evolution
- Organismal Biology and Ecology

Although this exam is essay-based, the concepts you are expected to discuss with a high level of mastery are the same as those tested in the Biology question bank that follows. Therefore, in preparation for this test, it is worthwhile to review the basic writing skills discussed in the PPST Writing Review in tandem with the Biology question bank.

CHEMISTRY TESTS

The tests described in this section focus on Chemistry. If you are required to take one of the tests in this section, be sure to work through the Chemistry question bank that follows.

Chemistry: Content Knowledge (0241)

Test Format: 50 multiple-choice questions
Test Length: 1 hour

Content Covered:

- Atomic Structure, Chemical Periodicity, and Thermodynamics of Chemical Reactions: 12 questions, 24 percent of the test
- Nomenclature, the Mole, Bonding, and Geometry: 11 questions, 22 percent of the test
- Solutions and Solubility: 13 questions, 26 percent of the test
- Chemical Reactions/Biochemistry: 14 questions, 28 percent of the test

This test covers many of the basic concepts addressed in the Chemistry question bank that follows. Working through that question bank paying special attention to the concepts discussed above will give you a good sense of what you will encounter on this test.

Chemistry: Content Knowledge (0245)

Test Format: 100 multiple-choice questions
Test Length: 2 hours

Content Covered:

- Matter and Energy; Heat, Thermodynamics, and Thermochemistry: 16 questions, 16 percent of the test
- Atomic and Nuclear Structure: 10 questions, 10 percent of the test
- Nomenclature; the Mole, Chemical Bonding, and Geometry: 14 questions, 14 percent of the test

- Periodicity and Reactivity; Chemical Reactions; Biochemistry and Organic Chemistry: 23 questions, 23 percent of the test
- Solutions and Solubility; Acid/Base Chemistry: 12 questions, 12 percent of the test
- History and Nature of Science; Science, Technology and Social Perspectives: 11 questions, 11 percent of the test
- Mathematics, Measurement, and Data Management; Laboratory Procedures and Safety: 14 questions, 14 percent of the test

This test covers many of the key concepts addressed in the Chemistry question bank that follows. Working through that question bank with special attention to the concepts discussed above will give you a good sense of what you will encounter on this test.

Chemistry: Content Essays (0242)

Test Format: 3 short-answer essay questions

Test Length: 1 hour

Content Covered:

- Structure/Property Correlations
- Chemical Reactions
- The Impact of Chemistry on Technology and Society

Although this exam is essay-based, the concepts you are expected to discuss with a high level of mastery are the same as those tested in the Physics question bank that follows. Therefore, in preparation for this test, it is worthwhile to review the basic writing skills discussed in the PPST Writing Review in tandem with the Chemistry question bank.

PHYSICS TESTS

The tests described in the section focus on Physics. If you are required to take one of the tests in this section, be sure to work through the Physics Question bank that follows.

Physics (0260)

Test Format: 100 multiple-choice questions

Test Length: 2 hours

Content Covered:

- Major Concepts, Heat and Thermodynamics, Environmental Issues: 28 questions, 28 percent of the test
- Mechanics: 25 questions, 25 percent of the test

- Electricity and Magnetism: 20 questions, 20 percent of the test
- Wave Motion; Atomic and Nuclear Physics: 27 questions, 27 percent of the test

This test covers a wide range of Physics content and concepts. Therefore, it is worthwhile that you review the Physics question bank that follows in preparation for the test.

Physics: Content Knowledge (0261)

Test Format: 50 multiple-choice questions

Test Length: 1 hour

Content Covered:

- Mechanics: 20 questions, 40 percent of the test
- Electricity and Magnetism: 17 questions, 34 percent of the test
- Optics and Waves; Special Topics in Modern Physics: 13 questions; 26 percent of the test

This test covers a wide range of Physics content and concepts. As a result, working through the Physics question bank that follows will give you a sense of what you might encounter on your test.

Physics: Content Knowledge (0265)

Test Format: 100 multiple-choice questions

Test Length: 2 hours

Content Covered:

- Mechanics: 32 questions, 32 percent of the test.
- Electricity and Magnetism: 23 questions, 23 percent of the test
- Optics and Waves: 17 questions, 17 percent of the test
- Heat and Thermodynamics: 8 questions, 8 percent of the test
- Modern Physics, Atomic and Nuclear Structure: 8 questions, 8 percent of the test
- History and Nature of Science; Science, Technology, and Social Perspectives: 12 questions, 12 percent of the test

This test covers a wide range of Physics content and concepts. Therefore, it is worthwhile that you review the Physics question bank that follows in preparation for the test.

Physics: Content Essays (0262)

Test Format: 3 short-answer essay questions
Test Length: 1 hour

Content Covered:
- Matter and Energy
- Fields and Waves
- Science, Technology, and Society

Although this exam is essay-based, the concepts you are expected to discuss with a high level of mastery are the same as those tested in the Physics question bank that follows. Therefore, in preparation for this test, it is worthwhile to review the basic writing skills discussed in the PPST Writing Review in tandem with the Physics question bank.

Earth Science: Content Knowledge (0571)

Test Format: 100 multiple-choice questions
Test Length: 2 hours

Content Covered:
- Basic Scientific Principles of Earth and Space Sciences: 8–12 questions, 8–12 percent of the test
- Tectonics and Internal Earth Processes: 18–22 questions, 18–22 percent of the test
- Earth Materials and Surface Processes: 23–27 questions, 23–27 percent of the test
- History of the Earth and its Life-Forms: 13–17 questions, 12–17 percent of the test
- Earth's Atmosphere and Hydrosphere: 18–22 questions, 18–22 percent of the test
- Astronomy: 8–12 questions, 8–12 percent of the test

This test covers a wide range of content from both Earth and Space Sciences. As a result, the Earth and Space Science question bank that follows is a valuable preparation tool for this exam.

Earth Science: Content Knowledge (0571)

Test Format: 100 multiple-choice questions
Test Length: 2 hours

Content Covered:
- Basic Scientific Principles of Earth and Space Sciences: 8–12 questions, 8–12 percent of the test
- Tectonics and Internal Earth Processes: 18–22 questions, 18–22 percent of the test

- Earth Materials and Surface Processes: 23–27 questions, 23–27 percent of the test
- History of the Earth and its Life-Forms: 13–17 questions, 12–17 percent of the test
- Earth's Atmosphere and Hydrosphere: 18–22 questions, 18–22 percent of the test
- Astronomy: 8–12 questions, 8–12 percent of the test

This test covers a wide range of content from both Earth and Space Sciences. As a result, the Earth and Space Science question bank that follows is a valuable preparation tool for this exam.

Earth/Space Science (0570)

Test Format: 120 multiple-choice questions

Test Length: 2 hours

Content Covered:

- Physical Geology: 24 questions, 20 percent of the test
- Historical Geology: 18 questions, 15 percent of the test
- Oceanography: 18 questions, 15 percent of the test
- Meteorology: 22 questions, 18 percent of the test
- Astronomy and Space Science: 20 questions, 17 percent of the test
- Environment, Natural Resources, and Natural Hazards: 18 questions, 15 percent of the test

This test covers a wide range of content from both Earth and Space Sciences. As a result, the Earth and Space Science question bank that follows is a valuable preparation tool for this exam.

This concludes our overview of PRAXIS II Science Subject Tests. The question banks that follow provide in-format practice with some of the basic concepts covered on the PRAXIS II Science Subject Tests. The question banks are provided as additional study aids and are not intended to directly reflect the content that will appear on any given test.

Science Question Bank

BIOLOGY

1. The columns in the chart below (A, B, C, and D) represent four different chemical compounds. The rows represent elements that could be found in these compounds. An X indicates the presence of a particular element. Which compound could be a carbohydrate?

Elements	Compound			
	A	B	C	D
Calcium	X			
Carbon		X		X
Sodium				
Hydrogen	X	X		X
Magnesium			X	
Nitrogen			X	X
Oxygen		X	X	

2. Which element is found in all proteins but not in all carbohydrates and lipids?

   (A) Carbon
   (B) Nitrogen
   (C) Oxygen
   (D) Hydrogen

3. Which list of molecules is arranged in order of increasing molecular size?

   (A) oxygen, starch, glucose, sucrose
   (B) sucrose, oxygen, starch, glucose
   (C) oxygen, glucose, sucrose, starch
   (D) starch, glucose, sucrose, oxygen

4. In general, plants and animals are similar in that they both

   (A) change light energy into the chemical bond energy of carbohydrates
   (B) use atmospheric oxygen to release the chemical bond energy of carbohydrates
   (C) are able to trap light energy in building carbohydrates
   (D) require a source of carbon dioxide to build up carbohydrates

5. 25 plants were placed in each of four closed containers. All environmental conditions such as amount of watering and light were held constant for a period of three days. At the beginning of the investigation, the quantity of CO_2 present in each closed container was 250 cm^3. The data table shows the amount of CO_2 remaining in each container at the end of the three days.

Container	Temperature (C°)	CO_2 (cm^3)
1	25	60
2	30	40
3	15	150
4	20	100

The independent variable in this investigation was the

   (A) temperature
   (B) light
   (C) number of days
   (D) amount of CO_2 in each container at the end of the investigation

Questions 6–7

(A) parasitism

(B) commensalism

(C) mutualism

(D) competition

6. Plants with nitrogen-fixing bacteria in root nodules of legumes grow faster and larger than plants without them. The bacteria obtain their nourishment from the plant.

7. Two species of algae-eating turtles are introduced to the same pond. One increases in number, whereas the other decreases in number.

8. Geographers discover tundra at the equator. Which of the following must be true?

   (A) The tundra is located at a high altitude.

   (B) The temperatures must be similar to a rainforest.

   (C) Most of the equator is comprised of tundra.

   (D) None of the above. This is not possible.

9. In mitosis, distribution of one copy of each chromosome to each of the resulting cells virtually guarantees

   (A) reduction of the chromosome number to half of the original chromosome number

   (B) formation of daughter cells with identical DNA sequences

   (C) cell growth

   (D) maximum cell size

10. The molecule pictured below could be found in all the following places EXCEPT

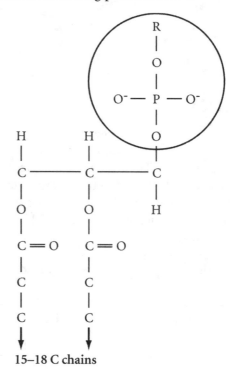

15–18 C chains

(A) the nuclear membrane

(B) cell walls in fungi

(C) Golgi vesicles

(D) secretory vesicles

11. A major difference between ectotherms and endotherms is that

    (A) as ambient temperature rises, ectotherms maintain nearly constant body temperature
    (B) endotherms receive most of their body heat from their surroundings
    (C) endotherms derive body heat from metabolic reactions and use energy derived from metabolic reactions to cool their bodies
    (D) ectotherms maintain their body at lower temperatures than endotherms, therefore leading to the term "cold-blooded"

12. Which of the following must be true regarding a sex-linked recessive disorder that is 100% lethal in infancy?

    (A) Females are unable to carry the recessive allele.
    (B) The disease will cause death in both males and females.
    (C) Male children of male carriers will also be carriers.
    (D) The condition will cause death only in males.

13. In the earthworm and the grasshopper, the gizzard is an organ that increases the surface area of food for faster chemical digestion. In humans, this increase in digestible surface area is accomplished by

    (A) the large intestine
    (B) the small intestine
    (C) the esophagus
    (D) teeth

Questions 14–15

    (A) alveoli
    (B) trachea
    (C) nasal cavity
    (D) diaphragm

14. Location for the exchange of oxygen and carbon dioxide through thin membrane walls.

15. Muscular tissue that contracts to permit air to enter lungs.

EARTH AND SPACE SCIENCE

1. The salinity of the ocean has remained relatively constant over billions of years, even though salt-bearing minerals continue to dissolve into it through erosion processes. Which of the following processes would be most likely to contribute to the maintenance of a stable oceanic salinity?

    (A) Evaporation of seawater in the open ocean
    (B) Suboceanic volcanic events melting minerals deposited on the ocean floor
    (C) Evaporation of "trapped" bodies of water with former inlets from the sea closed off
    (D) Coastal residue deposited by ocean currents

2. Which of the following samples would be best suited to carbon dating?

    (A) Hominid skull, 500,000 B.C.
    (B) Preserved fish skeleton fossil
    (C) Living redwood tree, sample taken three inches from perimeter
    (D) Felled redwood tree, sample taken from core

Questions 3–4

The city of Atlanta experiences an unusually high number of localized, intense thunderstorms that cannot be explained through classic environmental weather patterns.

3. Which of the following facts, if true, would best begin to explain the unusual number of small thunderstorms in Atlanta?

    (A) Automobile exhaust in the city creates a dense, low-hanging cloud of smog.

    (B) The air temperature in metropolitan Atlanta is 5–8 degrees hotter than the surrounding regions.

    (C) The number of trees in Atlanta is significantly less than that in most other major United States cities.

    (D) Greenhouse gas emissions within the city of Atlanta are higher by several factors of magnitude than those released in the surrounding regions.

4. Which of the following mechanisms would best explain the formation of these localized thunderstorms?

    (A) Smog released in the city increases the saturation of the air, leading to an increased release of moisture.

    (B) Greenhouse gases above the city of Atlanta warm the surrounding air, causing it to rise and release moisture.

    (C) Warmer air from the city rises, creating a vacuum that cold air fills, creating wind. The rising warm air cools and releases moisture.

    (D) The lack of trees in the city results in a higher concentration of carbon dioxide, which warms the upper atmosphere to a sufficient degree to release precipitation.

5. The flow of a large aquifer in Texas was determined by scientists to be exhibiting a slow northward flow between the years 1977 and 1997. Which of the following is the most likely explanation for this phenomenon?

    (A) Water use is higher on the northern side of the aquifer than on the southern side.

    (B) Inflow into the aquifer from the Gulf of Mexico has gradually pushed the body of water northward.

    (C) Isostatic forces leading to a depression in the northern half the land draw the bulk of the aquifer's water northward through simple gravity.

    (D) Hotter temperatures inland cause the aquifer to evaporate at a faster rate on its northern side.

6. Rocks categorized as vesicular are characterized by tiny holes formed by gas bubbles. They are extremely porous, and some types have the unusual property of floating on water. What general type of rock would vesicular rocks be categorized as?

    (A) Metamorphic
    (B) Igneous
    (C) Sedimentary
    (D) Both metamorphic and igneous

7. Jet streams can reach speeds up to 300 miles per hour and are thousands of kilometers long. The position and strength of the jet stream generally is dependent upon temperature contrasts between different latitudes in the earth. When will jet streams tend to be the strongest?

    (A) Summer
    (B) Fall
    (C) Winter
    (D) Spring

8. Which of the following statements is NOT true of the ozone layer?

   (A) The hole in the ozone layer allows ultraviolet light to pass through, significantly increasing the magnitude of global warming.

   (B) Chlorofluorocarbons, the primary source of artificial ozone breakdown, remain in the atmosphere long after their initial release.

   (C) The degradation of ozone molecules is necessary to achieve the ultraviolet-shielding effect of the ozone layer.

   (D) Ozone breakdown is primarily caused by the chain reaction initiated by chlorine molecules.

9. Which of the following is NOT true regarding the solar system's planetary orbits?

   (A) Planetary orbits can be modeled using laws formulated by Johannes Kepler.

   (B) The outermost and innermost planets have the greatest and least eccentricities of orbit, respectively.

   (C) The line joining a planet to the sun sweeps out equal areas in equal times as the planet travels around its orbit.

   (D) One focus of any planetary ellipse in the solar system is always the sun.

10. Which of the following methods would be most appropriate and accurate in the dating of a dinosaur fossil?

    (A) Carbon-14 dating

    (B) Radio-isotope dating of the fossil in question

    (C) Radio-isotope dating of surrounding rocks

    (D) Age determination through the Law of Superposition

11. Which of the following features of the earth contains the greatest total amount of carbon dioxide by mass?

    (A) Liquid oceans

    (B) Polar caps

    (C) The atmosphere

    (D) Rainforests

12. Water's solid state is slightly less dense than its liquid state. Which of the following results would likely occur if this were not true?

    I. The earth's oceans would consist of a sheet of ice with a very thin liquid surface.

    II. The overall surface albedo of the earth would decrease.

    III. The overall size of the polar caps would decrease.

    IV. The boiling point of water would be significantly lower, leading to increased oceanic evaporation.

    (A) I only

    (B) I and II only

    (C) II, III, and IV only

    (D) III only

13. Which of the following exhibit tidal pull?

    I. Oceans

    II. Lakes

    III. Land masses

    IV. Streams

    (A) I only

    (B) I and II only

    (C) I and III only

    (D) I, II, III, and IV

14. During the crescent phase of the moon, the dim face of the rest of the moon can often be made out in addition to the brightly-lit crescent portion. This phenomenon, called earthshine, is particularly common in spring months. Why is this most likely the case?

    (A) The regular progression of the moon's phases ensures that the crescent phase occurs most often during spring months.
    (B) The surface albedo of the earth during spring months is higher because of greater cloud cover.
    (C) During spring, the earth's tilt is at a perpendicular angle to the sun, ensuring maximum reflectivity.
    (D) The greater size of both polar ice caps during the spring leads to greater reflectivity.

15. Which of the following statements regarding the sun is false?

    (A) The sun is constantly losing mass.
    (B) Sunspots are higher in temperature than the surrounding areas of brightness.
    (C) Energy release in the sun is accomplished through the fusion of hydrogen to helium atoms.
    (D) Neutrinos released by the sun are nearly impossible to detect without sophisticated observational equipment.

CHEMISTRY

1. A 100-g substance is known to contain 32 percent SO_4 by weight. Approximately how many grams of lead are required to completely convert all available SO_4 to Pb SO_4?

    (A) 34.5 g
    (B) 69.0 g
    (C) 103.5 g
    (D) 169.0 g

2. The sun's core consists primarily of ^1H and ^4He, as well as various other trace elements and isotopes. Which of the following statements is NOT true regarding the fusion reaction that occurs within the core?

    (A) Electrons are released as a product of the fusion reaction.
    (B) The mass of the products is less than the mass of the reactants in the balanced fusion equation.
    (C) Six photons are emitted as a product of the fusion reaction.
    (D) Four hydrogen atoms combine to form a single helium atom.

3. Lead is a critical element of most automotive batteries. The reactions at the negative and positive anode of a typical battery are

    1. $Pb(s) \rightarrow PbSO_4 + 2e^-$

    2. $PbO_2(s) + SO_4^{2-} + 4H^+ + 2e^- \rightarrow PbSO_4(s) + 2H_2O$

    Is the first reaction above the reaction at the anode or the cathode, and does it represent oxidation or reduction?

    (A) Anode, oxidation
    (B) Anode, reduction
    (C) Cathode, oxidation
    (D) Cathode, reduction

4. A chemist performs an experiment involving the given reaction with given solubility constant:

   What will be the molar solubility of calcium fluoride in a solution containing 0.01 M $Ca(NO_3)_2$?

   (A) 3.1×10^{-10}
   (B) 3.1×10^{-5}
   (C) 9.8×10^{-5}
   (D) 9.8×10^{-10}

5. What is the principal reason for adding acid to water in a laboratory setting, rather than adding water to acid?

   (A) Adding water to acid would result in a very concentrated water-acid reaction, potentially releasing a great deal of heat and boiling the acid.
   (B) Adding water to acid can skew the calculations associated with the reaction because it is simpler to titrate acid.
   (C) Adding acid to water concentrates the acid within the surrounding water, preventing it from spreading too quickly and creating a runaway reaction.
   (D) Adding acid to water allows the chemist to observe any resultant color changes more accurately than would be possible by adding water to acid.

6. Potassium bromide is a common anticonvulsant used in veterinary medicine. The frequently used upper guidelines for administration of the anticonvulsant recommend a 2.5-mg/mL dosage. What is the molality of a solution of KBr in which the full, recommended dose is added to 2 liters of water?

   (A) 0.058 m
   (B) 0.105 m
   (C) 0.210 m
   (D) 0.119 m

7. A liter of sand is added to a liter of small rocks, with a final total volume of 1.8 liters. Which of these additions is most analogous to this situation?

   (A) 75 mL H_2O (g) + 75 mL EtOH (l)
   (B) 40 mL H_2O (l) + 40 mL CH_4 (l)
   (C) 50 mL H_2O (l) + 50 mL $CH_3(CH_2)_4CH_3$ (l)
   (D) 60 mL H_2O (l) + 60 mL EtOH (l)

8. What are the likely electronic and molecular geometric properties, respectively, of XeF_2?

   (A) Trigonal bipyramidal, linear
   (B) Linear, bent
   (C) Trigonal bipyramidal, bent
   (D) Bent, linear

9. Given the reaction $4NH_3 + 3O_2 \rightarrow 2N_2 + 6H_2O$ and bond enthalpies NH=389 kJ/mol, OO=498 kJ/mol, and NN=941 kJ/mol, which of the following is the enthalpy of the OH bond?

   (A) 67 kJ/mol
   (B) 253 kJ/mol
   (C) 462 kJ/mol
   (D) 986 kJ/mol

10. Which of the following will act as a Lewis acid but not a Bronsted-Lowry acid?

    I. $AlCl_3$
    II. H_2PO_4
    III. BF_3
    IV. NO

    (A) I only
    (B) IV only
    (C) I and III only
    (D) II and III only

11. Which of the following is NOT true of geometric isomers?

    (A) They are a subclass of diastereomers.
    (B) They are mirror images around a double bond.
    (C) They are not superimposable.
    (D) Two geometric isomers have the same molecular formula.

12. The rate for a given reaction is dependent upon the concentrations of two compounds, A and B. Given the table below, what are the respective rate constants of A and B?

[A]	[B]	Reaction rate (mmol/L*se
0.2	0.2	10
0.4	0.2	20
0.6	0.6	270

    (A) 1, 1
    (B) 1, 2
    (C) 2, 2
    (D) 1, 3

13. Which of the following is the primary function of ultraviolet spectroscopy?

    (A) UV spectroscopy determines the conjugation level in a substance through selective reflection of UV rays based on bond strength.
    (B) UV spectroscopy is used to determine the chemical composition of a substance through varying levels of atomic UV absorption.
    (C) UV spectroscopy is used to determine conjugation level in a substance by increasing electrons to a higher energy level.
    (D) UV spectroscopy is useful for determining the half-life of a substance by ionizing atoms within a given compound.

14. A reaction's spontaneity is temperature-dependent for which of the following sets of enthalpy and entropy changes?

    (A) I and II only
    (B) I and IV only
    (C) II and III only
    (D) II and III only

15. Which substance will, when 20 mL is added to a beaker containing 50 mL of pure water at room temperature, result in the highest electric conductivity of the resulting solution?

    (A) HCl
    (B) HBr
    (C) HI
    (D) HF

PHYSICS

1. Scientists attempt to measure a possible new force by examining the force of two neutral particles separated by a small distance in the absence of any other known force. Based on the experimental data collected (see table below), what can we conclude about the relationship between the force in question and the distance between the objects?

Distance between objects A and B (10^{-13} m)	Measured Force on B ($\times 10^{-9}$ J)
1.13 ±. 02	3.41 ± .005
2.74 ±. 02	.583 ± .003
5.32 ± .03	.156 ± .002
6.78 ± .04	.094 ± .002
10.66 ± .05	.038 ± .001

   (A) They are inversely related.
   (B) They are directly related.
   (C) The force is inversely related to the square of the distance.
   (D) No relationship can be determined from the data.

2. When electrons are in an excited state they can fall to a lower energy state by emitting a photon with the difference in energy between the two states. This can happen spontaneously or through stimulated emission by a passing photon of the requisite energy. In a standard HeNe laser, the stimulated emission of photons is used to produce a coherent beam of light. Which of the following statements best explains why the stimulated emission of photons is necessary in the laser instead of spontaneous emission?

   (A) Stimulated emission produces photons of higher energy than those produced by spontaneous emission.
   (B) Stimulated emission produces photons that travel in the same direction as the photon that induces their emission.
   (C) Stimulated emission produces photons with longer wavelengths than those produced by spontaneous emissions.
   (D) Either spontaneous or stimulated emission alone would be sufficient to produce laser light.

3. The position of a particle as a function of time is given by the equation:
$$x(t) = x^3 - 4x^2 + 3$$

   Starting from $t = 0$, where would the particle have both a positive velocity and acceleration?
   (A) $t > 0$
   (B) $0 < t < 1.33$
   (C) $t > 1.33$
   (D) $t > 3$

4. An object at rest with the shape of an equilateral triangle is subject to the three external forces as shown in the diagram. If the object does not exhibit translational motion, what must F and θ be, respectively?

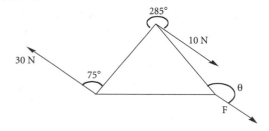

(A) 20 N, 120°
(B) 20 N, 165°
(C) 10 N, 120°
(D) 10 N, 165°

5. Two cylinders, one a hollow copper pipe and the other a solid plastic tube, are placed on an inclined ramp and released from the same height. Assuming both cylinders roll without slipping, what can we say about the resulting motion?

(A) Both reach the bottom of the ramp at the same time.
(B) The copper pipe reaches the bottom of the ramp first.
(C) The plastic tube reaches the bottom of the ramp first.
(D) It cannot be determined from the information given which cylinder will reach the bottom of the ramp first.

6. Two identical rockets of length 20m (as measured on earth) are in outer space. If rocket A is at rest and rocket B passes by at a speed of 0.5c, what is the length of rocket B as measured by the astronauts in rocket B?

(A) 17.3 m
(B) 20 m
(C) 23.1 m
(D) 28.3 m

7. If Earth's orbit around the sun has a radius of 1.5×10^{11} m and a period of 1 year, what is the period of Mars's orbit if it has a radius of 2.3×10^{11} m?

(A) 0.55 years
(B) 1 year
(C) 1.5 years
(D) 1.9 years

8. If oxygen has a molecular weight of 32 g/mol, and hydrogen has a molecular weight of 2 g/mol, what is the ratio of the rms speed of an oxygen atom to a hydrogen atom if both are at 300 K?

(A) 1:1
(B) 1:2
(C) 1:4
(D) 1:16

9. A turbine in a steam power plant has an efficiency that is 80% of the ideal Carnot engine efficiency. The turbine works by condensing water vapor at 520° C into water at 100° C. How much energy does the turbine require in order to produce 50 MJ of usable energy?

(A)   94 MJ
(B)   118 MJ
(C)   212 MJ
(D) 6250 MJ

10. Suppose a wire of length 2.0 m is conducting a current of 5.0 A toward the top of the page and through a 30 Gauss ($1\ T = 10^4\ G$) uniform magnetic field directed into the page (see diagram below). What is the magnitude and direction of the magnetic force on the wire?

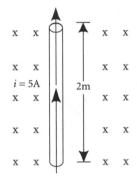

(A) 300 N towards the left
(B) 300 N into the page
(C) .03 N toward the right
(D) .03 N towards the left

11. The plates of a capacitor are originally separated by a vacuum. If a dielectric K > 1 is introduced between the plates of the capacitor, and the capacitor is allowed to charge up, which of the following statements are true?

   I. The capacitance of the capacitor will increase.
   II. The voltage across the capacitor plates will increase.
   III. The charge stored on the capacitor will increase.

(A) I only
(B) I and II
(C) II and III
(D) I and III

12. A Hydrogen atom is in its first excited state ($n = 2$). How many associated angular momentum states does the atom have?

(A) two states corresponding to one vertical and one horizontal
(B) three states corresponding to the orientation in space of the angular momentum
(C) three states corresponding to the three possible spin states
(D) four states corresponding to n^2

13. An 8 kg bowling ball rolls down a hill (height = 10 m) and collides elastically with an identical bowling ball at rest. If the moment of inertia for a spherical object is $\frac{2}{5}Mr^2$, and the diameter of the bowling ball is 20cm, what is the speed of the second bowling ball after the collision?

(A) 5.8 m/s
(B) 6.9 m/s
(C) 11.8 m/s
(D) 14 m/s

14. The cornea in a human eye acts like a lens, focusing the incoming light on the retina. The retina lies approximately 1.8 cm behind the iris. What can we say about the human eye?

(A) It acts like a convergent lens with an inverted image on the retina.
(B) It acts like a convergent lens with an upright image on the retina.
(C) It acts like a divergent lens with an inverted image on the retina.
(D) It acts like a divergent lens with an upright image on the retina.

15. An airplane wing is constructed so as to minimize turbulent flow over the wing and to ensure that the air flowing over the top surface of the wing travels a greater distance in a given amount of time than the air flowing over the bottom wing surface. Such a design will generate a lift force when air flows over the top and bottom wing surfaces because:

   (A) The velocity of the air on the top surface is greater than the velocity of the air on the bottom surface.

   (B) The velocity of the air on the top surface is less than the velocity of the air on the bottom surface.

   (C) The density of the air on the top surface is less than the density of the air on the bottom surface.

   (D) The density of the air on the top surface is greater than the density of the air on the bottom surface.

Science Question Bank
Answers and Explanations

BIOLOGY EXPLANATIONS

1. B

The word carbohydrate literally means carbon and water. All carbohydrates therefore only contain only carbon, "C", and water, "H_2O."

2. B

Carbohydrates and lipids contain only carbon, hydrogen, and oxygen. Carbohydrates contain these three elements in the ratio of 1 carbon to 1 water (CH_2O), whereas lipids contain much less oxygen relative to the other two elements. Proteins also contain carbon, hydrogen, and oxygen but also contain nitrogen in a chemical group called an amino group.

3. C

Glucose, sucrose, and starch are all carbohydrates that contain the element oxygen. Therefore, oxygen is the smallest of the four choices. Of the three carbohydrates listed, glucose is a monosaccharide, sucrose is a disaccharide, and starch is a polysaccharide. As the names indicate, disaccharides are made up of two monosaccharides, and polysaccharides are made up of many monosaccharides.

4. B

Plants are unique and vitally important to life on our planet because they have the ability to capture light energy and build high-energy macromolecules from atmospheric carbon dioxide. Animals must eat to receive their high-energy macromolecules. But both plants and animals need to break down the macromolecules to use their energy for cell functions. This process is called cellular respiration and requires atmospheric oxygen, which is why the process carries the name "respiration."

5. A

The amount of light, the number of days, and the initial levels of CO_2 were constant for all plants. The experimenter varied the temperature for each plant at the beginning of the investigation.

6. C

The terms listed in the key refer to various ways in which organisms interact with one another. The first three terms fall into the category of symbiosis, which means two organisms existing in a continually intimate way. In each of the relationships, at least one of the organisms benefits. In parasitism, the benefit comes at the detriment of the other organism. In commensalism, the benefit comes with negligible effect to the other organism. In mutualism, both organisms benefit from the relationship.

7. D

The last two terms refer to a less intimate relationship between organisms. Predation refers to one organism consuming another, and competition refers to two organisms vying for the same resources. The statements indicate that the turtles are in competition with one another. One of the species is using the existing resources in abundance and therefore increasing in number. The other species is left with fewer resources and is not reproducing at an adequate rate.

8. A

A distinguishing characteristic of tundra is an average monthly temperature near 10°C. Near the equator, such temperatures occur at high altitudes. Remember that there are glaciers in the Andes located on the equator.

9. B

Mitosis is often used interchangeably with cell division. Technically, mitosis is the process of chromosomal replication that results in two daughter nuclei with identical DNA sequences. Because of this process, all of the cells in your body contain the same DNA, even though you started out as one cell. Sexually reproducing organisms also undergo another cellular replication that happens in sex cells. The process is called meiosis.

10. B

The molecule pictured is a phospholipid found in all membranes that make up cells and their organelles. Because secretory and Golgi vesicles derive from the membranes of organelles, they too are made of phospholipids. The only structure listed that is not made of lipid, but rather of the amino sugar chitin, is the chitinous cell wall of fungi.

11. C

The major difference between endo- and ectotherms comes not from the temperature at which either type of organism maintains its body, but rather from the source of body heat that each type of organism uses. Ectotherms derive most of their body heat from the surrounding environment—surrounding temperature is termed the ambient temperature. However, endotherms can generate body heat or cool themselves off using metabolic reactions to keep their body temperature fairly constant.

12. D

Recall that a sex-linked (or X-linked) allele is carried on the X-chromosome and can be passed from fathers to daughters only and from mothers to both sons and daughters. An early-acting lethal disease will kill all males in infancy because males can never carry sex-linked alleles (they have only one X chromosome). Because of this, there will be no males of reproductive age to pass along the allele to daughters, so only female carriers, who will pass the allele to 50 percent of their sons and daughters, can pass on the disease. A female can never be homozygous because she could never have received an allele from her father (males don't survive past infancy with the disease).

13. D

Teeth are responsible for the mechanical breakdown of food, just like the gizzard in some organisms. Mechanical digestion begins in the mouth, where food is chopped into bits by the teeth so that enzymes in the stomach and small intestine can work more quickly and more effectively.

14. A

The alveoli are the location for the exchange of oxygen and carbon dioxide at the lungs. It is here, in these grape-like clusters, that gas exchange takes place between the lungs and the blood through thin membranes.

15. D

The diaphragm is a muscular band of tissue that contracts to permit air to enter the lung. As the diaphragm contracts, the pressure in the chest cavity decreases, and air rushes in through the nose or mouth. As the diaphragm relaxes, pressure in the chest cavity returns to normal, and air is pushed out.

EARTH/SPACE SCIENCE EXPLANATIONS

1. C

This question requires a good deal of critical thinking both in understanding the information given in the question and in analyzing the answers. If minerals continue to dissolve in the ocean, and yet its salinity remains relatively constant, there must be a process that removes minerals as well. Evaporation would be an unacceptable method because the minerals would be left in the ocean as water evaporated. Likewise, (B) and (D) provide less-than-convincing mechanisms. If, however, "pieces" of ocean are trapped and evaporate completely, leaving dried beds (such as the salt plains in the Western United States), the overall mineral content of the oceans will remain constant.

2. D

The key to answering this question is to remember that carbon dating is only useful for dating relatively recent samples that do in fact contain carbon from the atmosphere. The first two answer choices, being fossils, will not contain significant amounts of carbon. Furthermore, remember that oceanic creatures and those that feed primarily upon them are unreliable for carbon dating because of carbon variations in the ocean. Given the two remaining answer choices, remember that trees grow by adding layers to the outside. Therefore, the most accurate determination of a tree's age will come from its core, so the answer is (D).

3. B

Thunderstorms are created when warm air rises, cools, and releases precipitation because of its reduced capacity to hold moisture. Therefore, the fact that Atlanta is significantly warmer than the surrounding regions means that cool air would push the warmer air up, which would in turn cool and cause precipitation.

4. C

This is a "gimme" question if the mechanism has been predicted in the last question. The other answers can be eliminated also as mechanisms that might contribute to overall global warming or environmental effects but would not cause the localized effects observed in Atlanta.

5. A

Aquifers generally display movement based on the direction that water is draining. In heavily populated areas or areas that use a particular aquifer heavily, the water is being drained through the extensive use of wells. Therefore, a general northward flow of a large aquifer will usually indicate that water is being drawn from above the northern portion of that aquifer. Answer choices such as (D) can be eliminated easily; evaporation will of course not be a significant factor for a subterranean aquifer.

6. B

It is not necessary to be familiar with the type of rock mentioned in the question to answer it quickly and efficiently. By asking where gas bubbles would occur (in areas of high heat), the correct answer can be quickly deduced to be igneous. Moreover, the pressures associated with metamorphic rock would surely not allow for a rock of low enough density to float on water.

7. C

Again, a question in which it is important to ask what is being tested. The information about jet streams serves only to set up the fact that they are strongest when temperature contrasts between different latitudes on earth are the most pronounced. This will of course be the case when the tilt of the earth is most dramatic because the more extreme latitudes will receive far less sunlight than more central latitudes (compare New York to Miami in winter versus summer). The question ultimately becomes one less about meteorology than an earth-sun systems question.

8. A

This question can be answered by getting rid of everything you know to be true, which, depending on the extent of your knowledge, may or may not be the fastest way to go about it. However, choice (A) articulates the common misconception that the ozone layer contributes to global warming, when in fact the two are not related.

9. B

Elimination is likely the fastest way to answer this question. The last two answer choices are an expansion on the first; they are paraphrases of Kepler's first two laws. Specific knowledge about Mercury and Pluto might also help to narrow the answer choice down to (B). Both planets have the most eccentric orbits of any of the planets.

10. C

For the reasons described in the previous dating question, (A) is out immediately. Whereas the law of superposition might be useful for determining a general age, it will not be as accurate as radioactive dating. Radioactive dating of the rocks surrounding the fossil will be more accurate than the dating of the fossil itself because the fossil's composition has not been stable for a long enough time to use radioactive isotopes with confidence.

11. A

The oceans are the largest reservoir of carbon dioxide on earth, containing many, many times more carbon dioxide than the atmosphere.

12. A

The critical aspect of water is that liquid water is denser than solid water, allowing ice to float to the top of oceans. If this were not the case, ice would settle to the bottom, and eventually, only a thin upper layer of water would be warmed sufficiently to be liquid. If ice did sink, surface albedo would increase from the increase in ice, and the polar caps would increase in size commensurately. The difference between the states will not affect the overall boiling point of the water. When encountering a tough answer choice to evaluate, remember to think about overall trends. The trend associated with a heavier solid state will be an ice planet, which is the opposite of what would happen with a lower boiling point.

13. D

In fact, everything exhibits tidal pull, which is caused by the difference in the moon's and sun's gravities on one side of the earth as opposed to the other. In smaller masses, the difference is less pronounced, and so in anything less massive than oceans, such as lakes, or with less liquid than oceans (such as rock), the difference is barely noticeable. Lake Michigan has a tide of approximately half an inch to an inch and a half daily.

14. B

The dim outline of the moon can be inferred to be caused not directly by the sun itself, but rather by the reflection of light from the earth off the moon and back again to earth. This reflection will be greatest when the amount of light reflected off the earth is the greatest. Whereas all answer choices but (A) discuss reflectivity, only (B) offers a mechanism that does not contradict fact.

15. B

This question can be attacked by elimination, although it may be quicker to look for an answer that clearly jumps out as false. Sunspots are in fact darker because of their lower temperature. It is important to remember that the area just around sunspots is particularly bright and hot, far hotter than the normal surface of the sun. This might lead some to be confused and think that the entire sunspot is higher in temperature, but in fact, just the outer rim of the sunspot is higher in temperature.

CHEMISTRY EXPLANATIONS

1. B

If the 100-g substance contains 32 percent SO4, then there are 32 g of the compound to react with the lead. Calculate the molar weight of SO4 to be 96, which means that there is one-third mol in the substance. Lead will react with it in a 1:1 ratio, which means that a third of a mol of lead is required. A quick check on the periodic table and division by 3 will result in a mass of lead of 69.0 g.

2. A

Electrons are in fact required for the fusion reaction, which makes sense because the hydrogen is being converted into helium. In fact, the core of the sun is so hot, that any electrons around atoms are stripped away. The remaining three answers are all properties of the standard fusion reaction.

3. A

Don't be thrown off by the long equation; this can be made very simple. Because the first reaction is releasing electrons, it is by definition an oxidation. Further, the anode always contains the oxidation half-reaction, and the answer must be (A). Note that (A) and (D) are the only meaningful answers; the others can be eliminated even without reading the equation.

4. B

This problem requires a bit more calculation than the ones before. The key to solving this problem is to recognize that it is a common ion problem. Because the solution already contains a great deal of calcium ion, the amount of calcium added will be small enough to be neglected in calculations. The equation should be set up like this:

$$3.9 \times 10^{-11} = [Ca^{2+}][F^-]^2 = (x + 0.010)(2x)^2$$

$$3.9 \times 10^{-11} = (0.010)(2x)^2$$

$$x^2 = \frac{3.9 \times 10^{-11}}{4(0.010)} = 9.8 \times 10^{-10}$$

$$x^2 = 3.1 \times 10^{-5} \, M$$

5. A

This is a standard laboratory-safety question. Acid is always added to water so as to dilute the acid as it reacts. If water were added to acid, the concentration of acid around the water would result in a possibly violent reaction. Recall that the combination of water and acid is exothermic, and the acid might spill outside the vial as it boils.

6. B

If the full dose is used in 2 L of water, 2,500 mg, or 25 g, will be present in the solution. The mols must be calculated next. Because KBr has a molar weight of 119 g/mol, 0.210 mols are present. Dividing by the two kilograms of water yields the molality: 0.105 m.

7. D

Recall that certain substances, when mixed together, will "fall between the cracks" much as sand does through rocks. If they are immiscible liquids, this obviously will not happen. Therefore, answers (B) and (C) can be eliminated; mixing water with a hydrocarbon will not yield a high level of miscibility. Answers (A) and (D) are identical except for states; water is a gas in (A) and so cannot be miscible with the liquid EtOH.

8. A

The best way to answer this question is to draw out a quick Lewis diagram, consulting the periodic table to ensure accuracy. Xenon will have three empty spaces containing three lone pair electron groups in addition to the two fluorines that it binds. To determine the electronic geometry, the three lone pair groups must be taken into account in addition to the fluorines. Having five groups around the central xenon will result in trigonal bipyramidal geometry. The two fluorine atoms are all that need be considered along with the xenon atom in the molecular geometry; they will oppose each other and will not bend because of the presence of the three equatorial lone pair groups, resulting in a linear geometry.

9. C

This problem can be solved by calculating the bond energies on each side of the equation, but such a time-consuming process should drive you to search for a quicker way. The bond enthalpy of OH should be greater than that of NH, as oxygen is more electronegative than hydrogen. Everything below the bond energy of NH can be eliminated, getting rid of (A) and (B). The enthalpy of OH will also be lower than the strong oxygen double bond, and so everything above that enthalpy can be eliminated. (C) is all that remains. Always be on the lookout for a conceptual way to answer a tough question.

10. C

Remember that Lewis acids act as electron acceptors. A Lewis acid can be a Bronsted-Lowry acid as well, but it must have hydrogen ions to donate. Both I and III are frequently used Lewis acids, neither of which have a proton to donate. Notice that IV is not an acid at all, whereas II is a Bronsted-Lowry acid. As a side note, make sure you are familiar with diprotic acids like II; many questions will test your ability to recognize that these compounds can contribute two hydrogen ions.

11. B

Geometric isomers are a subclass of stereoisomers, with all the implications that go with it, knocking out (A), (C), and (D). Whereas geometric isomers do deal with double bonds, stereoisomers are not mirror images, and neither, consequently, can geometric isomers be mirror images.

12. B

The easiest place to start is with compound A. Because the rate of the reaction doubles when the concentration of A does, the rate constant of A must be linear, or 1. B is a little trickier. Look at the last two rows of the table. Because an increase in A from 0.4 to 0.6 mol should increase the reaction rate from 20 to 30 by virtue of the rate constant we just calculated, any further increase in reaction rate must be caused by B. Therefore, as B increases in concentration from 0.2 to 0.6 mol, the reaction rate increases from 30 to 270, a factor of 9x. Be careful not to jump to the conclusion that the rate of the reaction is 3 because we are taking an exponent rather than multiplying. Three squared gives us the 9x factor, meaning that the rate constant of B must be 2.

13. C

UV spectroscopy is primarily used to determine conjugation within a substance, and it does this by absorbing the rays and increasing electrons to a higher level.

14. B

The Gibbs free energy equation is helpful here. Because temperature and entropy change are multiplied together and subtracted from the change in enthalpy, a temperature dependent reaction will be one in which the Gibbs free energy could be positive or negative depending on whether the temperature is relatively high or low. This only occurs when both enthalpy and entropy changes are either positive or negative.

15. C

This question is essentially a complicated way of asking what the strongest acid is. The highest electric conductivity will result from the solution that has the highest degree of ionization. Because each of these compounds consists of a halide and hydrogen ion, high dissociation will by definition be equivalent to high acidity. The less electronegative the atom holding the hydrogen, the easier it will be for the hydrogen ion to escape into the surrounding solution. Iodine, being the largest halide, will be least able to hold onto the hydrogen ion. This acid, incidentally, is rarely seen in laboratory use because of its high cost.

PHYSICS

1. C

This problem can be backsolved by testing the answer choices. First, eliminate (B) since the force gets smaller as the distance gets larger. Second, use the formula $F = \dfrac{x}{r}$ with x representing an unknown constant and plug in the pairs of force and distance from the chart. If x is a constant for all pairs then we have an inverse relationship. Since x is NOT constant, eliminate (A). Try $F = \dfrac{x}{r^2}$, which gives an approximate value of $x = 4.34$ for all pairs. This proves that (C) is the correct response.

2. B

Stimulated emission is necessary because it produces identical photons: the same energy, direction, and wavelength of the original. This results in a coherent beam of light.

We can eliminate (A) and (C) because stimulated and spontaneous emission both produce the same energy and wavelength photons. (D) is wrong because without the stimulated emission, the photons produced would have every possible direction, and thus no coherent beam would be created.

3. D

The first derivative of the equation yields the velocity: $v(t) = 3x^2 - 8x$. The second derivative gives us acceleration: $a(t) = 6x - 8$.

The equations do not need to be solved exactly—try some possible numbers based upon the answer choices. At $t = 0.5$, both equations are negative; eliminate (A).

At $t = 1$ both equations are negative—eliminate (B).

At $t = 2$ the velocity is negative—eliminate (C).

4. B

It is not necessary to break the forces down into their $x - y$ components. Start by finding the angles based upon the fact that an equilateral triangle has 60° angles at each corner. From this we get the fact that the 30 N force is antiparallel to the 10 N force. So we need a force of 20 N parallel to the 10 N force: eliminate (C) and (D). The correct θ that makes F parallel to the 10 N force is 165°.

5. C

When rolling down the ramp, the objects will gain rotational kinetic energy ($E = \dfrac{1}{2}I\Omega^2$) as well as translational kinetic energy ($E = \dfrac{1}{mv^2}$). The gravitational potential energy is converted into both forms of kinetic energy and the object with less rotational energy will thereby have a greater translational energy and a higher translational velocity, thus reaching the bottom first. The plastic tube will have more mass closer to its center which equates to a smaller moment of inertia, I. So the plastic tube has less rotational energy and greater translational energy, and reaches the bottom first.

6. A

According to special relativity, an observer in a stationary inertial frame will measure the length of a moving frame to be *shorter* by a factor of $\dfrac{1}{\gamma} = \gamma\left(1 - \dfrac{v^2}{c^2}\right)$. From this we can eliminate (B), (C), and (D) since they are longer than the rest length. We could also do the actual calculation to prove (A) is correct:

$$L\gamma = 20\sqrt{1 - \dfrac{v^2}{c^2}} = 20\sqrt{1 - 0.5^2} = 20\sqrt{0.75} = 17.3\,\text{m}$$

7. D

Use Kepler's third law: the square of the period of any planet is proportional to the cube of the radius. So $\dfrac{T_E^2}{r_E^3} = \dfrac{T_M^2}{r_M^3}$. Plugging in the

number from the problem gives us

$TM = 1.9$ years. $\left(T^2 = \left(\dfrac{4\pi^2}{GMr^3}\right)\right)$.

8. C

The kinetic theory of gases states that $\dfrac{1}{2}mv^2 = \dfrac{3}{2}kT$. Since the gases are at the same temperature they must have the same kinetic energy per atom:

$$\frac{1}{2}m_H v_H^2 = \frac{1}{2}m_O v_O^2$$

Which leads to $\dfrac{v_O}{v_H} = \sqrt{\dfrac{m_H}{m_O}} = \sqrt{\dfrac{2}{32}} = \dfrac{1}{4}$.

9. B

Start with the efficiency of a Carnot engine:

$\dfrac{(T_H - T_C)}{T_H}$ and remember to use temperature in

Kelvin ($K = °C + 273$):

$$\frac{(793 - 373)}{793} = 0.53.$$

The turbine then has an efficiency of: $0.8 \times 0.53 = 0.424$. So to create 50 MJ of usable energy, the turbine will require $\dfrac{50}{0.424} = 118$ MJ of energy; (B) is the correct answer.

10. D

The magnetic force on a wire is given by $F = il \times B$. The direction is given by the right-hand-rule. Since the current is perpendicular to the magnetic field, the magnitude of the force is given by $ilB =$ (5 A)(2 m)(3×10^{-3} T) = 0.03 N. The right-hand rule gives the direction: to the left.

11. D

The purpose of a dielectric is to increase the capacitance of a capacitor, so the correct answer must include statement I—eliminate (C). But the voltage across a capacitor depends only upon the circuit it is in, so the voltage will not change—eliminate (B). Finally, recall that capacitance is defined as the ratio of charge to voltage, so increasing capacitance without changing the voltage must mean an increase in the charge—the correct answer is (D).

12. B

In general, for the primary quantum number n, there are $l = 0, 1, (n-1)$ orbital quantum numbers. For each l there are $m_l = 0, \pm 1, \pm 2, \pm l$ magnetic quantum numbers. For $n = 2$, we have $l = 1$ and $m_l = 0, \pm 1$. The orbital angular momentum states are given by m_l, and represent the three possible orientations of the angular momentum with respect to the z-axis: up, down, and zero. (B) is correct.

13. C

This problem requires energy conservation to calculate the velocity of the first ball at the bottom of the ramp, and then momentum conservation during the collision.

Using $mgh = \frac{1}{2}mv^2 + \frac{1}{2}I\Omega^2$ with $I = \frac{2}{5}Mr^2$ and $\Omega = \frac{v}{r}$ yields $mgh = \frac{1}{2}mv^2 + \frac{1}{5}mv^2$ and

$$v = \sqrt{\left(\frac{10}{7}\right)gh} = \sqrt{\left(\frac{10}{7}\right)(9.8)(10\ m)} = 11.8\ \frac{m}{s}$$

This is the speed of the first ball at the bottom of the ramp. But since the second ball is identical to the first and it is an elastic collision, you should recognize that the result of the collision will be to transfer all of the linear velocity to the second ball. Thus the correct answer is (C).

14. A

From our review of lenses, you should remember that only converging lenses produce real images, which is necessary for the human eye. We can therefore eliminate (C) and (D). And since the eye focuses on the object, we use the diagram where the object is placed at the focal length, which results in an inverted image. Choice (B) is correct.

15. A

The information in the question allows us to conclude that the air on the top of the wing must travel at a higher velocity than the air below. The density of air will not change on either surface, so we can eliminate (C) and (D). Remembering from our studies that the faster a fluid moves the less pressure it offers, and the fact that we want less pressure on top of the wing, you see that (A) is the correct answer.

CHAPTER SEVEN

ENGLISH

In this section, we will cover several key English Subject Assessments. We will begin with a brief summary of the major English Subject tests and an outline of the content covered on them. The section concludes with a question bank that will allow you to brush up on your content knowledge and test-taking skills in English. Depending on the test you are preparing for, some or all of the questions in this question bank will apply to you.

PRAXIS II ENGLISH SUBJECT TESTS

This section applies to you if you are taking one of the following tests:
- English Language, Literature, and Composition: Content Knowledge (0041)
- English Language, Literature, and Composition: Essays (0042)

PRAXIS II ENGLISH LANGUAGE, LITERATURE, AND COMPOSITION SUBJECT TESTS

Several PRAXIS II Subject assessments target English Language, Literature, and Composition. These tests pull questions from a wide range of English content areas. Consequently, much of the material covered in the English question bank that follows applies to the English subject tests. Be advised that the question bank focuses primarily on content knowledge with some reference to pedagogy. Nonetheless, the content covered provides a solid review of this broad and varied subject.

English Language, Literature, and Composition Content Knowledge (0041)

Test Format: 120 multiple-choice questions
Test Length: 2 hours

Content covered:
- Reading and Understanding the Text: 66 questions, 55 percent of the test
- Language and Linguistics: 18 questions, 15 percent of the test
- Composition and Rhetoric: 36 questions, 30 percent of the test

This test covers the broad range of concepts typically covered in a bachelor's program in English or English Education. Working through the question bank that follows should give you a good sense of how English content is tested on this exam.

English Language Literature, and Composition Essays (0042)

Test Format: 4 essay questions
Test Length: 2 hours

Content Covered—1 Essay in each of the following subject areas:
- Interpretation of a work of poetry
- Interpretation of a work of prose
- Evaluation of the argument and rhetorical features of a passage that addresses an issue in the study of English
- Assume and defend a position on an issue in the study of English using references to works of literature

Although this exam is essay-based, the concepts you are expected to discuss with a high level of mastery are the same as those tested in the question bank that follows. The interpretive tasks required in three of the essays are similar to passage and poem-based questions in the question bank. However, rather than choosing from answer choices, the actual test will require you to articulate your own interpretation or evaluation of these works. All four essays will require you to demonstrate mastery of written English. Therefore, in preparation for this test, it is worthwhile to review the basic writing skills discussed in the PPST Writing Review in tandem with the content covered in the question bank that follows.

Note: this question bank is designed to provide test-like practice with the wide range of content knowledge covered on the PRAXIS Subject tests in English. It is NOT designed to be a simulation of any single PRAXIS Subject test.

English Question Bank

Question 1 refers to the following passage.

Proverbs are hard to define, but one could do worse than the pithy definition offered by an 18th-century British statesman, Lord John Russell. A proverb, Russell is said to have
(5) remarked at breakfast, is "one man's wit and all men's wisdom." Proverbs have been identified in all the world's spoken languages, and—unlike Lord Russell's adage—they are almost always anonymous. Interestingly,
(10) similar sayings seem to have developed independently in many parts of the world. For example, the English saying, "A bird in the hand is worth two in the bush," has counterparts in Romania, Spain, and Iceland.

1. Which of the following best expresses the author's attitude toward Lord Russell's definition of a proverb?

   (A) dismissive
   (B) skeptical
   (C) loyal
   (D) favorable
   (E) exuberant

2. Arthur Miller's play, *Death of a Salesman*, has been called a "tragedy of the common man" because it

   (A) depicts the fall from grace of an important person
   (B) fits Aristotle's formal definition of tragedy
   (C) gives an ordinary salesman's life weight and meaning
   (D) is written in a poetic and serious style

3. Which outline correctly organizes and categorizes information pertaining to the work of William Shakespeare?

(A) **I. Plays**
   a) Tragedies
    1) *King Lear…*
   b) Histories
    1) *Richard III…*
   c) Comedies
    1) *Twelfth Night…*
   II. Poems

(B) **I. Plays**
   a) Tragedies
    1) *Hamlet…*
   b) Poems
    1) *My Mistress' Eyes…*
   c) Comedies
    1) *All's Well That Ends Well…*
   II. Histories

(C) **I. Plays**
   a) Tragedies
    1) Comedies
   b) Histories
    1) *Henry V…*
   c) Poems
    1) *Not Marble Nor the Gilded Monuments…*
   II. *The Tempest*

(D) **I. Plays**
   a) Tragedies
    1) *Hamlet…*
   b) Histories
    1) *King Lear…*
   c) Comedies
    1) *Titus Andronicus…*
   II. Poems

4. To be considered a poem, a work of literature must use which of the following?

   I. verse
   II. rhythm
   III.   rhyme
   IV.   metaphor

(A) I and II only

(B) I and IV only

(C) II and III only

(D) I only

5. Which of the following is an example of the "slippery slope" fallacy?

(A) "Of course you oppose divorce; you're a priest."

(B) "I admit I cheated on the test—but half the class did, too."

(C) "God must exist, because the Bible says so, and the Bible was written by God."

(D) "If you allow the government to censor the Internet today, they'll be banning books tomorrow."

Questions 6–7

I continued for the remainder of the day in my hovel in a state of utter and stupid despair. My protectors had departed and had broken the only link that held me to the world. For the first time, the feelings of revenge and hatred filled my bosom, and I did not strive to control them, but allowing myself to be borne away by the stream, I bent my mind towards injury and death. When I thought of my friends, of the mild voice of De Lacey, the gentle eyes of Agatha, and the exquisite beauty of the Arabian, these thoughts vanished, and a gush of tears somewhat soothed me. But again when I reflected that they had spurned and deserted me, anger returned, a rage of anger, and unable to injure anything human, I turned my fury towards inanimate objects. As night advanced, I placed a variety of combustibles around the cottage, and after having destroyed every vestige of cultivation in the garden, I waited with forced impatience until the moon had sunk to commence my operations.

As the night advanced, a fierce wind arose from the woods and quickly dispersed the clouds that had loitered in the heavens; the blast tore along like a mighty avalanche and produced a kind of insanity in my spirits that burst all bounds of reason and reflection. I lighted the dry branch of a tree and danced with fury around the devoted cottage, my eyes still fixed on the western horizon, the edge of which the moon nearly touched. A part of its orb was at length hid, and I waved my brand; it sank, and with a loud scream I fired the straw, and heath, and bushes, which I had collected. The wind fanned the fire, and the cottage was quickly enveloped by the flames, which clung to it and licked it with their forked and destroying tongues.

As soon as I was convinced that no assistance could save any part of the habitation, I quitted the scene and sought for refuge in the woods.

And now, with the world before me, whither should I bend my steps? I resolved to fly far from the scene of my misfortunes; but to me, hated and despised, every country must be equally horrible. At length the thought of you crossed my mind. I learned from your papers that you were my father, my creator; and to whom could I apply with more fitness than to him who had given me life?

But how was I to direct myself? I knew that I must travel in a southwesterly direction to reach my destination, but the sun was my only guide. I did not know the names of the towns that I was to pass through, nor could I ask information from a single human being; but I did not despair. From you only could I hope for succour, although towards you I felt no sentiment but that of hatred. Unfeeling, heartless creator! You had endowed me with perceptions and passions and then cast me abroad an object for the scorn and horror of mankind. But on you only had I any claim for pity and redress, and from you I determined to seek that justice which I vainly attempted to gain from any other being that wore the human form.

from *Frankenstein*, by Mary Shelley

6. The narrator of this passage is

   (A) Victor
   (B) Elizabeth
   (C) the monster
   (D) the author

7. "A part of its orb was at length hid, and I waved my brand; it sank, and with a loud scream I fired the straw, and heath, and bushes, which I had collected."

   Which of the following is a correct restatement of the above?

   (A) "When my branding iron sank, I screamed and shot at the bushes."
   (B) "When the moon set, I screamed and burned the cottage."
   (C) "When I could not find the orb, I screamed and kicked at the straw and the bushes."
   (D) "I waited until the sun set, then I screamed and set fire to the forest."

8. A Marxist interpretation of *Waiting for Godot* would probably focus on

   (A) the poverty and despair of its working-class characters
   (B) the use of archetypes in the portrayals of the characters
   (C) the power imbalances in the relationships of the characters
   (D) the reliance of the two main characters on the eventual arrival of a "savior"

9. "You will have 30 minutes to complete the assignment. When you're finished, give it to Ms. Fletcher or myself."

   What is the error in the sentences above?

   (A) "30" should be spelled out as "thirty"
   (B) The clauses should be joined by a semicolon, not a period
   (C) "Myself" should be "me"
   (D) "You're" should be "your"

Questions 10–12

The following passage analyzes one of Willa Cather's (1873–1947) novels.

Sapphira and the Slave Girl was the last novel of Willa Cather's illustrious literary career. Begun in the late summer of 1937 and finally completed in 1941, it is often regarded
(5) by critics as one of her most personal works. Although the story takes place in 1856, well before her own birth, she drew heavily on both vivid childhood memories and tales handed down by older relatives to describe
(10) life in rural northern Virginia in the middle of the 19th century. She even went on an extended journey to the area to give the story a further ring of authenticity.

Of all of Cather's many novels, *Sapphira*
(15) *and the Slave Girl* is the one most concerned with providing an overall picture of day-to-day life in a specific era. A number of the novel's characters, it would seem, are included in the story only because they are
(20) representative of the types of people to be found in 19th-century rural Virginia; indeed, a few of them play no part whatsoever in the unfolding of the plot. For instance, we are introduced to a poor white woman, Mandy
(25) Ringer, who is portrayed as intelligent and content, despite the fact that she has no formal education and must toil constantly in the fields. And we meet Dr. Clevenger, a country doctor who, with his patrician
(30) manners, evokes a strong image of the pre-Civil War South.

The title, however, accurately suggests that the novel is mainly about slavery. Cather's attitude toward this institution may best be
(35) summed up as somewhat ambiguous. On the one hand, she displays almost total indifference to the legal and political aspects of slavery when she misidentifies certain crucial dates in its growth and development.
(40) Nor does she ever really offer a direct condemnation of slavery. Yet, on the other hand, the evil that was slavery gets through to

us, albeit in typically subtle ways. Those characters, like Mrs. Blake, who oppose the
(45) institution are portrayed in a sympathetic light. Furthermore, the suffering of the slaves themselves and the petty, nasty, often cruel, behavior of the slaveowners are painted in stark terms.

(50)   Although *Sapphira and the Slave Girl* was certainly not meant to be a political tract, the novel is sometimes considered to be a denunciation of bygone days. Nothing could be further from the truth. In spite of her
(55) willingness to acknowledge that particular aspects of the past were far from ideal, Willa Cather was, if anything, a bit of a romantic. Especially in the final years of her life, an increasing note of anger about the emptiness
(60) of the present crept into her writings. Earlier generations, she concluded, had been the real heroes, the real creators of all that was good in America.

10. In the discussion of Willa Cather's *Sapphira and the Slave Girl*, the author refers to the book primarily as a

   (A) heroic tale of the Civil War
   (B) sweeping epic of the old South
   (C) story based on personal material
   (D) political treatise on slavery
   (E) veiled condemnation of 1930s America

11. In paragraph 2, Mandy Ringer and Dr. Clevenger are mentioned in order to emphasize which point about *Sapphira and the Slave Girl*?

   (A) A number of the characters in the novel are based on people Cather knew in her childhood.
   (B) The novel displays Cather's mixed feelings about slavery.
   (C) Cather took four years to complete the novel because she carefully researched her characters.
   (D) One of Cather's purposes in writing the novel was to paint a full portrait of life in rural Virginia in the years before the Civil War.
   (E) The characters in the novel are portrayed in a positive light since Cather was a great admirer of the old South.

12. In context, "a bit of a romantic" (line 57) suggests that Willa Cather

   (A) condemned the evils of slavery
   (B) favored the past over the present
   (C) disliked writing about life in the 1930s
   (D) denounced certain aspects of 19th-century life
   (E) exaggerated the evils of earlier generations

13. In English, you can tell whether a word is being used as a noun or a verb based on its placement in a sentence relative to other words. In the Slovak language, there are no placement rules; usage is determined by word endings. This is an example of a difference in

    (A) syntax
    (B) semantics
    (C) morphology
    (D) phonemes

14. The works of Charles Dickens, Harriet Beecher Stowe, and Upton Sinclair

    (A) examined 19th century cultural values
    (B) broke with the literary traditions of the past
    (C) fought against the mistreatment of the working class
    (D) awakened readers to social wrongs

15. The writing style used by Salman Rushdie and Gabriel Garcia Márquez is most often referred to as

    (A) Stream of Consciousness
    (B) Magical Realism
    (C) Socialist Realism
    (D) Minimalism

16. It is essential that we reject the proposed changes to the company's insurance plan. If we don't protest against these changes now, we'll soon end up with no health coverage at all.

    Which type of logical fallacy is demonstrated by this argument?

    (A) Slippery slope
    (B) Red herring
    (C) Strawman
    (D) Circular reasoning

Questions 17–18

Come live with me and be my Love,
And we will all the pleasures prove
That hills and valleys, dale and field,
And all the craggy mountains yield.

There will we sit upon the rocks
And see the shepherds feed their flocks,
By shallow rivers, to whose falls
Melodious birds sing madrigals.

There will I make thee beds of roses
And a thousand fragrant posies,
A cap of flowers, and a kirtle
Embroider'd all with leaves of myrtle.

A gown made of the finest wool
Which from our pretty lambs we pull,
Fair linèd slippers for the cold,
With buckles of the purest gold.

A belt of straw and ivy buds
With coral clasps and amber studs:
And if these pleasures may thee move,
Come live with me and be my Love.

Thy silver dishes for thy meat
As precious as the gods do eat,
Shall on an ivory table be
Prepared each day for thee and me.

The shepherd swains shall dance and sing
For thy delight each May-morning:
If these delights thy mind may move,
Then live with me and be my Love.

The Passionate Shepherd to his Love,
by Christopher Marlow

17. Which of the following is the most accurate classification of the poem?

    (A) Ballad
    (B) Ode
    (C) Pastoral
    (D) Dramatic monologue

18. Which of the following poetic devices are used in the first stanza of the poem?

    I. Alliteration
    II. Iambic pentameter
    III.   Hyperbole
    IV.   Personification

    (A) I and III only
    (B) I and IV only
    (C) III and IV only
    (D) I, II, and III only

19. Each of the 18 students in a graduate course is required to make a 15-minute presentation on a given topic. The professor has informed students that the use of effective nonverbal communication will make up a portion of the grade received on the presentation. Which of the following is the best example of effective nonverbal communication that a student should use during his or her presentation?

    (A) Maintaining eye contact with the professor
    (B) Using no notes
    (C) Standing still behind a podium
    (D) Establishing eye contact throughout the presentation with all members of the audience

20. Which of the following are key components of brainstorming?

    I. Organizing ideas
    II. Generating questions to be researched
    III.   Listing examples associated with a given topic
    IV.   Evaluating information

    (A) I and II only
    (B) II and III only
    (C) I, II, and IV only
    (D) I, II, III, and IV

21. Which of the following works of literature was originally written in Modern English?

    (A) *The Decameron*
    (B) *Sir Gawain and the Green Knight*
    (C) *War and Peace*
    (D) *Paradise Lost*

Questions 22–23

In the following passage, a nineteenth-century American writer recalls his boyhood in a small town along the Mississippi River.

My father was a justice of the peace, and I supposed he possessed the power of life and death over all men and could hang anybody that offended him. This was distinction
(5) enough for me as a general thing; but the desire to be a steamboatman kept intruding, nevertheless. I first wanted to be a cabin boy, so that I could come out with a white apron on and shake a tablecloth over the side, where
(10) all my old comrades could see me. Later I thought I would rather be the deck hand who stood on the end of the stage plank with a coil of rope in his hand, because he was particularly conspicuous.
(15) But these were only daydreams—too heavenly to be contemplated as real possibilities. By and by one of the boys went away. He was not heard of for a long time. At last he turned up as an apprentice engineer or
(20) "striker" on a steamboat. This thing shook the bottom out of all my Sunday-school teachings. That boy had been notoriously worldly and I had been just the reverse—yet he was exalted to this eminence, and I was left
(25) in obscurity and misery. There was nothing generous about this fellow in his greatness. He would always manage to have a rusty bolt to scrub while his boat was docked at our town, and he would sit on the inside guard
(30) and scrub it, where we could all see him and envy him and loathe him.

He used all sorts of steamboat technicalities in his talk, as if he were so used to them that he forgot common people could
(35) not understand them. He would speak of the "labboard" side of a horse in an easy, natural way that would make you wish he was dead. And he was always talking about "St. Looy" like an old citizen. Two or three of the boys
(40) had long been persons of consideration among us because they had been to St. Louis once and had a vague general knowledge of its wonders, but the day of their glory was over now. They lapsed into a humble silence,
(45) and learned to disappear when the ruthless "cub" engineer approached. This fellow had money, too, and hair oil, and he wore a showy brass watch chain, a leather belt, and used no suspenders. No girl could withstand his
(50) charms. He "cut out" every boy in the village. When his boat blew up at last, it diffused a tranquil contentment among us such as we had not known for months. But when he came home the next week, alive, renowned,
(55) and appeared in church all battered up and bandaged, a shining hero, stared at and wondered over by everybody, it seemed to us that the partiality of Providence for an undeserving reptile had reached a point
(60) where it was open to criticism.

This creature's career could produce but one result, and it speedily followed. Boy after boy managed to get on the river. Four sons of the chief merchant, and two sons of the
(65) county judge became pilots, the grandest position of all. But some of us could not get on the river—at least our parents would not let us.

So by and by I ran away. I said I would
(70) never come home again till I was a pilot and could return in glory. But somehow I could not manage it. I went meekly aboard a few of the boats that lay packed together like sardines at the long St. Louis wharf, and very
(75) humbly inquired for the pilots, but got only a cold shoulder and short words from mates and clerks. I had to make the best of this sort of treatment for the time being, but I had comforting daydreams of a future when I
(80) should be a great and honored pilot, with plenty of money, and could kill some of these mates and clerks and pay for them.

22. As used in line 4, the word *distinction* most nearly means

   (A) difference
   (B) variation
   (C) prestige
   (D) desperation
   (E) clarity

23. At the end of the passage, the author reflects on

   (A) his new ambition to become either a mate or a clerk
   (B) the wisdom of seeking a job in which advancement is easier
   (C) the prospect of abandoning a hopeless search for fame
   (D) the impossibility of returning home and asking his parents' pardon
   (E) his determination to keep striving for success in a glorious career

Questions 24–25

From the very beginning, at Tuskegee, I was determined to have the students do not only the agricultural and domestic work, but to have them erect their own buildings. My plan was to have them, while performing this service, taught the latest and best methods of labour, so that the school would not only get the benefit of their efforts, but the students themselves would be taught to see not only utility in labour, but beauty and dignity; would be taught, in fact, how to lift labour up from mere drudgery and toil, and would learn to love work for its own sake....

At first many advised against the experiment of having the buildings erected by the labour of the students, but I was determined to stick to it. I told those who doubted the wisdom of the plan that I knew that our first buildings would not be so comfortable or so complete in their finish as buildings erected by the experienced hands of outside workmen, but that in the teaching of civilization, self-help, and self-reliance, the erection of the buildings by the students themselves would more than compensate for any lack of comfort or fine finish.... Mistakes I knew would be made, but these mistakes would teach us valuable lessons for the future.

During the now nineteen years' existence of the Tuskegee school, the plan of having the buildings erected by student labour has been adhered to. In this time forty buildings, counting small and large, have been built, and all except four are almost wholly the product of student labour. As an additional result, hundreds of men are now scattered throughout the South who received their knowledge of mechanics while being taught how to erect these buildings. Skill and knowledge are now handed down from one set of students to another in this way, until at the present time a building of any description or size can be constructed wholly by our instructors and students, from the drawing of the plans to the putting in of the electric fixtures, without going off the grounds for a single workman.

Not a few times, when a new student has been led into the temptation of marring the looks of some building by leadpencil marks or by the cuts of a jack-knife, I have heard an old student remind him: "Don't do that. That is our building. I helped put it up."

From *Up from Slavery: An Autobiography*, by Booker T. Washington

24. Which of the following sentences from the passage provides an example, detail, or reason that directly supports the central argument of the passage?

(A) From the very beginning, at Tuskegee, I was determined to have the students do not only the agricultural and domestic work, but to have them erect their own buildings.

(B) At first many advised against the experiment of having the buildings erected by the labour of the students, but I was determined to stick to it.

(C) During the now nineteen years' existence of the Tuskegee school, the plan of having the buildings erected by student labour has been adhered to.

(D) As an additional result, hundreds of men are now scattered throughout the South who received their knowledge of mechanics while being taught how to erect these buildings.

25. Which of the following authors expressed direct disagreement with Booker T. Washington's views on education for African Americans?

(A) Toni Morrison
(B) Frederick Douglass
(C) W. E. B. DuBois
(D) Ishmael Reed

Questions 26–28

Hog Butcher for the World,
Tool Maker, Stacker of Wheat,
Player with Railroads and the Nation's
Freight Handler;
Stormy, husky, brawling,
City of the Big Shoulders:

They tell me you are wicked and I believe
them, for I have seen your painted women
under the gas lamps luring the farm boys.

And they tell me you are crooked and I
answer: Yes, it is true I have seen the
gunman kill and go free to kill again.

And they tell me you are brutal and my
reply is: On the faces of women and
children I have seen the marks of wanton
hunger.

And having answered so I turn once more to
those who sneer at this my city, and I give
them back the sneer and say to them:

Come and show me another city with lifted
head singing so proud to be alive and coarse
and strong and cunning.

Flinging magnetic curses amid the toil of
piling job on job, here is a tall bold slugger
set vivid against the little soft cities;

Fierce as a dog with tongue lapping for
action, cunning as a savage pitted against
the wilderness,

Bareheaded,
Shoveling,
Wrecking,
Planning,
Building, breaking, rebuilding,

Under the smoke, dust all over his mouth,
laughing with white teeth,

Under the terrible burden of destiny
laughing as a young man laughs,

Laughing even as an ignorant fighter laughs
who has never lost a battle,

Bragging and laughing that under his wrist
is the pulse, and under his ribs the heart of
the people,
Laughing!

Laughing the stormy, husky, brawling
laughter of Youth, half-naked, sweating,
proud to be Hog Butcher, Tool Maker,
Stacker of Wheat, Player with Railroads and
Freight Handler to the Nation.

Chicago, by Carl Sandburg

26. Which of the following most accurately
    identifies the form of this poem?

    (A) Blank verse
    (B) Ode
    (C) Narrative
    (D) Free verse

27. The line, "They tell me you are wicked and I
    believe them, for I have seen your painted
    women under the gas lamps luring the farm
    boys" is an example of which of the
    following?

    I. Apostrophe
    II. Personification
    III.   Hyperbole
    IV.   Metonymy

    (A) II only
    (B) I and II only
    (C) I, III, and IV only
    (D) II and IV only

28. This poem was most likely influenced by
    which of the following?

    (A) Industrialization
    (B) Increased immigration
    (C) Western expansion
    (D) World War II patriotism

Question 29

Everything was in confusion in the Oblonskys' house. The wife had discovered that the husband was carrying on an intrigue with a French girl, who had been a governess in their family, and she had announced to her husband that she could not go on living in the same house with him. This position of affairs had now lasted three days, and not only the husband and wife themselves, but all the members of their family and household, were painfully conscious of it. Every person in the house felt that there was no sense in their living together, and that the stray people brought together by chance in any inn had more in common with one another than they, the members of the family and household of the Oblonskys. The wife did not leave her own room; the husband had not been at home for three days. The children ran wild all over the house; the English governess quarreled with the housekeeper, and wrote to a friend asking her to look out for a new situation for her; the man-cook had walked off the day before just at dinner-time; the kitchen-maid, and the coachman had given warning.

Three days after the quarrel, Prince Stepan Arkadyevitch Oblonsky—Stiva, as he was called in the fashionable world—woke up at his usual hour, that is, at eight o'clock in the morning, not in his wife's bedroom, but on the leather-covered sofa in his study. He turned over his stout, well-cared-for person on the springy sofa, as though he would sink into a long sleep again; he vigorously embraced the pillow on the other side and buried his face in it; but all at once he jumped up, sat up on the sofa, and opened his eyes....

from *Anna Karenina*, by Leo Tolstoy

29. This excerpt is most likely from the novel's

(A) exposition
(B) rising action
(C) climax
(D) denouement

30. Which of the following authors are generally recognized as part of the Irish Renaissance?

I. William B. Yeats
II. Lady Gregory
III. James Joyce
IV. John M. Synge

(A) I and III only
(B) I, III, and IV only
(C) II and III only
(D) I, II, III, and IV

31. The poetry of Walt Whitman is significant in the development of American literature primarily because Whitman

(A) used the epic form to tell distinctly American tales
(B) developed his own poetic form and style instead of adhering to the traditional poetic forms
(C) commemorated in verse the lives of public leaders like Abraham Lincoln
(D) was heavily influenced by Emerson's call for a new national poet

English Question Bank
Answers and Explanations

1. D

The simple fact that the author cites Russell's definition is a clue that she considers it a good one. She also writes, "but one could do worse than…," which is an indirect way of showing her approval. In other words, she is saying that there are worse definitions than this [out there in the world]. Pithy means concise, to-the-point. (A) and (B) are the opposite case. The writer is not dismissive or skeptical. (C) is out-of-scope; loyalty is irrelevant to the discussion. And (E) is extreme. The writer seems positive, but *exuberant* implies high spirits that aren't consistent with the paragraph's tone.

2. C

Miller described his play as a "tragedy of the common man" because it gave the dramatic weight and importance once reserved for kings and warriors to a small and seemingly insignificant salesman. (A) is the definition of classical tragedy. "Important person" contradicts the "common man" of the question stem. (B) can be eliminated along with (A). Formal, classical tragedy was *never* about the "common man," so Miller's play must be something different. (D) may be tempting. The play is certainly serious, but it is not written in a poetic style. Also, this style independent of the subject matter is not what defines a tragedy.

3. A

Outlines can be thought of as nested boxes—sets and subsets. In a real outline, each step down would be indented, for easier reading. Here, you will have to read carefully to make sure you understand which item is a subset of which category. To eliminate incorrect answer choices, you should focus on the largest categories first to

see if there are any errors at this surface level. This can save you a great deal of reading time. In this example, the two broadest categories, labeled I and II, should be *plays* and *poems*. Everything Shakespeare wrote fits into these two general categories. Therefore, (B) and (C) can be eliminated right away without having to look any deeper. (D) is incorrect because *King Lear* is listed as a History play when it is a Tragedy. *Titus Andronicus* is listed as a Comedy when it is a Tragedy also.

4. D

The key word in this question stem is "must." As you know, not all poetry has to rhyme. Therefore, any answer choice that includes option III must be incorrect. That rules out (C). Free verse does not use a set rhythm. This rules out (A). (B) is tempting, but you should look back at the word "must." Do *all* poems really have to use metaphor? In fact, the only absolute, definitional requirement of poetry is that it be written in verse.

5. D

Each answer choice is an example of a different kind of logical fallacy. You should use the imagery in the name "slippery slope" to help you remember the fallacy. It is a fallacy of taking things to extremes—going too far (or taking one step and sliding all they way down the hill). (D) is the best example of this. (A) is an *ad hominem* fallacy, assigning an opinion to people based on their role or title. (B) is an "appeal to common practice" or "bandwagon"—other people do it, therefore it is acceptable. (C) is an example of "begging the question"—using the matter under question as the answer to the question.

6. C

Clues in the passage that can alert you to the answer include "you were my father, my creator," and "then cast me abroad an object for the scorn and horror of mankind." Clearly this is the monster speaking. (B) and (D) can be eliminated easily. There is nothing to indicate that a woman is speaking these lines; nor is there any hint that this is the author's voice instead of a character's. (A) may be confusing if you do not know the novel. However, the knowledge that everyone knows about *Frankenstein* includes the fact that the main character creates life—a monster. If you're familiar only with the Boris Karloff movie, you may be misled by the monster's eloquence. Yet, it is clearly he, not Victor, who is speaking.

7. B

This question may seem daunting to you if you have trouble deciphering older texts. However, the question is actually much easier than it first seems. You do not need to read each choice carefully. If you go back to the passage you will find that there are enough context clues in the sentences preceding the quoted text to help them quickly eliminate some wrong answer choices. The *orb* described here is the moon. If you go back to the passage you will see the moon referred to in the sentence before this quoted text. This should help you eliminate (A) and (D) right away. The cottage is also referred to in the preceding text, which will help you choose (B).

8. C

If you do not know much about Marxist theory or Samuel Beckett, you may feel hopeless in tackling this question, but you shouldn't. What is the "greatest hit" about Marxism, in terms of literary theory? It is that all relationships are power relationships, based on economic class standing. This points to either (A) or (C). Of the two, (C) is more closely aligned with Marxist ideas. (A) talks about class, but not about class conflict. (B) would correspond to Jungian or mythical analysis more than Marxist theory. (D) will seem tempting to you if you remember the basic plot

of *Godot*. However, this choice is more about the philosophical/existential interpretation of the play, and it has nothing to do with Marxist theory.

9. C

The incorrect use of "myself" is rampant in spoken English, and it may escape your notice. You should remember that "myself" is only to be used reflexively—when the speaker is both the subject *and* the object of the sentence (I gave myself a raise). In all other cases, "I" or "me" should be used. (C) is correct. (A) will seem tempting, but the use of numerals instead of words is not necessarily wrong. Typical style guidelines suggest spelling out numbers under ten. (B) is tempting. The sentences *could* be joined by a semicolon, but they are not incorrect as written. (D) is wrong. "Your" is possessive. The meaning here is "you are."

10. C

Paragraph 1 holds the answer. It tells us that *Sapphira* is one of Cather's most personal works and drew heavily on her childhood memories. The answer is almost certainly (C). With (A), paragraph 2 tells us that the novel is largely a portrait of the pre-Civil War South, and paragraph 3 tells us that *Sapphira* is mainly about slavery. With (B), there is nothing in the text to suggest that *Sapphira* is a sweeping epic. If anything, it's the opposite, a very personal novel. As for (D), this can't be right, because the first line in paragraph 4 says *Sapphira* is "not meant to be a political tract." And though (E) is less obviously wrong, it is still wrong. Also in paragraph 4, the author tells us Cather was dissatisfied with the present, but this is not the focus of her novel. (C) is the right answer.

11. D

Go back to paragraph 2 and see what's going on. The author mentions two characters who are included mainly to help complete Cather's portrait of rural Virginia.

(A) and (C) are discussed in paragraph 1. (B) is discussed in paragraph 3. (E) is an overstatement of the content in paragraph 4. (D) is a good match. Other answer choices might agree with points the author makes elsewhere in the passage, but this question asks specifically about paragraph 2.

12. B

The last paragraph refers to Cather as "a bit of a romantic" who cherished past creativity over the present emptiness. (A) can't be right, because the passage says Cather's views of slavery are "*ambiguous*." Ambiguous means "not clear; capable of being understood in two or more ways. With (C), nothing suggests Cather disliked writing about the 1930s. As for (D), Cather did dislike certain aspects of mid-19th-century life, but that's the opposite of romanticizing those times. And with (E), Cather didn't exaggerate the evils of the past; if anything, she underestimated them.

13. A

This question depends on some previous knowledge because it uses a lot of jargon in the answer choices. The correct answer is (A), syntax, which relates to the grammatical structure of a language. (B) relates to the meanings of individual words. (C) deals with the structure and formation of words, including such things as derivation and inflection. (D) refers to the smallest building blocks of languages—individual sounds.

14. D

In a comparison question like this, any answer choice that does not apply to *all* of the things being compared can immediately be eliminated. (A) can be eliminated because Upton Sinclair was a 20th century author. (B) can be eliminated because it does not apply to *any* of them. (C) can be eliminated because Harriet Beecher Stowe was concerned with the issue of slavery, not the working class. (D) is the only choice general enough to apply to all three authors.

15. B

You do not need to know *both* of these authors to get the correct answer. The question states that they share a writing style, so any answer that is correct for one *should* be correct for the other. Knowledge of either Márquez or Rushdie should point towards the phrase "Magical Realism." (A) applies more to turn-of-the-(last) century authors like James Joyce. (C) refers to artists of the Stalinist era in communist countries. The work was garishly realistic, touting science, technology, and the happy working classes. (D) can be eliminated by anyone who has even held a book written by either author. There is nothing minimalist about their writing. Quite the contrary.

16. A

The slippery slope argument involves reasoning that because of an initial event, a second, more extreme event must inevitable follow. In this example, the speaker argues that if any changes to the insurance plan are allowed (initial event), then it is inevitable that employees' health coverage will be terminated (second event). A red herring (B) involves the introduction of an irrelevant issue to an argument. The strawman fallacy (C) involves distorting a position taken in an argument. Circular reasoning (D) involves using the conclusion of an argument as evidence to prove the validity of the argument.

17. C

A pastoral poem is characterized by a simplicity of thought and action in a rural, rustic setting. The shepherd's desire to please his love with the beauty of this rural setting categorizes this as a pastoral poem. A ballad, (A), refers to a narrative poem that was originally sung. This is a lyric poem. An ode, (B), would typically deal with a more serious or elevated topic than this poem does. A dramatic monologue, (D), is also a narrative poem.

18. A

Alliteration is used in phrases like "pleasures prove." The statement that "we will all the pleasures prove" can be classified as a hyperbole or exaggeration for effect. This makes (A) the best answer. (II) can be eliminated because iambic pentameter requires ten beats per measure. The first line of this poem has eight beats. By eliminating (II), test takers can also eliminate (D). Personification (IV) is not used in the first stanza, so (B) and (C) can also be eliminated.

19. D

In a small group setting such as this, establishing eye contact with several or all members of the audience is an effective way of maintaining the audience's focus on the presentation. Maintaining eye contact with only the professor (A) will not encourage the other students to focus on the presentation. Although eye contact is important, it is not necessary to give a presentation of this length without the use of brief notes (B). In fact, it is usually a good idea for a speaker to have brief notes to refer to in order to convey all of the information planned for a presentation. Standing behind a podium can provide a focal point for the audience, but hand gestures should be used as an additional method of nonverbal communication.

20. B

Brainstorming and freewriting are steps taken at the very beginning of the writing process. In this step, the goal is to generate as many ideas or questions related to a given topic as possible. During brainstorming and freewriting, it is important to focus only on generating ideas, not evaluating or organizing those ideas. These steps come later in the writing process.

21. D

Although you might not know the exact dates of the publication of Milton's *Paradise Lost* (1667) and the beginning of Modern English (1500s), you can get to the answer through elimination. (A) can be eliminated because *The Decameron* was written in Italian in the 1300s. (B) is an Arthurian tale written in Old English. You should be able to identify Leo Tolstoy as the author of *War and Peace* (C); it was originally written in Russian.

22. C

Distinction has several meanings, including those in (A), (B), (C), and (E). The key to its use here is context: In the previous sentence the author is talking about his naive ideas of his father's great power. (C) *prestige*, suggesting high status and honor, fits this context; the other three don't. (D) *desparation*, is not a meaning of *distinction* at all.

23. E

The last paragraph discusses the author's failed attempts to become a pilot, and his daydreams that he will still become one, so (E) works best. Mates and clerks are mentioned as ignoring the author, but he never considers becoming either a (A) mate or a clerk, looking for some other job (B), giving up his aim of being a pilot (C), or asking his parents' forgiveness (D).

24. D

The central argument of this passage is that having the students construct the buildings at the Tuskegee school would benefit the students by teaching them "civilization, self-help, and self-reliance." Only (D) provides a direct example of how students were benefited by constructing the buildings. Many of the students went on to learn a trade in mechanics through their work on the buildings.

25. C

During the early 1900s, W. E. B. DuBois argued against Booker T. Washington's strategies for improving the lives of African Americans. In *The Souls of Black Folk*, DuBois argued that Washington's methods focused on economic advancement at the expense of social equality. After the Civil War, Frederick Douglass (B) had made efforts to create opportunities for former slaves to learn technical trades. Douglass' efforts greatly influenced Washington. Toni Morrison (A) and Ishmael Reed (D) are contemporary African American authors.

26. D

A free verse poem has no formal pattern or structure of rhythm or rhyme. A blank verse poem (A) is not rhymed, but it is written in iambic pentameter. (*Paradise Lost* is an example of blank verse.) An ode (B) is typically a much more formal poem. Although this poem praises Chicago, it is more accurate to describe the poem as free verse than as an ode. A narrative poem (C) tells a story with identified characters and action.

27. B

The "you" in this line is Chicago itself. This is a form of apostrophe, an address to a person or thing that is incapable of answering. It is also a form of personification. Sandburg gives the city human qualities, such as wickedness. Hyperbole is extreme exaggeration. Metonymy replaces a person or thing with a word closely associated with that person or thing. For example, "no news from the White House" indicates that the president has not released a statement.

28. A

This poem was written during the early 1900s, a time when Midwestern cities such as Chicago, Kansas City, and St. Louis experienced increased industrialization and population growth. Descriptions such as "Hog Butcher, Tool Maker, Stacker of Wheat" indicate that industrialization of Chicago influenced this poem. A poem from the mid 1800s would be more likely to have been influenced by the western expansion (C). Sandburg wrote and published this poem before World War II (D).

29. A

The exposition of a work of fiction provides important background information about characters, setting, etc. In this excerpt, Stiva Oblonsky is introduced for the first time. The conflict is also introduced in this excerpt. Rising action (B) involves the building of a conflict. The climax (C) is the highest point of the conflict. The denouement (D) is the resolution of the conflict.

30. D

The Irish Renaissance spans the late 19th and early 20th centuries. During this period, many Irish writers revived Irish folklore and legends in their works. Lady Gregory is best known for her recordings of folklore and her work in establishing the Abbey Theater. William B. Yeats, who wrote the poems "The Second Coming" and "Sailing to Byzantium," was generally thought of as the leader of the Irish Renaissance. James Joyce, famous for his stream of consciousness prose in *Ulysses*, was also an Irish writer during this time period. John M. Synge wrote plays, such as *The Playboy of the Western World*, that were performed at the Abbey Theater.

31. B

Whitman's *Leaves of Grass* is a sharp departure from the metered, traditional poetic forms. In the introduction to this work, Whitman writes that "the expression of the American poet is to be transcendent and new." Whitman popularized free verse, and his work influenced later poets such as Wallace Stevens and Allen Ginsberg. Whitman did not use the epic form (A). Although Whitman did write of Lincoln's death in *O Captain! My Captain!* (C), this is not his most significant contribution to the development of American literature. Similarly, Whitman was deeply influenced by Emerson, (D), but this influence is not his key contribution to the development of American literature.

CHAPTER EIGHT

MATHEMATICS

In this section we will cover several key concepts in the Mathematics Subject Assessments including a question bank of relevant Mathematics questions. Several tests are not included below because they do not conform to the multiple-choice format of the question bank that follows. Nonetheless, much of the content covered in the question bank that follows is addressed on other PRAXIS II Mathematics subject tests.

PRAXIS II MATHEMATICS SUBJECT TESTS

This section applies to you if you are taking one of the following tests:

- Mathematics: Content Knowledge (0061)

Mathematics: Content Knowledge (0061)

Test Format: 50 multiple-choice questions

Test Duration: 2 hours

- Arithmetic and Basic Algebra, Geometry, Trigonometry, and Analytic Geometry: 17 questions, 34 percent of the test
- Functions and their Graphs, Calculus: 12 questions, 24 percent of the test
- Probability and Statistics, Discrete Mathematics, Linear Algebra, Computer Science, and Mathematical Reasoning and Modeling: 21 questions, 42 percent of the test

This test is designed to assess the mathematical knowledge and ability of an examinee interested in teaching mathematics at a secondary school level. The mathematical content covered conforms to the curriculum, evaluation, and professional standards of the National Council of Teachers of Mathematics. The content on this test focuses on problem solving, communication, reasoning, and mathematical connections.

As you can see, the range of Mathematical knowledge tested varies from test to test. However, there is significant overlap between the Mathematics (0060) test and the Mathematics: Content Knowledge (0061) tests. The question bank that follows begins with a review of the basic formulas and symbols associated with these tests. It is then followed by a question bank testing many of the concepts that might appear on either of these tests.

Note: The Question Bank that follows is not designed to be a simulation of a PRAXIS II subject test. Rather, it is a study aid that should acquaint you with many of the concepts tested on the Mathematics (0060) and Mathematics: Content Knowledge (0061) tests.

For both tests, you are permitted to use a calculator. For the Mathematics: Content Knowledge (0061) test, you are required to use a graphing calculator.

Mathematics Question Bank

1. Provide a complete solution set for the equation $x^3 + 25 = 33$.

   (A) $\{2, 1 + \sqrt{3}i, 1 - \sqrt{3}i\}$
   (B) $\{2, -1 + \sqrt{3}i, -1 - \sqrt{3}i\}$
   (C) $\{-2, 1 + 2\sqrt{3}i, 1 - 2\sqrt{3}i\}$
   (D) $\{-2, 2 + 2\sqrt{3}, 2 - 2\sqrt{3}\}$

2. Identify the inflection point(s) of the curve $f(x) = x^3 - 12x^2 + 21x + 4$

   (A) $(4, -40)$
   (B) $(0, 4)$
   (C) $(1, 0), (7, 0)$
   (D) $(1, 14), (7, -94)$

3. If the function $f(x) = \dfrac{1}{(1 - |\sin x|)}$ is graphed for all x such that $-2\pi < x < 2\pi$, how many asymptotes are there?

   (A) 2
   (B) 3
   (C) 4
   (D) 6

4. What is the sum of the coefficients for the expansion of $(x + y)^8$?

   (A) 10
   (B) 254
   (C) 256
   (D) 264

5. Find the first term, a_1, of a geometric sequence where the common ratio is $\dfrac{1}{3}$ and the sum of the first six terms is 10,920.

   (A) 4,860
   (B) 6,075
   (C) 7,290
   (D) 8,505

6. What is the equation of an ellipse centered at $(6, -4)$ with a major axis of 18 that is parallel to the y–axis and a minor axis of 14 that is parallel to the x–axis?

   (A) $\dfrac{(y+4)^2}{81} + \dfrac{(x-6)^2}{49} = 1$
   (B) $\dfrac{(y-4)^2}{81} + \dfrac{(x+6)^2}{49} = 1$
   (C) $\dfrac{(y+4)^2}{324} + \dfrac{(x-6)^2}{196} = 1$
   (D) $\dfrac{(y-4)^2}{324} + \dfrac{(x+6)^2}{196} = 1$

7. What is the approximate area under the curve of $f(x) = \dfrac{1}{x}$ from 1 to 10?

   (A) 2.30
   (B) 2.93
   (C) 3.17
   (D) 3.44

8. Suppose that $f(x) = e^{2x}$ and $g(x) = 2x^2 - 7x + 6$. If $g(f(x)) = 0$, what is the solution set?

   (A) $\{1.5, 2\}$

   (B) $\left\{\dfrac{\ln 1.5}{2}, \dfrac{-\ln 2}{2}\right\}$

   (C) $\left\{\dfrac{\ln 1.5}{2}, \dfrac{\ln 2}{2}\right\}$

   (D) $\{\ln 1.5, \ln 2\}$

9. Which of the following is not a continuous function where $\mathbb{R}$ is mapped into $\mathbb{R}$?

   (A) $f(x) = x^2$
   (B) $f(x) = \sin(e^x)$
   (C) $f(x) = e^{\cos x}$
   (D) $f(x) = \sec(x)$

10. Find the inverse of the following matrix:
    $$Z = \begin{vmatrix} 4 & 2 \\ 5 & 3 \end{vmatrix}$$

    (A) $\begin{vmatrix} 3 & -2 \\ -5 & 4 \end{vmatrix}$

    (B) $\begin{vmatrix} \dfrac{3}{2} & -1 \\ \dfrac{-5}{2} & 2 \end{vmatrix}$

    (C) $\begin{vmatrix} \dfrac{1}{4} & \dfrac{1}{2} \\ \dfrac{1}{5} & \dfrac{1}{3} \end{vmatrix}$

    (D) $\begin{vmatrix} -4 & -2 \\ -5 & -3 \end{vmatrix}$

11. A coin is flipped nine times. What is the probability that heads will be flipped at least three times?

    (A) $\dfrac{23}{256}$

    (B) $\dfrac{123}{512}$

    (C) $\dfrac{389}{512}$

    (D) $\dfrac{233}{256}$

12. If a cube with edges of 12 is divided into 27 smaller cubes of equal size and each of the smaller cubes contains a sphere whose volume occupies the maximum possible space, what is the total surface area of the spheres?

    (A) 288π
    (B) 384π
    (C) 432π
    (D) 648π

13. Find $\dfrac{d}{dx} \dfrac{x \ln x}{\sin(\ln x)}$

    (A) $\dfrac{(\sin(\ln x)(1 + \ln x) - x(\ln x)(\cos(\ln x))}{\sin^2(\ln x)}$

    (B) $\dfrac{(\sin(\ln x)(1 + \ln x) - (\ln x)(\cos(\ln x))}{\sin^2(\ln x)}$

    (C) $\dfrac{\dfrac{1}{x}}{\cos(\ln x)}$

    (D) $\dfrac{(1 + \ln x)}{\cos(\ln x)}$

14. Consider the function $f(x) = e^{2x}$. If the area under the curve between $x = 1$ and $x = 3$ is rotated around the x–axis, what will be the volume of the solid?

    (A) $\dfrac{\pi e^4}{4} \cdot (e^3 - 1)$

    (B) $\dfrac{\pi e^2}{3} \cdot (e^4 - 1)$

    (C) $\pi e^2 \cdot (e^4 - 1)$

    (D) $\dfrac{4\pi}{3} \cdot (e^{18} - e^6)$

15. Find the inverse of the function $f(x) = \ln \cos (3x - 2) + 3$

    (A) $f^{-1}(x) = \dfrac{\arccos(e^{x-3}) + 2}{3}$

    (B) $f^{-1}(x) = \dfrac{(e^x) - \arccos 3 + 2}{3}$

    (C) $f^{-1}(x) = \dfrac{\arccos(e^{3x-2})}{3}$

    (D) $f^{-1}(x) = \arccos(e^{2x-3}) + 1$

16. If $\log_{16}(x) + \log_4(2x) = 5$, what is the value of x?

    (A) 16
    (B) 32
    (C) 64
    (D) 128

17. $\displaystyle\int \cot(x)\,dx =$

    (A) $\tan(x)\sec(x) + C$
    (B) $\ln|\sin(x)| + C$
    (C) $-\csc(\ln(x)) + C$
    (D) $\ln|\csc(x)| + C$

18. In a circle, one side of a right triangle is constructed by choosing a random point on the circumference of the circle and drawing a line from that point to the other side that passes through the center of the circle. If the area of the circle is 36π and one of the angles in the triangle is 34 degrees, what is the triangle's approximate area?

    (A) 26.6
    (B) 33.4
    (C) 38.9
    (D) 56.5

19. Working alone, Sam, Fred, Ernest, and Jacqueline each take 24, 20, 16, and 15 hours, respectively, to paint a house. All four start working together on the same job, but Ernest quits after 2 hours. If Sam, Fred, and Jacqueline finish the job, how many hours did it take the group to paint the house?

    (A) $\dfrac{20}{7}$

    (B) $\dfrac{22}{7}$

    (C) $\dfrac{67}{19}$

    (D) $\dfrac{105}{19}$

20. What is the equation of the line perpendicular to $f(x) = -\frac{1}{4}x + 8$ that goes through the point $(20, 3)$?

(A) $f(x) = 4x - 77$

(B) $f(x) = \frac{1}{4}x - 2$

(C) $f(x) = 2x - 37$

(D) $f(x) = \frac{1}{2}x - 7$

21. A student draws marbles from a bag containing 6 blue marbles, 5 red marbles, and 10 green marbles. If the marbles are selected without replacement, what is the smallest number of marbles that the student must draw to have at least a 50% chance of having drawn a blue marble?

(A) 2

(B) 5

(C) 9

(D) 10

22. The function $f(x) = x^3 - \frac{1}{2}x^2 - 2x + 2$ has maxima and minima at what points?

(A) $\left(\frac{2}{3}, \frac{20}{27}\right), \left(1, \frac{1}{2}\right)$

(B) $\left(\frac{2}{3}, \frac{20}{27}\right), \left(-1, \frac{5}{2}\right)$

(C) $\left(-\frac{2}{3}, \frac{76}{27}\right), \left(1, \frac{1}{2}\right)$

(D) $\left(-\frac{2}{3}, \frac{76}{27}\right), \left(-1, \frac{5}{2}\right)$

23. Solve the following equation for all values of x in the interval $[0, 2\pi]$.

$$\sin^2 x + \frac{1}{2}\sin x = \frac{1}{2}$$

(A) $\frac{3\pi}{2}, \frac{\pi}{6}, \frac{5\pi}{6}$

(B) $\frac{\pi}{2}, \frac{11\pi}{6}, \frac{\pi}{4}$

(C) $\frac{\pi}{2}, \frac{\pi}{6}, \frac{5\pi}{6}$

(D) $\frac{\pi}{4}, \frac{3\pi}{4}, \frac{11\pi}{6}$

24. $\lim\limits_{n \to \infty} (1 + \frac{1}{n})^n$

(A) 1

(B) $2n$

(C) e

(D) n^2

25. A rectangular prism has dimensions of $10 \times 5 \times 10$. If the longest diagonal between two points in the prism is used as the radius of a sphere, what is the surface area of the sphere?

(A) 675π

(B) 900π

(C) $3{,}375\pi$

(D) $4{,}500\pi$

Mathematics Question Bank
Answers and Explanations

1. B $\{2, -1 + \sqrt{3}i, -1 - \sqrt{3}i\}$

Strategy: Step-by-Step

$x^3 + 25 = 33$

$x^3 - 8 = 0$

$(x - 2)(x^2 + 2x + 4) = 0$

Therefore, one root is 2.

Using the quadratic formula on the second factor:

$$\frac{-2 + \sqrt{4 - 16}}{}, \frac{-2 - \sqrt{4 - 16}}{}$$

$$\frac{-2 + 2\sqrt{-3}}{}, \frac{-2 - 2\sqrt{-3}}{}$$

$$2, -1 + \sqrt{3}i, -1 - \sqrt{3}i$$

2. A $(4, -40)$

Strategy: Step-by-Step

To determine the inflection point(s), if any exist, the second derivative test must be applied. Set the second derivative equal to zero to find values of x. These values will be the points where the curve changes from facing up to facing down or vice–versa.

If $f(x) = x^3 - 12x^2 + 21x + 4$, then $f(x) = 3x^2 - 24x + 21$.

If $f(x) = 3x^2 - 24x + 21$, then $f(x) = 6x - 24$

If $6x - 24 = 0$, $x = 4$

At $x = 4$, $f(x) = -40$.

3. C 4

Strategy: Picking Numbers

The function will be undefined at any value of x where $|\sin x| = 1$. Over the interval $[-2\pi, 2\pi]$, there are four values of x where the sine of x will be either 1 or –1. These values are $(\frac{-3\pi}{2}, \frac{-\pi}{2}, \frac{\pi}{2}, \frac{3\pi}{2})$.

4. C 256

Strategy: Cut the Jargon

The sum of the coefficients in any standard binomial expansion $(x + y)^n$ is 2^n. Here, $n = 8$. The sum of the coefficients is $2^8 = 256$.

5. C 7,290

Strategy: Backsolving

Although the formula for the sum of a geometric ratio can be used, it is easier in this case to pick an answer and test the choices. Try answer (B) first.

$6,075 + 2,025 + 675 + 225 + 75 + 15 = 9,090$. Too small: try the next largest.

$7,290 + 2,430 + 810 + 270 + 90 + 30 = 10,920$. Correct.

6. A $\dfrac{(y + 4)^2}{81} + \dfrac{(x - 6)^2}{49} = 1$

Strategy: Cut the Jargon

Put the ellipse into its standard form, distinguishing between the major and minor axes.

7. A 2.30

Strategy: Cut the Jargon

The area under the curve will be the integral of the function over the interval [1,10].

$$\int \frac{1}{x}\, dx = \ln x \,\Big|_{1}^{10}$$

$\ln(10) \approx 2.30$

$\ln(1) = 0$

$2.30 - 0 = 2.30$

8. C $\left(\dfrac{\ln 1.5}{2}, \dfrac{\ln 2}{2}\right)$

Strategy: Step-by-Step

Substituting one function into the other,

$2(e^{2x})^2 - 7(e^{2x}) + 6 = 0$

$2e^{4x} - 7e^{2x} + 6 = 0$

$(2e^{2x} - 3)(e^{2x} - 2) = 0$

Therefore, $e^{2x} = 1.5$ or $e^{2x} = 2$

$2x = \ln 1.5$, or $2x = \ln 2$

$x = \dfrac{\ln 1.5}{2}$, or $x = \dfrac{\ln 2}{2}$

9. D $f(x) = \sec(x)$

Strategy: Cut the Jargon

For a function to be continuously mapped from a domain to a range, all members of the domain must have a corresponding value in the range. Because $\sec(x)$ is undefined at $\dfrac{\pi}{2}$ as well as other values, it cannot be continuous.

10. B $\begin{vmatrix} \dfrac{3}{2} & -1 \\ \dfrac{-5}{2} & 2 \end{vmatrix}$

Strategy: Step–by–Step or Backsolving

The inverse of a matrix is done as follows:

$$\begin{vmatrix} a & b \\ c & d \end{vmatrix} = \frac{1}{\text{determinant}} \times \begin{vmatrix} d & -b \\ -c & a \end{vmatrix}$$

The determinant of the 2 by 2 matrix $= ad - bc$. The determinant of the matrix in this question is $(4)(3) - (2)(5) = 2$

Rearranging and multiplying by the determinant, you get the correct answer.

One may also multiply the answer choices by the given matrix and determine which product gives the identity matrix.

11. D $\dfrac{233}{256}$

Strategy: Step-by-Step

If a coin is flipped nine times, the total sample space is $2^9 = 512$.

Flipping at least three heads encompasses the possibility of flipping three, four, five, six, seven, eight, and nine heads. It is easier in this case to calculate the probability of this not happening, and then subtract from 1.

$${}_9C_2 \binom{9}{2} = \frac{9!}{2!7!} = 36$$

$${}_9C_1 \binom{9}{1} = \frac{9!}{1!8!} = 9$$

$${}_9C_0 \binom{9}{0} = \frac{9!}{0!9!} = 1$$

The probability of failure is $= \dfrac{46}{512} = \dfrac{23}{256}$.

Therefore, $Pr(H > 3) = 1 - \dfrac{23}{256} = \dfrac{233}{256}$.

12. C 432π

Strategy: Step–by–Step

If the cube is being divided into 27 smaller cubes, the change in the dimensions will be the cube root of $\frac{1}{27}$ (the scale factor), or $\frac{1}{3}$.

Because each cube will have edges of $12 \times \frac{1}{3} = 4$, the radius of the largest sphere that can fit in the smaller cubes is 2. The formula for the surface area of a sphere is $4\pi r^2$; $4\pi(2)^2 = 16\pi$. Because there are 27 cubes, $27 \times 16\pi = 432\pi$.

13. B $\dfrac{\sin(\ln x)(1 + \ln x) - (\ln x)(\cos(\ln x))}{\sin^2(\ln x)}$

Strategy: Step-by-Step

The derivative rule for quotients states:

$$\frac{d}{dx}\left(\frac{u}{v}\right) = \frac{v\dfrac{du}{dx} - u\dfrac{dv}{dx}}{v^2}$$

In addition, you need to follow the chain rule.

14. A $\dfrac{\pi e^4}{4} \cdot (e^3 - 1)$

Strategy: Step-by-Step

The distance between the curve and the x–axis will be the radius of a single circle. Because the formula for the area of a circle is πr^2, a differential volume element is $\pi[f(x_k)]^2(\Delta x)_k$. The volume is

$$\int_3^1 \pi(e^{2x})^2 dx = \int_3^1 \pi e^{4x} dx = \frac{\pi e^{4x}}{4}\bigg|_1^3$$

$$\frac{\pi e^{12} - \pi e^4}{4} = \frac{\pi e^4(e^3 - 1)}{4}$$

15. A $f^{-1}(x) = \dfrac{\arccos(e^{x-3}) + 2}{3}$

Strategy: Step-by-Step

To solve for the inverse function, simply solve the original equation for the domain in terms of the range.

$f(x) = \ln \cos (3x - 2) + 3$

$f(x) - 3 = \ln \cos (3x - 2)$

$e^{f(x) - 3} = \cos(3x - 2)$

$\arccos (e^{f(x) - 3}) = 3x - 2$

$\arccos (e^{f(x) - 3}) + 2 = 3x$

$\dfrac{\arccos (e^{f(x) - 3}) + 2}{3} = x = f^{-1}(x)$

so, $f^{-1}(x) = \dfrac{\arccos(e^{x-3}) + 2}{3}$

16. C 64

Strategy: Backsolving

Plugging in (B) as the middle answer choice,

$\log_{16}(32) + \log_4(64) = 1.25 + 3 = 4.25$. Incorrect.

Plugging in (C)

$\log_{16}(64) + \log_4(128) = 1.5 + 3.5 = 5$. Correct.

To solve this question algebraically, use the identity $\log_a c = (\log_a b)(\log_b c)$.

Here $\log_{16} x = \log_{16} 4\log_4 x = \frac{1}{2}\log_4 x$

So $\log_{16} x + \log_4 2x = 5$ becomes

$\frac{1}{2}\log_4 x + \log_4 2x = 5$.

Solve this equation for x.

$\log_4 x^{\frac{1}{2}} + \log_4 2x = 5$

$\log_4 (x^{\frac{1}{2}})(2x) = 5$

$\log_4 2x^{\frac{3}{2}} = 5$

$$2x^{\frac{3}{2}} = 4^5$$
$$2x^{\frac{3}{2}} = (2^2)^5$$
$$2x^{\frac{3}{2}} = 2^{10}$$
$$x^{\frac{3}{2}} = 2^9$$
$$x^{\frac{1}{2}} = (2^9)^{\frac{1}{3}}$$
$$x^{\frac{1}{2}} = 2^3$$
$$x = 8^2$$
$$x = 64$$

17. B $\ln|\sin(x)| + C$

Strategy: Step-by-Step

By knowing that the cotangent function is equivalent to the cosine divided by the sine, the problem can be rewritten as $\int \frac{\sin x}{\cos x}$. Applying the chain rule, where $u = \sin x$ and $\frac{du}{dx} = \cos x$, $\int \frac{1}{u} \frac{du}{dx}$ $= \ln|4|+C$. Substituting, one gets the designated answer.

18. B 33.4

Strategy: Step-by-Step

If the area of the circle is 36π, the radius is 6; therefore, the diameter must be 12 (which is equivalent to the hypotenuse of the triangle). The side opposite the 34 degree angle can be calculated as $12 \times \sin(34)$. The side adjacent to the 34 degree angle can be calculated as $12\cos(34)$. Plugging into the formula for the area of a triangle, $A = \frac{1}{2}bh \approx 33.4$.

19. D $\frac{105}{19}$

Strategy: Step-by-Step

Since all four people work on the same job, their cumulative rate is equal to:

$$\text{Rate} = \frac{1}{24} + \frac{1}{20} + \frac{1}{16} + \frac{1}{15}$$
$$= \frac{10}{240} + \frac{12}{240} + \frac{15}{240} + \frac{16}{240}$$
$$= \frac{53}{240}$$

All four complete in two hours: $\frac{53}{240} \times 2 = \frac{53}{120}$.

There will be $\frac{67}{120}$ of the job remaining. After Ernest quits, the new rate will be:

$$\frac{1}{24} + \frac{1}{20} + \frac{1}{15} = \frac{38}{240} = \frac{19}{120}$$
$$\frac{19}{120} \times \text{time remaining} = 1 - \frac{53}{120} = \frac{67}{120}$$
$$\text{time remaining} = \frac{67}{19}$$

The total numbers of hours the group spent to paint the house was $\frac{67}{19} + 2 = \frac{105}{19}$.

20. A $f(x) = 4x - 77$

Strategy: Cut the Jargon

Because the slope of a perpendicular line is the negative reciprocal of the original, (A) is the only choice.

21. A 2

Strategy: Step-by-Step

Because we are looking for when the probability of having drawn a blue marble climbs above 50%, it is easier to calculate the cumulative probability of when not drawing a blue marble hits 50% or below.

First draw: $\dfrac{15}{21}$ (the number of marbles that are not blue divided by the total)

Cumulative probability: $\dfrac{5}{7}$

Larger than $\dfrac{1}{2}$, keep going.

Second draw: $\dfrac{14}{20} = \dfrac{7}{10}$

Cumulative probability: $\dfrac{5}{7} \times \dfrac{7}{10} = \dfrac{1}{2}$

At least two marbles are needed to drive the cumulative probability of drawing a blue marble to 50% or above.

22. C $\left(-\dfrac{2}{3}, \dfrac{76}{27}\right), \left(1, \dfrac{1}{2}\right)$

Strategy: Step-by-Step

The maxima and minima are determined by setting the first derivative equal to zero.

$$f(x) = x^3 - \frac{1}{2}x^2 - 2x + 2$$

$$f'(x) = 3x^2 - x - 2 = 0$$

$$(3x + 2)(x - 1) = 0$$

The x-values are $-\dfrac{2}{3}$ and 1; just plug into the original function to get the y-values.

23. A $\dfrac{3\pi}{2}, \dfrac{\pi}{6}, \dfrac{5\pi}{6}$

Strategy: Step-by-Step

$$\sin^2(x) + \frac{1}{2}\sin(x) = \frac{1}{2}$$

$$\sin^2(x) + \frac{1}{2}\sin(x) - \frac{1}{2} = 0$$

$$(\sin(x) + 1)(\sin(x) - \frac{1}{2}) = 0$$

$$\sin(x) = -1 \text{ or } \sin(x) = \frac{1}{2}$$

Therefore, in the interval $[0, 2\pi]$, $\sin\dfrac{3\pi}{2} = -1$, $\sin\dfrac{\pi}{6} = \dfrac{1}{2}$, and $\sin\dfrac{5\pi}{6} = \dfrac{1}{2}$. So all the possible values of x are $\dfrac{3\pi}{2}, \dfrac{\pi}{6}$, and $\dfrac{5\pi}{6}$.

24. C e

Strategy: Cut the Jargon

This is the definition of e.

25. B 900π

Strategy: Step-by-Step

In a rectangular prism with dimensions $10 \times 5 \times 10$, calculating the long diagonal requires calculating the diagonal of the base and then using that value for the main calculation. Assume that 10 and 5 represent length and width. Using the Pythagorean theorem

$$10^2 + 5^2 = d^2$$
$$d = \sqrt{125} = 5\sqrt{5}$$
$$(5\sqrt{5})^2 + 10^2 = 225$$
$$\text{long diagonal} = 15$$
$$\text{Surface area} = 4\pi(15)^2 = 900\pi$$

CHAPTER NINE

SOCIAL STUDIES

In this section, we will cover several key concepts in Social Studies Subject Assessment. A brief summary of some of the relevant tests will be followed by a question bank of Social Studies questions. Depending on the test you are preparing for, some questions will apply to you.

PRAXIS II SOCIAL STUDIES SUBJECT TESTS

This section applies to you if you are taking one of the following tests:

- Social Studies: Content Knowledge (0081)
- Social Studies: Analytical Essays (0082)

Overview of Social Studies: Content Knowledge (0081)

Test Format: 130 multiple-choice questions
Test Duration: 2 hours

Content Covered:
- United States History: 29 questions, 22 percent of the test
- World History: 29 questions, 22 percent of the test
- Government/Civics/Political Science: 21 questions, 16 percent of the test
- Geography: 19 questions, 15 percent of the test
- Economics: 19 questions, 15 percent of the test
- Behavioral Sciences: 13 questions, 10 percent of the test

This test is designed to assess whether an examinee has the skills and knowledge necessary to teach social studies at a secondary school level. The test draws from a wide range of social science content areas with special emphasis on United States and World History. The question bank that follows includes questions from each of the content areas described above and is a useful study aid in preparation for this test.

Overview of Social Studies: Analytical Essays (0082)

Test Format: 2 essay questions
Test Duration: 1 hour

Content Covered:

- United States: History or Contemporary Issues: 1 essay, 50% of the test
- World: History or Contemporary Issues, 1 essay, 50% of the test

The Social Studies: Analytical Essays (0082) test is designed to test the knowledge and skills necessary for a secondary school social studies teacher. The test consists of two essay questions requiring analysis of contemporary and historical issues, an understanding of interdisciplinary relationships, and the synthesis and integration of information within an analytical essay. Questions may require the ability to make comparisons and contrasts, synthesize a wide body of knowledge, or argue one side of an issue.

Although the question bank that follows does not contain sample essay questions, the content areas covered are consistent with the topics you may encounter on the essay test. Therefore, in preparation for this test, it is worthwhile to review the basic writing skills discussed in the PPST Writing Review in tandem with the content covered in the Social Studies question bank that follows.

Social Studies Question Bank

1. A drop in interest rates will most likely lead to which of the following pairs of trends?

   (A) Increased debt, increased home ownership

   (B) Decreased debt, decreased home ownership

   (C) Increased debt, decreased home ownership

   (D) Decreased debt, increased home ownership

2. The purpose of the Dawes Act passed by the U.S. Congress in 1887 was to encourage Native Americans to

   (A) live on reservations

   (B) adopt European Americans' style of dress, culture, and religion

   (C) cease their efforts to retake the Great Plains region

   (D) abandon tribal ways and have privately owned land

3. A researcher studying the motives behind the dropping of the atomic bomb on Japan in World War II would find which of the following types of resources most useful?

   I. Novels
   II. Primary sources
   III.   Encyclopedias
   IV.   Online resources

   (A) I and II only

   (B) I and IV only

   (C) II and III only

   (D) II and IV only

4. The partition in Pakistan in 1947 resulted most directly from which of the following circumstances?

   (A) Oppression of Muslims in India by the presiding British government

   (B) Laws depriving Hindus of the right to vote

   (C) Demands of Muslim nationalists in India for an independent state

   (D) Conditions placed by the British government on Indian independence

5. The Code of Hammurabi and the Justinian Code of the Byzantine Empire were similar in that they both

   (A) were some of the earliest expressions of basic democratic rights

   (B) provided a consistent rule of law

   (C) became blueprints for religious doctrine

   (D) dictated very strict guidelines for trade

6. Which of the following features was developed most fully during the American colonial period?

   (A) Universal suffrage

   (B) Representative assemblies

   (C) An independent court system

   (D) Separation between church and state

Questions 7–8

"To the Honorable Senate and House of Representatives in Congress Assembled: We the undersigned, citizens of the United States, but deprived of some of the privileges and immunities of citizens, among which is the right to vote, beg leave to submit the following Resolution:…"

–Susan B. Anthony and
Elizabeth Cady Stanton

7. The statement is an example of a citizen's constitutional right to

   (A) seek election to public office

   (B) assemble peacefully

   (C) exercise the right to vote

   (D) petition for a redress of grievances

8. The strongest support for the cause of women's rights in the 1800s came from those mostly tied to

   (A) Social Darwinist thinking

   (B) the abolitionist movement

   (C) the settlement house movement

   (D) civil service reform

9. The parliamentary system's primary disadvantage in comparison to a bipartisan system of legislative organization is

   (A) infrequent elections
   (B) greater difficulty building governing coalitions
   (C) less accountability of officials to public demands
   (D) less representation by elected officials

10. The outcome of the Opium War showed that in the 19th century,

    (A) the Chinese army was the most highly disciplined army in the world
    (B) the Chinese people were successful in eliminating foreign influence
    (C) the Chinese government was no longer strong enough to resist western demands for trading rights
    (D) the Chinese government preferred to continue the opium trade

Line	Scientific Theory	Relevance	Time Period
1	Theory of Relativity	Theoretical basis for use of atomic energy	20th century
2	Theory of Universal Gravitation	Made possible the calculation of the speed of falling objects and movement of planets	17th century
3	Heliocentric Theory center of universe	Church supported view that sun was center of universe	18th century
4	Evolutionary Theory	Species arise and develop through natural selection	19th century

11. Which line *incorrectly* matches the scientific theory with its significance and correct time period?

    (A) Line 1
    (B) Line 2
    (C) Line 3
    (D) Line 4

12. The United States Federal Reserve most directly influences the American economy through

    (A) periodic fiscal forecasts

    (B) alterations in marginal tax brackets

    (C) recommendations on long-term interest rates

    (D) influence on American monetary supply

13. The tropical rainforests of the world are threatened by all of the following EXCEPT:

    (A) government policies that encourage road building

    (B) those who want to take advantage of the mineral-rich soil

    (C) loggers interested in selling wood products

    (D) landless peasants seeking economic opportunity

14. The most frequently proposed solution to the problem shown in the cartoon is to

    (A) establish poll taxes

    (B) use public funds to pay for political campaigns

    (C) eliminate primaries from the election system

    (D) have candidates finance their own campaigns

15. The situation shown in the map threatened the United States policy of

    (A) intervention

    (B) containment

    (C) neutrality

    (D) collective security

16. Which of the following is an accurate description of environmental conditions in the savanna biome?

    (A) High rainfall and exceptionally cold temperatures

    (B) Extensive grassland and moderate rainfall

    (C) Desertlike and sparse vegetation

    (D) Heavily forested and very low rainfall

17. The work of John Maynard Keynes most influenced fiscal policies under which leader?

    (A) George III
    (B) Vladimir Lenin
    (C) Lyndon Johnson
    (D) Andrew Jackson

18. A major effect of the decline of the Roman Empire was that western Europe

    (A) came under the control of the Muslims
    (B) returned to a republican form of government
    (C) entered a period of disorder and chaos
    (D) was absorbed by the Byzantine Empire

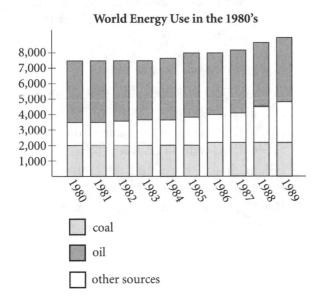

World Energy Use in the 1980's

coal

oil

other sources

19. Which statement is accurate according to this graph?

    (A) Energy use has declined in the 1980s.
    (B) Nuclear energy has become the most common form of energy source.
    (C) Natural gas has become a less important energy source.
    (D) Oil is the energy source the world most depends on.

Statement A: Each person must be able to voice his or her concerns on all issues that involve this new nation and bear the responsibility for the decisions made.

Statement B: The power of this new nation must rest in a strong, stable group that makes important decisions with the approval, but not the participation, of all.

Statement C: There must be several governments within one nation to ensure adequate voice and responsibility to all.

Statement D: Individuals must not allow their freedoms to be swallowed by an all-powerful government.

20. Which statement best represents the ideas of the Bill of Rights?

    (A) Statement A
    (B) Statement B
    (C) Statement C
    (D) Statement D

21. Camill di Cavour, Giuseppe Mazzini, and Otto Von Bismarck are similar in that they

    (A) strengthened the power of the Catholic Church
    (B) appealed to nationalistic sentiment
    (C) adopted communist philosophy
    (D) led nations that faced economic depression

22. The Magna Carta and the Glorious Revolution contributed to the development of

    (A) imperialism
    (B) absolute monarchy
    (C) civil rights
    (D) parliamentary democracy

23. One of the political consequences of the Korean War was

    (A) the increase in presidential powers in determining foreign policy
    (B) the increase in the powers of Congress over foreign policy
    (C) strengthened support for the Democratic party in 1952
    (D) the increase in bipartisan support for the use of atomic weapons

24. Which one of the following is the best example of a thesis statement?

    (A) In 1964 the Warren Commission concluded that Lee Harvey Oswald acted alone in the assassination of President John F. Kennedy.
    (B) The European Industrial Revolution had an enormous impact on the lifestyles of laborers, the middle class, the upper class, as well as the environment.
    (C) Martin Luther's posting of his 95 Theses in the 16th century was the pivotal event that forever changed the path of Christianity.
    (D) At the height of World War II, the United States devoted approximately 50 percent of its production capacity to the war effort.

25. The gross national product is a

    (A) means of calculating the next year's national debt
    (B) basic estimate of the value of the nation's natural resources
    (C) method of calculating the profits of the nation's largest corporations
    (D) barometer of the nation's economic growth

26. President Franklin Roosevelt's New Deal programs and policies were successful according to most supporters because they

    (A) prohibited speculation in corporate stocks and bonds
    (B) set a precedent for future balanced budgets
    (C) accelerated the government's move away from laissez-faire policies
    (D) increased employment by creating a larger bureaucratic government structure

27. A graph showing that output per worker-hour has increased from 50 in the base period of 1975 to 65 by 1985. A labor union in 1985 could best use these statistics to support

    (A) an expansion of its apprenticeship program
    (B) a drive for a shorter work week
    (C) a campaign against sexual discrimination
    (D) an increase in membership dues

28. All of the following helped to limit the power of the English monarchy except the

    (A) Act of Supremacy
    (B) Magna Carta
    (C) Glorious Revolution
    (D) Petition of Right

29. The issuance of King James II's Charter of Liberties and Privileges allowed New York

    (A) to limit slavery
    (B) limited self-government
    (C) representation in the House of Commons
    (D) to trade freely with Dutch and French merchants

30. The construction of the Erie Canal did all of the following except

    (A) deny the British the fruits of western trade
    (B) dramatically lower the cost of shipping goods from Albany to New York City
    (C) open up the Ohio Valley to trade
    (D) ensure that New York City would be the most important port on the East Coast

Social Studies Question Bank Answers and Explanations

1. A

This is an economics question that relies on somewhat abstract principles. If interest rates drop, more capital is made available for lending, and so debt goes up as more people take loans. Home ownership goes up because the payments on the homes go down and mortgages are easier to obtain. Putting the situation into a real-world scenario is helpful: think about what a decreased interest rate on a credit card invites or what friends give as their reason for finally buying a house. Abstract questions can almost always be made more tangible and related to current events.

2. D

In 1887, Congress passed this act to "Americanize" the Native Americans by cultivating the desire to own property and to farm. The act broke up the reservations and distributed some of the reservation land to each adult head of a family. The actual result of this act was the seizing of most reservation land for white settlers.

3. D

Primary sources and online sources would be the best of the four. In fact, there are many primary sources online, which can aid in research. Novels (historical) are fictionalized accounts of events. Encyclopedias are not the best resources for research. They can be useful as an initial research tool, but encyclopedias do not go into enough depth.

4. C

Overall, trends are more important than the event itself. Which answer choices simply don't make sense? You might have eliminated (D) very quickly.

Why would the British demand a Muslim state as a condition of Indian independence? Likewise, why would laws discriminating against Hindus trigger Muslim nationalism? Scratch (B). Between (A) and (C), both answers look tempting. However, (C) would seem to be a more direct and in fact inevitable cause of Pakistani independence. Once again, previous knowledge will help to answer the question; any student familiar with the situation surrounding Pakistani independence will get this question in very short order. However, even a passing knowledge of the situation in that area in the 1940s is sufficient to answer the question with complete accuracy.

5. B

This is one of those questions that compares (not contrasts) two items. Sometimes it is enough to know about just one of the items to answer the question. Both items were sets of laws that made for consistency throughout these empires. You should have been able to quickly eliminate (A) because these items sound too old to be democratic. Choices (C) and (D) might have been tempting for some. Previous knowledge is important here.

6. B

Representative assemblies like the Virginia House of Burgesses and other colonial assemblies were important precursors to America's independent representative assemblies like the Congress. Universal suffrage was not developed at all in the colonial period. Enslaved people, women, and in many cases men without property were not allowed to vote. Church and state were not separated in the colonies, and there wasn't an independent court system.

7. D

Although (D) is the correct one, (C) is thrown in there to confuse you. The document is using the right to vote as an example of a right deprived of women. However, the document itself represents an attempt at a redress of grievances, which is any citizen's constitutional right.

8. B

This is another women's rights question. Most of the people involved in the women's rights movement in the 1800s were involved in abolitionist campaigns. They sought the freedom of enslaved persons as well as women. Many male abolitionists supported women's rights. (C) and (D) were progressive era reforms in the final years of the 1800s and early 1900s. Choice (A), Social Darwinism, is the economic and social belief that unrestrained competition will ensure that only the strongest will survive. This is true of individuals and businesses.

9. B

Governments in parliamentary systems are sometimes weak because of the need to build party coalitions to rule. If parties withdraw their support from a governing coalition, the government in power can collapse or be ineffective. The need to build coalitions in a parliamentary system is usually very strong but can be very difficult to achieve at times.

10. C

The Chinese government was defeated in the Opium Wars with western nations. The Chinese government wanted to eliminate the opium trade and western trading influence. Instead, these nations gained full access to the Chinese market. It demonstrated the weakness of the Chinese armed forces as well.

11. C

Line 3 is incorrect because the Catholic Church did not support this accurate view that the sun was the center of the universe. Also, the time period is inaccurate. Copernicus (1473–1543) is credited with advocating this theory, and Galileo (1564–1642) helped to prove his theory. The other three lines are correct.

12. D

This question requires the knowledge that taxation (B) is exclusively the province of Congress, whereas (A) and (C) would be lacking in fiscal clout. You may have predicted something close to (D) before looking at the answer choices, which is the best way of attacking this question. If you looked at the answer choices first, you might have gone with (C) because it is talked about often in the news and might seem tempting.

13. B

The reason (B) is the correct answer is because rainforests are not known for their mineral-rich soil. In fact, farmers have discovered that the land is rather infertile. That is often why landless peasants farm a plot of land for a few years and have to move onto another plot of land because the soil's mineral content is used up quickly.

14. B

(D) may be tempting, especially if you have seen high-profile candidates finance their own campaigns. Campaign reform laws in places around the country have begun to implement programs that use limited public funds to pay for campaigns.

15. C

Despite the fact that this is a map question, previous knowledge is very useful in answering this question. The date on the map indicates that this is WWI. The U.S. tried to stay neutral during the initial years of the war but eventually entered in 1917. The Lusitania was a British liner that was sunk off the coast of Ireland by a German U-boat in 1915.

16. B

You may agree that savanna evokes images of Africa or lions. You may know immediately that (B) accurately represents the savanna. Even if you don't, you will be able to use your associations of the savanna to eliminate all answer choices except for (B) and possibly (C). (A) and (D) include environmental conditions that do not make sense: cold temperatures and high rainfall or heavy forestation with little rainfall simply do not go together. Therefore, even without knowledge of this particular biome, you should be able to narrow the answer down to a 50/50 choice.

17. C

Knowing the time period that Keynes lived would be helpful in eliminating (A) and (D). Lenin and Johnson are the only two 20th century figures along with Keynes. You may have eliminated (B) because Keynes is associated with capitalism, not communism. Keynes was a British economist who proposed that high unemployment, being a result of insufficient consumer spending, could be relieved by government-sponsored programs such as the Great Society programs. He also advocated deficit spending by governments to stimulate economic activity, which was a hallmark of the Johnson years.

18. C

Europe entered the Middle Ages after the fall of centralized authority under Rome. Europe entered a feudal period where local (land)lords had authority over the people on their lands. Europe was not taken over by Muslims armies or the Byzantines.

19. D

According to the graph, oil, which is represented by the solid dark shading, accounts for the majority of energy used in the world. Other sources have increased their percentages of the total but have not equaled oil. Coal has remained steady throughout the period shown in the graph.

20. D

The Bill of Rights was created in the first place because many people feared that the new national government created by the Constitution would be too powerful. This could lead to a usurpation of the rights of individuals. The Bill of Rights is essentially a set of protections against our government. Statement D expresses this idea.

21. B

You may not remember all of these men, but if you know one, you may be able to answer the question correctly. All three were nationalist leaders who wanted to unite their countries. Cavour and Mazzini were 19th century Italian leaders, whereas Bismarck was a 19th century German leader.

22. D

Both were opportunities for the British Parliament to cede power from the king. Choice (B) contradicts this, whereas (C) doesn't fit the time periods associated with these two items.

23. B

In 1950, President Truman ordered naval and air support for South Korea after they were invaded by the north. To some in Congress, this meant a usurpation of the power of Congress to declare war. Presidential administrations after this continued to follow in the footsteps of Truman with the Vietnam conflict. The War Powers Act was enacted in 1973, which stipulated that a president must inform Congress within 48 hours if U.S. forces are sent into a hostile area without a declaration of war. In addition, the troops cannot remain there past 90 days unless Congress approves the action or declares war.

24. C

(C) is a good example of a thesis statement. It is an argument that needs to be proven. (A) and (D) are simply factual statements that don't need to be proven. (B) tries to tackle too many topics. It should be narrowed dramatically.

25. D

The GNP is a macroeconomic term that is the total market value of all the goods and services produced by a nation during a specified period. (C) could be eliminated because gross takes into account the whole amount of something. That choice only considers the nation's largest corporations. (B) refers to natural resources that are not products.

26. C

Most supporters of F.D.R.'s New Deal believed that the government should come to the aid of those in need, particularly under the economic circumstances of The Great Depression. This meant a move away from the government's still rather laissez-faire attitude toward the economy. Laissez-faire policies of the 19th century meant that the government left businesses and the economy alone. The progressive legislation at the end of the 19th and beginning of the 20th century began that retreat away from laissez-faire policies, and the New Deal accelerated it greatly. (A) is incorrect because speculation remains an integral part of the stock market. (B) is incorrect because the New Deal produced huge deficits and not a balanced budget. The government borrowed money to pay for the New Deal programs. (D) is incorrect because the expansion of the government bureaucracy was not a goal of New Deal supporters. It happened to be a consequence of the reforms instituted.

27. B

Because workers are producing at a higher rate, the union would see this as a justification to shorten the work week. Having an apprenticeship program (A) and increasing membership dues (D) are clearly within the purview of the union and are thus not related to using increased productivity as a bargaining tool. The increased production rate would be a bargaining tool in getting a shorter work week. (C) is unlikely related to higher production levels.

28. A

The Act of Supremacy granted King Henry VIII of England the authority over the Church of England. This effectively created the Anglican Church, which was separate from the Roman Catholic Church. The other three choices all provided the opportunity for the English Parliament to wrest power from the crown. The Magna Carta guaranteed that free born Englishmen could not be fined or imprisoned except according to the laws of the land. The Glorious Revolution was a time when King James II fled, and his daughter and her husband were invited by the leaders of Parliament to take his place. The Petition of Right finally established Parliament's supremacy over the king.

29. B

The Charter granted limited self-government to the New York colony. Slavery was never limited, and no colony was given representation during the colonial period. Representation became an important issue in the independence struggle. The mercantilist system of the British would not allow American colonists to trade with foreign nations without specific permission.

30. B

Costs for shipping were lowered with the construction of the Erie Canal. However, the Albany to New York route was along the Hudson. A shipper would not necessarily save much more than he did before the construction of the canal. All the other three answer choices were a result of the building of the canal.

PRAXIS RESOURCE: STATE CERTIFICATION INFORMATION

State Certification Information*

State	Teacher Certification Division	Praxis State Requirements Link
Alabama	Department of Education 50 North Ripley Street PO Box 302101 Montgomery, AL 36130-2101 alsde.edu	ets.org/praxis/prxal.html
Alaska	Teacher Education and Certification 801 West 10th Street Suite 200 Juneau, AK 99811-0500 (907) 465-2831 eed.state.ak.us/teacherscertification	ets.org/praxis/prxak.html
Arkansas	Office of Professional Licensure Arkansas Department of Education 4 State Capitol Mall Little Rock, AR 72201 (501) 682-4475 arkedu.state.ar.us	ets.org/praxis/prxar.html
California	Commission on Teacher Credentialing P.O. Box 944270 1900 Capital Avenue Sacramento, CA 94233 (916) 445-7254 ctc.ca.gov	ets.org/praxis/prxca.html
Colorado	Educator Licensing Department of Education 201 E. Colfax Avenue, Room 105 Denver, CO 80203-1799 (303) 866-6628 cde.state.co.us	ets.org/praxis/prxco.html
Connecticut	Connecticut State Department of Education Bureau of Certification and Teacher Preparation PO Box 150471-Room 243 Hartford, CT 06115-0471 (860) 713-6969 Fax (860) 713-7017 state.ct.us/sde/dtl/cert/index.htm	ets.org/praxis/prxct.html

State	Teacher Certification Division	Praxis State Requirements Link
Delaware	Delaware Department of Education Licensure/Certification Office 401 Ferderal Street, Suite 2 Dover, DE 19901 (302) 739-4686 deeds.doe.state.de.us	ets.org/praxis/prxde.html
District of Columbia	Office of the State Superintendent of Education Educator Licensing and Quality 51 N St., NE – 3rd Floor Washington, DC 20002 (202) 741-5881 osse.dc.gov	ets.org/praxis/prxdc.html
Georgia	Georgia Professional Standards Commission 2 Peachtree Street, Suite 6000 Atlanta, GA 30303 (404) 232-2500 gapsc.com	ets.org/praxis/prxga.html
Hawaii	Hawaii Department of Education Hawaii Teacher Standards Board 650 Iwilei Rd. #201 Honolulu, HI 96817 (808) 586-2600 htsb.org	ets.org/praxis/prxhi.html
Idaho	Idaho Department of Education Teacher Certification 650 West State Street PO Box 83720 Boise, ID 83720-0027 (208) 332-6880 sde.idaho.gov/teachercertification	ets.org/praxis/prxid.html
Indiana	Indiana Division of Professional Standards Indiana Department of Education Room 229, State House Indianapolis, IN 46204-2798 (317) 232-9010 doe.state.in.us/dps/	ets.org/praxis/prxin.html
Iowa	Iowa Department of Education Grimes State Office Building 400 E 14th St Des Moines IA 50319-0146 boee.iowa.gov	ets.org/praxis/prxia.html

State	Teacher Certification Division	Praxis State Requirements Link
Kansas	Certification and Teacher Education Kansas State Department of Education 120 SE 10th Avenue Topeka, KS 66612-1182 (785) 296-2288 ksde.org/cert	ets.org/praxis/prxks.html
Kentucky	Education Professional Standards Board 100 Airport Road, 3rd Floor Frankfort, KY 40601 (502) 564-4606 kyepsb.net/certification/index.asp	ets.org/praxis/prxky.html
Louisiana	Louisiana Department of Education Division of Certification and Preparation P.O. Box 94064 Baton Rouge, Louisiana 70804-9064 (877) 453-2721 teachlouisiana.net	ets.org/praxis/prxla.html
Maine	Maine Department of Education Certification Office 23 State House Station Augusta, ME 04333-0023 (207) 624-6603 maine.gov/education/cert/index	ets.org/praxis/prxme.html
Maryland	Maryland State Department of Education Attn: Certification Branch 200 West Baltimore Street Baltimore, MD 21201 (410) 767-0412 marylandpublicschools.org/msde/divisions/certification	ets.org/praxis/prxmd.html
Minnesota	Minnesota Department of Education Personnel Licensing Team 1500 Highway 36 West Roseville, MN 55113-4266 (651) 582-8691 education.state.mn.us/html/mde_home.htm	ets.org/praxis/prxmn.html
Mississippi	Educator Licensure/Certification PO Box 771 359 North West Street Jackson, MS 39205 601-359-3483 mde.k12.ms.us/ad_licensure/index.htm	ets.org/praxis/prxms.html

State	Teacher Certification Division	Praxis State Requirements Link
Missouri	Teacher Education and Certification P.O. Box 480 Jefferson City, MO 65102 (573) 751-0051 dese.state.mo.gov	ets.org/praxis/prxmo.html
Nebraska	Teacher Education and Certification 301 Centennial Mall South PO Box 94987 Lincoln, NE 68509 (402) 471-2496 nde.state.ne.us/tcert/tcmain.html	ets.org/praxis/prxne.html
Nevada	Nevada Department of Education Teacher Licensing Office 1820 East Sahara Avenue, Suite 205 las Vegas, NV 89104 (702) 486-6458 doe.nv.gov	ets.org/praxis/prxnv.html
New Hampshire	New Hampshire Department of Education 101 Pleasant Street Concord, NH 03301 (603) 271-3494 ed.state.nh.us	ets.org/praxis/prxnh.html
New Jersey	New Jersey Department of Education Office of Licensing and Credentials P.O. Box 500 Trenton, NJ 08625 (609) 292-2070 state.nj.us/njded/educators/license	ets.org/praxis/prxnj.html
New Mexico	Professional Licensure Unit New Mexico Public Education Department 300 Don Gaspar Santa Fe, NM 87501-2786 (505) 827-5800 sde.state.nm.us/index.html	ets.org/praxis/prxnm.html
North Carolina	Department of Public Instruction Licensure Section 301 North Wilmington Street Raleigh, NC 27601-2825 (919) 807-3310 ncpublicschools.org	ets.org/praxis/prxnc.html

State	Teacher Certification Division	Praxis State Requirements Link
North Dakota	Department of Public Instruction 600 East Boulevard Avenue, Dept. 201 Bismarck, ND 58505 (701) 328-2260 dpi.state.nd.us/	ets.org/praxis/prxnd.html
Ohio	Office of Certification/Licensure 25 South Front Street, Mail Stop 105 Columbus, OH 43215-4183 (614) 466-3593 ode.state.oh.us	ets.org/praxis/prxoh.html
Oklahoma	Professional Standards Section Oklahoma Department of Education Hudge Education Building, Room 211 2500 North Lincoln Boulevard Oklahoma City, OK 73105 (405) 521-3337 sde.state.ok.us	ets.org/praxis/prxok.html
Oregon	Oregon Teacher Standards and Practices Commission 465 Commercial St. NE Salem, OR 97301 (503) 378-3586 tspc.state.or.us	ets.org/praxis/prxor.html
Pennsylvania	Bureau of Teacher Certification and Preparation Pennsylvania Department of Education 333 Market Street Harrisburg, PA 17126-0333 (717) 787-3356 pde.state.pa.us	ets.org/praxis/prxpa.html
Rhode Island	Rhode Island Department of Education 255 Westminster Street Providence, RI 02903 (401) 222-4600 ridoe.net	ets.org/praxis/prxri.html
South Carolina	Division of Teacher Quality South Carolina Department of Education 3700 Forest Drive, Suite 500 Columbia, SC 29204 (803) 734-8446 scteachers.org	ets.org/praxis/prxsc.html

State	Teacher Certification Division	Praxis State Requirements Link
South Dakota	Department of Education Office of Accreditation and Teacher Quality 700 Governors Drive Pierre, SD 57501 (605) 773-6934 doe.sd.gov.oatq/	ets.org/praxis/prxsd.html
Tennessee	State Department of Education Office of Teacher Licensing 4th Floor, Andrew Johnson Tower 710 James Robertson Parkway Nashville, TN 37243-0377 (615) 532-4885 tennessee.gov/education/lic	ets.org/praxis/prxtn.html
Utah	Utah State Office of Education Certification and Personnel Development 250 East 500 South Salt Lake City, UT 84111 (801) 538-7500 usoe.k12.ut.us	ets.org/praxis/prxut.html
Vermont	Professional Standards and Licensing Office Vermont Department of Education 120 State Street Montpelier, VT 05620 (802) 828-2445 state.vt.us/educ/new/html/maincert.html	ets.org/praxis/prxvt.html
Virginia	Department of Education P.O. Box 2120 Richmond, VA 23218 (800) 292-3820 doe.virginia.gov	ets.org/praxis/prxva.html
Washington	Washington Professional Educator Standards Board Old Capital Bldg. P.O. Box 47236 Olympia, WA 98504-7236 (360) 725-6275 k12.wa.us/certification	ets.org/praxis/prxwa.html
West Virginia	West Virginia Department of Education Office of Professional Preparation 1900 Kanawha Boulevard East Building 6, Rm 252 Charleston, WV 25305 (304) 558-7826 wvde.state.wv.us/certification	ets.org/praxis/prxwv.html

State	Teacher Certification Division	Praxis State Requirements Link
Wisconsin	Department of Public Instruction 125 South Webster Street PO Box 7841 Madison, WI 53707-7841 (800) 266-1027 dpi.state.wi.us/	ets.org/praxis/prxwi.html
Wyoming	Professional Teaching Standards Board 1920 Thomas Avenue, Suite 400 Cheyenne, WY 82002 (307) 777-7291 ptsb.state.wy.us	ets.org/praxis/prxwy.html

*The states represented in the table use one or more tests in the PRAXIS series for teacher certification. If your state is not listed, it does not currently use the PRAXIS exams.

PRAXIS RESOURCE: GETTING STARTED: ADVICE FOR NEW TEACHERS

Getting Started: Advice for New Teachers

So you've passed the PRAXIS with flying colors and fulfilled all the requirements for becoming a teacher in your state. Now it's time to put all your learning into practice!

FINDING THE RIGHT POSITION

It is common knowledge that more good teachers are needed across the country. According to the National Center for Education Statistics, approximately 2 million new teachers will be needed in the United States by 2008–2009 (nces.ed.gov). But finding the right job for you can be a daunting process.

1. Do Your Research

First, determine the grade levels and/or subjects you are most interested in teaching. Make sure you have fulfilled all the qualifications for your state.

2. Identify Where You Would Like to Work

Next, make a list of the districts and/or schools where you would most like to work. Many school districts have websites on which they post job openings. In addition, you should call the district office to find out if there are any positions open and what their application procedures are.

Use the Internet as a resource. In addition to the many general websites for job hunters, there are websites devoted solely to teaching jobs. A few websites will ask you for a subscription fee, but there are many others with free listings. A list of some of these sites is included at the end of this chapter.

3. Attend Job Fairs

Job fairs are a good way to learn about openings and to network with other education professionals. Several of the websites for job-seekers listed at the end of this chapter also have job fair listings by state.

Remember that you are assessing potential employers as much as they are assessing you. Consider asking the following:

- What is the first professional development opportunity offered to new teachers?
- What additional duties outside the classroom are expected of teachers?
- When can I expect to meet my mentor?

- What is the top school-wide priority this year?
- What kinds of materials or resources would be available in my classroom? (if applicable)
- What is your policy on lesson planning?

You may also want to ask about the demographics of the student population and what kinds of unique challenges they present.

4. Sign Up for Substitute Teaching

Substitute teaching can be another good strategy for getting your foot in the door in a particular school or district, even if there are no permanent jobs available. Think of this as an opportunity to impress principals and to learn from other teachers about possible openings. You can even submit your resume to the principals in the schools where you are substitute teaching and give them the chance to observe you in the classroom.

STARTING IN THE CLASSROOM

Don't get disillusioned if you're not immediately comfortable in your role as a teacher. Give yourself time to adjust, and don't hesitate to ask for advice from others. Be persistent about finding a mentor who can provide support during your first year and beyond. Try to find one in your subject area and determine how much experience you would like that person to have. For the sake of convenience, it's a good idea to find someone who has a similar class schedule or daily routine.

Teach Rules and Respect

With students, be friendly but firm. Establish clear routines and consistent disciplinary measures early on. This way, the students have a firm understanding of what is expected of them and when certain behaviors are appropriate. Have the principal review your disciplinary plan to make certain that he or she will support it and that there aren't any potential legal issues. Be aware of how cliques and social hierarchies impact classroom dynamics, and don't underestimate the power of your own advice.

Although disciplinary issues vary according to grade level, there are some general tips you may find helpful in setting rules in the classroom:

- Often, troublesome students misbehave merely to get your attention. Reduce this negative behavior by paying the least amount of attention when a student is acting out and giving that child your full attention when he or she is behaving.
- When it comes to establishing classroom rules, allow your students to have some input. This will increase their sense of empowerment and respect for the rules.
- Convince all of your students that they are worthwhile and capable. It is easy to assume that struggling students are lazy or beyond help–do not allow yourself to fall into this trap.

- When disciplining students, absolutely avoid embarrassing them in any way, shape, or form, especially in front of their peers.
- Double standards and favoritism will lose you the respect of all your students-always be firm, fair, and consistent. Never talk down to your students.
- Avoid becoming too chummy with your students. Young teachers often feel that they must make "friends" with students, particularly in the older grades. However, it's important to maintain some professional distance and to establish yourself as an authority figure.
- Admit your mistakes. If you wrongly accuse a student of doing something she did not do, make an inappropriate joke, or reprimand a student more harshly than necessary, be sure to apologize and explain. If a parent or administrator criticizes you for your mistake, calmly explain how you felt at that moment and why. Also, explain how you plan on handling that kind of situation in the future.

Do Your Homework

Any veteran teacher will tell you that you will spend almost as many hours working outside the classroom as you do with your students. Preparing lessons and grading homework and tests can take an enormous amount of time, so it's a good idea to be as organized as possible.

Also, consider what your expectations will be:

- Will you grade every homework assignment or just some of them?
- Will you give students an opportunity to earn extra credit?
- What kind of system will you use for grading tests?

Design Lesson Plans Early

Before you start planning, be aware of holidays off, assemblies, and similar interruptions. Design your lessons accordingly. Similarly, be sure you know your content, your state's standards, your school's expectations, and the ins and outs of child development. Be prepared with multiple learning styles and differentiated teaching strategies.

Try to develop time-saving strategies. Saving your lesson plan outline as a template on the computer can be very helpful–instead of rewriting the whole plan everyday, you can just fill in the blanks.

Establish Rules for Grading Homework

Along with establishing a consistent disciplinary policy early on, it's important to develop grading guidelines. Some teachers set the bar high at the beginning of the year by grading a little tougher than they normally would. Just as many students will underachieve if they think you are a soft grader, they will work hard to meet your expectations if your standards are high. However, it's important to assess your students' abilities and set realistic standards.

Grading every single assignment can get overwhelming; sometimes verbally assessing comprehension is enough. Rubrics are another useful tool for outlining expectations and scoring, as well as making sure you cater to the needs of all your students. They are also effective when students grade each other.

Returning graded assignments as soon as possible sets a good example, keeps your workload manageable, and prevents students' interest from waning. However, you should never use a student's work as an example of what not to do.

Consider sending grades home on a regular basis and getting them signed by a parent in order to keep everyone aware of students' progress. This prevents students and parents from being blindsided by poor grades.

Don't confuse quietness for comprehension. Check in with all students because some may be afraid to admit that they don't understand what's going on. If you feel there is a problem, don't wait to address a student's needs. If you believe that a student may have an undiagnosed disability, let your principal know and follow your school's procedure.

Finding tangible rewards for students' achievements is a great way to keep them motivated, particularly if you focus their efforts around gradually earning the rewards. These types of incentive systems work particularly well in the elementary grades.

Deal with Parents Early On

Establish a relationship with parents from the beginning–frequent, positive communication is essential to helping the children attain the best education possible. Here are a few tips for keeping in touch with parents:

- Make phone calls, even if you're just going to leave a message. Doing so will allow you to share good news and help guardians become more familiar with you.
- Give students homework folders that frequently travel between school and home.
- Be ready to deal with breakdowns in communication: it may be necessary to send multiple messages home.
- Send home a short newsletter of things to come.

Set Up Parent-Teacher Conferences

Meeting with parents can often be intimidating for new teachers, particularly if a student is not performing well. It's a good idea to seek guidance from experienced teachers, and communicate with administrators if you encounter problems. In addition, try to follow these general guidelines when talking with parents:

- Remain professional. Don't take heated words personally, have good things to say about the student, choose your words carefully, keep examples of the student's work on hand, and document what is said during the meeting.
- Allow parents to ask the first question. This will help you understand their tone and their concerns.
- Be as thick skinned as possible when dealing with problems: some parents want to vent a little before getting to the crux of the issue. Let them vent, try to put them at ease, and then look for a solution or compromise.

- If a parent becomes excessively confrontational, inform an administrator.
- Be confident. Listen to what the parents suggest, but also stand up for what you believe is the best course of action.

Building Relationships with Colleagues

Meet as many teachers in the building as you can: not only will you gain valuable insights about the inner workings of the school, but you'll also make new friends. Don't be afraid to step up and ask questions when information isn't offered. Veteran teachers are a tremendous resource for all kinds of information, ranging from labor contracts to strategies for staying sane under pressure. Also, get to know the other new teachers. These people will be valuable sounding boards and will help you feel less alone.

Earn the respect of your colleagues by stepping up to committee work, and by proving yourself to be a reliable, competent teacher. You should also be polite and friendly with the staff and custodians: you'll need their help for all sorts of reasons.

Finally, be professional, timely, and unafraid to calmly share your opinions or disagree with administrators. Your professionalism and enthusiasm will earn you their respect and ensure that your needs are met.

Dealing with Paperwork

Be aware of what kinds of paperwork you need to fill out and file, including the school Improvement Plan, special education forms relating to Individualized Education Plans, budget requests, reading and math benchmarks, and permanent record cards. Try to sit with fellow teachers when filling out forms. Their companionship will make these tedious tasks more fun.

Understanding Unions

Depending on your school district, you may be part of a teacher's union. It is important to gain a clear understanding of union requirements. You'll want to know:

- How much money will be deducted from your paycheck for union dues
- How you can obtain a copy of the most recent union contract

Allow Yourself "Down Time"

Finally, always give yourself time to wind down and distance yourself from the classroom. This is essential to prevent burnout or resentment over a lack of free time, and will allow you to pursue other interests and personal relationships.

ADDITIONAL RESOURCES

Books

Capel, Susan, Marilyn Leask, and Terry Turner, *Learning to Teach in the Secondary School:* A Companion to School Experience. Taylor & Francis, 2005.

Dillon, Justin. *Becoming a Teacher.* McGraw Hill, Open University Press, 2001.

Goodnough, Abby. *Ms. Moffett's First Year: Becoming a Teacher in America.* Public Affairs, 2004.

Howe, Randy. *First-Year Teacher: What I Wish I Had Known My First 100 Days on the Job: Wisdom, Tips, and Warnings from Experienced Teachers.* Kaplan, 2007.

Maloy, Robert W., and Irving Seidman. *The Essential Career Guide to Becoming a Middle and High School Teacher.* Bergin & Garvey, 1999.

Parkay, Forrest W., and Beverly Hardcastle Stanford. *Becoming a Teacher 6th edition.* Allyn & Bacon; 6th edition, 2003.

Shalaway, Linda, and Linda Beech (Editor). *Learning to Teach...Not Just For Beginners (Grades K-8).* Scholastic, 1999.

Starkey, Lauren. *Change Your Career: Teaching as Your New Profession.* Kaplan, 2007.

Staff of U.S. News and World Report. *U.S. News Ultimate Guide to Becoming a Teacher* Sourcebooks, 2004.

Wong, Harry K., and Rosemary T. Wong. *The First Days of School: How to be an Effective Teacher.* Harry K. Wong Publications, 2001.

Magazines and Journals

American Educator

Harvard Educational Review

The *New York Times* "Education Life"

The *Phi Delta Kappan*

Internet Resources

teachernet.com/htm/becomingateacher.htm
Community for K–8 educators

pbs.org/firstyear/beaTeacher/
PBS: How to become a teacher

newsweekshowcase.com/teacher-training/Newsweek
Teacher education and recruitment, teaching as a second career

eric.ed.gov/
Education Resources Information Center; large teaching and education database

aft.com
American Federation of Teachers

proudtoserveagain.com/pages/808014/indcx.htm
Troops to Teachers program–gives former members of the U.S. military the opportunity to become public school teachers–can help with certification, job searching, etc.

ed.gov
U.S. Department of Education

theteachersguide.com

behavioradvisor.com

teach-nology.com
Free and easy-to-use resources for teachers

kidsource.com
Sites with tips from teachers

ncrel.org/he/tot/teach.htm
Teachers' input on teaching, learning how to teach

teachingtips.com
Tips from an experienced teacher

atozteacherstuff.com
A teacher-created site listing online resources and tips

Lesson Plan Sites

education-world.com

theteacherscorner.net

lessonplansearch.com

moteachingjobs.com/lessons/mainsearch.cfm

teachnet.com

General Teaching Job Sites

schoolspring.com

teachers-teachers.com

job-hunt.com/academia.shtml

educationjobs.com

abcteachingjobs.com

k12jobs.com

jobs2teach.doded.mil/Jobs2Teach/J2TDefault.asp
Part of the Troops to Teachers website

wanttoteach.com/newsite/jobfairs.html
National teaching job fair website

udel.edu/csc/teachers.html
MBNA Career Services Center: A list of resources for teachers

NOTES

NOTES

NOTES

NOTES

How Did We Do? Grade Us.

Thank you for choosing a Kaplan book. Your comments and suggestions are very useful to us. Please answer the following questions to assist us in our continued development of high-quality resources to meet your needs.

The title of the Kaplan book I read was: _____

My name is: _____

My address is: _____

_____

My e-mail address is: _____

What overall grade would you give this book?   Ⓐ Ⓑ Ⓒ Ⓓ Ⓕ

How relevant was the information to your goals?   Ⓐ Ⓑ Ⓒ Ⓓ Ⓕ

How comprehensive was the information in this book?   Ⓐ Ⓑ Ⓒ Ⓓ Ⓕ

How accurate was the information in this book?   Ⓐ Ⓑ Ⓒ Ⓓ Ⓕ

How easy was the book to use?   Ⓐ Ⓑ Ⓒ Ⓓ Ⓕ

How appealing was the book's design?   Ⓐ Ⓑ Ⓒ Ⓓ Ⓕ

What were the book's strong points? _____

How could this book be improved? _____

Is there anything that we left out that you wanted to know more about?

Would you recommend this book to others?   ☐ YES   ☐ NO

Other comments: _____

_____

_____

Do we have permission to quote you?   ☐ YES   ☐ NO

Thank you for your help.
Please tear out this page and mail it to:

Content Manager
Kaplan Publishing
1 Liberty Plaza, 24th Floor
New York, NY 10006

KAPLAN)

Thanks!